Revelation
and Reason

Revelation and Reason

New Essays in
REFORMED
APOLOGETICS

EDITED BY

K. SCOTT OLIPHINT
AND LANE G. TIPTON

P&R PUBLISHING
P.O. BOX 817 • PHILLIPSBURG • NEW JERSEY 08865-0817

Page design and typesetting by Lakeside Design Plus.

Printed in the United States of America

Library of Congress Control Number: 2006934632

To

Rev. David T. Brack

Pastor, Mentor, Friend

Contents

Introduction

K. SCOTT OLIPHINT
LANE G. TIPTON

Christian apologetics is, at root, a biblical discipline. To some, this may sound so obvious as to be redundant. To others, however, it is a hotly contested proposition. At least part of the purpose of this collection of essays is to set in the foreground the necessity of exegetical and theological foundations for any Reformed, Christian apologetic. A Reformed apologetic is only Reformed to the extent that its tenets, principles, methodology, and so forth are formed and re-formed by Scripture.

One aspect of apologetics that has been lacking in the literature, to the point of near extinction, is the *ground* for the discipline of apologetics itself. Of course, the general reason for apologetics is given in the meaning of the term; the reason to engage in the discipline of apologetics is to defend the faith. But why be engaged in such an enterprise? Does the Christian faith really need defending? Doesn't defending the

1

faith smack of defensive*ness*? Or is the primary purpose of apologetics simply to give Christian philosophers something to do?

Because the defense of Christianity has, at least historically, taken place in the context of philosophical objections to the faith, apologetics has taken on a reputation as, in the first place, a philosophical discipline. Much of the history of apologetics has been concerned to show, philosophically, that Christianity can stand intellectual scrutiny and emerge without too many bruises.

This trend, however, has had the effect, directly or indirectly, of undermining the discipline itself. It has led many to believe, and some to argue, that the most difficult issues of philosophical theology or theological philosophy should be engaged only by those philosophically trained, those whose minds have been able to meld together the best of theology with the best of philosophy.

To cite just one example, William Craig notes in *The Only Wise God* and again in *Time and Eternity* that those who want to know how the deep things of God relate to his creation should consult Christian philosophers. Says Craig:

> Some readers of my study of divine omniscience, *The Only Wise God*, expressed surprise at my remark that someone desiring to learn more about God's attribute of omniscience would be better advised to read the works of Christian philosophers than of Christian theologians. Not only was that remark true, but the same holds for divine eternity.[1]

This line of thinking is most unfortunate. As happened in the medieval period, such thinking will inevitably lead to the need for a radical, biblical reformation of those ideas and concepts developed by philosophers. If one wants to know about God's omniscience or his eternity, if one wants to think deeply about God and his relationship to the world, if one wants to do apologetics, the first place to look is

---

1. William Lane Craig, *Time and Eternity: Exploring God's Relationship to Time* (Wheaton, IL: Crossway, 2001), 11. It is interesting to note that Craig references the medieval period as a time when students were required to master philosophy before tackling theology; today's theologians, according to him, are ill-equipped to think about the deep things of God. Craig seems not to be aware that the medieval period, in its attempt to synthesize Christianity with philosophy, was in desperate need of biblical reformation, which, in God's providence, brought back the primacy of Scripture for such discussions. For a review of Craig's *Time and Eternity*, see K. Scott Oliphint, *Westminster Theological Journal* 63 (2001): 439–45.

to Scripture, and then to those theologians who faithfully articulate its teachings. Philosophy, even Christian philosophy, has a long and resolute history of turning its back on a consistent Reformed theology.[2] It, therefore, has not faired well with regard to theological (or philosophical-theological) discussions.[3]

What, then, can we learn from Scripture about the ground (and the task) of Christian apologetics? One of the best places to begin is in 1 Peter, especially chapter 3. As Peter begins his first epistle, note the designation of those to whom he writes:

> Peter, an apostle of Jesus Christ, To those who are elect exiles of the dispersion in Pontus, Galatia, Cappadocia, Asia, and Bithynia, according to the foreknowledge of God the Father, in the sanctification of the Spirit, for obedience to Jesus Christ and for sprinkling with his blood: May grace and peace be multiplied to you. (1 Peter 1:1–2)[4]

It is best to read these verses as one long designation. This is who Peter's recipients are; this is how he views them. They are elect exiles, chosen ones who are dispersed. Because dispersed, they may feel as though they do not belong. But they do belong—to God, according to his foreknowledge, *in* the sanctification of the Spirit, *unto* (*eis*/εἰς) obedience to Christ.

Notice, most especially, that these readers, while being elect (*eklektois*/ἐκλεκτοῖς), are nevertheless exiles (*parepidēmois*/παρεπιδήμοις). They are those who have no land—aliens, strangers, and not residents. The place wherein they reside is not their home.

Scripture gives abundant witness to the importance of land and home for God's covenant people. Without land, God's people are not

2. One of the reasons philosophy, especially philosophical theology, has too often undermined theology is that its *principium* is reason, not revelation. This too is most unfortunate. Particularly when much of philosophy seeks to understand who God is, a better recipe for error could hardly be imagined. See K. Scott Oliphint, *Reasons for Faith: Philosophy in the Service of Theology* (Phillipsburg, NJ: P&R, 2006).

3. Thus, Craig's conclusion in *Time and Eternity* that God was eternal when there was no creation, but since, according to Craig, he simply could not relate himself to time and remain eternal, he needed to set his eternity aside at creation.

4. Scripture quotations in this introduction are from The Holy Bible, English Standard Version, copyright © 2001 by Crossway Bibles, a division of Good News Publishers. Used by permission. All right reserved.

"a people." What are the current wars in the Middle East all about? Land. Why? Because of the continued belief that a people are identified and set apart by the land they possess. This, as we know, hearkens all the way back to that great salvific event of the Old Testament, the Exodus. God's people were set free from Egypt to possess a land. And it was God who would give them that land.

But Peter is writing to scattered people in order to remind them of new covenant priorities. They are now, because chosen and elected by God in Christ, who is himself the King, *aliens* in this world. This world is not their home. The "land" of God's people is now the *new* heavens and the *new* earth. Their home is in Christ, and in his kingdom. So, the fact that they are scattered is really an incidental matter in the end. Even if they were *not* scattered, even if they were "home," they would still not be home.

This notion is of paramount importance when we think of apologetics specifically, and of our Christian identity more generally. As Christians, we know what it is like to be aliens. It is much like traveling to another country. Everything seems strange: the language is different, the customs are different, the values are often different, it is difficult to think that we really "belong." But that is Peter's point. These Christians do not belong to a physical place. They are united to Christ and are seated with him in the heavenlies. They are elect in him, secure only in the Father's sovereign act of grace and mercy in salvation. They belong, first and foremost, to him.

Peter notes that he is writing to those "who by God's power are being guarded through faith for a salvation ready to be revealed in the last time" (1 Peter 1:5). Notice that, as Christians, we "are being guarded" (*phrouroumenous*/φρουρουμένους). The Greek word is a military term; it is battle terminology. It means we are shielded *by* God's power and *through* our faith in Christ. When we think of apologetics, then, we are not to see it as in itself a shield or guard from the attacks of the world. God is our shield; he alone guards us by his power because of, and through, our union with Christ.

The reason it is important *not* to see apologetics as our guard and shield is that we will immediately begin to think that warding off attacks from the world, or shielding ourselves, is really in our hands. We might begin to think that it all depends on our own efforts, our own apologetic expertise, whether or not we can defend the faith. But God guards us *while* we defend.

Our apologetic defense is not our shield. We do not rely on what we say or on our methodology or our gifts and skills when we defend the Christian faith. That would be a defense that is centered on us. But our defense is not man-centered, it is God-centered from beginning to end. Our defense of the faith, therefore, is *through faith*. That is, we trust in God as we defend, not in ourselves. Our trust is in him and his power, both to guard us and to change hearts and minds.

Peter then moves to the reality of suffering for Christians. That reality frames the quintessential passage on apologetics, 1 Peter 3:15. Suffering is the context in which the *locus classicus* of apologetics comes. Notice the passage:

> Finally, all of you, have unity of mind, sympathy, brotherly love, a tender heart, and a humble mind. Do not repay evil for evil or reviling for reviling, but on the contrary, bless, for to this you were called, that you may obtain a blessing. For
>
> > "Whoever desires to love life
> >   and see good days,
> > let him keep his tongue from evil
> >   and his lips from speaking deceit;
> > let him turn away from evil and do good;
> >   let him seek peace and pursue it.
> > For the eyes of the Lord are on the righteous,
> >   and his ears are open to their prayer.
> > But the face of the Lord is against those who do evil."
>
> Now who is there to harm you if you are zealous for what is good? But even if you should suffer for righteousness' sake, you will be blessed. Have no fear of them, nor be troubled, but in your hearts regard Christ the Lord as holy, always being prepared to make a defense to anyone who asks you for a reason for the hope that is in you; yet do it with gentleness and respect, having a good conscience, so that, when you are slandered, those who revile your good behavior in Christ may be put to shame. For it is better to suffer for doing good, if that should be God's will, than for doing evil. (1 Peter 3:8–17)

The section beginning in verse 8 through verse 12 addresses "all of you." Prior to verse 8, Peter has been addressing specific groups as to their behavior; now he wants to sum up his exhortation by addressing all of them together. As Peter finishes the general address, encouraging these suffering Christians to do what is honorable to God in the midst of suffering, he begins, in verse 13, a more specific application of what they should do as they are abused from the outside, just how best to respond to their enemies.

The first important thing to notice about verses 13–17 is the way in which Peter *grounds* his instruction in the verse that immediately follows: "For Christ also suffered once for sins, the righteous for the unrighteous, that he might bring us to God, being put to death in the flesh but made alive in the spirit" (1 Peter 3:18). Here Peter gives the primary and foundational *reason* (*hoti*/ὅτι) that we are to act in a certain way toward outsiders. That reason is that Christ himself suffered. *He* was righteous, and he suffered, not only *for* the unrighteous, but also *by the hands* of the unrighteous.

In verse 13, Peter asks, "Who is there to harm you . . . ?" This is a double-edged question. It is meant to encourage his readers by reminding them that, while there are those who can harm the body, the readers need fear (as Peter had heard his Master say) only the One who can destroy both body and soul in hell (Matt. 10:28). But it is also meant to remind them that, in fact, there are those who may want to harm them. The word Peter uses here for harm (*kakōsōn*/ κακώσων) is the word used of Herod Agrippa in Acts 12, which tells of Herod's putting James to death and seeking to harm Peter. So, Peter has in mind the kind of persecution that he himself experienced, and the kind he was likely experiencing even as he wrote this epistle. He is reminding his readers, and us, that the suffering we all experience is penultimate, and that it is not worthy to be compared to the glory that will be revealed in us.

The specifically apologetic section of this passage actually begins in the latter part of 1 Peter 3:14. There Peter refers to Isaiah 8:12–13: "Do not call conspiracy all that this people calls conspiracy, and do not fear what they fear, nor be in dread. But the LORD of hosts, him you shall regard as holy. Let him be your fear, and let him be your dread." This passage issues a change of perspective. It calls the Lord's people to fear *him* rather than those who persecute them. You will note that there is purposed equivocation in the word *fear*. We are not to fear the Lord in the same way that we fear those who persecute us, but we are to fear him as the one who is holy; we fear him with reverence and awe (as Peter will explain in a moment).

So, our focus changes from the persecutors and what they can do, to the Lord and who he is. Note in Isaiah 8:13 that it is Yahweh (יהוה) whom we are to fear. Peter picks this up in 1 Peter 3:15 and refers it to Jesus Christ without hesitation. It is Yahweh, Christ himself who is the Lord, whom we are to set apart *as Lord* in our hearts.

The only finite verb used in this section is the verb *sanctify* (*hagiasate*/ἁγιάσατε), and it is used as an imperative. This command serves to provide the imperatival force to the rest of the verse. The focus of the command is on our responsibility to sanctify *Christ* as Lord in our hearts as a requirement for the apologetic task (how distant this seems to be from so much of the history of apologetics).

It is worth emphasizing that Peter's use of Isaiah 8 is given a Christological (and therefore, eschatological) emphasis. As we noted above, while Isaiah 8 has Yahweh (יהוה), "the LORD," and the Septuagint has *kyrios* (κύριος), Peter without hesitation gives the command to sanctify *Christ* as Lord. There can be no question in Peter's mind as to whom we are to serve in these last days.[5] Because Jesus' work is completed in his death and resurrection, he now has been made both Lord and Christ. We are to set Christ apart as Lord, even as he now *is* Lord and has sat down at the right hand of God (Mark 16:19; Heb. 1:3; 10:12).

So the essence of who we are is servants (and children) of Christ (1 Peter 2:16), who is himself Yahweh, the Lord. If we get that straight, then we know at least one of the ways we are to demonstrate the lordship of Christ: by defending the Christian faith.

Peter then tells us that we are to be "ready" (NASB). The word used in 3:15, *hetoimoi* (ἕτοιμοι), is in adjectival form and thus is not, strictly speaking, an imperative. Some have wanted to construe its force as imperatival, given its dependence on the imperative, "sanctify" (NASB).

5. This hearkens back, you may remember, to Peter's sermon on the day of Pentecost in Acts 2:36: "Let all the house of Israel therefore know for certain that God has made him both Lord and Christ, this Jesus whom you crucified."

Others have seen it as simply adjectival, so that, while it depends on the imperative, is it better translated, "by being ready," so that it modifies the imperative rather than extends it. Whatever the case, there is no question that it carries the force of something we *must* do. Either we must do it because it is a way of setting Christ apart as Lord, or we must do it because it carries the force of a command. To set Christ apart as Lord, therefore, is (in part) to ready ourselves.

And we are always to be ready, says Peter, to give an answer, a defense, an apology (*pros apologian*/πρὸς ἀπολογίαν). The term here is a legal one. It is the technical term for a defendant's rebuttal against charges in a court of law.[6] There is no question, then, that the context here is apologetic in nature.

It must be said here, in case it is not obvious, that one of the primary ways to ready ourselves for the apologetic task is by our study and knowledge of Scripture. We may also desire to study philosophy or culture or some other relevant area in order to strengthen or deepen or broaden our defense. There is nothing wrong with such study. Some of the essays in this book hope to show the relevance and importance of such study. But if we study those things to the neglect of Scripture, then we have not adequately prepared ourselves for the apologetic task.

We should note here, as well, Peter's use of a phrase that can be translated "to require an account," that is, a *logos* (λόγος). That word, too, carries legal connotations. Peter sees our responsibility of setting Christ apart as Lord and therefore of answering charges brought against the faith, as if they were brought to us in a court of law. He wants the answers and responses to be taken that seriously.

Notice that the defense, in this context, is not specifically of "the faith," but rather of "the hope" (*elpidos*/ἐλπίδος). This is likely Peter's way of summarizing the Christian life (cf. Acts 23:6; 26:7; Col. 1:23; 1 Tim. 1:1; Heb. 3:6; 6:18; 7:19; 10:23).[7]

It is also Peter's way of reminding us of the lordship of Christ. That lordship is both a present reality, as we have seen, and his future,

6. It is used in this sense in Acts 25:16; Phil. 1:7, 16; 2 Tim. 4:16, as is the verb *apologeo-mai*/ἀπολογέομαι in Luke 12:11; 21:14; Acts 24:10; 25:8; 26:1, 2, 24. We could note also Paul's use of the word in 1 Cor. 9:3; 2 Cor. 7:11.

7. Note that in the epistle to the Hebrews, especially, hope is a way of summarizing the entirety of the Christian life.

consummated reign over all things. The hope of the suffering Christian is that Christ is coming to judge the quick and the dead. Peter reminds us that the invisible things are the lasting, permanent, essentially "real" things.

All of this is just to say that the word *apologia*, along with its derivatives, expresses a situation in which we are called on to defend ourselves, more specifically, to defend Christianity, against those who would seek to undermine or destroy it. In the context of 1 Peter 3, we are commanded to do so.

As important as the injunction to sanctify and to defend is, the injunction in verse 16 is equally important: "Yet do it with gentleness and respect, having a good conscience, so that, when you are slandered, those who revile your good behavior in Christ may be put to shame." Peter uses here the stronger conjunction "but" (*alla*/ἀλλα), in order to stress that when we defend the faith, it is to be defended with meekness and reverence. That is, our defense ought to be patterned after Christ himself, who was meek (see Matt. 11:29; 2 Cor. 10:1), and it is to be done not in the fear of those who oppose us, but in the fear of the Lord (see 2 Cor. 5:11).

So there is a three-step progression in this passage, a three-step approach to apologetics that Scripture gives us and that is absolutely essential. (1) We are first to have firmly resolved in our own minds that even though there may be attacks and persecution, Christ is on the throne. Jesus is Lord, and we must establish that in our own hearts. (2) We are to do apologetics in the context of those attacks; we are to defend the faith, making plain the truth of the gospel, the hope that is in us. This can be done only as we explicitly rely on Scripture. This will, inevitably, take us beyond and around issues of bare theism, to the centrality of Christ. (3) We are to do this with gentleness and fear. That is, we should not be threatened, nor will we be, if we remember who is in charge of the universe, who is *really* in control.

Imagine how difficult conditions must have been when Peter wrote these instructions. This epistle was directed to a group of scattered Christians who themselves were suffering persecution. The emperor Nero was a tyrant whose life left much to be desired. During his reign, the Roman world was chaotic and falling apart. Though it would take years for the empire finally to collapse, the turmoil that marked this stage in Rome's history was the beginning of the end. Not only were there wars and attacks from without—in Britain and Judea, for example—but there was turmoil within. Whether or not the emperor's personal ethics mattered to the empire was debated. Not only had Nero divorced his first wife and married another, but when he was tired of his second wife, he kicked her to death and then married a woman whose husband he executed. It would not have been easy, to say the least, to be gentle in such circumstances, to have no fear of man, to be bold in defense.

That, however, is our mandate; it is our duty. We are to be bold in our defense, yet gentle and meek in our manner of defense. As Cornelius Van Til used to say, we must be *suaviter in modo, fortiter in re*.

This, then, is our ground; this is why we do apologetics. It is a discipline that has as its content and context, not bare theism, as much of apologetics wants to maintain (and which, by the way, is foreign to Christianity), but the glorious gospel of Christ—his death, resurrection, ascension, and coming again. And it is our task, our mandate, our privilege to be engaged in it as soldiers of the Divine Warrior King, the Lord of Hosts.

It is our hope that this book will demonstrate the necessity of the truth of Scripture, and the implications of that truth, for apologetics. As we said above, Reformed apologetics is "reformed" to the extent that it takes its cue from Scripture and the theology that flows therefrom. The following essays are meant to spell out more clearly the need for, and the beauty of, an apologetic surrounded by the rich truths of the Reformed faith.

PART 1

REFORMED APOLOGETICS
Exegetical Considerations

I

Epistemological Reflections on 1 Corinthians 2:6–16

RICHARD B. GAFFIN JR.

*I*n the *Festschrift* for Cornelius Van Til, *Jerusalem and Athens*, G. C. Berkouwer expressed disappointment over the criticism that Van Til had made of his views. He had expected that "*exegesis of Holy Scripture would play a decisive role.*" Instead, not only did Van Til misunderstand him, he believed, but "of far greater consequence" was "the total lack of biblical reflection and the absence of a *reply* to all the exegetical questions."[1]

In responding briefly, Van Til conceded Berkouwer's point. His critique of Berkouwer's theology "should have had much more exege-

This chapter is a slightly revised version of an article that appeared originally as "Some Epistemological Reflections on I Cor. 2:6–16," *Westminster Theological Journal* 57 (1995): 103–24. That issue of the journal commemorated the hundredth anniversary of the birth of Cornelius Van Til. My thanks to Eric Sigward for numerous editorial suggestions. Scripture quotations are my translations.

1. G. C. Berkouwer, "The Authority of Scripture (A Responsible Confession)," in *Jerusalem and Athens: Critical Discussions on the Philosophy and Apologetics of Cornelius Van Til*, ed. E. R. Geehan (Nutley, NJ: Presbyterian and Reformed, 1971), 200, his italics (in view primarily is Van Til's, *The Sovereignty of Grace an Appraisal of G. C. Berkouwer's View of Dordt* [Philadelphia: Presbyterian and Reformed, 1969]).

sis in it than it has. This is a defect."[2] He then went on to generalize, "The lack of detailed scriptural exegesis is a lack in all of my writings. I have no excuse for this."[3]

This interchange highlights a frequent perception amounting to a charge: Van Til talks repeatedly about "the Christ of the Scriptures"; his uncompromising concern is to let "the self-attesting Christ of Scripture" speak. Yet his writings provide precious little, if any, argumentation based on a careful treatment of key biblical passages; his approach is assertive and dogmatizing, rather than exegetical.

In my view Van Til was too hard on himself and conceded too much to his critics. Many of them have not read him as carefully as they might. He was, more than may appear at a first glance, well read in the commentaries of Dutch Calvinism such as the Bottenberg series; conversant, say, with the exegetical work of his colleague John Murray; and not only knowledgeable in but thoroughly committed to the kind of biblical theology fathered by his Princeton Seminary professor and friend Geerhardus Vos. A reflective reading of Van Til shows a mind (and heart) thoroughly permeated by Scripture. Issues of its interpretation substantially shaped his thinking, if not his manner of presentation.

Still, there is some substance to criticism like Berkouwer's. Van Til did not make the biblical basis for the characteristic emphases in his thought as clear as he might; that basis needs to be made more explicit. What follows here is the effort to show, primarily from the teaching of Paul, some of the exegetical support for several key emphases in Van Til's epistemology.

Kingdom Epistemology: The Outlook of Jesus

"It can be rightly said that Paul does nothing but explain the eschatological reality which in Christ's teachings is called the Kingdom." This perceptive observation of Herman Ridderbos[4] is certainly applicable

---

2. "Response by C. Van Til," in Geehan, ed., *Jerusalem and Athens*, 203. He adds, "I wish I could have given better exegetical justification for this position than I have" (204).

3. Ibid., 203.

4. *When the Time Had Fully Come: Studies in New Testament Theology* (Grand Rapids, MI: Eerdmans, 1957), 48–49. This statement strikes me as especially helpful for appreciating

to 1 Corinthians 2:6–16. There, if anywhere, Paul is the interpreter of Jesus. In particular, this passage is a virtual commentary on teaching in Matthew 11:25–27/Luke 10:21–22.[5] The different placing of this unit in each Gospel raises questions that we may pass over here. Most likely Luke gives us the right chronology by connecting it directly with the return of the seventy (-two) ("at that same hour," *En autē tē hōra/*Ἐν αὐτῇ τῇ ὥρᾳ, Luke 10:21; cf. v. 17). Matthew's indefinite temporal indicator, "at that time" (*En ekeinō tō kairō/*Ἐν ἐκείνῳ τῳ καιρῷ, Matt. 11:25), probably reflects his less chronologically oriented concern at this point.

In terms of internal structure and wording the two accounts are virtually identical. The only noteworthy variation, beyond the time indicators just noted, is also in the introductory clauses. Matthew's prosaic "Jesus answered and said" (v. 25) contrasts with Luke's "he rejoiced in the Holy Spirit[6] and said" (10:21). The latter, which might be rendered, "jubilant in the Holy Spirit," accents the intensity of Jesus' involvement and the climactic nature of the words that follow. We are at a high point in Jesus' earthly ministry.

This passage is often cited in discussing the deity of Christ because of what it discloses about his unique identity as the Son of God and his equality in being with the Father. Particularly in the past one hundred years or so this text has been focal in debates about the messianic self-consciousness of Jesus. Here, however, our primary interest is not in the person of Christ—the issue of his essential deity—but in what he says about the activity of Father and Son and the content of that action.

The Activity of Revelation: The Sola *of Revelation*

In Luke 10:21 "have hidden" stands in stark contrast with "chooses to reveal," verse 22. This contrast clearly points up the sense of this

---

the overall doctrinal or didactic unity of the New Testament in its historically differentiated diversity.

5. We proceed here on the premise that, with tradition and the redactional activity of the respective evangelists duly taken into account, this material provides us with a reliable record of what Jesus said. Authenticity is argued (on historical-critical grounds), e.g., by R. Riesner, *Jesus als Lehrer: Eine Untersuchung zum Ursprung der Evangelium-Überlieferung*, Wissenschaftliche Untersuchungen zum Neuen Testament (Tübingen: J. C. B. Mohr, 1981), 220–21, 330, 335–37, 344–45, 434, 478.

6. Even if *tō hagiō/*τῷ ἀγίῳ is not original, a reference to the (Holy) Spirit is most likely.

primary word for revelation (*apokalyptō*/ἀποκαλύπτω) in the New
Testament. What is revealed is otherwise hidden, a disclosure of the
previously veiled. Revelation is making known what heretofore has
been unknown, kept a secret; in that sense it may be said to be an
"open secret."

Further, what is revealed remains hidden from "the wise and the
intelligent" (*sophōn kai synetōn*/σοφων καὶ συνετων); the latter word may
also be rendered "learned," "having understanding." What is revealed,
then, is beyond all human capacity and competence, whether rational
or intuitive; revelation is inaccessible to human potential in its highest actualizations. In other words, Jesus asserts the absolute, exclusive
necessity of revelation.

There is nothing here to suggest that revelation is an alternate, and
therefore essentially dispensable, means of communicating what could
also be arrived at by the use of reason or some other human capacity.
In fact, everything is decisively against such a notion. Nor is there even
the slightest indication that the problem necessitating revelation is
moral but not intellectual. The categories in view are cognitive; those
"having understanding" are as such, respecting revelation, those who
do not and cannot *understand*.

The exclusive necessity of revelation is reinforced by the "infants,"
"little children" (*nēpiois*/νηπίοις, Matt. 11:25) as the recipients of revelation, in counterpoint to the "wise and intelligent." This reference
is explicated by what Jesus teaches elsewhere about the necessity of
repenting and becoming like a little child for entering the kingdom of
heaven and of becoming humble like a child to be great in the kingdom
(Matt. 18:3–4), and about receiving the kingdom like a little child in
order to enter it (Mark 10:15).

In other words, Jesus speaks of the need for *faith*. Just as revelation
is necessary, because what is revealed is not an intellectual attainment
or any other human accomplishment, so the necessary condition in
its recipients is faith, the receptive humility that stems from faith
alone; the necessity of revelation involves the necessity of faith. In
this sense there is an unbreakable correlation between revelation and
its reception, and faith.

The necessity of revelation appears from the side of the recipients, as we have seen, in their absolute dependence. But, further, the

revealer is under no outside compulsion to reveal. No claim arising from the (potential) recipients necessitates revelation. Rather, the act of revealing is free, sovereign, of entirely uncoerced divine initiative; it is a matter of the Father's *eudokia* (εὐδοκία), his "good pleasure," "purpose," "choice" (cf. Eph. 1:5, 9). Correlatively, the Son does not merely reveal but "*chooses* to reveal" (Luke 10:22; cf. what is said about the gratuitous disclosure of "the mysteries of the kingdom," Matt. 13:11/Luke 8:10). Both Father and Son are sovereign in revelation, and that sovereignty is unrestricted, unqualified by anything outside themselves.

The Content of Revelation: The Tota of Revelation

The scope of what is revealed is designated here as "these things" (*tauta*/ταῦτα, Luke 10:21) and "all things" (*panta*/πάντα, v. 22). *Tauta* has no explicit grammatical antecedent, either within the passage or in the preceding verses. That suggests a looser, more general reference back to the "things" (miracles) done by Jesus in Chorazin, Bethsaida, and Capernaum (Matt. 11:20–24; Luke 10:13–15). Additionally, Luke brackets the passage, on the one side (vv. 17–20), with what he intends his readers to understand as the eschatological overthrow of Satan and his rule, which Jesus perceives as having taken place in the mission of the seventy-two. On the other side (vv. 23–24), Jesus speaks of the new realities of fulfillment experienced by the disciples ("what you see, . . . what you hear . . ."), in contrast to the old order (the "many prophets and kings").

All told, from these indications in the immediate context and within the overall framework provided by the Synoptic Gospels, we are on sound footing in saying that "these things" are, in other words, the things of the kingdom of God/heaven (cf. in the immediate context, Matt 11:11–13; Luke 10:9).

With that sort of summation the wider ramifications of this passage begin to emerge. According to the Synoptics, the kingdom of God is at once the central and all-encompassing theme of the proclamation of Jesus during his earthly ministry. As such it is not limited in scope or confined to some restricted sector or dimension of concerns. Rather, the kingdom is an eschatological reality, comprehensively considered.

It embodies the consummation of God's covenant—the realization of the ages-long hopes of his people, the fulfillment of the sweeping promises made to them (cf., again, Luke 10:24). More specifically, the kingdom is a matter of the eschatological lordship of God in Jesus, the Christ, presently being realized in his arrival and to be consummated fully at his return.[7]

Consequently, "these things," as the content of revelation, are to be considered comprehensively. They are in fact "all things" (v. 22)—that is, all that has its origin in the unique fellowship of knowledge between Father and Son and is purposed by them for revelation in and by the Son (v. 22). Or, as already noted, they are all that is revealed and brought to realization in the coming of the kingdom.

It might appear that this kingdom qualification somehow limits the scope of "all things." But, to the contrary according to the New Testament, there is nothing in the entire creation that is irrelevant to the kingdom; absolutely nothing falls outside the eschatological rule of Christ. Availing ourselves of some Pauline commentary at this point, the reality of the kingdom is the reality that God has "placed all things under his [Christ's] feet and appointed him to be head over everything for the church"; it is the reality, already underway, of "bringing all things, things in heaven and things on earth, under Christ as head" (Eph. 1:22, 10).[8] The kingdom of God is totalitarian in the most ultimate sense we can know and experience. It is not a partial or part-time allegiance, involving only some of our efforts or just one sector of our experience, or merely a part of our knowledge.

The implications of Jesus' words, in context, are entirely decisive. Their momentousness, though often missed, is inescapable. There is

7. Many helpful treatments of Jesus' kingdom proclamation have appeared over the course of the twentieth century to the present. Among those of book length, some of the older ones are still the best. See Herman Ridderbos, *The Coming of the Kingdom* (Philadelphia: Presbyterian and Reformed, 1962), and the much earlier (1903) classic of Geerhardus Vos, *The Teaching of Jesus Concerning the Kingdom of God and the Church* (repr., Nutley, NJ: Presbyterian and Reformed, 1972).

8. The NIV's rendering of *eis oikonomian tou plērōmatos tōn kairōn*/εἰς οἰκονομίαν τοῦ πληρώματος τῶν καιρων in v. 10a, "to be put into effect when the times will have reached their fulfillment," is unfortunate because it masks that the heading-up of all things in Christ (v. 10b) has already begun, as (presently being) "head over everything for the church" (v. 22) makes plain (cf. Gal. 4:4).

no area or dimension of human knowledge that lies outside the scope of the revelation in view in these verses, or for which that revelation is irrelevant. Any epistemological endeavor true to these verses recognizes its absolute, exclusive dependence on such revelation. To be truly "wise and learned" in the creation, one must become a "little child" and receive the revelation of God in Christ. Involved here is the epistemological ultimacy of the Creator-creature distinction, the unconditional dependence of creatures made in God's image, a dependence upon him for knowing as well as being.

In sum: according to Jesus, revelation is the exclusive and comprehensive *principium* for human knowledge, its foundation and norm. In terms of classical Reformation predicates, revelation involves both a *sola* and a *tota*.

Paul's Epistemology

It is difficult not to see 1 Corinthians 2:6–16, within and including its immediate context, especially 1:26–28, as a commentary on the Matthew/Luke passage. Whatever may have been in Paul's mind as he wrote, the connection between the two is close; common themes, as we will see, tie them together.

Within the first main part of the letter (1:10–4:21),[9] 1:18–3:23 has a high order of importance in the Pauline corpus as a whole. To counter the disastrous misconception of the gospel at Corinth, resulting in sharp divisions within the church and an entrenched party spirit (1:10–17), Paul highlights the true nature of the division that the gospel does create by drawing attention to some fundamentals of his apostolic ministry and message.

Within this passage a key word, perhaps the most prominent, is wisdom (*sophia*/σοφία). As we move to the end of chapter 1 and on into chapter 2, two points, among others, come to the fore.

1. A clash—a sharp, unrelieved antithesis—exists between "the wisdom of God" (1:21) and the wisdom of unbelief. What has been effected by God in the cross of Christ is the transvaluation of wis-

---

9. We may leave to the side here the question of the basic outline of 1 Corinthians. More than one proposal is defensible, and no one ought to be pressed; see the various commentaries and volumes on special introduction.

dom—in fact its countervaluation—as measured by the standards of "the world,""this age" (1:20), constituted by unbelief and sinful rebellion. In terms of the rhetorically balanced antithetical parallelism of 1:26–28, foolishness and weakness in the eyes of the world are wisdom and power before God; conversely, what the world judges to be wise and powerful, God considers to be foolish and weak. Echoes of the contrast between the "wise and learned" and the "little children" in Matthew 11:25/Luke 10:21 are unmistakable.

2. The wisdom of God is not ultimately cognitive or merely intellectual. Though a body of doctrinal knowledge is certainly integral to that wisdom (e.g., Rom. 6:17; 2 Tim. 1:13), and it would be quite perverse to deny that,[10] its controlling point of reference is Christ, himself "the power of God and the wisdom of God" (1 Cor. 1:24; cf. Col. 2:3). Hence, the resolve "to know nothing . . . except Jesus Christ and him crucified" (1 Cor. 2:2). Christ, in his death and resurrection, is Paul's ultimate epistemic commitment.[11]

Worth noting is the recent and salutary turn in the interpretation of 1 Corinthians 2:6–16 within the historical-critical tradition. With the rise of the history-of-religions approach toward the close of the nineteenth century, the view emerged and eventually became more or less standard, especially in German scholarship, that this passage reflects the basic outlook of the Hellenistic mystery religions of Paul's day. Following Wilhelm Bousset, Rudolf Bultmann proved especially influential in his *Sachkritik* of 2:6ff.: Paul has betrayed himself by a disastrous accommodation to the thought-world of Gnosticism; the cross-based concept of "wisdom" in 1:18–26 may not be made the basis for interpreting the mystery-concept of "wisdom"

10. Suffice it here to say that Kantian/post-Kantian polarizations of rational and personal knowledge, of whatever variety—modern or postmodern—are foreign to Paul.

11. Care must be taken not to read a narrow, one-sided theology of the cross out of (or into) 1 Cor. 2:2. It has to be connected with equally sweeping and aphoristic assertions like 2 Tim. 2:8: "Remember Jesus Christ raised from the dead . . . according to my gospel." As Calvin notes, in Scripture references to the death alone or to the resurrection alone are synecdochic (*Institutes of the Christian Religion*, ed. John T. McNeill, trans. Ford Lewis Battles [Philadelphia: Westminster, 1960], 2.16.13). This is certainly true for Paul. On balance, the center of his gospel ("of first importance") is Christ's death and resurrection in their significance as the fulfillment of Scripture (1 Cor. 15:3–4), entailing ultimately the soteriological-eschatological renewal of nothing less than the entire creation (Rom. 8:19–22; 2 Cor 5:17).

in 2:6ff., because the two are not merely at odds but fundamentally irreconcilable.

More recent exegesis, however, has questioned this assessment. The consensus forming in the past several decades is that 2:6–16 has its background in the merging of wisdom and apocalyptic traditions, primarily within Hellenistic Judaism, which Paul interprets christologically, in the light of the cross and resurrection. On this view 2:6–16 expands on and does not contradict "the word of the cross" in 1:18ff. It is now widely accepted, and so need not be argued here, that the passage is a direct, even essential, continuation of the previous argumentation with its basic antithetical theme.[12]

So far as the internal flow of the passage is concerned, I find Stuhlmacher's proposal persuasive: verses 6a and 6b set the direction so that, in chiastic sequence, verses 7–9 expand on 6b, verses 10–16 on 6a; in this way 2:6–16 enlarges on 1:18–25 especially.[13]

God's Wisdom as Eschatological (1 Cor. 2:6–9)[14]

The antithesis created by the wisdom/foolishness of gospel-preaching is nothing less than eschatological in its dimensions. That sweep, intimated already in 1 Corinthians 1 in references to "the disputant of this age" (v. 20) and "the wisdom of the [=this, cf. 3:19] world" (1:20, 21), is accented beginning in 2:6: the wisdom spoken to believers, identified as the *teleioi* (τέλειοι),[15] is "not of this age nor of

12. This brief overview is largely based on the survey of P. Stuhlmacher, "The Hermeneutical Significance of I Cor 2:6–16," in *Tradition and Interpretation in the New Testament*, ed. G. F. Hawthorne (Grand Rapids, MI: Eerdmans, 1987), 330–32; see also, e.g., the discussion of the passage in F. Lang, *Die Briefe an die Korinther*, Neue Testament Deutsch 7 (Göttingen: Vandenhoeck & Ruprecht, 1986), 38–48; and W. Schrage, *Der erste Brief an die Korinther*, Evangelisch-katholischer Kommentar zum Neuen Testament, 7, 1 (Zürich: Benziger, 1991), 242–45, 268f; cf., among English-language treatments, the similar stance of Gordon D. Fee, *The First Epistle to the Corinthians* (Grand Rapids, MI: Eerdmans, 1987), 99–101.

13. Stuhlmacher, "The Hermeneutical Significance of I Cor 2:6–16," 333.

14. Among the considerable secondary literature pertinent to this section, I mention especially W. D. Dennison, *Paul's Two-Age Construction and Apologetics* (Lanham, MD: University Press of America, 1985), esp. 55–85, a work with the same emphases as this section.

15. The rendering "mature" in most recent translations, though apparently supported by Paul's usage of the word elsewhere (e.g., 1 Cor. 14:20; Phil. 3:15), blunts and relativizes Paul's eschatological point here, which is better captured by "perfect," "complete." In view is not their (relative) subjective spiritual and moral condition. Rather, the thought is along the lines of the definitive sanctification "in Christ" affirmed of the *whole* church in 1 Cor. 1:2. Accordingly, the *teleioi* are not just some in the church in distinction from the rest, an in-group of Gnostic-like

the rulers of this age, who are passing away," along with this world-age in its entirety (cf. 7:31).

The background here, of course, is the contrast between the two aeons, coined within intertestamental Judaism and taken up by Paul and other New Testament writers—a comprehensive conceptual framework that, as it encompasses the whole of history, from creation to consummation, accents its eschatological *telos*.[16] The plain implication, then, of verses 6, 7, and 9 (whatever the source of the supporting citation in the latter[17]) is that "God's wisdom" (2:7), granted to believers, is of the aeon to come, the new and final world-age; it is, in a word, eschatological wisdom.[18]

Verse 8, which expands on the negative point of verse 6b, is to be read in that light: "which [God's mystery-wisdom] none of the rulers of this age understood, for if they had understood it, they would not have crucified the Lord of glory." While "the rulers of this age" may have in view primarily those directly responsible for the crucifixion (cf. the specific mention of Herod and Pontius Pilate in Acts 4:27), there is surely a broader association with the wise, powerful, and well-born (*eugeneis*/εὐγενεῖς) in 1 Corinthians 1:26–28 (cf. 1:20).[19] The rulers of this age are representative; in them we see the most impressive achievements of the present world-order, measured by the standards of human pride and unbelief. Within the creation, as presently subject to the curse on sin (cf. Rom. 8:20–22), they exemplify the most that it has to offer and is capable of attaining.

---

initiates, but all believers as such—those, as Paul has just said (v. 5), whose "faith rest[s] not on men's wisdom, but on God's power." Beyond the commentaries, see especially the excellent discussion of P. J. Du Plessis, *TELEIOS: The Idea of Perfection in the New Testament* (Kampen: Kok, 1959), 178–85, 204–5, 243–48.

16. Among the best introductory discussions of the two-aeon construct is, still, Geerhardus Vos, *The Pauline Eschatology* (Grand Rapids, MI,: Baker, 1979), 1–41.

17. See, e.g., Fee, *The First Epistle to the Corinthians*, 108f.

18. Despite what might be the surface impression from the language employed ("wisdom in a mystery" "hidden"), v. 7 is not a lapse into the thought-world of Gnosticism. If anything, Paul uses (proto-)Gnostic terminology here and elsewhere (e.g., the *psychikos-pneumatikos* [ψυχικὸς-πνευματικὸς] distinction in vv. 13–14) to make decidedly anti-Gnostic emphases; cf. Rom. 16:25f.; Col. 1:26. On Paul's redemptive-historical, eschatological understanding of *mystērion*/μυστήριον, see especially Herman N. Ridderbos, *Paul: An Outline of His Theology*, trans. John Richard DeWitt (Grand Rapids, MI: Eerdmans, 1975), 46–49.

19. For a brief but incisive and convincing refutation of the view that the "rulers" are demonic powers, see Fee, *The First Epistle to the Corinthians*, 103f.; cf. John Murray, *The Epistle to the Romans*, 2 vols. (Grand Rapids, MI: Eerdmans, 1965), 2:254.

All the more striking, then, is Paul's disqualification of the rulers of this age, in the face of the age-to-come, eschatological wisdom of the gospel. Moreover, the specific terms of this disqualification are clear: they do not *understand* the gospel; their failure is not only moral but epistemological, a point we will see made even more emphatically in 1 Corinthians 2:14.

Coming to light in this passage, then, is the epistemological difference between believers and unbelievers, a difference of the most radical and far-reaching sort, in that it does not go too far to say believers and unbelievers belong to two different worlds; they exist in not only separate but antithetical "universes of discourse."

Such rhetoric is subject to distortion and must be qualified, as Paul in fact does qualify. In the period until Christ's return, the two aeons overlap,[20] so that in terms of psycho-physical makeup ("in the body," as "outer man," e.g., 2 Cor. 4:10, 16) believers continue to exist in the present, sinful aeon. In that respect their resurrection is a still future hope (see esp. 1 Cor. 15:35ff.). Until then they must not suppose, as Paul's opponents at Corinth apparently did, that they are beyond or can override the eschatological *Vorbehalt* of 1 Corinthians 13:12 ("now we see but a poor reflection").

But such reservations, along with the anthropological complexities undeniably involved, must not obscure that at the core of their being ("heart," as "inner man," e.g., Rom. 2:29; 2 Cor. 4:16), believers are "alive from the dead" (Rom. 6:13) and so, as already raised with Christ (Eph. 2:5–6; Col. 2:13; 3:1), are presently within the eschatological "new creation" (2 Cor. 5:17). More particularly, such qualifications as are necessary must not be used to tone down the unrelieved antithesis between "the wisdom of God" and "the wisdom of the world" in this passage, nor to soften the nothing-less-than aeonic clash between them. Again, fundamentally believers and unbelievers are in two different worlds.

With the gospel and its implications as the point of reference, there is no point of contact epistemologically between believers and unbelievers, however understood, whether by empirical observation or by rational reflection and speculation. When Paul says, "Jews require

20. See, e.g., Vos, *The Pauline Eschatology*, 36–41, including the diagrams in n. 45.

signs, Greeks seek wisdom" (1 Cor. 1:22), the exclusion intended is universal. The notion of such a common ground or capacity, rational or otherwise, that can be used to build a bridge toward the gospel, or otherwise prepare and dispose unbelievers to accept its truth, is not only not present in this passage; it is alien to it, jarringly so.

Clear enough here already, in other terms, is what 2:10a states: "but God has revealed it to us. . . ." God's wisdom is revelation and is as such, as in the Matthew 11/Luke 10 passage, not merely an alternative track, not just another, second way of arriving at knowledge that human beings are otherwise quite capable of achieving on their own. God's wisdom-revelation, focused in the cross of Christ, is beyond the human competence and capacity to grasp and determine, of whatever kind—reason, intuition, observation, feeling.

The Activity of the Spirit (1 Cor. 2:10–16)

Seen as commentary on Matthew 11:25–27/Luke 10:21–22, 1 Corinthians 2:10–16 advances our understanding in a significant respect. The Gospels pericope speaks of the activity of Father and Son. Paul places added emphasis on the activity of the Holy Spirit. All told, the fully Trinitarian character of revelation emerges. Verses 10b–16 expand on "through the Spirit" of verse 10a, which picks up on "in the demonstration of the Spirit and power" in verse 4, the letter's first explicit reference to the Spirit, where his activity opposes this-age, human wisdom (v. 5).

This emphasis on the Spirit, it needs to be appreciated, does not move us beyond but continues and even reinforces the eschatological dimension of the argument. Paul's overall conception of the work of the Holy Spirit is decidedly eschatological.[21] That is clear from the metaphors he uses for the Spirit's work in believers: he is the "deposit" on our eschatological inheritance and the resurrection body (2 Cor. 1:22; 5:5; Eph. 1:14), the "firstfruits" toward the resurrection body

---

21. This became widely recognized during the past century; see, e.g., Gordon Fee, *God's Empowering Presence: The Holy Spirit in the Letters of Paul* (Peabody, MA: Hendrickson, 1994), 803–26; and the 1912 essay, well ahead of its time, of Geerhardus Vos, "The Eschatological Aspect of the Pauline Conception of Spirit," in *Redemptive History and Biblical Interpretation: The Shorter Writings of Geerhardus Vos*, ed. R. B. Gaffin Jr. (Phillipsburg, NJ: Presbyterian and Reformed, 1980), 91–125; see also Vos, *The Pauline Eschatology*, 162–66.

(Rom. 8:23). The adjective "spiritual," having reference to the work of the Spirit, is the single, comprehensive designation not only of the resurrection body (1 Cor. 15:44) but of the entire eschatological order (v. 46). Inherent in the soteriological activity of the Spirit are "the powers of the age to come" (Heb. 6:5).

First Corinthians 2:10–16 also brings out the comprehensive role of the Spirit in revelation. He initiates both the giving and the receiving of revelation; he is both knower and communicator.

Verses 10–11 address the former. The Spirit functions in revelation because he has the requisite investigative competence. He has the capacity for the comprehensive probing and searching (*erauna*/ἐραυνᾷ) adequate to "all things," including "even the deep things of God." As investigator he is omnicompetent.

Verse 11 offers a supporting argument from analogy, involving a word-play on *pneuma* (πνεῦμα), an argument from the lesser to the greater, from our experience to the issue at hand. "The spirit of man which is within him" is an anthropological use of *pneuma*, one of the terms Paul uses for the inner side of human personality, referring to self-consciousness and self-awareness, to the self as knowing and willing.[22]

The basic point of verse 11 is to compare the unique self-knowledge of God to the exclusive knowledge each of us has of ourselves. Just as no one knows me with my concerns, "the things of man," as I know myself from the inside out, so no one knows God with his concerns, "the things of God," referring here primarily to his wisdom revealed in Christ, as God himself does. Specifically, the Spirit of God is viewed here as the principle of self-knowledge in God. This is for the sake of the analogy with the human *pneuma* and with a view to the stress on the Spirit's activity in the immediate context, not to exclude Father and Son from this self-knowledge.

Verse 11 also shows that the Spirit's searching and probing (v. 10) is not permanently without resolution. It is not some sort of open-ended divine search without end. As a "discovering," it is simultaneously a possession.

Consequently, the Spirit is not only the principle of knowledge in God but also (vv. 12–13) the principle and means for communicat-

---

22. See Ridderbos, *Paul*, 117ff. esp. 120f.

ing that knowledge. The Spirit now comes into view as given to and indwelling believers ("we have received . . ."), specifically so that they may understand "the things freely given to us by God." The latter has a comprehensive reference; they are "the things of God" (v. 12) determined for revelation, God's eschatological gospel-wisdom, centered in Christ's cross and resurrection (vv. 2, 6–9), or, in terms of Matthew 11/Luke 10, "these things" of the kingdom of God.

"The spirit of the world" occurs only here in the New Testament. Despite what might be an initial impression, the reference is almost surely not to Satan as "the god of this age" (2 Cor. 4:4) or to some other spiritual being. Rather, coined to sharpen the antithesis to the Spirit and his eschatological activity, the phrase captures the world as humanity in rebellion against God (cf. 1 Cor. 1:20, 21, 27, 28; 2:6b, 8), with the attitudes and standards that characterize it as a whole. It is close, perhaps identical, to the *phronēma* (φρόνημα, "mind-set," "disposition," "attitude") of the flesh in opposition to that of the Spirit in Romans 8:6. As we speak of "the spirit of the times" or "the spirit" that controls a culture, so here Paul speaks in effect, sweepingly, of "the spirit of this world-age." This serves to point up, once again, the inability of sinful humanity, the constitutional incompetence of sinners in themselves to attain to a true knowledge of God, and so the absolute necessity of the revelation through the Spirit in view.

First Corinthians 2:13 expands on the Spirit's revelatory role as that involves the apostle. "We," inclusive of all believers in verses 10 and 12, now distinguishes Paul from them, as in verses 6 and 7.[23] His speaking is a function of the Spirit's controlling activity; his words are not human, this-age wisdom, but gospel-wisdom, "taught by the Spirit." The participial clause at the end, whatever its exact meaning,[24] accents this didactic activity of the Spirit.[25]

23. Although, by implication, other apostles—and even all believers, when they faithfully communicate apostolic teaching—are in view.

24. For the exegetical issues involved, see, e.g., Fee, *The First Epistle to the Corinthians*, 114f.

25. It is hardly correct to argue that throughout this passage Paul's dominant interest is the Spirit's activity, through him, in producing Scripture (as does Walter Kaiser, "A Neglected Text in Bibliology Discussions: I Corinthians 2:6–16," *Westminster Theological Journal* 43 [1981]: 301–19; see the pertinent rejoinder of Fee, *The First Epistle to the Corinthians*, 112–13n63). At

Verses 14–16 focus on the response to revelation, the believer's Spirit-worked reception of the apostle's Spirit-taught words. In so doing they put that response in the most fundamental possible perspective. Here again, as in Jesus' teaching, but in an even more emphatic, antithetic fashion, emerge the twin factors of exclusiveness and comprehensiveness, both the *sola* and the *tota* of revelation.

Only two responses are possible: acceptance or rejection; there is no middle ground, no temporizing third alternative.[26] This unrelieved state of affairs is captured by the contrast between *psychikos anthrōpos* (ψυχικὸς ἄνθρωπος) and *ho pneumatikos* (ὁ πνευματικὸς)—again, a distinction that, without exception, covers every hearer.

The former, as Paul's only other pairing of these Greek adjectives, in 1 Corinthians 15:44, 46, makes clearer, is "living" (*psyxē*/ψυξη, 15:45a), that is, everyone who bears the image of the first Adam (v. 49a), who now, since the fall (Rom. 5:12ff.), is under the control of sin with its enervating and corrupting consequences (1 Cor. 15:42–43; cf. vv. 21–22). As such this person is devoid of the Spirit ("the man without the Spirit")

---

the same time, however, there are important implications for the doctrine of inspiration in v. 13, on the justified assumption that it applies equally to what the apostle writes, as well as to what he says. Striking here, particularly with a view to ongoing debate about the doctrine of Scripture, is that the specific *content* of Paul's message is *not* in view, at least not directly. Rather, it is considered in a purely *formal* fashion, and then not merely as resulting from a revelatory encounter or in terms of underlying ideas or promptings, but as a *plurality of words*. The *words* of Paul, as such and ultimately considered, are not of human origin but inculcated by the Spirit (cf. 2 Peter 1:20–21).

26. This is contrary to the persistent, widespread misreading of 1 Cor. 3:1, where Paul tells Corinthian believers ("brothers") that he must address them not as *pneumatikois*/πνευματικοῖς but as *sarkinois*/σαρκίνοις, and of v. 3, where he calls them *sarkinoi*. In 3:1–3 Paul is not seeking to rationalize or even concede as normal a two-level distinction between spiritual and carnal Christians. Whatever slight semantic difference there may be between the two adjectives used on the one side of the contrast, both may be translated "fleshly" and are parallel to *psychikos*/ψυχικὸς in 2:14 ("Here ψυχή approaches the second meaning of σάρξ, namely flesh as existence turned away from God," J. van Genderen and W. H. Velema, *Beknopte gereformeerde dogmatiek* [Kampen: Kok, 1992], 323). The specific reason that Paul must write as he does is the presence of "jealousy and quarreling" (*zēlos kai eris*/ζῆλος καὶ ἔρις), a combination (in reverse sequence) that occurs elsewhere in Paul only in describing "the works of the flesh" (Gal. 5:19), in sharp opposition (vv. 16–17) to "the fruit of the Spirit" (vv. 22–23), and "the works of darkness," in conflict with "the weapons of light" (Rom. 13:12–13). The point of the imagery in 1 Cor. 3:1c–2, then, is not that in their immature behavior the Corinthians, regrettably but as must be expected, are acting like young, low-level Christians, but that they are not acting like Christians at all. Their behavior is the flat antithesis of Christian conduct; the figurative language points to abnormal, deformed development and likely carries the nuance "infantile," "puerile," in that sense, "childish." Sin is sin wherever it is found, even in God's people.

and so "does not accept the things of God's Spirit." In fact, "to him," that is, in terms of the standards of this age to which he is committed, God's wisdom-revelation is (demonstrable) "foolishness" (cf. 1:27).

What Paul goes on to say about this person must not be overlooked: "he cannot understand them." It is not simply that such a person will not or refuses to accept what he right well knows to be true. No, he won't because he can't. Expressed here is a total cognitive inability, an incapacity that exists "because they [the things of the Spirit] are spiritually discerned," that is, they are properly appraised and assessed only through the Spirit's activity. Here, again, yawns the unbridgeable epistemological gulf between this age and the age to come, the nothing-less-than eschatological chasm between belief and unbelief. Calvin's pungent comment on 1:20 comes to mind: faced with God's revelation, the unbeliever is like an ass at a concert.[27]

With this negative description the positive side of the picture is emerging. Revelation is understood only where the Spirit provides the requisite discernment. Unmistakably, so far as the granting and receiving of God's wisdom are concerned, we are shut up within the closed circle of the Spirit's working.

Verse 15 makes that explicit. "The one who is spiritual" is such because indwelt, renewed, enlightened, directed by the Holy Spirit.[28] Such persons, believers, are transformed by the Spirit so that they are enabled to do what *psychikos anthrōpos* can't. Believers are granted the Spirit-worked capacity for appraisal and discernment so that, however imperfectly and even inadequately (13:12), they can truly understand God's revelation and know it for what it is. In other words, the believer is taken up into the "closed circle" of the Spirit's activity.

Along with the exclusiveness of the Spirit's activity, the comprehensiveness of that activity, the *tota* of revelation, also comes out in 2:15. The discernment produced by the Spirit contemplates *panta*

27. " . . . atque asinus ineptus est ad symphoniam," *Opera . . . Omnia* (Brunsvigae: C. A. Schwetschke, 1892), 49:325.

28. By now the long-standing effort ought to have been put to rest to enlist this passage in support of an anthropological trichotomy (with *pneumatikos*/πνευματικὸς here taken to refer to the human *pneuma*/πνεῦμα come to its revived ascendancy); see John Murray, *Collected Writings of John Murray: Vol. 2, Selected Lectures in Systematic Theology* (Edinburgh: Banner of Truth, 1977), 23–33, esp. 23–29.

(πάντα), "all things." This echoes *panta* as the object of the Spirit's searching activity in verse 10. Both, in turn, pick up on the *panta* in Matthew 11:27/Luke 10:22, discussed above with its implications.

Paul's point is not that *ho pneumatikos*, by the Spirit, transcends every human limitation and so shares in God's exhaustive self-knowledge. Nor is he suggesting that believers have expert, encyclopedic knowledge in every area of human investigation—as if they know all there is to know about God, self, and the universe; becoming a Christian does not make one a polymath, a sort of renaissance man.

At the same time, however, we must not tone down this passage or domesticate Paul's *panta*. His point is hardly that revelation is restricted in its relevance to only a part of life, or, following Kant, concerns only the moral-religious dimension of human experience. Rather, God's eschatological wisdom, focused in Christ's cross and resurrection, is still in view here, as that elaborates Jesus' sweeping kingdom vision in Matthew 11/Luke 10. Such wisdom, Paul is saying, has a bearing on, in fact is essential for, a true knowledge of everything there is to know about God, ourselves, and the world.

The sense of this Spirit-worked assessment of *panta*, the full, comprehensive proportions involved, is further pointed up by the use of Isaiah 40:13 in 1 Corinthians 2:16. The reference to the nonderivative "mind of the Lord," God as ultimate knower, brings into view as well a context (Isa. 40:12–31) that, in the Scripture at Paul's disposal, is difficult to match for rhetorical sweep and power as a description of God's sovereign, all-inclusive control of everything that transpires in the universe.

To that Paul adds, as the concluding note of the passage, "But we have the mind of Christ." To have "the Spirit who is from God" (1 Cor. 2:12), without overlooking the consequences and qualifications already made in verses 13–15, is to have "the Spirit of Christ" (Rom. 8:9) and so, too, the mind (*nous*/νοῦς) of Christ,[29] the exalted Christ, "in whom" as "the mystery of God" now revealed in the church, "are

---

29. On this interchange of *pneuma* and *nous*, note that the Hebrew of Isa. 40:13 has "spirit of the Lord" (רוח יהוה). The LXX reads *noun kyriou*/νουν κυρίου (but in other ways the citation differs; the citation in Rom. 11:34 varies from both the Hebrew and the LXX, as well as 1 Cor. 2:16); see E. E. Ellis, *Paul's Use of the Old Testament* (Grand Rapids, MI: Baker, 1981) 12n10, 20n5, 151, 174f.

hidden all the treasures of wisdom and knowledge" (Col. 2:2–3). This link in comprehensive scope between the nonderivative knowledge of God and the Spirit-derived, Christ-centered wisdom of the gospel emerges yet again in the rhetorical flourish with which the larger section closes: "For all [*panta*] are yours . . . all [*panta*] are yours, and you are of Christ, and Christ is of God" (1 Cor. 3:21–23).

A controlling viewpoint in this passage, a theistic, fully Trinitarian point, is that the saving revelation of God in Christ, taught by the Holy Spirit, is the indispensable key to rightly understanding God himself and, with that understanding, literally everything (*panta*) in his creation. Right knowledge is saving knowledge. Anything else, every other knowledge, no matter how operationally effective or functionally productive, is essentially *mis*understanding.

A final comment, on 1 Corinthians 2:15b (note, again, how sweeping the assertion is): "he ['the one who is spiritual'] is subject to appraisal [=judgment][30] by no one." Obviously, this is not an assertion of fideistic autonomy or individualistic independence. Rather, in context, Paul is affirming that the believer submits to no ultimate authority other than the Spirit of God working with the revelation of God, and to authority legitimately deriving from that unbreakable bond between Word and Spirit (to say it with the Reformation). Here again, in other terms, is the reality of enclosure within the sovereign circle of the Spirit's activity. For Paul, this "bondage" to the Spirit is in fact the only real freedom and integrity, intellectual or otherwise, a human being can know (cf. Rom. 6:15–22).

Van Til's Epistemology and the Current Theological Scene

First Corinthians 1:17–3:22/4:21 is a significant apostolic *apologia*. In it come to expression specific convictions decisive for the matrix of thought that shapes Paul's teaching as a whole and in every aspect; nowhere in the Pauline corpus are his basic concerns more on the line than here.

This is the thought-matrix that captured Cornelius Van Til. These were his basic concerns too. No passage of Scripture, especially the

30. Paul's use of *anakrinō*/ἀνακρίνω, with its semantic possibilities, in vv. 14–15 is difficult, if not impossible, to capture in English translation.

closed circle of the Spirit's work in 2:10–16, has had a more determinative impact on his life and thought. In his time, in a singular and most resolute fashion, he contended for this and related truth.[31]

In his lifelong efforts, radiating an evident love for Christ and his church, Van Til challenged two fronts primarily: (1) the mainstream of modern and contemporary theology, flowing from the Enlightenment with its commitment to rational autonomy and "historical-critical" *Sachkritik*[32] of Scripture, and (2), coming closer to home, apologetics committed to the notion of a rationally grounded natural theology, with its essential tenets held in common by believer and unbeliever alike and serving as an adequate basis for convincing unbelievers of the distinctive truths of Christianity. In light of the epistemological considerations from Scripture brought out above, both these fronts prompt several further observations.

1. Virtually from its beginning the church has wrestled with the implications of 2:10–16 for determining the relationship of the gospel

31. There are numerous places throughout his writings where Van Til sets out his basic concerns; perhaps the best brief statement, coming toward the close of his career, is "My Credo," in *Jerusalem and Athens: Critical Discussions on the Philosophy and Apologetics of Cornelius Van Til*, ed. E. R. Geehan (Phillipsburg, NJ: Presbyterian and Reformed, 1971), 3–21.

32. That is, criticism of its subject matter or content (*Sache*) in the sense of the right, even the mandate, to decide, if deemed warranted, that the Bible is wrong, in error. Stuhlmacher's very helpful article "The Hermeneutical Significance of I Cor 2:6–16" is marred in this respect. He begins his brief conclusion (342f.) with the emphatic assertion, "Theological *Sachkritik* must remain silent with regard to this passage [1 Cor. 2:6–16]." What he goes on to say, however, about a circumscribed role for "the historical critical method" as "a special human talent that may be put to the service of faith" is confusing at best. Everything here depends on how "critical" is understood. If in view is "scholarly seriousness and gifts [applied] to the clarification of the linguistic form of Paul's letters and the biblical books in general," who would object? But he continues: it is "both dangerous and wrong to abandon critical thought and judgment in interpreting Scripture and deciding matters of faith in general" (with a parenthetical reference to 1 Peter 3:15), which means that "theological thinking must proceed from the gospel. As such it must be—and continue to be—critical in the light of its subject matter." Now, it appears, *Sachkritik* of Scripture may in fact be necessary at points (just for the sake of the gospel!). Such *Sachkritik*, however, standing in judgment on Scripture, can only be a function of rational autonomy, and, if our passage teaches us anything, human autonomy (wisdom *kata sarka*/κατὰ σάρκα) resists all attenuation. By its very nature it seeks to control everything (and certainly cannot be enlisted in the service of faith, at least not faith in the Christ of Scripture as God's inspired Word). So far as "Paul's letters and the biblical books in general" are concerned (in their original text form, as well as content, cf. 1 Cor. 2:13), *Sachkritik* admitted at one point means, in principle, that it cannot be excluded at any point. At any rate (though Stuhlmacher would likely disagree), such *Sachkritik* is not what the Reformers had in mind when they vigorously affirmed the external clarity of Scripture (to which he appeals, cf. 328f.).

to non-Christian knowledge and reasoning.[33] Consequently, there is a long line of efforts (e.g., as early as Clement of Alexandria, Aquinas and the medieval synthesis, Kant in the modern era) to define the scope of what Paul says here in order to make room for the more or less peacefully partitioned ("schiedlich-friedlich," Schrage) coexistence of Christian and non-Christian wisdom. Repeatedly, especially beginning with the Enlightenment, attempts have been made to accommodate the exercise of human reason as in some sense autonomous.[34]

All such efforts, however, run aground on the immovable rock of Paul's unqualified *panta*. Every attempt to read our passage in partial terms or to restrict its scope by categorical distinctions, of whatever kind, clashes with the sweeping totality of Paul's vision. The antithesis in view leaves no room for an amicable division of territory or a neutral terrain. The wisdom of God is eschatological; it opposes *all* the wisdom of this age, *all* human wisdom according to the flesh (*kata sarka*/κατὰ σάρκα).[35]

Especially popular but damaging has been the notion that the passage is limited to the "religious" sphere, as if Paul's concern is "spiritual" truth in distinction from other kinds ("secular"), which are beyond his purview. The pernicious consequences of this view are nowhere more palpable than in its highly influential Kantian version.[36] The noumenal-phenomenal disjunction supposedly functions to circumscribe (pure)

33. Schrage, *Der erste Brief an die Korinther*, 269f., provides a brief survey; the entire section, "Auslegungs- und Wirkungsgeschichte" (269–78), repays careful reading and reflection; see also A. C. Thiselton, "The Posthistory, Influence, and Reception of 2:6–16," in *The First Epistle to the Corinthians*, New International Greek Testament Commentary (Grand Rapids, MI: Eerdmans, 2000), 276–86.

34. Postmodernism does not diminish occasions for such accommodations. So far as I can see, while postmodern epistemology may have abandoned the Enlightenment pretense to the neutrality and objectivity of reason, it is, if anything, even more resolutely committed to human autonomy—rational or otherwise.

35. In an otherwise fine and penetrating treatment of our passage, D. A. Carson is at best misleading in saying, "But Paul is not addressing general questions of epistemology. He is not even addressing how one comes to a knowledge of what some specific passage of Scripture really means." *The Cross and Christian Ministry* (Grand Rapids, MI: Baker, 1993), 64. Certainly, as Carson immediately adds, "His focus is the fundamental message of the crucified Messiah." But present as well are profound and essential considerations for any sound epistemology, considerations, for instance, that exclude, as Carson himself does, an "ostensibly neutral epistemology" (p. 65).

36. As a measure of how convoluted and even inverted the history of interpretation can become, J. H. Jung-Stilling, a contemporary of Kant's, believed Kant's philosophy to be a confirmation of Paul; the *Critique of Pure Reason*, he held, is a virtual commentary on 1 Cor. 2:14 (cited in Schrage, *Der erste Brief an die Korinther*, 271n288)!

reason and limit its autonomous exercise, thus making room for faith and its free exercise. But the effect, as Western culture of the past two centuries makes all too evident, has been exactly the opposite. Increasingly, faith, especially faith in Christ and the Scriptures, has been marginalized and eventually banished into irrelevance. The lesson is plain: give "secular" (=autonomous) reason an inch and it will not rest content until it controls everything (which, by the way, simply demonstrates the truth of our passage). Or, as Paul would warn the church, "all things are yours . . . or nothing is yours" (cf. 1 Cor. 3:21–23).

2. Still, the nettlesome question of the knowledge of the unbeliever remains, a particularly controversial matter between Van Til and his critics (although it strikes me that this has always been much more of an issue for the latter). Van Til is charged with being unclear: most often roundly denying that unbelievers have any true knowledge, but then sometimes suggesting that they do know.[37]

I make no effort to enter into this debate here in any full way. Nor do I want to suggest that Van Til has had the last word and could not have expressed himself any better.[38] But I do propose that what he says, in its essence, about the unbeliever's knowledge, far from betraying a vitiating flaw in his thinking, points up a singular and important strength. Van Til, following Paul and the Reformers, does not deny the resourceful and valuable know-how unbelievers can display (building highways, decoding DNA, writing textbooks on logic, and much more, often better than believers). But, following Scripture with Calvin, and even more consistently than he, Van Til captures the equivocal tone of the Bible's, especially Paul's, assessment of the unbeliever's knowledge.

The "problem" begins with Scripture itself. In describing how and what the unbeliever knows, it does so in a deliberately ambiguous, paradoxical, "dialectical" fashion, precisely and necessarily in order to

37. See, e.g., *An Introduction to Systematic Theology* (Nutley, NJ: Presbyterian and Reformed, 1974), 24–28; *A Christian Theory of Knowledge* (Nutley, NJ: Presbyterian and Reformed, 1969), 43ff.; cf. John M. Frame, *The Doctrine of the Knowledge of God* (Phillipsburg, NJ: Presbyterian and Reformed, 1987), 49–61; and *Cornelius Van Til: An Analysis of His Thought* (Phillipsburg, NJ: P&R, 1995), 116, 232–33, 307–9, 398, 412–13 and especially the extended discussion, 187–213.

38. Frame's discussions are for the most part illuminating and helpful in this regard, although I would have liked him to give some explicit attention to 1 Cor. 1:18–2:16 in discussing and criticizing what he classifies as Van Til's "Extreme Antithetical Formulations"; see especially *Cornelius Van Til*, 192–97.

make a crucial point unambiguously and powerfully plain. According to Romans 1:18ff., a passage Van Til is sometimes charged with downplaying or treating one-sidedly, unbelievers both know and are ignorant; they understand and do not understand, and they do so in the same *cognitive* moment. The knowledge of God, of "his eternal power and divine nature," in other words, who he is as the true and living God, is (a) clearly revealed in and around them, (b) made evident to them, and (c) understood by them (vv. 19–20). But this truth is suppressed or repressed (*katechontōn*/κατεχόντων, v. 18) such that their *thinking* is futile and their *uncomprehending* hearts darkened (v. 21). As presumably wise—the ironical "wise and understanding" in Luke 10:21 and "wise *kata sarka*" in 1 Corinthians 1:26—they are in fact foolish, the point made in 1 Corinthians 1:20ff.[39] What they really believe is God's truth exchanged for a lie (Rom. 1:25), and their *minds* are corrupted, worthless (*adokimon*/ἀδόκιμον, v. 28).[40]

The categories in verses 21ff., no less than in verses 18–20, are cognitive or contain a cognitive element. It is gratuitous to maintain, as some do, that 18–20 describes an adequate intellectual knowledge, while in 21ff. the knowledge in view is defective only in a more-than-intellectual respect of not being intimate or saving knowledge.[41] Where is the exegetical basis for finding a disjunction here between cognitive and more-than-cognitive knowledge? The knowledge of verse 21 is disqualified cognitively, as well as in a more-than-cognitive respect; its intellectual or cognitive aspect must not be diminished. That knowledge is a matter of "thoughts," "reasonings" (*dialogismois*/διαλογισμοῖς) said to be "futile," "worthless." In addition, the heart is "foolish," that is, literally "without understanding" (*asynetos*/ἀσύνετος), lacking in comprehension.

The full impact of "their foolish heart was darkened" (v. 21) must not be missed. "Heart" brings the individual into view as a totality, considered from the center, the self as a whole, with all its capacities,

---

39. Rom. 1:22 and 1 Cor. 1:20 are the only two uses of *mōrainō*/μωραίνω in Paul.

40. It is important to keep in mind that, while every human being without exception is in its purview, this passage does not describe the actual, individual experience of every unbeliever, particularly at the level of conscious psychology. Paul paints in bold, sweeping strokes, capturing the collective human condition as a result of the fall, the universality of solidarity in sin and its consequences.

41. E.g., Henry E. Allison, *Benedict de Spinoza: An Introduction*, rev. ed. (New Haven, CT: Yale University Press, 1987); there are more exegetical options to consider than they pose (pp. 49f.).

purposefully directed, especially as a religious being, whether to or away from God.[42] "Heart" captures the self in its integrity, or in this passage we may better say, unbelievers in their "broken wholeness." The heart, Paul says, is "without understanding," not just one aspect of the unbeliever but every function, and the attendant circumstance is darkness—total darkness, cognitive, and otherwise.

For Paul, it is not a matter of the primacy of the intellect, but of the heart. His point here is hardly that the basic problem is one of refusing to acknowledge but not of understanding, of the will rather than the intellect, moral instead of philosophical. Distinctions like intellect, will, and emotions have their place, but they are always and ultimately functions of the heart, directed either toward or against God. "The heart *only* has its reasons" (to modify Pascal); all reasoning is reasoning from the heart.

Elsewhere, in Ephesians 4:17–18,[43] Paul is equally, if not more, forceful; cognitive language is emphatic. The sinful rebellion and moral insensitivity of unbelievers involves "the futility of their mind" (*nous*/νους) and their "darkened understanding" (*dianoia*/διάνοια), multiple echoes of Romans 1:21. This expressly cognitive inability stems from their deeply rooted "ignorance" (*agnoian*/ἄγνοιαν), rooted in "the hardness of their heart."

All told, what Paul ascribes to unbelievers is "knowledgeable ignorance," "uncomprehending understanding." The unbeliever both knows and does not know, and there are no categories for neatly distinguishing the one from the other. This "dialectical" dilemma of the unbeliever is the genius of Paul's teaching.

However capable of better formulation, this analysis is not to be dismissed as self-contradictory nonsense. Unbelievers do know—they know God—and, within the parameters of unbelief, there are *no* categories or distinctions in terms of which that is *not* true; they know profoundly, that is, they know from the heart. But this knowledge in its actual possession and exercise, however otherwise effective, is ultimately always confused, inevitably unstable. To use Paul's language, it is in every respect

---

42. On Paul's use of "heart" (*kardia*/καρδία), see Ridderbos, *Paul*, 119f.

43. Not even cited in R. C. Sproul, John H. Gerstner, and Arthur Lindsley, *Classical Apologetics* (Grand Rapids, MI: Zondervan, 1984), even in a context where we might most expect it (p. 49).

fundamentally "futile"; it can serve no useful, constructive epistemological purpose, either in understanding God or, in that light (or better, that darkness), ourselves and the rest of the creation. Specifically and surely Paul would spare the church and have it never forget: such knowledge is not sound and adequate as a point of contact for bringing unbelievers even a step closer to accepting the truth of the gospel.

Perhaps a helpful parallel to the unbeliever's knowledge is what we find in contemplating the effects of the fall on the image of God. Is the unbeliever still the *imago*? Yes and no. Established distinctions for addressing the difference—broader and narrower senses, natural and moral, structural and functional—all leave something to be desired. The unbeliever is/has the image of God, and the consequent image-bearing but sin-blinded need, deeply rooted and ineradicable in unbelievers, provides the point of contact, the capacity for being addressed by the gospel and, through the resurrection, faith-creating power of the Holy Spirit, for recognizing and accepting its truth, "the light of the knowledge of the glory of God in the face of Christ" (2 Cor. 4:6). But, apart from that working of the Spirit, being the divine image in no way alleviates or extenuates human sinfulness; being that image is the presupposition for being a sinner. The unbeliever remains the image of God, entirely, but only "in a negative mode."[44] Every single capacity enjoyed as an image-bearer is engaged in rebellion against God.

In this respect, common grace, with its restraining effects, is not to be overlooked or minimized, and certainly deserves more attention than I give it here.[45] But, contrary to a frequent misconception, the maintenance of the divine image is not simply an unmitigated benefit of common grace; the image, however exactly it is to be defined, makes human sin, *human* sin.[46] Common grace does moderate the consequences of the antithesis between belief and unbelief, but not the

44. Van Genderen and Velema, *Beknopte gereformeerde dogmatiek*, 308, 332; the entire treatment of the image of God in chap. 8 (292–352) is most penetrating. (The early appearance of an English translation of this book is greatly to be desired.)

45. See especially the various writings of Van Til published together in *Common Grace and the Gospel* (Philadelphia: Presbyterian and Reformed, 1972); for an excellent survey of pertinent biblical teaching, see Murray, *Collected Writings of John Murray*, 2:93–119.

46. "The higher is our conception of man in his intrinsic essence, the greater must be the gravity of his offense in rebellion and enmity against God. . . . Man conceived of as in the image of God, so far from toning down the doctrine of total depravity, points rather to its gravity, intensity, and irreversibility"; "It may seem paradoxical, but the higher our view of man's nature,

antithesis itself—a crucial distinction; common grace and the antithesis do not function in inverse proportion to each other. Common grace may make unbelievers genuinely "nicer" but does not reduce their enmity toward God one whit (Rom. 8:7). Common grace renders our present life in the world tolerable, even enjoyable, but does not bring unbelievers even one step closer to the new creation. Common grace, unlike special, gospel grace, is of "this age"; it is not eschatological.

After all the many words on this issue, Calvin's word-picture is difficult to improve on:[47] Unbelievers are like travelers on a pitch-black, moonless night, after a momentary lightning flash. For an instant the surrounding terrain has been illumined far and wide; but before they can take even one step, they are plunged back into darkness and left groping about aimlessly. To vary the figure slightly, this is the unbeliever's situation: frozen perpetually in the split second following the firing of a flash attachment in a darkroom, with a blurred and fading, still indelible impression of everything just illumined and yet now no longer seeing anything—knowing and yet not knowing. This too, I take it, is the basic, controlling point that Van Til, in his day, was concerned to make about the knowledge of the unbeliever.

3. The unbelievers in view in Romans 1:18ff. are those in view in 1 Corinthians 1:18ff., though considered from different perspectives; they are not two different groups. Paul's scope in both passages is universal; the general considerations of each apply, collectively, to all unbelievers; the two passages supplement and reinforce each other. Paul would not have us be in any doubt: those under the impact of God's general revelation (Rom. 1:19–20)—in all of its necessity, authority, sufficiency, and clarity[48]—are those who, just as an expression of their rebellious struggle against the unrelenting, inescapable pressure of that revelation, "require signs . . . and . . . seek wisdom" (1 Cor. 1:22). All such efforts are *kata sarka* (v. 26); the apostle disqualifies and opposes them for what they are: the inevitable truth-suppression (cf. Rom.

---

the more aggravated becomes the depravity that characterizes man as fallen" (Murray, *Collected Writings of John Murray*, 2:38f., 45f).

47. Calvin, *Institutes*, 2.2.18.

48. See Van Til's masterful treatment of general revelation, "Nature and Scripture," in *The Infallible Word: A Symposium by the Members of the Faculty of Westminster Theological Seminary*, ed. N. B. Stonehouse and Paul Woolley (Nutley, NJ: Presbyterian and Reformed, 1978), 255–93, esp. 261–75.

1:18) of "this age" (v. 20), attempts that will never be able to conclude that the gospel of Christ and any epistemological considerations truly conducive to its truth are anything but a "stumbling block," (provable and verifiable) "foolishness" (v. 23).

Among the dissenting critiques of Van Til's epistemology and apologetics, one of the more recent, and most massive, is *Classical Apologetics*.[49] At the heart of its proposal for "A Rational Defense of the Christian Faith" is an extensive defense of natural theology, based primarily, so far as Scripture is involved, on an appeal to Romans 1:18ff.

Remarkably, the authors virtually ignore 1 Corinthians 2:6–16.[50] In chapter 9 ("The Spirit, the Word, and the Church"), there is a passing reference to 1 Corinthians 2:9 (as well as similar references to the Matthew 11/Luke 10 passage, pp. 162f., 167); on pages 170–72, 1 Corinthians 2:9–13 is quoted and discussed briefly for its bearing on the doctrine of Scripture.[51] Elsewhere, where we might most expect 1 Corinthians 2:6–16 or the Gospels pericope to be treated,[52] there is nothing, not even a parenthetical reference. Most remarkably, verse 14 concerning the inability of the unbeliever to understand and the antithesis in verses 14–15 are not even mentioned, much less addressed.[53]

It may be a fair criticism of this chapter that more attention could have been given to Romans 1:18ff. But it will hardly do, in trying to make a case for natural theology, simply to bypass 1 Corinthians 2:6–16. Apparently the authors of *Classical Apologetics* consider the passage irrelevant. If so, then they at least needed to show us how that is the case; for example, how the epistemological gulf between belief and unbelief is really something less than eschatological, or how the cogni-

---

49. Full bibliographic details are above, n. 43.

50. That is, unless I've overlooked something substantive. (The book has no Scripture index.)

51. "This passage may well be the best in all of Scripture for putting together the revelation of God, the inspiration of God, and the illumination of God" (*Classical Apologetics*, 171). This, while certainly true, narrows the scope of the passage; see above, n. 25, especially the first sentence.

52. Chap. 4, "The Biblical Evidence Confirming Natural Theology" (where Rom. 1:18ff. is discussed in some detail); chap. 13, "The Noetic Influence of Sin"; chap. 16, "The Self-Attesting God"; chap. 17, "The Internal Testimony of the Holy Spirit."

53. This omission is all the more perplexing in authors who are committed Reformed theologians, men whom we otherwise recognize for their important contributions in effectively communicating important truths of the Reformed tradition in our time.

tive inability of unbelievers in verse 14 does not exclude the rational competence to arrive at a sound natural theology, or, again, how the "all things" of verse 15 must be circumscribed and does not include the truths of such a theology. That demand does not seem "unreasonable."

In fact, however, 1 Corinthians 2:6–16 (1:18–3:23) is the death blow to all natural theology.[54] There is no knowledge of God resident in unbelievers or accessible to them that reduces the eschatological void that separates them from a saving knowledge of God. The failure to recognize that is sad, especially in the light of developments in theology and the church since the Reformation.

Until recently the prevailing reading of that history has been that seventeenth-century Reformed and Lutheran orthodoxy abandons the Reformation and prepares the way for the Enlightenment and then theological liberalism (until all is eventually made better by Karl Barth *cum suis*). This is a gross distortion.[55] It does, however, contain a significant germ of truth. The increasing preoccupation of orthodox dogmatics with natural theology, particularly after Descartes, worked to undermine itself and aided the rise of the very rationalism it was opposing. The tension is there, for instance, in Francis Turretin on the role of reason in theology.[56] And the out-

54. "Above all every natural theology, wherever it sees the divine *remoto spiritu Christi* [apart from the Spirit of Christ] resident in man or the world, has difficulty in coping with 1 Cor 2" (Schrage, *Der erste Brief an die Korinther*, 272f.).

55. This paradigm, dominant from the late nineteenth century over most of the twentieth, has been increasingly questioned and rejected in the past several decades. The work of Richard Muller, built on by a number of others, has been especially important in rehabilitating a sound understanding of the Protestant "scholastics" and redressing existing scholarly distortions by showing the deep and cordial continuity, despite all the differences in method and style of presentation, between the theology of the Reformers and that of the seventeenth century; see, e.g., R. A. Muller, *Post-Reformation Reformed Dogmatics: Prolegomena to Theology* (Grand Rapids, MI: Baker, 1987), including the primary sources and secondary literature cited throughout; *Scholasticism and Orthodoxy in the Reformed Tradition: An Attempt at Definition* (Grand Rapids, MI: Calvin Theological Seminary, 1995); and, more recently, *After Calvin: Studies in the Development of a Theological Tradition* (New York: Oxford University Press, 2003), chaps. 1, 2, 4, 5, afterword, and the literature cited there.

56. E.g., in topic 1, question 8 of his *Institutes of Elenctic Theology*, vol. 1, ed. James T. Dennison Jr., trans. George Musgrave Giger (Phillipsburg, NJ: P&R, 1994), 23–28. This discussion, in continuity with the Reformers, is for the most part a helpful treatment of the ministerial role of reason in theology ("an instrument of faith," par. 7, p. 25). Toward the end, however, he speaks of the use of arguments, both theological (based on Scripture) and philosophical, in the effort to see atheists "converted" (*converti*), "so that by the principles of reason the prejudices against the Christian religion drawn from corrupt reason may be removed" (par. 23, p. 28); cf.

come, a permanent lesson that we miss to our theological peril, is the startling swiftness with which in the span of a single generation at the Academy in Geneva, from Turretin father to son, Reformed orthodoxy was virtually displaced and rendered impotent in the face of a frank rationalism, bordering on Socinianism, that was quick to follow.[57] By now, too, we should have learned that natural theology may have a place in Roman Catholic and Arminian theologies, with their semi-Pelagian anthropologies and qualified optimism about the unbeliever's capacity to know God, but not in a theology that would be Reformed.[58]

Unbelievers undoubtedly know God, but that knowledge does not serve to silence their rebellion or otherwise dispose them to accept the truth of the gospel. That, too, is the *skandalon* of the cross (1 Cor. 1:23). And that, as much as any, is the scandalizing truth that Van Til, following Paul, labored to hold before the church, perhaps with unprecedented tenacity and rigor in the history of theology. Those efforts ought not to be ignored or to go unheeded. May that truth not prove to be a stumbling block to our generation and generations of the church yet to come.[59]

---

his not always clear comments on natural theology in question 3 (pp. 6–9; "natural theology" seems at points to be equivalent to general revelation).

57. See the informative account of Klauber, "Jean-Alphonse Turrettini and the Abrogation of the Formula Consensus in Geneva," and, more extensively, his *Between Reformed Scholasticism and Pan-Protestantism: Jean-Alphonse Turretin (1671–1737) and Enlightened Orthodoxy at the Academy of Geneva* (Selinsgrove, PA: Susquehanna University Press, 1994), 143–92.

58. See in this respect the perceptive discussion of van Genderen and Velema, *Beknopte Gereformeerde Dogmatiek*, 126–33.; cf. Schrage, *Der erste Brief an die Korinther*, 273n302, on Vatican I's grounding of a *duplex ordo cognitionis* on Rom. 1:20, on the one hand, and 1 Cor. 2:7–8, 10, on the other. All such "two-order" knowledge constructions can be maintained only at the expense or compromise of what these passages actually teach.

59. Despite the overall impression this chapter may leave, I have no desire to escalate, but hope to see reduced and clarified as much as possible, the conflict in apologetics between "evidentialists" and "presuppositionalists" (this designating nomenclature itself is already a source of some confusion). There is no doubt a certain amount of "talking by" each other and mutual misunderstanding, especially where the debate takes place on a common Reformed commitment. Nor do I think that Van Til has spoken the final word. But I am convinced that genuine rapprochement can take place only where there is a common appreciation of those biblical considerations drawn from Reformed anthropology and soteriology that control Van Til's epistemology and apologetics, considerations, as I see it, that are much less clearly present, even eclipsed, in the "classical" approach.

2

Resurrection, Proof, and Presuppositionalism

Acts 17:30–31

LANE G. TIPTON

The basic contention of this essay is that Paul's conception of the resurrection as proof[1] of final judgment in Acts 17:31b depends on revealed categories derived from redemptive history. This distinctive approach to proof places the evidential function of the resurrection in a redemptive-historical setting and supplies an exegetical line of support for presuppositional apologetics in the tradition of Cornelius Van Til. Five basic propositions summarize the argument developed in this section:

1. Paul the theologian of redemptive history is Paul the apologist for the resurrection of Christ.
2. Paul provides a covenant-historical conception of proof in 17:31, which rests on (a) Christ's resurrection as an eschatological

---

1. Greek: *pistin/πίστιν*.

event, and (b) Christ's resurrection as a covenantal (or solidaric) event.

3. Paul refuses to separate the denotation (fact) of the resurrection
from the connotation (meaning) of the resurrection, because
the fact and meaning of the resurrection are covenantally and
eschatologically qualified.

4. As such, Paul's notion of proof cannot be reduced to an ordinary,
standard, philosophical conception of proof (e.g., based on rational
reflection, empirical observation, or pragmatic utility), since it
rests on revealed categories derived from redemptive history.

5. Paul's argument requires us to rethink or at least reorient
the discipline of apologetics in light of redemptive-historical
categories.

Opening Observations

Paul's address to the Athenian philosophers on Mars Hill, recorded
in Acts 17:16–34, presents us with the *locus classicus* for understanding
the Pauline apologetic. The serious student of biblical theology and apologetics must come to terms with the programmatic theological message
of the address, as well as its bearing on the assumptions that inform the
use of reason, argument, and evidence in apologetical disputation. This
essay will focus on the influence of the Pauline theology on the nature of
the proof he presents in verse 31b, particularly the redemptive-historical
orientation of his argument, which construes the resurrection as proof
of the certainty and inescapability of final judgment.

In restricting the investigation to a small section of the passage
(vv. 30–31), I obviously am not attempting an exegesis of the passage
as a whole, nor do I intend to answer all of the questions relevant to
the function of verses 30–31 within the broader context of the passage. I will limit the investigation to the covenantal and eschatological
components in Paul's argument and will not focus on the important
but implicit Trinitarian contours of the argument.[2]

2. The Trinitarian character of the address appears implicitly in the fact that God has
appointed (*hōrisen*/ὥρισεν) a man to dispense judgment in righteousness, and the prerogative
to judge belongs *exclusively* to God. When we conjoin this insight with the fact that in Pauline
theology God's effective declaration (*horisthentos*/ὁρισθέντος, Rom. 1:4) constitutes Christ the

The argument is designed to demonstrate that Paul presupposed *the entire redemptive-historical framework* in the presentation of the fact of the resurrection of Christ from the dead. And this means that Paul did not reason from the fact of the resurrection to the God who raised Jesus; rather, Paul's reasoning about the fact of the resurrection already presupposes the God who raised him, that is, the meaning of the resurrection.[3]

Recent evangelical scholarship on the book of Acts is beginning to recognize the distinctively theological underpinnings of Paul's Areopagus address, along with the fact that he argues on the level of basic presuppositions or worldviews. For instance, Ben Witherington observes that in Paul's address on Mars Hill, "Conversion to a new *worldview*, not merely additional knowledge, is required."[4] In addition, D. A. Carson notes that in Paul's Mars Hill address "there is a massive *clash of worldviews*."[5] However, while there is a basic, and I believe, correct, recognition of the distinctively Christian presuppositions in Paul's address in general, and his conception of proof in particular,[6] the specific categories that contribute to the redemptive-historical conception of proof Paul offers have not been developed adequately. Nor have scholars such as Witherington and Carson tied Paul's argument to the development of presuppositional apologetics. Therefore, in this section I will attempt to point out more precisely the theological

---

eschatological Spirit (functionally, not ontologically) by his resurrection from the dead (1 Cor. 15:45; 2 Cor. 3:18), Christ's appointment as resurrected judge displays clearly an implicit Trinitarianism.

3. The reason I put it this way becomes clear in light of recent comments on the meaning and implications of Acts 17:31 for apologetics. Gary Habermas argues that in Acts 17:30–31 Paul presents an argument that moves "from history to the God who raised Jesus," *Five Views on Apologetics* (Grand Rapids, MI: Zondervan, 2000), 2. My contention is that Paul's argument *presupposes* the God who raised Jesus because Paul already understands the fact of the resurrection as a covenantal and eschatological event. Paul approaches the fact of the resurrection in terms of the entire redemptive-historical framework presented in Scripture. Hence, it is not adequate merely to say that Paul moved from history (i.e., the resurrection of Christ) to the God who raised Jesus.

4. Ben Witherington, *The Acts of the Apostles: A Socio-Rhetorical Commentary* (Grand Rapids, MI: Eerdmans, 1998), 531, emphasis mine.

5. D. A. Carson, "Athens Revisited," in *Telling the Truth: Evangelizing Postmoderns*, ed. D. A. Carson (Grand Rapids, MI: Zondervan, 2000), 390, emphasis mine.

6. "Paul says that resurrection *proves* that his audience themselves will one day face judgment." Witherington, *The Acts of the Apostles*, 530, emphasis mine. However, Witherington does not develop precisely the theological framework that accounts for such a uniquely redemptive-historical concept of proof.

constructs that underlie Paul's notion of the resurrection as proof of final judgment, and spell out the implications for the development of presuppositional apologetics.

The argument proceeds in terms of the five propositions already noted. The first two of the five propositions deal with Paul's argument in Acts 17:30–31. Propositions 3 and 4 demonstrate the correlation between Paul's argument and the presuppositional approach to apologetics advocated by Van Til. The fifth proposition suggests some ways that redemptive-historically regulated exegesis bears on the development of presuppositional apologetics. Let us examine each proposition in turn.

Proposition 1

> Paul the theologian of redemptive history is Paul the apologist for the resurrection of Christ.

It becomes clear in the development of Paul's argument that Paul the theologian of redemptive history is Paul the apologist for the resurrection of Christ. This means that Paul does not argue with one set of presuppositions as a *theologian* and another set of presuppositions as an *apologist*.[7] He is not methodologically schizophrenic. Paul does not alter his fundamental theological approach to covenant history in his address to the Athenian philosophers; rather, he presents in a compressed, terse manner the central core of covenant history as it has reached its climax in the humiliation and exaltation of Christ. No abstract, formal, philosophical reasoning appears in Paul; rather, he argues as a covenant theologian, or a theologian of redemptive history.

Regarding Paul's preaching in general, Herman Ridderbos notes, "The whole content of Paul's preaching can be summarized as the proclamation and explication of the eschatological time of salvation

7. Witherington observes that Paul's argument is "thoroughly biblical *from the start*, and is not unlike other early Jewish examples of apologetics for monotheism. The conclusion follows naturally from the argument." *Acts*, 531 (emphasis mine). Witherington's observation is basically sound but underdeveloped, as the following exegetical and theological considerations will suggest.

inaugurated with Christ's advent, death, and resurrection."[8] This means that it is "from this principal point of view and under this denominator that all the separate themes of Paul's preaching can be understood and penetrated in their unity and relation to one another."[9] What we will see in Acts 17:30–31, then, is that what holds true of Paul the theologian of redemptive history holds true of Paul the apologist for the resurrection of Christ.[10]

In order to grasp this assertion more clearly, let us move on to the second proposition.

Proposition 2

Paul provides a covenant-historical conception of proof in Acts 17:31, which rests on (a) Christ's resurrection as an eschatological event, and (b) Christ's resurrection as a covenantal (or solidaric) event.

(a) Christ Resurrection as an Eschatological Event

As an eschatological event, Christ's resurrection is an epoch-changing occurrence that guarantees the certainty of a universal, future, and final act of God's righteous judgment against sin.

The resurrection of Christ as an epoch-changing event. The eschatological character of Paul's thought emerges clearly throughout the address, but is accentuated in verse 30, where Paul elaborates on the epoch-changing significance of the resurrection of Christ. The text reads, "Therefore, although God overlooked[11] the times of ignorance, he now[12] commands all men everywhere to repent." The specific call to repentance is grounded in a decisive intervention by God in redemptive history (v. 31), an intervention that, contrary to the

8. Herman N. Ridderbos, *Paul: An Outline of His Theology*, trans. John Richard DeWitt (Grand Rapids, MI: Eerdmans, 1975), 44.

9. Ibid.

10. Witherington argues that "the conclusion of the speech in vv. 30–31 should not be seen as anomalous, or a mere tacking on of a Christian addendum to an otherwise Hellenistic piece of rhetoric." *Acts*, 531.

11. Scripture quotations in this chapter are my translations. The rendering "although" reflects my judgment that the aorist participle, *hyperidōn*/ὑπεριδών, is concessive.

12. Greek: *ta nyn*/τὰ νῦν.

past, now, in the sense of realized eschatology in Christ, heightens the responsibility of his hearers. This implies that Paul grounds the gospel imperative to repent in the redemptive-historical indicative of God's decisive activity in history—the resurrection of Christ as judge. In particular, Paul argues that the exaltation of Christ inaugurates a new redemptive-historical era, so that after the resurrection of Christ, covenant history has in principle reached its climax.[13]

In light of these observations, we can begin to understand the inference[14] Paul makes in verse 30, that "although God has overlooked" (*hyperidōn ho theos*/ὑπεριδὼν ὁ θεὸς) such "times of ignorance" (*chronous tēs agnoias*/χρόνους τῆς ἀγνοίας), "he now commands all men everywhere to repent." Paul focuses on the radical change that coincides with the new redemptive-historical era established by the resurrection of Christ (v. 31).[15] Ridderbos notes, "In it [the resurrection] the time of salvation promised in him [Christ], the new creation, dawns in an overwhelming manner, as a *decisive transition from the old to the new world*."[16] The former epochs of overlooking sin have given way to a new aeon in which God requires repentance of all men everywhere in light of Christ's resurrection from the dead (*ek nekrōn*/ἐκ νεκρῶν).

This is clear in that Paul characterizes the former epochs as "times of ignorance" (v. 30a), which stand in sharp contrast with now (*ta nyn*/τὰ νῦν), the present epoch (v. 30b). Notice that Paul does not state in verse 30 that only the Stoic and Epicurean philosophers were ignorant, although verses 23 and 29 prove that they in fact were ignorant in a significant sense; rather, he predicates ignorance of entire historical epochs prior to the eschatological era inaugurated by the resurrection of Christ. The times of ignorance refer best to a previous and indeterminate period of time. The reason Paul alludes to an indefinite time

13. We must remember that Christ's resurrection marks the inauguration of his eschatological kingdom, and his *parousia* will mark its consummation. This already/not-yet structure of Paul's eschatology is critical in understanding his theology in general, and the Areopagus address in particular; cf. Geerhardus Vos, "The Eschatology of the New Testament," in *Redemptive History and Biblical Interpretation: The Shorter Writings of Geerhardus Vos*, ed. R. B. Gaffin Jr. (Phillipsburg, NJ: Presbyterian and Reformed, 1980), 25–58.

14. *Oun*/οὖν is an inference indicator, suggesting that v. 30 is a conclusion reached from v. 29.

15. Witherington observes that "as a result of what has happened through Christ's death and resurrection, such ignorance will no longer be endured." *Acts*, 531.

16. Ridderbos, *Paul*, 56, emphasis mine.

period, which extends backward without clearly prescribed boundaries, rests in the fact that his concern is not the duration of the former epochs of ignorance, but their present termination, which coincides with "now" in verse 30.

The resurrection of Christ as judge therefore marks a pivotal change in the way that God deals with all men everywhere. Rather than indicating an existential moment of present decisional crisis, "now" marks the beginning of the new era in redemptive history.[17] As such, the phrase does not have an existential nuance, but has an *eschatological* nuance that derives its significance from the resurrection of Christ.[18]

The resurrection as guarantee of future judgment. In the Greek text, Paul uses a concessive participle, which means that God now commands repentance although he overlooked the times of ignorance. Prior to the call for repentance in the new era inaugurated by the resurrection of Christ, the text states that God overlooked in some sense the sins associated with idolatry. Paul means that before the inauguration of this semi-eschatological age, God had not brought a final or ultimate display of judgment against idolatry. To be sure, many provisional expressions of judgment appear in the old covenant, but nothing of truly eschatological significance appeared until "now."

What accounts for the transition from God's former overlooking the times of ignorance to his now commanding repentance from all men everywhere? The precise sense in which God overlooked previous sins of idolatry and consequently now commands repentance becomes clear in verse 31. God has set a day to judge the world in righteousness. The call to repentance finds its rationale in the emergence of a future act of universal judgment on the day God has appointed. In other words, the appointed day of judgment, which brings a definitive verdict

17. This notion of a distinctively redemptive history undermines the Stoic and Epicurean understanding of history at the most basic level conceivable. As Joseph Fitzmyer astutely remarks, Paul "views world history only from one perspective, vis., from that of the risen Christ." *The Acts of the Apostles*, The Anchor Bible (New York: Doubleday, 1998), 612.

18. Ridderbos notes, "It is to be maintained no less vigorously that in Paul's proclamation the resurrection of Christ in fact means the breakthrough of the new aeon in the real, redemptive historical sense of the word, and therefore cannot be understood *only* in forensic, ethical, or existential categories." *Aan de Romeinen*, Commentaar op het Nieuwe Testament (Kampen: Kok, 1959), 55.

against those who worship idols in ignorance, looms imminent on the horizon of redemptive history. The times of ignorance in which God overlooked the sin of idolatry have given way to a period of impending, eschatological judgment.

And what event grounds Paul's confidence in a future, final, universal judgment? Verse 31 makes it clear: the resurrection of Christ as judge. Christ's resurrection guarantees that all impenitent idolaters will find no escape from God's righteous judgment.

To summarize, then, Paul presents the resurrection of Christ to his hearers as an eschatological event that inaugurates a new stage in redemptive history and guarantees the certainty of a future act of universal judgment.

(b) The Resurrection of Christ as a Covenantal Event

Now let us consider the resurrection of Christ as a covenantal event. In this connection, I want to assess briefly the solidaric character of the resurrection in the context of Pentecost and discuss the resurrection as the event that inaugurates an eschatological covenant lawsuit against covenant-breakers who continue in sin and idolatry.

The solidaric character of the resurrection in the context of Pentecost. The covenantal character of Christ's resurrection appears clearly in the fact that it has implications for *all* men *everywhere* (*tois anthrōpois pantas pantachou metanoein/*τοῖς ἀνθρώποις πάντας πανταχοῦ μετανοεῖν, v. 30), whether covenant-breakers or covenant-keepers. It is precisely the solidaric aspect of Christ's resurrection for "all men everywhere" that *requires* us to see the resurrection as a covenantal event. This is so because the resurrection of Christ from the dead simultaneously guarantees salvation for the covenant-keeper and condemnation for the covenant-breaker. Jesus' resurrection is a concrete event in history with universal significance and implications.

It is precisely the universal implications of the resurrection that ground it as a covenantal event. Reformed theology traditionally has explained solidarity with the first Adam in covenantal terms, parallel to the explanation of the church's solidarity with the second Adam (cf. Rom. 5:12–20; 1 Cor. 15:22–58). From Paul's redemptive-historical perspective, it is precisely Christ's status and function as the second Adam that ensures his resurrection has implications for "all men everywhere." As second Adam, Christ stands in a solidaric relationship to all men, either as Redeemer or as judge. This becomes particularly clear when we consider the eschatological and solidaric dimensions of his humiliation and exaltation.

Richard B. Gaffin Jr. makes this very point when describing Christ's messianic baptism of death on the cross, in terms of both promise and fulfillment. From the perspective of promise (Luke 3:16–17), symbolized by John's water baptism, Christ's messianic baptism of death on the cross involves "*eschatological judgment* . . . [which is] *of a piece with God's great discriminating activity of cleansing the world-threshing floor* or, to vary the metaphor slightly, harvesting the world-field, at the end of history."[19] In terms of fulfillment, "Pentecost is . . . component with the fiery baptism of final judgment set by the New Testament to be executed by Christ at his return (e.g., Matt. 16:27; Acts 10:42; 17:31; II Thess. 1:7f.; II Tim. 4:1)."[20] In other words, whether viewed from the standpoint of promise or of fulfillment, Christ's messianic baptism of death on the cross involves the same judgment ordeal awaiting the world at the end of the age.

Therefore, Gaffin's formulation helps us grasp how the baptism ordeal that Christ endured in his messianic death is the *same ordeal* that awaits the "world-threshing floor" at the end of the age. This sort of theological formulation informs Paul's argument in Acts 17:31 at the nuclear level. This insight also helps explain why Luke would include Paul's speech in Acts 17. Paul's resurrection theology perfectly complements Luke's theology of Pentecost. In fact, Paul's address in Acts 17 brings Luke's theology of Pentecost into sharp focus and clear application. God's righteous judgment is bound up with the resurrection of Christ as judge as a solidaric, covenantal event, which is full of eschatological significance.

The resurrection and the covenant lawsuit. The necessity of a righteous judgment seems unavoidable when we consider that Paul

19. Richard B. Gaffin Jr., *Perspectives on Pentecost* (Phillipsburg, NJ: Presbyterian and Reformed, 1979), 15, emphasis mine.
20. Ibid., 17.

announces an eschatological covenant lawsuit against the Athenian idolaters.[21] Following the general pattern of a covenant lawsuit,[22] Paul identifies the Athenian idolaters as creaturely vassals of the Creator King, *ho theos*/ὁ θεὸς and *kyrios*/κύριος identifying the King by name (v. 24). Verses 24–26 provide the reasons why the Athenians ought to worship and serve the living God, rather than idols. The living God not only created all things, but sustains all he has created. Verse 28 identifies the culpable ignorance of the idol worshipers, since the living God is clearly present among them (Rom. 1:19–20). Then, in Acts 17:29, Paul brings the formal indictment of the lawsuit. This is the first phase of the process, which appears in the call to repent in verse 30. The second phase of the process will occur on the appointed day of judgment at the end of the age (v. 31), so that the two phases of the eschatological covenant lawsuit correspond to the two epoch making events of the New Testament: the first and second comings of Christ.

To state the matter differently, Paul announces an eschatological covenant lawsuit adjusted in terms of the already/not-yet categories of realized and future eschatology. Christ's resurrection and ascension provide the basis for the first phase of announced judgment, which culminates in the commandment to repent (v. 30). Christ's second coming (*parousia*) marks the second and final stage of the threatened judgment, which reaches its climax on the last day (v. 31). In this sense, Paul, the apostle to the Gentiles, charges the Athenians with

21. As Van Til says regarding Paul's intention for the Athenians, "he wanted them to become *covenant-keepers* instead of *covenant-breakers.*" *Paul at Athens* (Nutley, NJ: Presbyterian and Reformed, 1978), 10, emphasis mine.

22. For a more extensive summary treatment of the covenant lawsuit pattern, see M. G. Kline, *By Oath Consigned* (Eugene, OR: Wipf and Stock, 1998), 51–54. Notice also Paul's consistent allusions to Isaiah's language of covenant lawsuit (Acts 17:24–25, cf. Isa. 42:5; Acts 17:29, cf. Isa. 40:18–20). Regarding the lawsuit pattern, Kline observes that "when a vassal [subject] failed to satisfy the obligations of a sworn treaty, the suzerain [king] instituted a covenant lawsuit against him. The legal process was conducted by messengers. In the first of its two distinct phases, messengers delivered one or more warnings. . . . The vassal was reminded of the suzerain's benefits and of the treaty stipulations, explanation of his offenses was demanded, and he was admonished to mend his ways. He was also confronted anew with the curses of the covenant, now in the form of an ultimatum and warned of the vanity of all hope of escape through recourse to any alien quarter. If the messenger of the great king was rejected, imprisoned, and especially if he was killed, the legal process moved into its next phase. This was a declaration of war as an execution of the sacred sanctions of the treaty, and so as a visitation of the oath deities against the offender, a trial by ordeal" (pp. 51–52).

idolatry and announces an impending covenant lawsuit in terms that derive significance from the already and not-yet aspects of Christ's resurrection as judge. Failure to repent (v. 30) constitutes a rebellious attitude toward the lawgiver and judge, thereby ensuring final judgment (v. 31).

In this context, Paul introduces the ultimate agent who will enforce this judgment, in verse 31: "in righteousness through a man whom he has appointed" (*en dikaiosynē en andri hō hōrisen*/ἐν δικαιοσύνῃ ἐν ἀνδρὶ ᾧ ὥρισεν). Therefore, verse 31 provides the reason for the transition from God's overlooking the ignorance of idolatry in verse 30a to the command for all men to repent in verse 30b. God has fixed a day to judge the world in righteousness by an appointed man who will end definitively the practice of idolatry.

It is helpful to note that Paul answers an anticipated question: How do we know that a radical transition has occurred in redemptive history that *guarantees* the righteous judgment of God against all idolaters? Verse 31 gives the answer: "God offered [*paraschōn*/παρασχὼν] proof [*pistin*/πίστιν][23] to all men by raising [*anastēsas*/ἀναστήσας][24] him from the dead." In other words, the event that guarantees the certainty of eschatological judgment is *the resurrection of Christ*—the event that constitutes him judge of the world.

However, it appears that we can find no immediate rationale for the transition between verse 31a and 31b. Specifically what accounts for the connection between them? To put the question differently, what precisely about Christ's resurrection "from the dead" guarantees the universal judgment and therefore grounds the requirement of universal repentance?

In order to see the answer, we need to understand first and foremost that we have an implicit premise that provides the connection between 31a and 31b, and establishes the force of the commandment to repent. That premise can be summarized as follows: the judgment that will befall all covenant breakers at the end of the age has already

23. *Pistin* is alternately translated as assurance, but the basic point remains the same: God has produced evidence which guarantees the judgment of all men. Witherington comments that "within a rhetorical argument such as this one, πιστιν here refers to a proof; cf. Aristotle, *Nic. Eth.* 1173A; Josephus, *Ant.* 15.69." *The Acts of the Apostles*, 532.

24. *Anastēsas* is best understood as an aorist participle of means, indicating precisely how the proof occurs.

befallen Christ at the beginning of the age. This implies that all who do not identify with the resurrected one by faith and repentance will bear personally the eternal judgment to be executed by him as judge at the end of the age, that is, at the end of *ta nyn*.

The hint of an implicit premise arises with the mention not of the resurrection *per se*, but of the resurrection of Christ "*from the dead*."[25] Christ's resurrection from the dead assumes that he has faced the judgment of God, since, "just as it is appointed for men to die once and then comes judgment. So also Christ . . ." (Heb. 9:27–28). This means that for Christ the resurrection from the dead entails a previous encounter with the consummate judgment of God (v. 27). Immediately before, in Hebrews 9:26, Christ is presented as a sacrifice for sins at the consummation of the ages. That is, the reality of *eternal* judgment befell Christ in his obedience and satisfaction. This point from Hebrews finds a close parallel in Paul's argument in Acts 17:31: the eschatological judgment threatened there has already been applied to one man, Christ. As Ridderbos notes, "To Paul, the eschatological reality of the divine judgment and the divine acquittal are revealed in the cross and in the resurrection of Christ."[26]

In summary, God the Father prosecuted the violated covenant of works against his Son as a substitute in his obedience and satisfaction at the beginning of this age, and it is the same broken covenant of works that God the Son will prosecute against all unbelievers at the end of the age.[27]

Consequently, when Paul appeals to Christ's resurrection from the dead as proof of the final judgment, he has in mind covenantal categories that give Christ's resurrection its unique and distinctive meaning. Paul announces eschatological judgment in covenantal categories and construes the resurrection as a solidaric event with implications for all men everywhere. Christ's resurrection is an eschatological and covenantal event.

25. Greek: *ek nekrōn*/ἐκ νεκρῶν.

26. Herman Ridderbos, *When the Time Had Fully Come: Studies in New Testament Theology* (1957; repr., ON: Paideia, 1982), 50–51.

27. Of course, another implicit premise is that the prerogative of deity belongs to the one constituted judge by means of his resurrection. This observation confirms the earlier observation regarding the implicitly Trinitarian structure of Paul's argument.

Proposition 3

> Paul refuses to separate the denotation (fact) of the resurrection from the connotation (meaning) of the resurrection, because the fact and meaning of the resurrection are covenantally and eschatologically qualified.

Consider the following, more philosophical, implication. Paul refuses to present the denotation of the resurrection (i.e., the fact of the resurrection) apart from the connotation of the resurrection (i.e., the covenant-historical meaning of the resurrection). The Christ whom Paul proclaims is the Christ of covenant history, and his resurrection is not presented in isolation from its significance for redemptive history. The deed revelation of the resurrection is never artificially abstracted from the interpretation provided by Word revelation. Accordingly, any apologetical procedure that artificially separates at any point the fact of the resurrection from the meaning of the resurrection is, from a biblical standpoint, defective.[28]

This implies that Paul is not interested in offering the resurrection as an isolated factual occurrence. Van Til notes the interrelationship between covenantal revelation and the resurrection when he says, "It takes the *fact* of the resurrection to see its proper *framework* and it takes the *framework* to see the *fact* of the resurrection."[29] Paul articulates this sort of relationship in his Areopagus address; he understands the resurrection of Christ in terms of its redemptive-historical framework. At no point does Paul entertain Christ's resurrection as a brute fact, that is, as a fact that exists independent of God's eternal decree and revelation in history. To argue for the fact of the resurrection is to presuppose its meaning, and to argue for the meaning of the resurrection is to presuppose its factuality. But the point is that the argument Paul presents regarding the resurrection of Christ from the dead presupposes *both* its fact *and* its meaning as a covenantal and eschatological event.

28. These approaches would include: new Reformed epistemology (e.g., Alvin Plantinga, Kelly James Clark), evidentialism (e.g., Gary Habermas, John Warwick Montgomery), natural theology (e.g., R. C. Sproul, Norman Geisler), and Wittgensteinian fideism (e.g., Norman Malcolm), among others.

29. Van Til, *Paul at Athens*, 16, emphasis mine.

In addition Van Til notes that when it comes to understanding the significance of the resurrection as a revelational event in redemptive history, "the setting is all important . . . [since it is] that which gives meaning to the fact of the resurrection."[30] This revelational "setting" is inherently covenantal, Trinitarian, and eschatological in nature, and, as such, involves a construal of the resurrection as proof of the final judgment.

Notice that Van Til's formulations are confirmed by a careful treatment of the text in Acts 17:30–31. Although Van Til himself did not provide such exegesis, it seems clear enough that his understanding of how the "setting" or "framework" of redemptive history relates to the fact of the resurrection is thoroughly Pauline. Perhaps Van Til himself failed to offer substantial exegetical support for his apologetic, but his approach is not for that reason unbiblical. Quite to the contrary, Van Til's language resonates with the theology of the inscripturated text.

Complementing this insight, let us consider the next proposition.

Proposition 4

> As such, Paul's notion of proof cannot be reduced to an ordinary, standard, philosophical conception of proof (e.g., based on rational reflection, empirical observation, or pragmatic utility), since it rests on revealed categories derived from redemptive history.

In Paul's presentation, the resurrection functions as proof of the final judgment. Christ's resurrection proves the certainty and inescapability of the judgment to be executed by him at the end of the age. This means that Paul presents the resurrection of Christ in terms of its function and bearing in redemptive history. The evidential function of the resurrection is not artificially isolated from its relationship to redemptive history. That is, the empirical and rational aspects of Paul's notion of proof are at every point subordinate to his theology of redemptive history, or to speak more philosophically, his revelational epistemology.

Van Til summarizes this point well:

30. Ibid., 13.

He [Paul] was not interested in having them endorse the Resurrection as an *isolated event*. . . . He was, rather, concerned that they accept it as the climax of the work of redemption from sin by Jesus, truly God and truly man. . . . In short, men should not existentially accept the resurrection unless, in doing so, they received it as part of the *entire biblical redemptive framework*.[31]

Consequently, Van Til observes that Paul called those present on Mars Hill to accept a "peculiar thought framework"[32] that "required a new, radically different view of history from its beginning to its end."[33] Basically, then, Paul presented to the Athenians the resurrection of Christ, articulated in consistently covenant-historical categories, never artificially separating the fact of the resurrection from its redemptive-historical meaning.

Paul's notion of proof therefore turns on what God has objectively effected in Christ's resurrection. Paul does not offer a proof in the ordinary sense of the term; rather, he appeals to what God has validated in Christ's resurrection. God has given assurance or proof of final judgment to all men by raising Christ from the dead. Van Til notes,

Paul proclaimed the *fact* of creation, the *fact* of the resurrection of Christ, and the *fact* of the coming judgment of all men by Christ as judge, as together constituting a philosophy of history which at every point challenged the philosophy of history of the natural man in general and of the Greeks in particular.[34]

As such, Paul offers a covenant-historical proof that stands antithetically over against the Stoic and Epicurean philosophies of history represented on Mars Hill.

Elaborating on the connection between Christ's resurrection and the judgment it effects, Van Til notes, "In His resurrection from the dead through the power of the Creator there stood before men the

---

31. Cornelius Van Til, *Who Do You Say I Am?* (Nutley, NJ: Presbyterian and Reformed, 1975), 8, emphasis mine.
32. Ibid.
33. Ibid.
34. Cornelius Van Til, *The Great Debate Today* (Nutley, NJ: Presbyterian and Reformed, 1970), 169.

clearest evidence that could be given that they who would still continue to serve and worship the creature would at the last be condemned by the Creator then become their judge" (Acts 17:31).[35] In Van Til's assessment, the resurrection of Christ is the clearest conceivable evidence of universal and final judgment against sin. But it is the "entire biblical redemptive framework" alone that accounts for such crystal clarity, because *in terms of no other framework does the fact of the resurrection bear such a meaning.*

In verse 31, then, *pistin* does not operate in the technical, philosophical sense of rational demonstration. Rather, Paul's notion of proof indicates that he understands and presents the resurrection in terms of the matrix of Trinitarian and redemptive-historical activity. For this reason, Paul's notion of proof is *inseparable* from the framework of redemptive-historical revelation—the framework that provides the theological and hermeneutical foundation for his construal of the resurrection as proof of the final judgment.

What makes Paul's unique conception of proof so relevant to a discussion of apologetics is simple. Paul's understanding of the meaning of the resurrection of Christ is not the only option for explaining the phenomenon of his bodily resurrection. For instance, the Epicurean philosophers present on Mars Hill (cf. Acts 17:18) would explain the resurrection of Christ as an adjustment in the falling of individual atoms. What would account for an event as unusual as the resurrection of a dead person but an unexpected "swerve" in the falling of atoms, that is, the basic stuff of reality? In other words, the philosophical explanation for understanding the resurrection in Epicurean categories would be the "Epicurean swerve." From that perspective, the resurrection is simply a curious and random episode in history.

However, this is simply impossible in Paul's approach, since the resurrection of Christ is understood in terms of covenantal and eschatological categories. It is not a brute fact that belongs in "Ripley's Believe It or Not." Rather, the resurrection proves that Christ is the righteous judge of the world. This redemptive-historical conception of the fact and meaning of the resurrection (i.e., how it functions as proof) puts Paul's conception of proof on a collision course with Greek thought

35. Van Til, *Paul at Athens*, 5.

in general and Epicurean philosophy in particular. The apologetical implication is obvious: Paul refuses to present the resurrection of Christ apart from its redemptive-historical context—a point emphasized by Van Til and central to his presuppositional approach to apologetics.

This helps us understand the fifth and final point.

Proposition 5

> Paul's argument requires us to rethink or at least reorient the discipline of apologetics in light of redemptive-historical categories.

As we have seen from the previous propositions, Paul the apologist for the resurrection is Paul the theologian of covenant history. His presentation of the resurrection as proof of eschatological judgment, both realized and future, depends for its plausibility on a theology of covenant history that lies at the heart of the Pauline apologetic. An apologetic regulated by covenant-historical categories forms the theological foundation for Paul's address on Mars Hill. It is, therefore, simply impossible to separate in any meaningful way Paul's apologetic from his covenant theology.

This means, at least, that we need to be willing to subject the discipline of apologetics to insights derived from the biblical theology of the inscripturated text. We will do well to heed Paul's argument on Mars Hill and appropriate his programmatic insights into the core of our apologetic. Taking Paul seriously means at least the following.

First, biblical theology requires that we regulate apologetics in light of exegesis, so that the discipline of apologetics depends ultimately on the theology contained in the inscripturated text and not a contemporary philosophical outlook (e.g., deconstructionism, pragmatism, phenomenology, existentialism, ordinary language philosophy). Of course, this does not mean that we fail to take into account contemporary philosophical trends in developing our apologetic, but it does remind us that apologetics, no less than biblical and systematic theology, must be regulated by the same *principium*—the text of Scripture alone.

Second, biblical theology helps us see that it is biblically inappropriate to appeal to the historical fact of the resurrection in isolation from its redemptive-historical meaning. Paul's presentation of the fact and the meaning of the resurrection as covenantally and eschatologically qualified rules out presenting the resurrection as a brute fact. It also requires that we remember the fundamental role of the entire redemptive-historical framework when defending both the fact and the meaning of the resurrection of Christ from the dead.

Third, biblical theology helps us realize the centrality of the resurrection as an eschatological and covenantal event, and, as a result, helps orient our apologetic along the same lines as our theology. So often in apologetics the defense of the faith proceeds in categories foreign to biblical and systematic theology. Apologetics is then construed as theological prolegomena, utilizing autonomous philosophical categories as a preamble to the revealed truths of Scripture and redemptive history. Biblical theology in general, as well as Paul's argument in Acts 17 in particular, reminds us that this is simply not the biblical (or the consistently Reformed) approach to the defense of Christian theism. Our apologetic is regulated by Trinitarian, covenantal, and eschatological categories just as much as our theology. In this sense apologetics is every bit as theological as theology, whether biblical or systematic.

Finally, biblical theology reminds us that in order to be faithful apologists for the resurrected Christ, we must be *first and foremost* faithful theologians of redemptive history. If this is so, then certainly the time has come to incorporate biblical-theological insights from the inscripturated text into the core of our presuppositional approach to apologetics. Paul's address in Acts 17, particularly his redemptive-historical conception of the resurrection as proof of the final judgment, helps us take some significant strides forward in that direction.

Paul's argument on Mars Hill therefore lends strong support to the development of presuppositional apologetics. A careful analysis of his conception of proof gives us an opportunity to enrich apologetics in light of redemptive-historically regulated exegesis. As we seize that opportunity, the disciplines of biblical and systematic theology will stand in a much more organic relationship to our defense of the faith, and will place us in a better position to demonstrate the deep lines of continuity between Reformed theology and Reformed apologetics.

3

The Irrationality of Unbelief

An Exegetical Study

K. SCOTT OLIPHINT

*I*n his monumental volume on sin (a volume impressive in both breadth and length), G. C. Berkouwer notes that, embedded in the *mysterium iniquitatis* is, fundamentally, foolishness and irrationality. The riddle of sin, according to Berkouwer, lies in its lack of rationale. Sin is essentially, and will remain, deeply unreasonable, utterly irrational.

> For the riddle of sin is the same as the essence of sin, with its antinormative character and illegality. It is the same as the senselessness of sin. Therefore, since every "unriddling" of sin implies a discovery of "sense" where no sense can possibly be found, the very notion of an "unriddling" is impossible. One cannot find sense in the senseless and meaning in the meaningless.[1]

My purpose in this chapter is to show that there is an exegetical foundation for this understanding of the irrationality of unbelief. Given

1. G. C. Berkouwer, *Sin*, Studies in Dogmatics, trans. Philip C. Holtrop (Grand Rapids: Eerdmans, 1971), 134.

that unbelief is at root the quintessential sin, it is therefore, necessarily, quintessentially irrational.

But what does it mean to be irrational? How can the effects and influences of sin be tied to such a sweeping and strong indictment? As we look at the apostle Paul's argument in the latter half of Romans 1, we will seek to show that, as a matter of fact, according to Paul, it is sin's irrationality that lies at the root of the thinking, and the behavior, of unbelief.

It should first of all be noted that in the history of thought, to the present day, no consensus exists on just how the notions of "rational" and "irrational" should be defined. This should not be surprising. Because the vast majority of that history has sought to develop its ideas and display its arguments without reference to the true God, confusion is bound to reign.[2]

With all of the confusion, however, it can be stated without much controversy that, whatever rationality is conceived to be, however the concept is defined and defended, it must have as its foundational concern the way in which a person (or group of people) relates to the world. Even in some aspects of Eastern philosophy, where the encouragement to deny the world of the senses is paramount, *that* concern nevertheless provides the starting point. Given that starting point, every discussion of rationality seeks to show some kind of corresponding relationship between what one believes or knows to be the case, on the one hand, and "the way things really are," on the other.[3]

With that in mind, our brief look at Romans 1 should give us some help in attempting to understand what irrationality actually is. For paramount in Paul's mind in verses 18–32 (and into chapter 2), is the interplay between God himself, in his revealing activity through

2. For a nice summary of some of the notions of rationality present in Western thought, see Alvin Plantinga, *Warranted Christian Belief* (Oxford: Oxford University Press, 2000), 108–34; for a sample of such discussions in the East, see Aziz Esmail, *Poetics of Religious Experience* (London: Institute for Ismaili Studies, 1998).

3. This is the case, it should be noted, even in those philosophies and religions (more prolific in the East than in the West) that seek to convince their adherents (1) that the empirical world is illusion and therefore (2) that one should believe in other, more transcendent (thus, more "real") truths, which alone can set one on the proper path. A coherence or correspondence with the "real" is just as important, and urgent, in this line of thinking, as in the more Western approaches.

creation, and those who, while remaining in their sin, respond to that activity in the world.

First, a few important preliminary matters are in order. At the heart of this epistle is Paul's declaration in 1:16–17: "For I am not ashamed of the gospel, for it is the power of God for salvation to everyone who believes, to the Jew first and also to the Greek. For in it the righteousness of God is revealed from faith for faith, as it is written, 'The righteous shall live by faith.'"[4] Embedded in this declaration are a host of themes, all of which reach their historical apex in the universal application of God's gospel righteousness. This righteousness, we should note, is not the righteousness that belongs to God, but rather the righteousness that comes *from* God to those who believe.[5]

In order to set the context for Paul's discussion beginning in 1:18, we should note that, in this central declaration, "those who believe" include the Jew, first, and also the Greek (*Hellēni*/Ἕλληνι). In other words, *all* people are now considered to be the objects of the gospel of God's righteousness to his people.

This is important for at least two reasons. First, it points us to the fact that God's righteousness in the gospel is universal in its scope. In other words, *because* this gospel, which was "promised beforehand" (v. 2) as the gospel "concerning his Son" (v. 3), is to "bring about the obedience of faith . . . among *all the nations*" (v. 5), it is now, in the fullness of time, in a way heretofore unknown in redemptive history, a *universal* gospel. It extends (and thus Paul can speak of its "power," its *dynamis*) to every "tribe and language and people and nation" (Rev. 5:9; 13:7; 14:6).

---

4. Unless otherwise indicated, Scripture quotations in this chapter are from The Holy Bible, English Standard Version, copyright © 2001 by Crossway Bibles, a division of Good News Publishers. Used by permission. All right reserved. Italics in subsequent quotations indicate emphasis added.

5. Significant debate centers on whether *dikaiosynē theou*/δικαιοσύνη θεοῦ should be taken as a subjective or possessive genitive, in which case the righteousness of God would refer to *his* righteousness, or whether it is to be taken as a genitive of relationship or source, in which case the righteousness would be from God, but would belong to the person. While Vos hints that both options are likely in view (*The Pauline Eschatology*, Grand Rapids, MI: Baker, 1979, 313f.), the latter option seems to be more consistent with v. 18. For an exegetical analysis see Herman N. Ridderbos, *Aan de Romeinen*, Commentaar op het Nieuwe Testament (Kampen: Kok, 1959), 35–38. See also Herman N. Ridderbos, *Paul: An Outline of His Theology*, trans. John Richard DeWitt (Grand Rapids, MI: Eerdmans, 1975), 163, for a helpful summary and sources of the debate itself.

Second, this righteousness to those who believe is eschatological at its core. It is a righteousness in the gospel that has its foundation in the eschatological resurrection of the Son of God (Rom. 1:1–4). That is, according to Paul, we should see this signal event of Christ's work as one in which a new humanity is inaugurated. This new humanity, in union with Christ, consists of those who are "be[ing] made alive" (1 Cor. 15:22) by virtue of the fact that, in Christ's resurrection, as the "last Adam" (1 Cor. 15:45), he becomes the "firstfruits of those who have fallen asleep" (1 Cor. 15:20).[6] Resurrection life, therefore, is the life that is inaugurated in Christ's resurrection, reaching its climax in the *eschaton*.[7]

The importance of these two emphases for our study revolves around the parallel concern of Paul both for this righteousness of God (universally and eschatologically revealed in the gospel) *and* for (what will be the controlling idea of our section) the wrath of God. It is just because the righteousness of God is universally and eschatologically revealed now in the gospel of the risen Son that the wrath of God is likewise revealed. This wrath, though present in the past (like God's gospel righteousness—see Rom. 4), now takes on both a universal and an eschatological character. It is universal, as Paul says, "For we have already charged that *all*, both Jews and Greeks, are under the power of sin, as it is written: 'None is righteous, no, not one . . .'" (Rom. 3:9–10). The point that Paul is beginning to make in 1:18ff. is that all, universally, both Jew and Greek, are bound by sin. Thus, God's wrath comes "from heaven" and extends over all the earth.

It is also eschatological in character, in that, as Paul says, "because of your hard and impenitent heart you are storing up wrath for yourself on the day of wrath when God's righteous judgment will be revealed" (Rom. 2:5). This wrath now revealed, like righteousness, is moving toward its ultimate fulfillment "on the day of wrath."[8]

---

6. As we will develop below, since the new humanity is the true humanity, inaugurated in Christ, humanity "in Adam" is, by definition, a false humanity in that its activity is centered in the subversion, perversion, and denial of the truth.

7. For a detailed analysis of the central significance and importance of Christ's resurrection, see Richard B. Gaffin Jr., *The Centrality of the Resurrection: A Study in Paul's Soteriology* (Grand Rapids, MI: Baker, 1978).

8. Speaking of the revelation of both righteousness and wrath, Herman Ridderbos notes: "In both cases it is a matter of an eschatological reality, which is 'revealed,' becomes visible,

To put the parallel in the starkest possible terms, as Paul will do in Romans 5:12ff., the revelation of God's gospel righteousness has inaugurated a redemptive-historical antithesis in which every single individual, universally and eschatologically, either remains covenantally bound to Adam or is, by faith, covenantally bound to Christ. Thus, "as one trespass led to condemnation for all men, so one act of righteousness leads to justification and life for all men" (Rom. 5:18). The context, then, for Paul's initial discussion of the parallel between righteousness revealed and wrath revealed is the covenant relationship that all people, each and every one, sustains—a relationship that is characterized by the one to whom all everywhere are united, either Adam or Christ.

In the latter half of Romans 1 and into Romans 2, Paul has one overarching concern, which is to explain just how the wrath of God is made manifest among those who are outside of Christ, those who remain in Adam. In order to make clear the effects of God's wrath, as it is now revealed, Paul directs us both backward, to the beginning of creation itself, and forward, to the outworking of God's wrath for those who are covenant-breakers in Adam.

There are a number of helpful and enlightening projects that could be pursued with great benefit, both theologically and apologetically, in this passage.[9] Given the limitations of space, however, we will confine ourselves in this brief study to those aspects of Paul's analysis that will help us understand how unbelief is inherently irrational. In

---

makes itself felt. That is not to say, so far as the wrath of God is concerned, that it would only now have become visible together with the righteousness that is by faith, but indeed that in it the final judgment of God to be expected upon sin is in process of revealing itself and coming to execution; and that in an unmistakable way. For it reveals itself 'from heaven,' i.e., before the eyes of all, in such a way that everyone is able to see it (cf. Acts 14:17; Luke 21:11; 17:24)." Ridderbos, *Paul*, 110.

9. Specifically, the question of the *objects* of this wrath has become important. Here Mark Seifrid's analysis is compelling: "The universality of Paul's argument is implicit. It rests on his unexpressed, but nevertheless profound assumption that each of us stands either in open rebellion against God or in the insidious rebellion of a religiosity which embraces the divine demand but goes on to apply it to the other and not to one's self. Paul's charge is not merely universal, it is also particular. It is not directed against humanity in general, but against each and every one of his hearers. . . . To speak with Paul of 'human beings' (Rom 1:18) is to say again that he does not deal with merely ethnic categories in Romans 1:18–32." "Unrighteous by Faith: Apostolic Proclamation in Romans 1:18–3:20," in *Justification and Variegated Nomism*, ed. D. A. Carson, Peter T. O'Brien, and Mark A. Seifrid (Grand Rapids, MI: Baker, 2004), 118.

order to do that, we should begin with the *cause* of God's wrath in the lives of those who remain in Adam, and then show the effects of that cause.

As noted, as Paul begins his discussion of the revelation of God's wrath from heaven,[10] he has two primary aspects of that wrath in view: the cause and the effects. He gives the universal scope of the cause itself in Romans 1:18. God's wrath is revealed from heaven "against all ungodliness and unrighteousness of men, who by their unrighteousness suppress the truth." It is ungodliness (*asebeian*/ἀσέβειαν) and unrighteousness (*adikian*/ἀδικίαν) against which God's wrath is revealed. But Paul goes on to define in a striking way what motivates God's wrath toward all who are in Adam, all who are covenant-breakers. He introduces a specificity to this unrighteousness; it is an unrighteousness that is defined essentially as a suppression of the truth.[11]

Verse 18, then, is a general announcement of the fact that God's wrath is revealed, and of the reason for that wrath. The cause of God's wrath toward us is our unrighteous suppression of the truth. In other words, God's wrath is revealed from heaven because, in our wickedness and unrighteousness (in Adam), we hold down (in our souls) that which we know to be the case.[12] Within the context of this general announcement, however, Paul knows that he has introduced two concepts, suppression and truth, that will necessarily need clarification. In verses 19–23 (and, to some extent, v. 25 as well), Paul develops and amplifies the notions of "suppression" and of "truth."[13]

10. The wrath of God from heaven (as in "the righteousness of God,") should be seen as that which comes *from* God *to* his creatures, resulting in the effects that Paul will outline in vv. 24f.

11. We are taking the prepositional phrase *en adikia*/ἐν ἀδικίᾳ here to be instrumental rather than adverbial. See John Murray, *The Epistle to the Romans: The English Text with Introduction, Exposition, and Notes*, The New International Commentary on the New Testament (Grand Rapids, MI: Eerdmans, 1995).

12. The word translated "suppress" here is the participial form of the verb *katechō*/κατέχω. This verb can mean suppress, but it can also be translated "possess" or "retain." While "suppress" is the best translation of this verb, given that the instrument of this activity is our unrighteousness, it seems likely as well that we should include, along with this suppression, the notions of retention and possession. There is, perhaps, here a purposeful ambiguity such that all connotations of this verb are implied. Paul's analysis of suppression will necessarily include the fact that the truth we suppress we nevertheless continue to retain and possess. See Douglas J. Moo, *The Epistle to the Romans*, The New International Commentary on the New Testament (Grand Rapids, MI: Eerdmans, 1996), 103.

13. Vv. 19 to 21 are to be seen as a part of the one declaration given in v. 18. Note the connections—*dioti*/διότι (v. 19), *gar*/γὰρ (v. 20), and *dioti*/διότι (v. 21).

If we take verses 18–32 as a unit,[14] we can see how Paul puts flesh on his (so far skeletal) notion of "truth" as he reiterates what he means by truth in verses 19, 20, 23, and 32 (with v. 25 simply repeating the notion of "the truth of God"). In each of these verses, Paul gives more specificity to the concept of truth mentioned in verse 18. We shall take these verses together in order to understand what Paul means by "the truth" that is suppressed.

In verse 19, Paul tells us that by "truth" he means that which is "known about God." The truth that is suppressed, therefore, is specifically truth *about God*.[15] The way in which we come to know this truth is twofold. We come to know it, in the first place, because it is evident (*phaneron*/φανερόν) among us.[16] Paul will expand this idea in the next verse. Before that, however, he wants us to understand just how this truth, this knowledge of God, is evident or clear among us.

This is vitally important for Paul. It is vitally important, as we will see, both because Paul is concerned with *God's* activity in revealing himself (more specifically, his wrath) and, in tandem with that, because Paul wants to highlight the contrast between what *God* is doing in this revelation, on the one hand, and what we (in Adam) do with it, on the other.

So, Paul says immediately (even before he explains the sweeping scope of what is evident among us) that the reason that God's revelation is evident among us is that *God has made it evident to us*.

We should be clear here about Paul's emphasis. What Paul is concerned to deny in this context is that we, in our sins, as covenant-breakers in Adam, would ever, or could ever, produce or properly infer this truth that we have, this knowledge of God, in and of ourselves. Paul

14. To break the passage off at v. 32 is somewhat artificial since crucial aspects of Paul's argument continue in chaps. 2 and 3. For our purposes here, however, we need not go beyond the first chapter.

15. By speaking of "truth," we should emphasize here, Paul means something that is known. Paul's use of *gnōstos*/γνωστός can be translated as "what is known" or "what can be known." The former is the more common rendering, though some would see it to be a redundancy when coupled with that which is clearly visible to us (cf. Moo, *The Epistle to the Romans*, 103). It seems, however, that since Paul is concerned to explicate just what this "truth" is that we all already possess, the more common translation is more fitting. In that case, Paul is simply saying that what *is* (not "can be") known, is, quite literally, right before our very eyes.

16. The preposition *en*/ἐν here is probably best translated "among." This does not, however, mean that there is no revelation of God in us, since, as we will see, God's revelation is in all that he has made.

wants to make sure that we are not tempted to think that the truth of God, as evident among us, is evident because we have marshaled the right arguments or have set our minds in the proper direction. His point, at least in part, in this entire section, is to remind us of the devastating effects sin continues to have on our thinking (in Adam). The truth that we know—that we retain, possess, and suppress—therefore, is truth that is, fundamentally and essentially, *given* by God to us. God is the one who ensures that this truth will get through to us. It is his action, not ours, that guarantees our possession of this truth.

The truth that we all, as creatures in Adam, know and suppress is a truth about God. Even more specifically (v. 20), it is a truth concerning the "invisible" things of God, his eternal power and deity. What might Paul mean by this description? While it is perhaps not possible to be absolutely definitive, it seems that Charles Hodge is right in his assertion that what Paul has in mind here are "all the divine perfections."[17] Had Paul wanted to limit his description, he would more likely have delineated exactly what characteristics of God were known through creation.

This truth that we all know, then, is the truth of God's existence, infinity, eternity, immutability, glory, wisdom, and so forth.[18] As Paul is developing this thought in verse 23, he speaks of this knowledge of the truth as "the glory of the incorruptible God" (NASB). It is this that we all know as creatures of God. It is this that God gives, and that we necessarily "take" as knowledge, which comes to us by virtue of his natural revelation.

Two important aspects to this knowledge of God are crucial to see. First, we should be clear about the context for this knowledge. It is not

17. Charles Hodge, *Commentary on the Epistle to the Romans* (Grand Rapids, MI: Eerdmans, 1994), 37.

18. As a matter of fact, it would be difficult to improve on the Westminster Larger Catechism's description of God (question 7) as an apt description of what we know by virtue of God's natural revelation: "God is a Spirit, in and of himself infinite in being, glory, blessedness, and perfection; all-sufficient, eternal, unchangeable, incomprehensible, every where present, almighty, knowing all things, most wise, most holy, most just, most merciful and gracious, long-suffering, and abundant in goodness and truth." This does not mean, of course, that every individual knows each and every one of these characteristics of God at all times. What it does mean is that they are all revealed in and through creation. Paul, in his Areopagus address in Acts 17:16ff., demonstrates how one might apply this revelational knowledge of God.

knowledge in the abstract of which Paul speaks. He is speaking here of a knowledge that ensues on the basis of a real relationship. It is not the kind of knowledge we might get through reading about someone or something in a book or in the newspaper. This is relational, *covenantal*, knowledge. It is knowledge that comes to us because, as creatures of God, we are always and everywhere confronted with God himself. We are, even as we live in God's world every day, set squarely before the face of the God who made us and in whom we live, and move, and exist. This, then, is decidedly *personal* knowledge. It is knowledge of a person, of *the* Person, whom we have come to know by virtue of his constant and consistent revealing of himself to us.

This personal aspect of the knowledge we have is made all the more prominent in verse 32. This verse serves as a transition between Paul's exposition of God's wrath revealed in chapter 1, and the revelation of God's law in chapter 2. Notice that Paul can affirm that those who are in Adam "know the ordinance of God" (NASB). This knowledge of the ordinance (*to dikaiōma*/τὸ δικαίωμα) of God is coterminous with our knowledge of God. To know God, in the way that Paul is affirming here, is to know (at least something of) God's requirements. Along with the knowledge of God, in other words, comes the knowledge "that those who practice such things are worthy of death" (NASB). Instead of repenting, however, we, in Adam, rejoice in our disobedience and attempt to gather together others who share in our rebellion. Therefore, because this knowledge is a relational knowledge, and because the relationship is between God and the sinner, God ensures that we all know that the violations of his law in which we willingly and happily participate are capital offenses; they place us under the penalty of death. Our knowledge of God is a responsible, covenantal, knowledge that brings with it certain demands of obedience.

Second, Paul is emphatic that this knowledge of God, as given to us, is abundantly clear and is understood. There is no obscurity in God's revelation.[19] It is not as though God masks himself in order to

19. In one of his most brilliant essays, Van Til argues that the attributes that we apply to Scripture, i.e., necessity, authority, sufficiency, and perspicuity, should be applied as well to God's natural revelation. We should understand natural revelation, therefore, to be perspicuous in that the information communicated in that revelation by God to us is never fuzzy or otherwise obscured. This, of course, does not mean that natural revelation is in any way a sufficient means of salvation. As it was in the beginning, is now, and ever shall be, special revelation is needed for

keep himself hidden from his human creatures.[20] The problem with the natural revelation of God, and on this we need to be as clear as possible, is *not* from God's side, but from ours.

With the preceding discussion in mind, and in the background, we can move to the material in Romans 1 that bears more directly on our announced topic, the irrationality of unbelief. In clarifying what is meant by "truth" in verse 18, Paul at the same time begins to clarify what he means when he says that, in Adam, we *suppress* that truth. It is this suppression, we will begin to see, that is the cause of and the impetus behind the irrationality that is our sin.

As Paul is explaining what he means by truth, he is also pouring content into the notion of suppression that he introduced in verse 18. It is in verses 22, 23, and 25 that we see Paul explaining what suppression is. What we immediately notice in these verses is that the notion of suppression is characterized by what Paul calls an *exchange*. The suppression, which is part and parcel of our own sinfulness, is worked out, says Paul, by the fact that we take this glory of God (which is the truth we have from him) and exchange it for an image.[21]

This, then, begins to explain the utter irrationality of creatures who remain in Adam. We have, as creatures made in God's image, the truth of God. To use Paul's strong and decisive terminology, we *know* God.[22] We have this knowledge of the truth by virtue of his (merciful) revela-

---

that. See Van Til, "Nature and Scripture," in *The Infallible Word: A Symposium by the Members of the Faculty of Westminster Theological Seminary*, ed. N. B. Stonehouse and Paul Woolley (Nutley, NJ: Presbyterian and Reformed, 1978).

20. It is true that God is hidden, in one sense, in that he is incomprehensible. Most discussions of God's hiddenness in the (post?)modern philosophical context, however, center on the virtual obscurity, if not nonexistence, of his revelation to us. See, for example, J. L. Schellenberg, *Divine Hiddenness and Human Reason*, Cornell Studies in the Philosophy of Religion (Ithaca, NY: Cornell University Press, 1993).

21. The language Paul uses here (*homoiōmati eikonos*/ὁμοιώματι εἰκόνος) hearkens back both to the creation of human beings in God's image and likeness, and to the perversion of that creation through idolatry (see Ps. 106:20; Jer. 2:11).

22. We should note that Paul's language in v. 21 (*dioti gnontes ton theon*/διότι γνόντες τὸν θεὸν) leaves no doubt as to whether he is thinking merely about a capacity for knowledge, or about knowledge itself. It is *not* that we could, or might, or have the *ability* to, know God. It is rather, says Paul, that *we know God*. Following Calvin, we call this natural knowledge of God the *sensus divinitatis*. Calvin's exposition of the *sensus* is unequaled. See John Calvin, *Institutes of the Christian Religion*, ed. John T. McNeill, trans. Ford Lewis Battles, Library of Christian Classics (Philadelphia: Westminster, 1960), book 1, esp. chaps. 3 and 5.

tion to us.[23] This knowledge of God comes to us through everything that God has made (which is as universal as one can imagine, since it includes everything but God himself).[24] Yet, instead of acknowledging God's revelation (and repenting on the basis of it), we twist and pervert it, turning it into (exchanging it for) something false, something of our own imaginings, something that we ourselves have invented. We take this truth, which should cause us to bow down and worship God, and to be thankful (v. 21), and we fashion it into an idol. All of us, in Adam, are experts in inventing idols.[25]

We should remember here that our idolatry stems not from ignorance, not from a futile attempt to fill a void in our lives. It results always from a perversion of the truth, a twisting of reality.[26] It stems from denying the way things are and attempting to create a world of our own making. It is idolatry, therefore, that lies at the root of our sin, and thus at the root of our irrationality. In Adam, we convince ourselves that what we know to be the case is untenable. What we necessarily understand, we sinfully attempt to hold down. We sinfully exchange our true knowledge of God, which he graciously gives, for false gods and images.

These images, Paul wants us to remember, are not simply things that we make and leave behind. Images, as idols, are not decorative mantel pieces or innocuous statues. Paul makes clear, in strong religious language, that, as a matter of fact, these images are made in order that we might worship (*sebazomai*/σεβάζομαι) and serve (*latreuō*/λατρεύω) them (v. 25). We should see, then, that the activity in which we are engaged as sinners apart from Christ is an activity that is rooted and grounded in an illusion. Instead of worshiping God, we make other things that we can worship. We bow down to those things as if they were the true God, and thus we create for ourselves a complex web of self-deception.

This is why Paul notes, in verse 25, that our suppression involves an exchange of the truth of God for a lie. However much we might

---

23. And this merciful revelation *should have* led us to repentance, as Paul will argue in Rom. 2:4f.

24. The revelation of God in nature comes *tois poiēmasin*/τοῖς ποιήμασιν (v. 19).

25. To paraphrase Calvin, our hearts are "idol factories."

26. Again see Paul's approach to the philosophers at Athens (cf. Acts 17:16–34).

want to retain certain elements of the truth we have been given, we only retain that which will serve our own idolatrous purposes.[27] The whole of our lives, in sin, is seen to be a running away from the obvious, a holding down of what is in front of us always and everywhere, in order to build a world based on lies and deception.[28]

If we think, therefore, of irrationality as a disjunction between ourselves and the world as it really is, this pattern of exchange and illusion is a quintessential expression of such a disjunction. It is what robs us of being truly human; it is what is always at work to dehumanize us.[29]

Lest there be any question about the irrationality of this idolatry, Paul turns us to the effects of God's wrath on those who persist in it. In his discussion of God's-wrath-as-a-result-of-suppression, Paul outlines the general parameters of the effects of this suppression in the lives of those who are covenant-breakers in Adam. In this discussion, a general pattern emerges. The pattern looks something like this: suppression (*katechō*/κατέχω, v. 18) is essentially an exchange (*allassō*/ἀλλάσσω, v. 23; *metallassō*/μεταλλάσσω, vv. 25, 26), which brings about God's giving over (*paredōken*/παρέδωκεν, vv. 24, 26, 28) those who are in Adam to more and more sinful behavior.

Just what does this "giving over" look like? The initial description that Paul gives of this expression of God's wrath is central for our purposes here. As in idolatry generally, so in the specifics of sinful behavior, when God gives his creature (in Adam) over to our sinful desires, it results, at least in part, in a denial (by way of self-deception)

---

27. Paul knows that this is what the philosophers have done in their assertion that we live and move and have our being in God, and that we are his offspring. He uses these quotations, not because the Greeks have got it right, but in order to show that their truth depends on a necessary reference to the true God. The idolatrous statements themselves, therefore, served as an entry way for Paul to the truth of the gospel.

28. As one example of this irrational deception, note Paul's admonition on Mars Hill when he says, "Being then God's offspring, we ought not to think that the divine being is like gold or silver or stone, an image formed by the art and imagination of man" (Acts 17:29). Here Paul points out to the philosophers that their own irrationality is evidenced in their contradictory affirmations that (1) we are God's offspring, and (2) we make our own gods; a brilliant, persuasive move by Paul. One cannot rationally have it both ways.

29. So, says Ridderbos, "as communion and life with God imply true manhood, so alienation from God means the corruption, indeed the destruction of human existence." Herman N. Ridderbos, *Paul*, 112.

of the world, a denial of the way things are. Paul's initial example of this is in homosexual relationships.

Just as the notion of exchange is central to our truth-suppression, so also does exchange find its expression in our irrational behavior. Central to Paul's description of homosexual behavior is his explanation that "women exchanged natural relations [*physikēn*/φυσικὴν] for those that are contrary to nature" (*para physin*/παρὰ φύσιν, v. 26) and that men "gave up natural relations [*physikēn*] with women" and turned to relations between the same sex (*arsenes en arsesin*/ἄρσενες ἐν ἄρσεσιν, v. 27).

The question we must face is just why Paul gives the account he does of same-sex relations in the context of God's wrathful giving over of those in Adam to their own sinful desires? The answer can be found (in part) in Paul's allusions to creation and to the created order. In verse 20, Paul reminds us that God's revelation in and through creation is not something that has just begun; rather it is something that has continued "since the creation of the world."[30] In our idolatry, we are denying, in effect, that which has been operative since creation and obvious through the created order. So, as Paul gives the list of images that we fashion into idols, he works backward from the order of creation (v. 23, "mortal man and birds and animals and reptiles"). This illustrates the sheer perversity, the *backward-thinking*, that idolatry is. It seeks fundamentally to change, to perversely reverse, the natural, created order of the world.

This is why Paul turns to same-sex relations as an initial demonstration both of God's wrath revealed and of our sinful suppression. These relations attempt to change the order of creation itself. They ignore the obvious order and intent of creation; they flaunt the way things are and seek, conversely and perversely, to overturn that order. In that way, these kinds of relationships serve as (at least one of) the most obvious example(s) of the revelation of God's wrath.[31] They are, as Paul puts it, "unnatural" (NASB), or, more literally, "against nature"

30. For an explanation and defense of the temporal interpretation of *apo*/ἀπὸ, see Moo, *The Epistle to the Romans*, 105.

31. Paul's use of *thēlys*/θῆλυς and *arsēn*/ἄρσην are intentional. The Septuagint uses these words to refer to the creation of male and female in Gen. 1. Thus, Paul is again referring his readers back to the creation order, the way things were, and are, meant to be.

(*para physin*, v. 26). The exchange that takes place in these relationships (and we should note this exchange as a specific example of the
more general exchanging of the truth of God for a lie) is an exchange
of that which is true, obvious, embedded in the very order of creation
itself (*tēn physikēn*/τὴν φυσικὴν), for that which is a lie, perverse, and
against the natural order of things. Thus, in Adam, we have essentially
irrational behavior.

Our irrational suppression (exchange), as an attempt to try to
disconnect from the real world (a world in which God is always and
everywhere revealed and known), results in God's giving us over,
as those who steadfastly refuse to acknowledge him, to the kind of
behavior that our irrational suppression (exchange) demands.

But Paul does not want us to think that only the most obvious of
perversions qualify as irrational. He gives us an impressive list of all
kinds of sins, so that we might see, as Jesus himself said, that it is out
of the heart (of suppression and exchange) that evil thoughts, murder,
adultery, sexual immorality, theft, false witness, slander, and other sins
come (see Matt. 15:18f.). All sin, *as sin*, is rooted in an irrationality
that seeks in earnest to deny what is obvious and to create a world
that is nothing more than a figment of a sinful imagination.

The apologetic implications of this passage are deep and wide.
Among the most important is the fact that every person on the face of
the earth is, by virtue of being created in God's image, a God-*knower*.
No person operates in a religious vacuum. No person is outside the
bounds of God's covenant relationship. Those who are in Adam are,
nevertheless, in a covenant-breaking relationship with the God who
made, and who sustains, them.

In our defense of Christianity, therefore, we may be confident in
the fact that, even before we begin our defense, God has been there,
dynamically and perpetually making himself known through every
single fact of the unbeliever's existence. Our apologetic is, then, in a
very real sense, a reminder to the unbeliever of what he already knows
to be the case.

Much more needs to be pursued, but space constraints draw this
to a close. We should note, however, in conclusion, that the end result
of God's revelation to his human creatures is that they are rendered,
centrally and essentially, without excuse. The word Paul uses here (used

here alone in the New Testament) can be rendered, literally, "without an apologetic" (*anapologētous*/ἀναπολογήτους, Rom. 1:20). If we think of what it means to have no excuse, no defense, we realize that there is, as a matter of fact, no reason to be given for a particular offense or violation. This is Paul's meaning here. In spite of any attempt to explain or give a rational account of sin, those outside of Christ will never be able to find a reason for the rejection of the obvious. The irrationality of unbelief, as Paul will go on to explain in the book of Romans, finds its only terminus in its own demise. That demise is met at the cross and becomes ours through faith in Christ.

The *mysterium iniquitatis*, as the suppression and grotesque exchange of the knowledge of God, is only defeated in the Great Exchange of the gospel, the *mysterium Christi* (Col. 1:27).

4

The Case for Calvinistic Hermeneutics

MOISÉS SILVA

The word *Calvinistic* in the title of this essay contains an ambiguity. Am I interested here in the methods of interpretation used by John Calvin in his biblical commentaries? Or does the title refer to that system of theology which, originating in Calvin's *Institutes of the Christian Religion*, was brought to full expression a century later by the Westminster Confession of Faith?

The ambiguity is deliberate, since one of my aims is to stress the close connection between biblical interpretation and systematic theology. True, it would be an exaggeration to claim that Calvin's exegetical method in the commentaries is absolutely identical to his use of the Bible in the *Institutes*, but one must recognize that during the course of over two decades, Calvin's theological thought guided his exegesis while his exegesis kept contributing to his theology. (The

This essay appeared originally in Walter C. Kaiser Jr. and Moisés Silva, "The Case for Calvinistic Hermeneutics," in *An Introduction to Biblical Hermeneutics* (Grand Rapids, MI: Zondervan, 1994), 251–69. It is reproduced here by permission of The Zondervan Corporation (with minor changes). There is more than a verbal coincidence between the title of this essay and that of Cornelius Van Til's book, *The Case for Calvinism* (Philadelphia: Presbyterian and Reformed, 1964).

first edition of the *Institutes* appeared in 1536, and the last one in 1559, and during those two decades most of the commentaries were produced.)

Again, some might object that there are significant differences between Calvin himself, on the one hand, and later Calvinism, on the other.[1] These differences, however, have been greatly overstated. While undoubtedly there are features that distinguish these two expressions of theology (e.g., organization, formulation, and emphases), such distinctions are far outweighed by the fundamental commitments that bind them together.

It may be worth mentioning that I myself was not raised in a Calvinistic environment and that my initial training in theology came from quite a different tradition. Curiously, the very conservative circles of which I was a part—indeed, American evangelicalism generally—has depended *heavily* on the publications of such Reformed scholars as B. B. Warfield, J. Gresham Machen, and E. J. Young, but has at the same time been rather critical of the alleged "cold intellectualism" in the Princeton-Westminster tradition and of the distinctively Calvinistic features in their theology.

We should, no doubt, be quick to retain what is valuable and reject what is damaging in any book we read. But is it only a coincidence that this theological tradition, more than any other, has furnished the means to preserve the intellectual integrity of evangelicalism? Does it make sense to cast aspersions at the academic rigor of these scholars while freely using the results of their academic labor? And could it be that what evangelicalism finds objectionable in their theology is precisely what has made possible their contribution to conservative scholarship?[2]

1. Particularly after the rise of so-called neoorthodox theology in the 1920s, it became common to dismiss the orthodox Calvinist theologians of the seventeenth and eighteenth centuries as scholastics who undermined the spirit of the Reformers. Subsequently, some writers have sought to draw a sharp wedge between Calvin and the Westminster Confession. For a criticism of these attempts, see Paul Helm, *Calvin and the Calvinists* (Carlisle, PA: Banner of Truth, 1982).

2. The argument can be made, for example, that Warfield's defense of the infallibility of Scripture, though widely adopted by non-Calvinist evangelicals, is intimately related to his commitment to divine sovereignty. See Cornelius Van Til's introduction to B. B. Warfield, *The Inspiration and Authority of the Bible* (Philadelphia: Presbyterian and Reformed, 1948), esp. 66.

Whatever our answer to these questions, we can certainly profit from considering the distinctives of "Calvinistic hermeneutics." Note, however, that in the brief space at my disposal I cannot adequately defend all of my claims, especially since some of them would require extensive theological discussion (the occasional bibliographical comments in the notes may be of value to readers who want to pursue these topics). Neither do I wish to suggest that the positive qualities described below are the exclusive property of Reformed scholarship. If I set Reformed distinctives over against broad evangelicalism, that is only to clarify the issues. It goes without saying—but I want to stress it anyway—that the Calvinistic tradition, which suffers from its own weaknesses, can learn a great deal from Christians of other persuasions.

Excellence and Clarity of Exposition

In attempting to make the case for a Calvinistic approach to biblical interpretation, one must first appeal to those biblical commentaries for which Calvin became justly famous. Numerous scholars, some of whom would be the least inclined to accept Calvinism, emphasize the extraordinary virtues of Calvin as an expositor of Scripture. A brief summary of opinions on this matter is given by Philip Schaff, the dean of nineteenth-century church historians:

> Calvin was an exegetical genius of the first order. His commentaries are unsurpassed for originality, depth, perspicuity, soundness, and permanent value. . . . Reuss, the chief editor of [Calvin's] works and himself an eminent biblical scholar, says that Calvin was "beyond all question the greatest exegete of the sixteenth century." . . . Diestel, the best historian of Old Testament exegesis, calls him "the creator of genuine exegesis."[3]

It is even more remarkable that professional exegetes in our day continue to refer to Calvin as a matter of course when commenting on the biblical text. Quite likely, no commentator prior to the middle

3. Philip Schaff, *History of the Christian Church*, 5th ed. (New York: Scribner, 1885–1920), 8:524–25.

of the nineteenth century is alluded to more frequently than Calvin is, even though he lived long before the development of the modern scientific outlook.

Among the characteristic features of Calvin's work as a commentator, none was so important as his desire for clarity and brevity.[4] These were not two separate aims, but rather twin ideals that he pursued in conscious distinction from much of the work that had preceded him. As he looked back on the history of commentary-writing, he found that one theologian stood out as a model for biblical expositors, and that was the fourth-century Antiochene preacher John Chrysostom. When compared against Chrysostom's expositions, most subsequent writers appeared verbose.

But if Calvin objected to long-winded commentaries, the reason was not merely impatience with a particular kind of style—it was rather the inevitable obscuring of the message of the text that concerned him. The task of the expositor is to clarify the author's meaning, whereas the accumulation of material normally moves the expositor away from this goal. In keeping with this principle, Calvin consciously refrained from dealing with contrary opinions (unless the omission were likely to confuse the reader) because, he said, "I have held nothing to be of more importance than the edification of the church." Moreover, it appears that he sought to write in a style that was patterned after the Scriptures themselves. The Bible has its own eloquence, and it is the eloquence of simplicity.

Not all of Calvin's followers imitated him in this matter. The seventeenth-century Puritans tended to write massive expositions, such as William Gurnall's influential work, *The Christian in Complete Armour*, a nearly 1200-page treatment of Ephesians 6:11–20. In the last couple of decades, the growth of learning has led many scholars to write lengthy works as well. It would be foolhardy to ignore the wonderful contribution that some of these commentaries have made to our understanding of the biblical text. Still, Calvin's example should remind us of what our primary goals ought to be. It is all too easy to

4. In a letter to Simon Grynaeus, he states that the interpreter's principal virtue resides in *perspicua brevitate*. See Richard C. Gamble, "*Brevitas et Facilitas*: Toward an Understanding of Calvin's Hermeneutic," *Westminster Theological Journal* 47 (1985): esp. 2–3; for what follows, see pp. 8–9 and 13–15.

become mesmerized either by exegetical problems or by perceived devotional needs; in both cases, we allow the central and simple message of the text to recede into the background. If, however, we keep in mind that no motive is more important than the edification of the church—the basis for which is God's own teaching and not our imagination—our efforts will remain focused on the historical meaning intended by the biblical author.

Common Grace

A second feature that distinguished Calvin's method of interpretation was his full appreciation of human learning. In this respect, Calvin was a child of the Renaissance and, inevitably, a follower of the humanism associated with Erasmus.[5] Prior to devoting his life to the Christian ministry, Calvin had been trained in the humanities and had produced a detailed commentary on *De clementia*, a philosophical work by Seneca, the first-century Spanish Stoic. Whatever else one may think of that commentary, it clearly reveals that Calvin had honed his skills in the best methods of philological and literary analysis available in his day. It is also clear that subsequently, far from abandoning his devotion to classical scholarship (as Jerome did—or so he claimed), Calvin put it to the service of biblical interpretation and theological reflection. As he expressed it in his *Institutes*, "men who have either quaffed or even tasted the liberal arts penetrate with their aid far more deeply into the secrets of the divine wisdom." And again: "But if the Lord has willed that we be helped in physics, dialectic, mathematics, and other like disciplines, by the work and ministry of the ungodly, let us use this assistance. For if we neglect God's gift freely offered in these arts, we ought to suffer just punishment for our sloths."[6]

Calvin's use of "secular" learning is of special significance because it reflected a key theological concept, namely, his view of so-called *common grace*. This is a crucial point, because Calvin's approach must be distinguished from that of many evangelical scholars who make

---

5. Cf. Quirinius Breen, *John Calvin: A Study in French Humanism* (Grand Rapids, MI: Eerdmans, 1931), esp. chaps. 4–5.

6. John Calvin, *Institutes of the Christian Religion*, ed. John T. McNeill, trans. Ford Lewis Battles, Library of Christian Classics (Philadelphia: Westminster, 1960), 1.5.2, 2.2.16.

free use of critical methods that have been developed without consideration of (sometimes in opposition to) biblical faith. The issue here is not whether such methods should be used, but whether it is appropriate to use them without careful reflection on their theological implications. To put it differently, one seldom sees an attempt to integrate the principles of critical scholarship with the distinctives of evangelical thought. The impression one usually gets is that, unless a specific conclusion of scholarship explicitly contradicts a tenet of "conservative" theology, we should freely appropriate the work of "liberal" critics.

This attitude, however, can only undermine the integrity of evangelicalism. For one thing, the very coherence of the evangelical faith is likely to be crippled as potentially incompatible elements are adopted without critical evaluation. In addition, the approach does not sit well with nonevangelical scholars, who argue, with some justification, that the credibility of conservative thinking becomes suspect.[7] In short, the desire to gain intellectual respectability backfires.

So how was Calvin's approach different? As is well known, the Swiss Reformer actually begins his *Institutes* by discussing epistemology, that is, by reflecting on fundamental questions of knowledge: just how can we know God? His answer is that the knowledge of God and the knowledge of ourselves are intimately related. We cannot look at ourselves, he argues, without thinking about God. "For, quite clearly, the mighty gifts with which we are endowed are hardly from ourselves; indeed, our very being is nothing but subsistence in the one God. Then, by these benefits shed like dew from heaven upon us, we are led as by rivulets to the spring itself." Of course, Adam's rebellion has brought ruin, but even that fact "compels us to look upward." On the other hand, he continues, we cannot expect to acquire a clear knowledge of ourselves—inclined to hypocrisy as we are—unless we look carefully at God and judge everything by his standard.[8]

7. Though not always accurate or fair, James Barr, in his *Fundamentalism* (London: SCM, 1977), esp. chap. 5, raises questions that demand our attention. See the discussion of this book in my Evangelical Theological Society presidential address, "'Can Two Walk Together Unless They Be Agreed?' Evangelical Theology and Biblical Scholarship," *Journal of the Evangelical Theological Society* 41 no. 1 (1998): 3–16.

8. Calvin, *Institutes*, 1.1.1–3.

In subsequent chapters, Calvin has much to say about general revelation and about the other evidences of God's grace toward humanity in general. Of special interest for us is his discussion of human learning as a gift of the Spirit:

> Whenever we come upon these matters [art and science] in secular writers, let that admirable light of truth shining in them teach us that the mind of man, though fallen and perverted from its wholeness, is nevertheless clothed and ornamented with God's excellent gifts. If we regard the Spirit of God as the sole fountain of truth, we shall neither reject the truth itself, nor despise it wherever it shall appear, unless we wish to dishonor the Spirit of God. For by holding the gifts of the Spirit in slight esteem, we contemn and reproach the Spirit himself. . . . No, we cannot read the writings of the ancients on these subjects without great admiration. . . . But shall we count anything praiseworthy or noble without recognizing at the same time that it comes from God? . . .
> . . . But lest anyone think a man truly blessed when he is credited with possessing great power to comprehend truth under the elements of this world, we should at once add that all this capacity to understand, with the understanding that follows upon it, is an unstable and transitory thing in God's sight, when a solid foundation of truth does not underlie it.[9]

It is essential to appreciate Calvin's balance here. By recognizing at once the marvel and praiseworthiness of human learning as a divine gift and also its basic instability because of the fallen and perverted mind of the sinner, he could do justice to the coherence of biblical teaching.

Later Reformed theology has not always been consistent in working out the implications of Calvin's ideas. In the Dutch tradition, however, the doctrine of common grace has played a prominent and controversial role, and few have given more attention to it than Cornelius Van Til. Without attempting to describe his apologetic system, we can point out certain features that are of particular relevance for biblical hermeneutics. Central to Van Til is the importance of pre-

9. Ibid., 2.2.15–16.

suppositionalism and thus the denial of neutrality. Over against the traditional Roman Catholic distinction between nature and grace—and thus between reason and faith—Van Til argues that, according to Scripture, all human beings know full well that God exists and that his power has created the world. Moreover, they have all rejected that knowledge and rebelled against him (see esp. Rom. 1:18–23). Human beings, therefore, are not neutral observers who need to be persuaded by natural and rational arguments that there is a God so that subsequently they can be brought to faith. On the contrary, they have willfully chosen to worship the creature rather than the Creator, and their whole thinking is distorted by the presence of sin. Readers will note that this formulation is a specific way of expressing the Reformed doctrine of total depravity.

Van Til also emphasizes, however, that men and women are not as sinful as they could be. Sin has fundamentally distorted, *but it has not destroyed*, their character as God's image. To put it differently, they are inconsistent both in their thinking and in their conduct. It is here that the doctrine of common grace shows up clearly. God continues to send the warmth of the sun to this sinful world; he restrains the progress of evil in human society as a whole. As a result, many people who reject God's goodness manage to live apparently exemplary lives, even though their starting point should lead them to full-blown licentiousness. Similarly, their minds, in spite of having spurned the knowledge of the only wise God, accomplish remarkable feats. To the extent that they make intellectual progress, however, they do so only on "borrowed capital," that is, by taking advantage of the very truths that contradict their most basic commitments. Van Til's approach, then, while radically antithetical, does not at all lead to contempt for human accomplishments but makes possible our appreciation of them.[10]

10. See Van Til, *The Defense of the Faith*, 3rd ed. (Philadelphia: Presbyterian and Reformed, 1967), chap. 8; and Cornelius Van Til, *Common Grace* (Philadelphia: Presbyterian and Reformed, 1947), esp. 91, on the correlative character of common grace and total depravity, and 95: "It is only when we thus press the objective validity of the Christian claim at every point, that we can easily afford to be 'generous' with respect to the natural man and his accomplishments. It is when we ourselves are fully self-conscious that we can cooperate with those to whose building we own the title." In other words, only if we are unequivocal about the antithesis

The history of both "Old Princeton"[11] and Westminster exemplifies how this Calvinistic understanding of sin and common grace can affect theological scholarship. The best-known theologians at Princeton Theological Seminary, Charles Hodge (1797–1878) and Benjamin B. Warfield (1851–1921), were not only fully abreast of contemporary progress in the sciences, the humanities, and critical biblical scholarship;[12] it is also clear that their own thinking was positively affected by those advances. While much of their work had a strong polemical edge against unbelieving scholarship, it is undeniable that their own thought reflected an integration of so-called "secular" knowledge and biblical teaching. This was not, however, a naive adoption of unbiblical ideas, but simply a recognition that Calvin was right when he insisted that the Spirit of God is the source of all truth and so we should not despise it, regardless of where it appears; in other words—to use a profound saying that for some has become an ambiguous cliché—"all truth is God's truth."

Specifically in the area of biblical scholarship, no one illustrates this principle more powerfully than J. Gresham Machen (1881–1937), who taught New Testament at Princeton until 1929 and then, because of the "modernist-fundamentalist" conflicts at that time, led several of his colleagues to found Westminster Theological Seminary in Philadelphia. Having studied under some prominent liberal theologians in Germany, Machen struggled with the challenges brought against the authority of Scripture and the integrity of his evangelical faith. In the end he became the leading intellectual opponent of modernism while at the same time making full use of the biblical scholarship associated with that movement.

Machen's two major works, *The Origin of Paul's Religion* (1925) and *The Virgin Birth of Christ* (1930), are brilliant examples of evangelical learning, in both of which he attempts to dismantle, logically and

---

between the Christian and the non-Christian viewpoint can we legitimately use the work of the unbeliever.

11. Ironically, much of Van Til's work was developed in reaction to the apologetic system that had been used at Princeton. By correcting certain features in the Warfieldian approach, however, Van Til was in effect bringing the apologetics of American Calvinism closer to its theology.

12. Cf. Mark Noll, "The *Princeton Review*," *Westminster Theological Journal* 50 (1988): 283–304, esp. 302–3.

patiently, major tenets of liberal theology. It is important to empha-size, however, that Machen did not master liberal scholarship merely to build his intellectual ammunition against it (as more than a few evangelical scholars are wont to do). The seriousness with which he regarded that scholarship is evident on every page—as is the fact that he was not at all afraid to *learn* from it. Not surprisingly, a well-known German critic who disputed Machen's thesis wrote a twenty-page review article of *The Virgin Birth of Christ* in which he described the book as "so circumspect, so intelligent in its discussions, that it must be recognized unqualifiedly as an important achievement."[13] Still, we cannot ignore the fact that Machen himself viewed his approach as "a thoroughgoing apologetic."[14]

In our day, the growing presence of evangelicals in scholarly forums, such as the Society of Biblical Literature, is at once encouraging and unnerving. Sometimes, one fears, this participation reflects a tendency to compartmentalize the intellect: commitments to biblical truth are suspended, not merely for the temporary purposes of discussion, but perhaps as a reflection of the view that the issues have a neutral char-acter. (In principle, it is quite proper to engage nonevangelical scholars on a whole spectrum of issues without having to raise the bugaboo of theological presuppositions. The question is rather whether, in the process of discussion, our own thinking becomes independent of our faith.) Apart from the occasional disagreement expressed against spe-cific ideas, one seldom detects an effort, or even a desire, to assess the fundamental character of critical approaches in the light of evangelical faith. Perhaps a consideration of how Calvin and his successors have related their study of Scripture to human learning can assist modern conservative scholars as they seek to do the same in these challeng-ing times.

---

13. F. Kattenbusch, "Theologische Studien und Kritiken" (1930), 454.

14. J. Gresham Machen, *The Virgin Birth of Christ* (New York: Harper & Row, 1932), x. It is sometimes thought that Machen's approach was incompatible with Van Til's; this misconcep-tion is adequately handled by Greg L. Bahnsen, "Machen, Van Til, and the Apologetic Tradition of the OPC," in *Pressing toward the Mark: Essays Commemorating Fifty Years of the Orthodox Presbyterian Church*, ed. C. G. Dennison and R. C. Gamble (Philadelphia: The Committee for the Historian of the Orthodox Presbyterian Church, 1986), 259–94. More to the point, however, I wish to suggest that the character of what Machen and some of his predecessors did (whatever their conscious apologetic principles) provided a model for Van Til regarding the proper use of unbelieving scholarship.

Theology and Exegesis

As the previous section may have suggested to the reader, it is not feasible to separate biblical interpretation from theology.[15] The relationship between exegesis and systematic theology has been one of the most controverted issues in the history of biblical scholarship. Many scholars doubt, or even deny, that it is really possible to use the Bible for the purposes of developing a systematic theology. In their view, the various biblical authors had different, indeed incompatible, theologies, so that the attempt to treat them as a unity can result only in distorting the text.

Evangelical biblical scholars, of course, would reject such an approach, but that does not mean they have a particularly high view of systematic theology. Exceedingly few of them show much interest in the subject—if anything, it is viewed with suspicion. Particularly objectionable to them would be the suggestion that systematics should influence our exegesis. Yet that is precisely the claim that I wish to make, and here again Calvin provides a remarkable model.

The first edition of the *Institutes* was published when Calvin was a very young man, and the subsequent revisions and expansions reflect both his growing knowledge of historical theology (references to the church fathers and medieval theologians increase sharply in each subsequent edition) and his greater attention to exegetical work. No one is likely to argue that these two sides of his work were independent of each other—as though he forgot about his theology when he exegeted (and that is why his commentaries are good!) or did not pay attention to the Bible when he did theology (and that is why the *Institutes* are so bad!). My own thesis is that both his expositions and his theology are superb precisely because they are related.[16] But even those who have little use for Calvin's system stand to gain, rather than to lose,

---

15. Some of the material in this section is taken from my "Systematic Theology and the Apostle Paul," *Trinity Journal* 15 (1994): 3–26.

16. Calvin himself saw his two projects as complementary. In his introductory statement to the *Institutes* ("John Calvin to the Reader"), he tells us that his aim in this work was to help "candidates in sacred theology" grasp "the sum of religion in all its parts" and thus guide them in the study of Scripture. Such a compendium would make it possible for him, when writing his commentaries, to avoid long doctrinal discussions. In his view, the proper use of the commentaries presupposed that the student was "armed with a knowledge of the present work, as a necessary tool" (pp. 4–5).

if their exegesis is consciously done within the framework of their theology.

Such an approach, admittedly, seems to be diametrically opposed to the aims of grammatico-historical exegesis. Three centuries ago scholars were already arguing, with great vigor, that systematic theology—especially in its classical form—must be kept quite separate from biblical interpretation. Indeed, it was not difficult to show that theological biases had frequently hampered the work of exegetes, even to the point of distorting the meaning of the text. True "historical" exegesis was understood, more and more, as interpretation that was not prejudiced by theological commitments. Leopold Immanuel Rückert, in the preface to his 1831 commentary on Romans, stated that the biblical interpreter must abandon his own perspective.

> In other words, I require of him freedom from prejudice. The exegete of the New Testament as an exegete . . . has no system, and must not have one, either a dogmatic or an emotional system. In so far as he is an exegete, he is neither orthodox nor heterodox, neither supernaturalist nor rationalist, nor pantheist, nor any other ist there may be. He is neither pious nor godless, neither moral nor immoral, neither sensitive nor insensible.[17]

And one of his contemporaries, the great New Testament exegete Heinrich August Wilhelm Meyer, expressed the same idea as follows:

> The area of dogmatics and philosophy is to remain off limits for a commentary. For to ascertain the meaning the author intended to convey by his words, impartially and historico-grammatically—that is the duty of the exegete. How the meaning so ascertained stands in relation to the teachings of philosophy, to what extent it agrees with the dogmas of the church or with the view of its theologians, in what way the dogmatician is to make use of it in the interest of his science—to the exegete as an exegete, all that is a matter of no concern.[18]

17. W. G. Kümmel, *The New Testament: The History of the Investigation of Its Problems* (Nashville: Abingdon, 1972), 110.
18. Ibid., 111.

Today most people would view these two formulations as strikingly naive. But we should not be fooled. The underlying commitment is alive and well. Moreover, there are plenty of exegetes around who might vigorously disown these statements, but whose work, unwittingly perhaps, is a perfect expression of the same viewpoint. In contrast, I wish to argue that proper exegesis should be informed by theological reflection. To put it in the most shocking way possible: my theological system should tell me how to exegete. Can such an outrageous position be defended? I would like to suggest three considerations that make that position not merely defensible but indeed the only real option.

In the first place, we should recognize that systematic theology is, to a large extent, an exercise in contextualization, that is, it is an attempt to reformulate the teaching of Scripture in categories that are meaningful and understandable to us. Sometimes, it is true, theologians have given the impression (or even claimed) that their descriptions are no more and no less than the teachings of Scripture and that therefore, being independent of the theologian's historical context, those descriptions have permanent validity. But the very process of organizing the biblical data—to say nothing of the use of a different language in a different cultural setting—brings to bear the theologian's own context. Even Charles Hodge, who claimed with great pride that no original ideas had ever been proposed at Princeton,[19] was a truly creative thinker, and his *Systematic Theology* reflects through and through an innovative integration of some strands of nineteenth-century philosophy with classic Reformed theology.

Intrinsically, there is nothing objectionable in attempting to understand and explain an ancient writing through contemporary categories, yet biblical scholars often assume that such an approach is off-limits. As one writer has put it, biblical exposition should be done "in terms of what the text itself has to say. . . . Resorting to . . . later formula-

---

19. The reference was specifically to the journal edited by him (see Noll, "The *Princeton Review*," 288). Of course, Hodge was not as naive as those words might suggest. His use of hyperbole was intended to focus on doctrinal *substance*, not on the way the doctrines were formulated. Indeed, some modern writers have emphasized—and severely criticized—the innovative use of Scottish realism made by Hodge. Though we need not deny that some aspects of that background had a negative effect, attention must be paid to the positive benefits as well. In any case, it is my opinion that the indebtedness of Hodge and later Princetonians to realism has been greatly overstated.

tions is not only anachronistic but obscures the impact of the specific words [the writer] chose to use on the occasion. In short, such an approach is methodologically indefensible."[20] In fact, however, the very use of English to explain the biblical text means resorting to subsequent formal expressions. If a modern writer wishes to explain Aristotle's thought, for example, we all acknowledge not only the legitimacy but also the great value and even the necessity of doing so by the use of contemporary philosophical terms that make it possible to express clearly an ancient thinker's writings. Someone who merely restated Aristotle's teachings using Greek words, or even strict English equivalents, would fail to explain those teachings precisely because no attempt was made to contextualize them.

In the second place, our evangelical view of the unity of Scripture demands that we see the whole Bible as the context of any one part. An appeal to the study of Aristotle is of help here too. The modern scholar looks at the whole Aristotelian corpus for help in understanding a detail in one particular work. To the extent that we view the whole of Scripture as having come from one Author, therefore, to that extent a systematic understanding of the Bible contributes to the exegesis of individual passages. Admittedly, there are some real dangers in this approach. On the basis of a questionable reading of Romans 12:6, Christians have often appealed to "the analogy of faith" in a way that does not do justice to the distinctiveness of individual writers of Scripture. Moreover, it is all too easy to fall into the trap of *eisegesis*, that is, reading into a particular text some broad theological idea because we (sometimes unconsciously) want to avoid the implications of what the text really says. It is therefore understandable that Walter Kaiser, for example, wishes to restrict the principle of the analogy of faith to the end of the interpretive process, and that only as a means of summarizing the teaching of the passage.[21] To do so, however, is to

20. Clinton E. Arnold, review of Silva, *Philippians*, in *Critical Review of Books in Religion 1991* (Atlanta: Scholars Press, 1991), 232.

21. In Kaiser and Silva, "The Case for Calvinistic Hermeneutics," chap. 11. Other writers are more negative, even to the point of undermining the coherence of Scripture. Cf., among others, Calvin R. Schoonhoven, "The 'Analogy of Faith' and the Intent of Hebrews," in *Scripture, Tradition and Interpretation: Essays Presented to Everett F. Harrison by His Students and Colleagues in Honor of His Seventy-Fifth Birthday*, ed. W. W. Gasque and W. S. LaSor (Grand Rapids, MI: Eerdmans, 1978), 92–110, esp. 105. Much more helpful is Henri Blocher, "The 'Analogy of Faith'

neglect God's most important hermeneutical gift to us, namely, the unity and wholeness of his own revelation.

Third, and finally, my proposal will sound a lot less shocking once we remember that, as a matter of fact, everyone does it anyway. Whether we mean to or not, and whether we like it or not, all of us read the text as interpreted by our theological presuppositions. Indeed, the most serious argument against the view that exegesis should be done independently of systematic theology is that such a view is hopelessly naive. The very possibility of understanding anything depends on our prior framework of interpretation. If we perceive a fact that makes sense to us, the simple reason is that we have been able to fit that fact into the whole complex of ideas that we have previously assimilated.

Of course, sometimes we *make* the fact fit our preconceptions and thus distort it. The remedy, however, is neither to deny that we have those preconceptions nor to try to suppress them, for we would only be deceiving ourselves. We are much more likely to be conscious of those preconceptions if we deliberately seek to identify them *and then use them* in the exegetical process. That way, when we come across a fact that resists the direction our interpretation is taking, we are better prepared to recognize the anomaly for what it is, namely, our interpretive scheme is faulty and must be modified. On the other hand, exegetes who convince themselves that, through pure philological and historical techniques, they can understand the Bible directly—that is, without the mediation of prior exegetical, theological, and philosophical commitments—are less likely to perceive the real character of exegetical difficulties.[22]

The old advice that biblical students should try as much as possible to approach a text without a prior idea as to what it means (and that therefore commentaries should be read after, not before, the exegesis) does have the advantage of encouraging independent thinking; besides, it reminds us that our primary aim is indeed to discover the historical

---

in the Study of Scripture: In Search of Justification and Guidelines," *Scottish Bulletin of Evangelical Theology* 5 (1987): 17–38, though I would wish to go a little further than he does.

22. It is perhaps worth pointing out that long before Rudolf Bultmann's emphasis on "preunderstanding" became a popular topic, and certainly before Thomas Kuhn challenged the neutrality of scientific investigation, Cornelius Van Til had, in an even more radical way, exposed the role of presuppositions for all of life.

meaning and that we are always in danger of imposing our meaning on the text. Nevertheless, the advice is fundamentally flawed, because it is untrue to the very process of learning. I would suggest rather that a student who comes to a biblical passage with, say, a dispensationalist background, should attempt to make sense of the text assuming that dispensationalism is correct. I would go so far as to say that, upon encountering a detail that does not seem to fit the dispensationalist scheme, the student should try to "make it fit." The purpose, of course, is not to mishandle the text, but to become self-conscious about what we all do anyway. The result should be increased sensitivity to those features of the text that disturb our interpretive framework and thus a greater readiness to modify that framework.[23]

God's Sovereignty in Biblical Interpretation

Calvin's theology is best known for its stress on divine sovereignty, particularly as expressed in the concept of election. For some people, it seems, that is all Calvin ever taught. The truth, however, is that few theologians have ever been as balanced as Calvin was in attempting to give expression to the breadth of biblical teaching. The very fact that he wrote commentaries on almost every book of the Bible should tell us something. Even in the midst of a strongly polemical setting, he managed to do justice to every theological *locus*.

His balance, ironically, is especially evident in his treatment of election. This doctrine does not have as prominent a place in the *Institutes* as many imagine. It is not covered in the first chapter or even the whole of book 1. One has to wait to book 3, chapters 21–24, and then the treatment consists of 44 pages, that is, about one half of one percent of the *Institutes*. In short, an understanding of Calvin's doctrine of divine sovereignty in salvation must take into account its place in the context of his whole teaching.

From another perspective, however, this doctrine was even more important to Calvin than is usually understood. The fact that it is not the explicit subject of discussion in books 1 and 2 hardly means that it is not present there. Quite the contrary. Calvin's sense of awe at

23. Or so one hopes—at this point, unfortunately, psychological disposition often takes over!

the majesty and power of God over all creation pervades the whole of his theology in a fundamental way. In the Calvinistic tradition, this emphasis has played a significant role. Far from annulling human freedom, total divine sovereignty alone makes such freedom meaningful.[24] Because only in God do we have our being, freedom outside of his will is inconceivable. Accordingly, in light of our slavery to sin (Rom. 6:16–23), it would be illusory to think that salvation can in any way depend on our effort or will (John 1:13; Rom. 9:14–16).

What bearing does all this have on biblical hermeneutics? Here we can only illustrate its significance with a few examples. With regard to exegetical practice, the doctrine of divine sovereignty makes us particularly sensitive to God's workings in the history of redemption. Biblical narrative nowhere suggests that the divine plan has been frustrated by historical accidents or human obstinacy. While free agency and responsibility are clearly assumed, these human realities are pictured as coordinate with—indeed, subsumed under—God's will for his people. Particularly striking is the description of events in the days of Rehoboam, whose wicked decision to oppress Israel led to the tragedy of a divided kingdom: "So the king did not listen to the people, for this turn of events was from the LORD, to fulfill the word the LORD had spoken to Jeroboam . . ." (1 Kings 12:15 NIV). The prophets understood well the significance of this principle:

> The LORD Almighty has sworn,
> "Surely, as I have planned, so it will be,
>   and as I have purposed, so it will stand. . . ."
> For the LORD Almighty has purposed, and who can thwart him?

24. As the Westminster Confession of Faith 3.1 puts it: "God from all eternity did, by the most wise and holy counsel of his own will, freely and unchangeably ordain whatsoever comes to pass; yet so as thereby neither is God the author of sin, nor is violence offered to the will of the creatures, nor is the liberty or contingency of second causes taken away, *but rather established*" (my emphasis). This is hardly the place to provide a philosophical defense of the doctrine. Note, however, that a world in which *anything at all* happens outside of God's will is a world inevitably ruled by contingency, that is, radical uncertainty. If God knows for certain what will take place in the future (the fundamental biblical doctrine of foreknowledge), then of course everything that takes place must take place. If, on the other hand, events are not "determined" in this sense, then God cannot know what will take place, which means that *anything* could take place and God would be quite limited as to what he could do about it.

His hand is stretched out, and who can turn it back?
(Isa. 14:24, 27 NIV)

The relevance of these concepts shows up unexpectedly in various exegetical problems. Redaction criticism, for instance, has pointed out how frequently biblical narrative colors and interprets historical events. For some scholars, this characteristic is evidence that the biblical writers have tampered with the facts. Conservative writers, afraid of the implications, often shy away from such features and prefer to downplay, for instance, the differences among the Gospels. Evangelical scholars who do appreciate the value of redaction-critical work have not always grappled with the serious theological challenges posed by this method. The Reformed view of biblical inspiration, however, goes hand in hand with a Reformed understanding of history. The God who controls the events of history is the God who interprets those events in Scripture, and thus there can be no inherent contradiction between the two. This hardly means that we are free to adopt any approach to the narratives even if it undermines their reliability, nor does it provide an automatic solution to many difficult problems. It does mean that we need not "protect" the credibility of Scripture by making sure it conforms to our expectations of history-writing.[25]

The doctrine of divine sovereignty also helps us to appreciate the centrality of the concept of covenant in Scripture. As is well known, Calvinism has been characterized by an approach known as *covenant theology*. The term means different things to different people, and to be sure it serves as a conceptual umbrella covering a rich and wide variety of emphases, some more clearly biblical than others. Fundamentally, it refers to God's dispositions in his plan of salvation. It is God who takes the initiative in forming a people for himself, so that the assurance, "I am your God and you are my people," provides an all-pervasive principle throughout the history of redemption (from Gen. 17:7–8 to Rev. 21:3).

Faithfulness to this principle should guide the exegete at numerous points, as in passages that bear on the doctrine of salvation by grace, or when assessing the function of the Mosaic law in relation to the

---

25. I have dealt with this problem in "Ned B. Stonehouse and Redaction Criticism," *Westminster Theological Seminary* 40 (1977–78): 77–88, 281–303.

Abrahamic covenant. The concept evidently has much to say about questions related to prophecy and the place of the people of Israel. Traditionally, for instance, dispensationalism has drawn a sharp distinction between Israel and the Christian church. More recent writers have recognized the important features common to both, but the organic unity of God's people throughout the ages is a distinctive emphasis of covenant theology. This emphasis in turn has profound implications for our understanding of ecclesiology (including questions of church government, baptism, etc.), of the Christian's use of the Old Testament, and much more.

Finally, an appreciation for the Calvinist or Augustinian—indeed, Pauline!—doctrine of divine sovereignty and election affects one's understanding of biblical interpretation as such.[26] It is not sufficient to recognize God's lordship over biblical history without submitting ourselves to that lordship as interpreters. It is in fact quite silly, on the one hand, to affirm that the events related in Scripture, as well as the actual writing of Scripture, are a fulfillment of God's will and, on the other hand, to assume that our interpretation of that material has some sort of neutral character or independent status. Yet some students of the Bible seem to think (or at least act as though they think) that God, after "going to all the trouble" of overseeing the writing of Scripture by many different individuals over the course of many centuries, decided to sit back and watch believers try to figure out what to do with it! On the contrary. The divine purposes are being worked out even now in the lives of believers as they listen to the Scriptures no less than when God was overseeing the events of redemptive history.[27]

The implications of this truth are rather far-reaching. If nothing else, it should fill us with a sense of humility before the majesty of God; truly, without him we can do nothing (John 15:5), and it is only because he anoints us with his Spirit that we are able to learn at all (1 John 2:27). This principle also sheds light on the difficult questions surrounding such issues as the proper application of Scripture, the

26. For a discussion of this issue in a more general way, see Vern Poythress, "God's Lordship in Interpretation," *Westminster Theological Journal* 50 (1988): 27–64.

27. It is important to point out again that, paradoxical though this principle may sound, the doctrine of divine sovereignty in history does not suspend human agency, nor does it render God in any sense responsible for human sin. Similarly, the truth of God's sovereignty in our Christian lives neither guarantees that we will always do right nor excuses us when we do wrong.

use of allegorical methods, and the claims of reader-response theorists. Although I neither approve of nor recommend Origen's hermeneutical methods, it is difficult for me simply to dismiss them without inquiring into the burning question, Why has allegorical interpretation spoken to the hearts of countless believers, and why does it continue to meet their needs even today?[28] Similarly, a reader-response approach to the Bible, especially when set in opposition to historical interpretation, can easily turn into a subtle excuse for finding what we are looking for, but the challenges of this new approach are too serious to be ignored.

If we believe that God's Spirit is truly at work as Christians explore the Scriptures, and if his work of illumination is something more than identifying a bare textual meaning, isn't it true then that interpreters in some sense contribute to the meaning of the Bible out of their own context? God does not wait for us to become masters of the grammatico-historical method before he can teach us something. Instead, he uses even our ignorance to lead us to himself, and he resorts to our capacity for associations as a means for us to recognize his truth. Some years ago I heard a learned minister testify to God's goodness through a rather trivial incident. In the midst of some discouragement, he came across a branch lying on a sidewalk. For some reason, this sight reminded him of the biblical image of the staff and the various comforting truths associated with it. Shall we condemn this pastor for his allegorical interpretation of that event and forbid him to use such hermeneutics again? Or shall we recognize that God, in his wisdom and sovereignty, delights to work in us at whatever level of "receptivity" we may find ourselves?

Of course, the fact that God can use our ignorance for his glory is hardly enough reason to remain as ignorant as we possibly can—and we dare never appeal to divine sovereignty to excuse our failings. Accordingly, we should do everything in our power to help believers appreciate the historical character of Scripture and thus respect its original meaning. But in their reading of the Bible, especially for devotional purposes, do believers need to suppress associations that come to mind? Previous exposure to other parts of Scripture inevitably lead

28. See my discussion in *Has the Church Misread the Bible? The History of Interpretation in the Light of Current Issues* (Grand Rapids, MI: Zondervan, 1987), chap. 3.

us to make "literary" connections that are, from an exegetical point of view, far-fetched. But as long as those connections are *biblical* in their own right—and as long as we do not make improper claims about the original meaning of the text we happen to be reading—need we really condemn this commonplace (and "time-honored"!) approach to finding solace and direction from Scripture? Should not a sense of God's power in our interpretive activity affect our evaluation of this problem?[29]

But there is one more conclusion to be drawn from the doctrine of divine sovereignty. If we acknowledge God's lordship in our interpretation, that is a fact that should fill us with confidence. There are, to be sure, many things to discourage us as we study the Scriptures. Acquainting ourselves with the history of biblical interpretation can sometimes be a baffling experience. Looking around us even today, we become aware of theological controversies among believers and find them unspeakably depressing. And as though all that were not enough, when we examine ourselves we detect ignorance, selfishness, obduracy, deceit—a host of obstacles that would seem to wipe out all hermeneutical hopes!

Yet, a moment's reflection on God's sovereignty ought to set us straight. If the Lord assures us that his Word will not return to him empty but will rather accomplish what he desires (Isa. 55:11), can we really think that his purposes will be thwarted and that his people will fail to "reach unity in the faith and in the knowledge of the Son of God" (Eph. 4:13 NIV)? May we learn to do all our biblical interpretation assured that "he who began a good work in [us] will carry it on to completion until the day of Christ Jesus" (Phil. 1:6 NIV).

---

29. For similar reasons, I am open to the possibility that the apostles, in their reading of the Old Testament, may have *in some occasions* used approaches that do not conform to what we usually consider "proper" exegetical method. Without for a moment blurring the distinction between the inspired work of the biblical writers and our use of Scripture, we must do justice to the continuity between them and us. Cf. Geerhardus Vos, *Biblical Theology: Old and New Testaments* (Grand Rapids, MI: Eerdmans, 1948), 325–36. Admittedly, if the apostolic understanding of the Old Testament was fundamentally flawed, it would be impossible to defend the intellectual viability of the gospel message. But neither can I accept that an occasional "free" or "associative" type of allusion—even in the midst of serious argumentation—necessarily reflects a misunderstanding of the literary work being alluded to. See my article, "The New Testament Use of the Old Testament: Text Form and Authority," in *Scripture and Truth*, ed. D. A. Carson and J. W. Woodbridge (Grand Rapids, MI: Zondervan, 1983), 147–65, esp. 157–58.

5

Paul's Christological Interpretation of Creation and Presuppositional Apologetics

LANE G. TIPTON

*I*n response to criticism from G. C. Berkouwer, Cornelius Van Til once lamented that "detailed scriptural exegesis is a lack in all of my writings."[1] Van Til understood that his uniquely Reformed approach to apologetics lacked a full-fledged line of exegetical argumentation. Instead, his method developed along dogmatic and theological lines, and he relied on the exegesis of theologians such as Charles Hodge, B. B. Warfield, Herman Bavinck, and John Murray. This essay will attempt to provide some direct exegetical and redemptive-historical support for Van Til's revelational epistemology and presuppositional apologetic.

1. *Jerusalem and Athens: Critical Discussions on the Philosophy and Apologetics of Cornelius Van Til*, ed. E. R. Geehan (Nutley, NJ: Presbyterian and Reformed, 1971), 203.

The central argument in this essay is that Paul's reference to a philosophy "according to Christ" (*kata Christon*/κατὰ Χριστόν) in Colossians 2:8 depends on his "christological interpretation of creation" in Colossians 1:15.[2] Paul's Christology both distinguishes and relates Christ's ontic status as the eternal Son and his redemptive historical function as the incarnate Son in a way that accents his exclusive preeminence as the source and substance of a Christian philosophy and apologetic. The theological formulations in Colossians 1:15–20, particularly the relationship between Christ's eternal person and his historical function, underlie Paul's conception of revelation (1:26, 28; 2:2), knowledge (2:3), and philosophy (2:4, 8), and supply the basic framework for his christological interpretation of creation.

Christ's Ontic Status and Redemptive-Historical Function

Among the many penetrating theological affirmations in Paul, perhaps none is more significant than the relationship between Christ's eternal ontic status and his redemptive-historical function. No matter how basic the realized and future eschatology of redemptive history may be in Paul's theology, the controlling importance of the redemptive-historical cannot for a moment be isolated from ontic christological considerations.

Regarding Paul's Christology along these lines, Herman Ridderbos observes that the centrality of the redemptive-historical concern, along with the supreme importance of the humiliation and exaltation of Christ,

> does not alter the fact that the whole of his preaching of the histori-
> cal and future revelation of Christ is supported by the confession of
> Christ as the Son of God, in the supra- and prehistorical sense of the
> word. It can even rightly be said that the sending of the Son by the
> Father in the fullness of time presupposes his pre-existence with God

2. For the sake of clarity, Paul's reference in Col. 2:8 is to a philosophy "not according to Christ" (*ou kata Christon*/οὐ κατὰ Χριστόν). Philosophy *kata Christon*, however, is implicit in Paul's language. As we will see, Paul's primary concern is that the "Colossian heresy," whatever its specific content, errs insofar as it has negated (*ou*) a philosophy *kata Christon*. All Scripture quotations in this chapter are my translations.

(cf. Gal. 4:4; Rom. 8:3 with such passages as 2 Cor. 8:9; Phil. 2:6ff.; Col. 1:15ff.; Rom. 8:32).[3]

Paul's conception of Christ in Colossians 1:15–20 both distinguishes and integrates his eternal status and his redemptive-historical function.

Reflecting further on precisely how Christ's ontic status as eternal Son and his redemptive-historical function as incarnate Son are both related to and distinguished from one another, Ridderbos notes that the exaltation of Christ "is at the same time not for a moment to be divorced from the significance of Christ's person as such."[4] Therefore, "one cannot, precisely because of this pre-existence (that is, the existing prior to revelation) of the Son, permit the being of the Son to be lost in his revelation as the Son of God."[5]

In this statement Ridderbos affirms the crucial distinction between the eternal being and the historical function of the Son of God. But in light of this, and equally important to emphasize, "when he speaks of Christ's pre-existence, Paul regards and designates this not as separate from, but precisely in its bearing on Christ's revelation in redemptive history."[6] While Christ's eternal being remains prior to and independent of his function in history, the latter in no way negates, denies, or marginalizes the former.

In addition to this, Ridderbos remarks that "undoubtedly what is said in Colossians 1:15ff. concerning Christ as the Image of God, Firstborn, and so forth, does not simply spring from Paul's conception of Christ as the second Adam in 1 Corinthians 15 and Romans 5."[7] In fact, he believes that a fundamental *difference* exists between Paul's conception of Christ in Colossians 1:15ff., on the one hand, and in Romans 5 and 1 Corinthians 15, on the other hand. He says, "Whereas in 1 Corinthians 15 and Romans 5 Christ is the second or last Adam, who *follows after the first* in the order of redemptive history, in Colossians 1:15 as the Firstborn, the Image of God, etc., he is

---

3. Herman N. Ridderbos, *Paul: An Outline of His Theology*, trans. John Richard DeWitt (Grand Rapids, MI: Eerdmans, 1975), 68.
4. Ibid.
5. Ibid., 69.
6. Ibid.
7. Ibid., 84.

antecedent to the first."[8] In sum, what is true about Christ *historically* as the one who *follows after* Adam does not subvert what is true about Christ *eternally* as the one who *precedes* Adam.

The exegetical basis for Ridderbos's argument turns primarily on his theology of Christ as "image of the invisible God" (1:15), "firstborn over all creation" (1:15), and "firstborn from among the dead" (1:18). It is specifically in the relationship between Christ as firstborn over all creation and Christ as firstborn from the dead that we can understand how both to distinguish and to relate the eternal being and redemptive-historical function of the Son of God.

To provide a terse summary of Ridderbos's basic point, we must affirm that Christ as the eternal Son is "firstborn over all creation" (1:15), and that this same *eternal reality* finds its *redemptive-historical* expression in the resurrected Christ as "firstborn from the dead" (1:18). In the second Adam, resurrected from the dead, we witness in history the unveiling of what is true of Christ in his eternal being prior to and apart from his incarnation in history. Ridderbos remarks that, "from Christ's significance as second Adam all the categories are derived which *further define* his significance as the Firstborn of every creature."[9] In other words, what Christ obtained by virtue of his resurrection from the dead (i.e., his redemptive-historical activity) discloses his significance as the firstborn over all of creation (i.e., his eternal ontic status).

Relating Christ's eternal ontic status to his redemptive-historical function would be incomplete without at least a brief discussion of the Pauline reference to Christ as the "image of the invisible God" in 1:15.[10] It is difficult to deny that Colossians 1:15 denotes the preexistent Christ.[11] In fact, it is impossible successfully to construe Paul's

8. Ibid., emphasis mine.

9. Ibid., emphasis mine.

10. M. G. Kline recognizes that the renewal of the image of God in creatures is "an impartation to them of the likeness of the archetypal glory of Christ." *Images of the Spirit* (Grand Rapids, MI: Baker, 1980), 28. Basic to the divine glory that provides the archetype after which Adam was created is "the glory of the royal-judicial office. In the Glory, God sits as King" (p. 27). Hence, we can discern in Paul's language of Christ as the eternal image of the invisible God a distinctively christological interpretation of Gen. 1 that recognizes the Son's cosmic vicegerency as the archetypal King. In fact, Ridderbos argues that Paul applies to Christ in his eternal glory language suited to the first Adam, who was created in the image of God. The glory and dominion of the first Adam finds its ultimate ontological ground in Christ as eternal Adam.

11. See James Dunn's *The Theology of Paul the Apostle* (Grand Rapids, MI: Eerdmans, 1998), 277; and Thomas Schreiner's *Paul, Apostle of God's Glory in Christ: A Pauline Theology*

language of Christ as image of God and firstborn over all creation in
1:15 merely as references to his exalted status as the second Adam or
firstborn from the dead.

This is so, first of all, because the language of Colossians 1:15–
17 speaks of Christ's role in a pre-redemptive—and therefore preincarnate—context of *creation*. Remarking on the language of "image
of God" in 2 Corinthians 4:4, Ridderbos observes that, "when in this
context he is called at the same time the Image of God, this is to say
nothing less than that in him the glory of God, indeed God himself,
becomes manifest."[12] In fact, "by calling Christ the Image of God he
[Paul] thus identifies Christ's glory with that of God himself. . . . And
the same thing applies to Colossians 1:15," so that there is special reference to "Christ's glory as the Pre-existent One in these passages."[13] This
means that "by the designation Image of God he is on the one hand
distinguished from God, and on the other hand identified with God
as Bearer of the divine glory."[14] In sum, Ridderbos concludes that "it is
evident here anew, therefore, to what extent the divine glory of Christ,
*even already in his pre-existence with the Father prior to his redemptive
revelation*, determines and underlies the Pauline Christology."[15]

This line of reasoning supports the idea that, at every point, Christ's
redemptive-historical activity is revelatory of his ontic status as the
eternal "image of the invisible God" (1:15).[16] The parallels between

---

(Downers Grove, IL: InterVarsity Press, 2001), 155–56. N. T. Wright, *The Climax of the Covenant: Christ and the Law in Pauline Theology* (Minneapolis: Fortress, 1992) takes Col. 1:15a as
a reference primarily to the incarnate Christ, but also recognizes, perhaps thinking in terms of
the *communicatio idiomatum* and recognizing that Christ is a divine person, that the "word εἰκών
though almost certainly referring primarily to Christ as being now the perfect human being,
carries with it . . . the idea of the appropriateness of the position he now enjoys. He has, in that
sense, become what he always was. The pre-existent lord of the world has become the human
lord of the world, and in so doing has reflected fully, for the eyes of the world to see, the God
whose human image he has now come to bear. This explains once more . . . the nature of the
language often used to describe this figure: as in 2 Corinthians 8:9, the pre-existent one, who
(strictly speaking) has not yet 'become' Jesus of Nazareth, can be referred to by that name in
advance, much as we might say 'the Queen was born in 1925'" (p. 116). Hence, Wright seems
to maintain that Col. 1:15 refers in some sense to Christ's preexistence, even though he believes
the reference to the image also denotes the incarnate Christ.

12. Ridderbos, *Paul*, 70.

13. Ibid.

14. Ibid.

15. Ibid., emphasis mine.

16. The bearing of Christ's eternal glory and ontic status on his redemptive-historical
function appears in several ways. First, the use of the *eikōn tou theou*/εἰκών τοῦ θεοῦ language in

Colossians 1:15a and 2 Corinthians 4:4, both of which refer to the creative activity of the Son,[17] point strongly in the direction of the Son's preexistence and therefore highlight his ontic status as the eternal Son.[18] Therefore, both the Son's eternal ontic status as the image of God and his activity in creation provide the context sufficient to warrant the conclusion, "We have before us, therefore, a christological interpretation of Genesis 1."[19]

Figure 1 may prove helpful in summarizing the basic relationships outlined up to this point. A denotes the eternal ontic status of Christ as the image of God and firstborn over all creation. B denotes the first Adam, who is a creaturely replica of the eternal Son, so that

---

2 Cor. 4:4 occurs in a context that cites Gen. 1:3 (in 2 Cor. 4:6), and in this context Paul refers to the divine "'glory' (*doxa*; 3:18; 4:4, 6), an idea that both in later Judaism and by Paul himself is closely linked with Genesis 1:26ff. (cf. 1 Cor. 11:7; Rom. 1:23; 3:23; 8:29ff.)." Ridderbos, *Paul*, 71. Moreover, the image of God is attributed not only to Christ but also to the church (cf. 2 Cor. 3:18), "which is obviously reminiscent of Genesis 1:27" (p. 71). Also, "with respect to Colossians 1:15 . . . the whole of the so-called hymn in that passage speaks of the creation. The expression Image of God is here clearly rooted in Genesis 1:27" (p. 71). Ridderbos then comments that this "is further corroborated by the fact that Christ is here likewise called the Beginning (*archē*) and the Firstborn (*prōtotokos*; 1:15, 18), and is set forth as World Ruler, an idea to be met with as well in the late Jewish Adam-theology" (p. 71). Even if the "image of God" language pertains to Christ's agency in creation, present implicitly is his eternal ontic status as the eternal Son, since Christ's existence clearly forms the presupposition for the actualization of the entire created order.

17. Along these lines, M. G. Kline suggests that "the eternal, firstborn Son furnished a pattern for man as a royal glory-image of the Father. It was in his creative action as the Son, present in the Glory-Spirit, making man in his own son-image that the Logos revealed himself as the One in whom was the life that is the light of men. Not first as incarnate word breathing on men the Spirit and re-creating them in his heavenly image, but at the very beginning he was quickening Spirit, creating man after his image and glory." *Images of the Spirit*, 24. While Kline's concerns lie with the development of the "image of God" idea, we can still observe something germane to our investigation. Given the parallels between the function of the Glory-Spirit as covenant witness in both creation and redemption, and given the functional identity of the Logos-Son as the Glory-Spirit in Gen. 1:2, Kline reasons that 2 Cor. 4:4, and by implication Col. 1:15, furnishes a distinctively covenantal and eschatological interpretation of Gen. 1. Christ's functional identification with the Spirit in redemption finds its pre-redemptive analogue in the original creation of man in the image of the Glory-Spirit.

18. In fact, it is virtually impossible to deny that Col. 1:15–16 affirms preexistence, since it cannot be the incarnate Christ *as incarnate* who created all things. The incarnation of the Son takes place long after the creation of the cosmos. Therefore, it seems utterly implausible to deny that it is the eternal Son, *prior to his incarnation*, who is the one through whom and unto whom all things have been created (Col. 1:16). Even if the present tense in 1:15a (*hos estin*/ὅς ἐστιν) applies primarily to the incarnate Son, by the application of the *communicatio idiomatum*, Christ is always an eternal person, so that as eternal Son he can create and rule over creation prior to his incarnation.

19. Ridderbos, *Paul*, 71.

B prefigures and anticipates in history **C**, because **B** is the "shadow" of **A**. **C** represents the incarnation, humiliation, and exaltation of the eternal Son, so that **A=C**.[20]

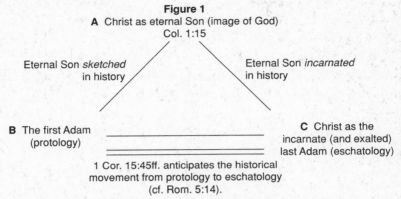

Figure 1

A Christ as eternal Son (image of God)
Col. 1:15

Eternal Son *sketched* in history

Eternal Son *incarnated* in history

B The first Adam (protology)

C Christ as the incarnate (and exalted) last Adam (eschatology)

1 Cor. 15:45ff. anticipates the historical movement from protology to eschatology (cf. Rom. 5:14).

Historical *anticipation* of the eternal and second Adam

What the diagram says is fairly simple: it is impossible to account adequately for the historical work of Christ apart from his eternal ontic status. To denote the incarnate Son in his redemptive-historical activity always and at every point invokes a horizontal connection to the first Adam (Rom. 5:12; 1 Cor. 15:44–49), as well as a vertical identification with the eternal Son (Col. 1:15–20; Phil. 2:6–12; 2 Cor. 8:9; etc.). The manifestation of Christ in redemptive history, that is, Christ as "the mystery," discloses aspects of both his historical identity as second and last Adam and his ontic status as the eternal Son.

The relationship between the Son's eternal being and his historical function therefore provides the ultimate justification for Paul's notion that "in him *all things* [*ta panta*/τὰ πάντα] hold together" (Col. 1:17).[21] Put differently, the "all things" that hold together or cohere

20. Compare this to Vos's chart that distills the philosophy of revelation in the book of Hebrews. *The Teaching of the Epistle to the Hebrews* (1956; repr., Phillipsburg, NJ: Presbyterian and Reformed, n.d), 57. By **A=C**, I do not mean to deny any difference between ontological and economic aspects of the Trinity. What I intend to accent is that Christ, even in his incarnate state, remains a divine person.

21. *Synestēken*/συνέστηκεν in 17b can mean either "in him all things cohere" or "in him all things subsist" (cf. Murray J. Harris, *Colossians and Philemon* [Grand Rapids, MI: Eerdmans, 1990], 47). However, on either interpretation the basic point remains Christ's preeminence over all things, which derives from both his ontic status as the eternal Son of God and redemptive-historical function as the incarnate Son of God.

in Christ encompass everything in creation and redemption, and it is the Son's eternal person and historical function that allow all things to hold together in him.

Moreover, this christological interpretation of creation underlies everything else Paul has to say about the significance of Christ in creation and redemption, including epistemological and philosophical implications (cf. Col. 2:3–4, 8). How can Christ have preeminence over all things if matters pertaining to knowledge and philosophy remain autonomous and neutral facets of human experience? Paul's christological interpretation of Genesis 1 therefore provides the comprehensive frame of reference for everything else he develops in Colossians 1–2. But before we attempt to suggest the way in which Paul's Christology informs his philosophy "according to Christ" (*kata Christon*) (2:8), we must turn our attention to the revelatory aspect of his Christology, which appears in Christ as "the mystery."

The Revelation of Christ, the Mystery (Col. 1:26; 2:3)

It is precisely in Paul's theology of Christ as "the mystery" that Paul moves into the epistemological and philosophical implications of his Christology, particularly as he speaks of Christ as the mystery in revelational categories that accent his preexistence (Col. 1:26).[22] Ridderbos comments that the revelation of the mystery (Col. 1:26; 2:2–3; cf. Rom. 16:25–26; 1 Cor. 2:7; Eph. 3:4–5) has in view "in addition to a noetic a plainly historical connotation: it is that which has not yet appeared, that which still exists in the counsel of God and has not yet been realized in history as fulfillment of that counsel."[23] The mystery is the "realized redemptive plan of God,"[24] which is "*entirely* defined and explained by the advent and the revelation of Jesus Christ."[25] Ridderbos gets to the very core of the matter when he observes that "for this reason the *whole content of the mystery* that has now been revealed can be qualified and summarized in *one word—Christ* (Col. 2:3)."[26] Christ

---

22. Cf. Col. 1:26b, *nyn de ephanerōthē*/νῦν δὲ ἐφανερώθη.
23. Ridderbos, *Paul*, 47.
24. Ibid.
25. Ibid., 49, emphasis mine.
26. Ibid., emphasis mine.

as the mystery accentuates the revelational focus of Paul's Christology, since Christ himself is the mystery that was hidden for ages past but has now been revealed to his saints (1:26).

In other words, the revelation of Christ as the mystery invokes *all* of the categories previously mentioned, including at the foundational level the relationship between Christ's eternal status and redemptive-historical function. Consequently, the "mystery" is revelatory of both Christ's ontic status as eternal Son and his redemptive-historical activity as incarnate Son, and it is *this conception of Christ* that stands at the center of Paul's notion of a philosophy "according to Christ" (2:8). On account of Christ's being himself the content of the revealed mystery, and on account of the way Christ's eternal status and historical function ground Paul's christological interpretation of Genesis 1, it is impossible to isolate any aspect of Paul's Christology from its bearing on knowledge (Col. 2:3) or philosophy (2:4, 8).

The Christological Interpretation of Creation and Philosophy according to Christ

As helpful as Ridderbos's exegesis may be in *Paul*,[27] he does not demonstrate in any sustained manner the relationship between Colossians 1:15–2:2 and the epistemological and philosophical implications Paul develops in 2:3–8. In other words, Ridderbos's insights in *Paul* are foundational but incomplete when we take into account the development of Paul's argument in Colossians 2:3ff. While we will not attempt to trace Paul's thought beyond verse 8, and while our development will be brief and only suggestive, it is important to note that Paul makes immediate epistemological and philosophical applications of his christological interpretation of creation.

Three lines of argument support the idea that Paul's christological interpretation of creation grounds his notion of philosophy according to Christ: (1) the *prima facie* implications of Paul's christological interpretation of creation in Colossians 1:15–20; (2) the epistemological and philosophical implications of Christ as the "mystery of God" in

---

27. Ridderbos's commentary on Colossians, which appeared in Dutch approximately five years before *Paul*, says nothing in substance that is not represented in *Paul*.

2:2–4; and (3) the denotation of "traditions of men" and the function of the three *kata* clauses in Colossians 2:8.

The Prima Facie *Implications of Paul's Christological Interpretation of Creation*

Paul's Christology is comprehensive in character, and it is precisely christological considerations that he brings to bear on his distinctive conception of "philosophy"[28] in Colossians 2:8. Given Paul's christological interpretation of creation, and what it presupposes regarding Christ's eternal ontic status and redemptive-historical function, it seems inevitable that he find in Christ the one who alone provides a fitting basis for a truly Christian philosophy. Whether viewed from an eternal and ontological standpoint or from a redemptive-historical standpoint—or, more accurately, the way the two are both distinguished from and related to one another—Christ is preeminent (1:17–18).

In other words, because of Christ's ontic status and redemptive-historical function, Paul's christological conception of philosophy (i.e., philosophy *kata Christon*) includes eternal and temporal aspects of reality that find their binding center in Christ, whether his preincarnate, eternal status as Creator is in view (cf. "in him all things consist or cohere,"[29] 1:17), or his incarnate, redemptive-historical function is in view (cf. "in order that he might be preeminent in all things,"[30] 1:18). Christ's preeminence over the orders of creation and redemption derives from his eternal person and function in redemptive history. It is this ontological state of affairs that grounds Paul's epistemological (2:3) and philosophical (2:4, 8) statements, both of which are

---

28. Dunn observes that *philosophias*/φιλοσοφίας means "literally 'love of wisdom,' but had long been used of a systematic treatment of a theme, practical as well as speculative, and so for various schools of 'philosophy' (see O. Michel, *TDNT* 9. 172–79). Jewish apologists made free use of it in this more technical sense in commending their own religious system. Thus, for example, *Aristeas* 256 provides a definition of 'philosophy' which begins: 'To have a well-reasoned assessment of each occurrence and not to be carried away by impulses,'" James D. G. Dunn, *The Epistle to the Colossians and Philemon*, The New International Greek Testament Commentary (Grand Rapids, MI: Eerdmans, 1996), 147. It appears that Paul uses the term in its application to the problem at Colossae, as well as his own understanding of the implications of Christ's ontic status and redemptive-historical function. The major difference between the two is the central and comprehensive character of Christ in Paul's "philosophy."

29. Greek: *ta panta en autō synestēken*/τὰ πάντα ἐν αὐτῷ συνέστηκεν.

30. Greek: *hina genētai en pasin autos prōteuōn*/ἵνα γένηται ἐν πᾶσιν αὐτὸς πρωτεύων.

christologically conditioned. Therefore, there is at least a *prima facie* expectation that Paul's conception of philosophy according to Christ will be every bit as far-reaching and all-inclusive as his Christology, which is clearly comprehensive in its scope.

The Epistemological and Philosophical Implications of Christ as the Mystery of God in Colossians 2:2–4

It is not necessary to leave the argument at the *prima facie* level, however, because Paul draws clear epistemological and philosophical implications from his theology of Christ as the mystery (Col. 2:2). Immediately following his affirmation of Christ as the mystery of God, Paul amplifies his thought: "In whom are hidden[31] all the treasures of wisdom and knowledge" (2:3). When this claim is understood directly in light of "the mystery," which is revelatory of *both* Christ's eternal ontic status *and* his redemptive-historical function, then we grasp more precisely the full connotation of "all" (*pantes*/πάντες) in 2:3. Those who are in Christ (v. 9) are in the one who is the fullness of wisdom and knowledge. This epistemological implication follows obviously from Paul's Christology, which is inclusive of eternal and temporal reality.

Christ as the mystery therefore underscores the revelational features not only of Paul's Christology, but also of his epistemology. If the mystery is revelatory of Christ, in whom all the treasures of wisdom and knowledge are hidden, and if this is so on the basis of Christ's eternal person and historical work, then Paul's Christology comes immediately to bear on his epistemology.

This means that the revelation of Christ as the mystery of God focuses the christological interpretation of creation on *epistemological* concerns. The "mystery" is revelatory of both Christ's ontic status as eternal Son and his redemptive-historical activity as incarnate Son, and it is *this conception of Christ* that lies at the center of Paul's notion of a

---

31. *Apokryphoi*/ἀπόκρυφοι accents the already/not-yet character of the mystery. In terms of future eschatology, what is now revealed in one sense (i.e., the already of eschatological inauguration) is hidden in another sense (i.e., the not-yet of future eschatological manifestation). In other words, the not-yet of the mystery will be publicly and openly revealed at Christ's *parousia*. But this in no way detracts from the realized eschatology inherent in the revelation of the mystery.

philosophy "according to Christ" (2:8). Consequently, it is implausible to detach any facet of Paul's Christology from its bearing on the rest of his observations in 2:4–8.

Moreover, in 2:4 Paul supplies the primary reason that he invokes the revelation of Christ as the mystery, along with its epistemological implications: "so that no one deceives you with enticing, but deceptive, speech."[32] The mystery is given for the precise purpose[33] of avoiding beguiling argument, which is obviously philosophical in character (cf. 2:8). Paul does not leave it to speculation that his Christology has epistemological and philosophical implications. He presents Christ's eternal person and redemptive-historical function in the framework of the mystery in order to avoid autonomous philosophical arguments and thought patterns.

To sum up, the revelation of Christ as the mystery has immediate epistemological and philosophical import, and *this is precisely what we would expect* given the theological implications of Paul's christological interpretation of creation.

The "Traditions of Men" and Three Kata Clauses in Colossians 2:8

In light of the preceding argument, we ought to anticipate a generalizing pattern in Paul's argument in Colossians 2:8 that takes into account the comprehensive character of his Christology developed in 1:15 and 2:2–4. This is precisely what we discover. Paul's generalizing concerns in 2:8, which are in keeping with the comprehensive scope of his Christology, emerge when we understand the function of the three *kata* clauses in 2:8 and the import of the reference to "the traditions of men and the basic principles of this world."[34]

The "traditions of men" most suitably should be viewed as standing over against the revelation of the mystery and a christological interpretation of creation. Ridderbos confirms this when he remarks that "the basic principles of this world" of 2:8 refers to the "sin domi-

---

32. Greek: *hina mēdeis hymas paralogizētai en pithanologia*/ἵνα μηδεὶς ὑμᾶς παραλογίζηται ἐν πιθανολογίᾳ.

33. The *hina* introduces a purpose clause.

34. Greek: *kata tēn paradosin tōn anthrōpōn, kata ta stoicheia tou kosmou*/κατὰ τὴν παράδοσιν τῶν ἀνθρώπων, κατὰ τὰ στοιχεῖα τοῦ κόσμου.

nated world of men, in which believers are no longer to 'live' (which can scarcely be said of the cosmos as universe); cf. also Colossians 2:8 where (the *stoicheia* of the) world is another expression for (the tradition of) men."[35]

Ridderbos's point is that the "sin dominated world of men" supplies a presuppositional frame of reference that negates in principle from the outset the content of the mystery, along with its bearing on a philosophy according to Christ. Whatever the precise identity and specific content of the heresy Paul faced in Colossae, its fundamental failure lies in the fact that it is "not according to Christ" (2:8). No deeper contrast in underlying presuppositions or worldviews is conceivable.

This becomes even clearer when we consider the function of the three *kata* clauses in 2:8. Murray J. Harris takes *kata* in *kata tēn paradosin tōn anthrōpōn* (κατὰ τὴν παράδοσιν τῶν ἀνθρώπων) as conveying the sense of "basis . . . or source . . . of the 'philosophy,' viz. 'the tradition of humans' . . . *as opposed to divine revelation*."[36] An observation similar to this is perhaps part of the reason why Dunn observes that "Paul may have left his warning vague or unspecific so that it could cover a *wider range* of possible alternatives to this gospel than the *more specific challenge at Colossae*."[37] In Paul's generalizing of the traditions of men we can detect that a philosophy according to Christ has implications far beyond the problem at Colossae.

In addition to this observation, if "it is preferable . . . to take the first *kata* as denoting the origin or source of the 'philosophy' ('human tradition,' as opposed to divine revelation), the second *kata* as describing its content or substance," then it is best to take "the third *kata* as introducing the negation of the two preceding clauses."[38] This would mean that the "essential weakness of this 'philosophy' was that Christ

35. Ridderbos, *Paul*, 149. Ridderbos qualifies immediately that Paul's language refers to the specific form of the Colossian heresy. It is possible to read the language of "traditions of men" as a genus of which the Colossian heresy was a species, and this would make sense in light of the concern Paul has for *any* approach which is *ou kata Christon*/οὐ κατὰ Χριστόν. Even more specifically, it seems that Paul gives the general depiction of philosophy which is *ou kata Christon* by designating its source and norm in the traditions of men [2:8b] and then moves on to describe with more precision the specific form of this philosophy *ou kata Christon* in 2:8c (the basic principles or "elemental spirits of the world"). See Harris, *Colossians and Philemon*, 93–94.

36. Harris, *Colossians and Philemon*, 92–93, emphasis mine.

37. Dunn, *The Epistle to the Colossians and Philemon*, 148, emphasis mine.

38. Harris, *Colossians and Philemon*, 93–94.

was neither its source nor substance."[39] As a result, Paul's theology of creation and redemption, as well as Christ's preeminence in both (1:17 and 18), makes the particular problem at Colossae the occasion for an *ad hoc* application of comprehensive "philosophy according to Christ."

Moreover, it is significant that Paul does not offer an exhaustive description of the specifics of the "Colossian heresy."[40] Paul does not provide a highly detailed account of the philosophical and theological assumptions of the heresy at Colossae,[41] but he does furnish an extremely well-developed account of the theological basis for a philosophy according to Christ (1:15–2:8). This observation enables us to recognize what is perhaps key for understanding Colossians 2:8: Paul is less interested in what the "Colossian heresy" affirms than in what it denies, that is, "Christ, the mystery of God" (2:2). In fact, a consistent affirmation of Christ as the mystery of God entails the utter rejection of the "Colossian heresy," along with every other philosophical approach that is not regulated from the outset by the Christ of Scripture.

For these reasons, it is seems rather strange when Harris argues that, in his reference to a philosophy based on empty deception, "Paul means neither philosophy in general nor classical Gk. philosophy specifically but so-called philosophy . . . what is falsely termed philosophy."[42] Dunn seems much closer to Paul's developed argument when he comments that "it was precisely the failure of such speculation to grasp the significance of Christ . . . that demonstrated their emptiness and deceitfulness."[43] Paul's concern with the philosophy at Colossae rests in what it opposes at the most basic level of fundamental presupposition,

39. Ibid., 94.

40. There are almost as many varieties of the "Colossian heresy" as there are commentators on the book of Colossians. For that reason, it certainly will not serve our purpose to determine the precise contours of the approach that Paul counters in Colossians. For some interesting treatments of this fascinating issue, see Clinton E. Arnold, *The Colossian Syncretism: The Interface between Christianity and Folk Belief at Colossae* (Grand Rapids, MI: Baker, 1996); and Troy W. Martin, *By Philosophy and Empty Deceit: Colossians as Response to a Cynic Critique* (Sheffield: Sheffield Academic Press, 1996).

41. Of course, he does list a few of the features of the heresy, but he comes nowhere close to a systematic identification and explanation of the heresy. In fact, it appears safer to say that he explains it by what it is not, namely, *kata Christon*/κατὰ Χριστόν.

42. Harris, *Colossians and Philemon*, 92.

43. Dunn, *The Epistle to the Colossians and Philemon*, 151.

namely, Christ, the mystery of God (2:2). Paul's method avoids any speculative approach that denies on the basis of deceptive philosophical presuppositions his christological interpretation of creation.

If this is so, then Paul's denunciation of vain philosophy applies to any and every philosophical approach that is "not according to Christ" (2:8). His language therefore would include any "Greek philosophy" or "philosophy in general" that is not governed at the worldview level by a christological interpretation of creation, together with its implications for redemption, epistemology, and philosophy.

Implications for Van Til's Approach

Let us now explore a few of the implications of the exegesis above for the development of Van Tilian apologetics. If the above exegesis is on the mark, then we have an opportunity to develop Van Til's approach in categories sensitive to biblical theology and redemptive history.

First, the theological implications of the earlier exegesis capture a basic concern of a general theological principle resident in the deep structures of Van Til's theology and apologetics: a refusal to commingle the eternal and the temporal in our theological formulations. Van Til insists "that we first think of the ontological trinity before we think of the economical trinity."[44] What this means for Christology is that we focus attention on the second person of the ontological Trinity, "who was, in . . . his essence, fully equal with the Father, who therefore existed from all eternity with the Father, who in the incarnation assumed a human nature."[45] We must give priority to the self-contained existence of the ontological Trinity, who exists apart from and prior to his relationship to creation. This ontological priority appears in Ridderbos's Christology, particularly in his theology of Christ as the image of God and firstborn over all of creation.

Second, the exegesis developed earlier brings a greater christocentric focus to the development of Van Til's revelational epistemology and apologetic. When we recognize the way the exegesis above lends support to a christological interpretation of creation that governs and

44. Cornelius Van Til, *The Defense of the Faith*, 3rd ed. (Philadelphia: Presbyterian and Reformed, 1967), 16.
45. Ibid.

underlies a philosophy "according to Christ," we can detect a redemptive-historical rationale for Van Til's language of the "self-attesting Christ of Scripture."[46] In fact, it allows us to bring a greater christocentric focus to bear on the matter than Van Til was able to achieve.

Third, the christological interpretation of creation lays the groundwork for what Van Til labeled a "revelational epistemology."[47] In Van Til's assessment, and I believe this is true in Paul as well, Trinitarian theology and Christology have immediate and vital epistemological consequences. According to our exegesis, *the philosophy according to Christ is as comprehensive as Paul's Christology, and Paul's christological interpretation of creation is all-inclusive*. Nothing is immune to the dominion of the exalted Christ, given his eternal ontic status and function in redemptive history, and Paul draws immediate epistemological (Col. 2:3–4) and philosophical (2:8) inferences from his christological interpretation of creation.

Fourth, Paul's argument eliminates every vestige of speculative, neutral, and autonomous reasoning. One reasons either in terms of a philosophy according to Christ or in "delusion" (2:4)[48] and "empty deceit" (2:8),[49] the latter being the direct philosophical consequence of denying a philosophy "according to Christ" (2:8). This is the Pauline way of articulating an argument for the truth of Christianity from the impossibility of the contrary.[50] In other words, there are decisive and destructive epistemological consequences for those who oppose philosophy "according to Christ" at the level of basic presupposition.

Finally, the argument above has attempted to demonstrate the bearing of biblical theology on the discipline of Christian philosophy and apologetics. While much more can and should be said, the arguments in this essay are designed exegetically to undergird Van Til's presuppositional apologetic. Paul's christological interpretation of creation

46. See Van Til's comments in "My Credo," in *Jerusalem and Athens*. It is possible to understand the exegesis above as supplying a more cohesive and consistently christological focus than Van Til was able to achieve. While by no means competing with Trinitarian theology, a christocentric focus allows us to concentrate on both the Trinitarian and the christological aspects of a truly Reformed apologetic.

47. Cornelius Van Til, *A Survey of Christian Epistemology* (Nutley, NJ: Presbyterian and Reformed, 1969), 1.

48. Greek: *paralogizētai*/παραλογίζηται.

49. Greek: *kenēs apatēs*/κενῆς ἀπάτης.

50. Van Til, *A Survey of Christian Epistemology*, 204–9.

proves foundational to epistemological (Col. 2:3–4) and philosophical (Col. 2:8) matters. Hence, a proper understanding of Colossians 1:15–2:8 turns up deep continuities between biblical theology and systematic theology, on the one hand, and Christian philosophy and apologetics, on the other.

Conclusion

Reformed apologetics in the tradition of Van Til recognizes that reasoning by presupposition is the best apologetical method, since the starting point, method, and conclusion are interrelated.[51] Van Til argued that we must reason in consistently Christian categories; and we have seen that Paul reasoned from the Christ of the mystery, to the Christ of the mystery, in terms of the Christ of the mystery, and he concluded that all other forms of reasoning are delusive and deceptive. Reformed apologetics can do no less.

As I indicated at the outset, this exegesis is not an attempt to exhaust the texts under consideration; rather, I have attempted simply to establish an exegetical trajectory for the further development of Van Til's approach along redemptive-historical lines of thought. We need to recognize that Paul's christological interpretation of creation—and its bearing on knowledge, philosophy and apologetics—ought to be pursued with a view toward integrating biblical and systematic theology in the service of presuppositional apologetics.

---

51. Cornelius Van Til, *Christian Apologetics*, 2nd ed., ed. William Edgar (Phillipsburg, NJ: P&R, 2003), 130.

PART 2

REFORMED APOLOGETICS

Theological Foundations

6

❧❦❧

Divine Aseity
and Apologetics

JOHN M. FRAME

The term *aseity* comes from the Latin phrase *a se*, meaning "from or by oneself." In the theological literature, the term designates a divine attribute by which God is "what he is by or through his own self."[1] Since God is *a se*, he does not owe his existence to anything or anyone outside himself, nor does he need anything beyond himself to maintain his existence. He is not like the idols that depend for their existence on select materials, skilled craftsmen, and ritual offerings (Isa. 40:19–20; 44:15–17; Ps. 50:8–15). Indeed, he has no needs at all (Acts 17:25).[2] So the terms *self-contained*, *self-existent*, *self-sufficient*, and *independent* are often used as synonyms for *a se*.

God's attributes are not abstract qualities that God happens to exemplify. They are, rather identical to God himself. That is sometimes

1. Herman Bavinck, *Reformed Dogmatics: God and Creation*, ed. John Bolt, trans. John Vriend (Grand Rapids, MI: Baker, 2004), 151.
2. I here summarize my exegetical case for this divine attribute. The word *aseity* is not found in Scripture, but Scripture clearly teaches that God has no need of creatures. For a more elaborate discussion, see my *The Doctrine of God* (Phillipsburg, NJ: P&R, 2002), 603–8.

called the doctrine of divine simplicity. For example, God's goodness is not a standard above him, to which he conforms. Rather, his goodness is everything he is and does. It is God himself who serves as the standard of goodness for himself and for the world. He is, therefore, his own goodness. But he is also his own being, wisdom, power, holiness, justice, and truth. These attributes, therefore, are concrete, not abstract; personal, not impersonal. Each describes the whole nature of God.[3] So to talk of God's attributes is simply to talk about God himself, from various perspectives.[4]

God's attributes, therefore, apply to one another: God's justice is holy, and his holiness just. His goodness is eternal, and his eternality is not an abstract concept, but rather the eternal life of a good person. So God's aseity, too, is the aseity of a person, one who is infinite, eternal, unchangeable, and so on. And all of God's attributes are *a se*. His infinity, goodness, wisdom, and justice are all self-existent and self-sufficient.

Aseity also applies in one sense to God's relationships with the creation, particularly his lordship, which I have defined as his control over the world, his authority over the world, and his presence in the world.[5] Of course, to be Lord one must have servants. In that sense God cannot be Lord without his having servants to rule. Nevertheless, his power and right to rule as Lord are not derived from the creation. As King, he is not the beneficiary of a social contract, nor is he bound to terms imposed upon him by creatures.[6] His lordship derives from his own being alone. God is such a God that he is necessarily Lord over anything and everything he creates.

So, considering the three attributes of lordship noted above, we may describe God's control as self-sufficient, his authority as self-justifying. His presence in the world is an implication of his universal power and authority. Wherever we go, we cannot escape from him (Ps. 139:7–12; Jer. 23:24). God's presence is inescapable, unavoidable,

---

3. For more discussion of divine simplicity as an affirmation of personalism, see ibid., 225–30.

4. Ibid., 387–92.

5. Ibid., 1–115.

6. He does, of course, voluntarily enter covenants with creatures, and in these covenants he binds himself to fulfill promises and threats. He is obligated to keep these covenants. But the obligations are self-imposed, not imposed by creatures.

and therefore not dependent on the will of creatures. This is to say that God's lordship is *a se*.

This chapter will discuss the relation of divine aseity to apologetics, the defense of the Christian faith. No one else has integrated these as fully as has Cornelius Van Til, professor of apologetics at Westminster Theological Seminary from 1929 to 1972. I will explore Van Til's teaching, drawing some inferences and applications for the work of apologetics today. I will suggest that the doctrine of aseity is helpful to the apologist in three ways: (1) It helps define the distinctive content of the Christian faith, which the apologist is called to defend. (2) It determines the epistemology of apologetics, how the apologist should seek to lead people to the knowledge of God. And (3) it suggests an important practical apologetic strategy.[7]

Aseity and the Distinctiveness of the Christian Worldview

For Cornelius Van Til, the doctrine of divine aseity is the key to a sound theology and apologetics. As he begins his discussion of the divine attributes, he says, "First and foremost among the attributes, we therefore mention the independence or self-existence of God (*autarkia, omnisufficientia*)."[8] He quotes Bavinck's statement that "in this aseity of God, thought of not merely as being by itself but as the fullness of being, all other virtues are included; they are but the setting forth of the fullness of God's being."[9] Van Til typically refers to aseity by means of the term *self-contained*.[10] So he writes, "Basic to all the doctrines of Christian theism is that of the self-contained God, or, if we wish, that of the ontological trinity."[11] And, "We must

7. For those who may be interested in the "three perspectives" I've expounded elsewhere, (1) is situational: the facts of the gospel; (2) is normative: the rules of apologetic thought; and (3) is existential: the actual process of apologetic dialogue.

8. Cornelius Van Til, *An Introduction to Systematic Theology* (Nutley, NJ: Presbyterian and Reformed, 1974), 206.

9. Ibid., 206. Van Til quotes Bavinck, *Reformed Dogmatics*, 152.

10. A search of "self-contained" on *The Works of Cornelius Van Til*, CD-ROM (New York: Labels Army Co., 1997) yielded 395 hits. He also uses as synonyms *self-sufficient, self-existent, self-referential, self-interpreting, self-determining*.

11. Cornelius Van Til, *The Defense of the Faith*, 3rd ed. (Philadelphia: Presbyterian and Reformed, 1967), 100.

take the notion of the self-contained, self-sufficient God as the most basic notion of all our interpretative efforts."[12]

Although Van Til puts aseity first among the doctrines of Christian theism, he finds it closely linked to other doctrines:[13] (1) In one of the quotations above, and in many other places, he links God's aseity to his ontological Trinity. These two concepts go together, for "ontological" here means that God's triunity is not derived from creatures, but is self-contained. God is a Trinity, not only in history, but in and of himself. God's triune character also implies that he cannot be construed merely as the aspect of unity within the world, correlative to the world's plurality. Rather, he has his own unity and plurality, which is distinct from the unity and plurality of the universe.

(2) Van Til reasons, then, from God's aseity and triunity to his all-controlling counsel: "Based upon this notion of the ontological trinity and consistent with it, is the concept of the counsel of God according to which all things in the created world are regulated."[14] If God is *a se*, then he has the resources within himself to carry out his purposes for history. His eternal plan does not depend on creatures for its formulation or implementation.

(3) Van Til also reasons from God's aseity to creation out of nothing: "If God is fully self-contained then there was no sort of half existence and no sort of non-being that had any power over against him. . . . and there was no sort of stuff that had as much even as refractory power over against God when he decided to create the world."[15] And he reasons also from creation to aseity: "The creation doctrine maintains that finite existence is wholly dependent upon God's rationality. And this is possible only if God is first self-contained."[16]

12. Cornelius Van Til, *Christianity and Idealism* (Philadelphia: Presbyterian and Reformed, 1955), 85; compare 88: "A truly Christian philosophy should, it seems to us, begin with the notion of God as self-contained." G. C. Berkouwer criticizes Van Til's emphasis on this concept in *The Triumph of Grace in the Theology of Karl Barth* (Grand Rapids, MI: Eerdmans, 1956), 390–91, but he is very vague as to how precisely he differs from Van Til's position.

13. I prefer not to regard any doctrine or divine attribute as "most basic." For the dangers in such proposals, see my *The Doctrine of God*, 392–94. I agree, however, that God's aseity is especially important for the work of formulating a Christian worldview in contrast with non-Christian alternatives.

14. Van Til, *The Defense of the Faith*, 100.

15. Ibid., 188.

16. Cornelius Van Til, *The New Modernism: An Appraisal of the Theology of Barth and Brunner* (Philadelphia: Presbyterian and Reformed, 1946), 373.

(4) In a summary of Christian metaphysics, he enumerates the above doctrines—the self-contained God, the ontological Trinity, and "the fact of temporal creation"—and adds two others, "the fact of God's providential control over all created reality," and (5) "the miraculous work of the redemption of the world through Christ."[17]

Van Til often says that the apologist should argue for Christianity "as a unit."[18] That is, in his view we must not defend a general theism first and then later defend Christianity. Rather, the apologist must defend only the distinctive theism of Christianity. As Van Til often put it, we should not try to prove *that* God exists without considering *what kind* of God we are proving. And that means, in turn, that we should not try to prove that God exists without defining God in terms of the doctrines of Scripture.

Does this principle imply that we must prove all the doctrines of Christianity in every apologetic argument we employ? Critics are sometimes tempted to understand Van Til this way, and Van Til's own expressions sometimes encouraged that misunderstanding.[19] But Van Til was too thoughtful to teach anything so absurd. Rather, I think what he meant was that (1) the apologist must "presuppose" the full revelation of the Bible in defending the faith. (2) He must not tone down any biblical distinctives in order to make the faith credible. (3) His goal should be to defend (by one argument or many) the whole of biblical theism, including the authority of Scripture, Trinity, predestination, incarnation, blood atonement, resurrection, and consummation. And (4) the apologist should seek to show that compromise in any of these doctrines leads to incoherence in all human knowledge.

But beyond these general principles, Van Til also had in mind a focus on divine aseity, the "self-contained ontological Trinity." For aseity designates what most clearly distinguishes the biblical worldview from

17. Cornelius Van Til, *The Defense of the Faith* (Philadelphia: Presbyterian and Reformed, 1955), 235. In these notes, citations of *The Defense of the Faith* without further specification will refer, not to this first edition, but to the revised and abridged edition of 1967 cited in the notes above.

18. Cornelius Van Til, *Christian Apologetics* (Phillipsburg, NJ: Presbyterian and Reformed, 1976), 72. "Unit" is another of Van Til's favorite terms. A search for this word on *The Works of Cornelius Van Til*, CD-ROM yielded eighty-eight hits.

19. See my *Cornelius Van Til: An Analysis of His Thought* (Phillipsburg, NJ: P&R, 1995), 183–84, 264–68.

its alternatives.[20] Thus it makes clear in what way Christian teachings are a system of truth, one "unit," and not just a fortuitous collection of ideas.

Only the Bible teaches that the universe is created and controlled by a personal[21] God who is *a se*, not dependent on the world in any way. Polytheistic religions teach the existence of personal gods, but those gods are not *a se*. Monistic worldviews, such as Hinduism, Taoism, and the philosophies of Parmenides, Plotinus, Spinoza, and Hegel, teach the existence of an absolute being, and indeed most polytheisms place a principle of absolute fate beyond the realm of the gods. But these "absolute" beings and fates are impersonal, and so they do not have personal control over the world. Indeed, as Van Til emphasizes, these absolutes are *correlative* to the nonabsolute sectors of the world. They could not exist without the world. They cannot be defined or described except as aspects of the universe. They serve as the element of unity in the world, correlative to the world's plurality, contrary to the biblical doctrine of the ontological Trinity. They serve as the unchanging aspect of the world, correlative to the changes of the world of our experience. So these supposed absolutes depend on the world as much as the world depends on them. They are not truly *a se*.[22]

In this way, the doctrine of divine aseity defines what is distinctive about the biblical worldview. To defend the faith is to defend its dis-

20. Van Til says in *The Triumph of Grace* (no publication data, 1958), 28, "There is no speculative system that entertains the idea of such a self-contained God. It is only the Scriptures which teach us about this God."

21. Van Til correlates "personal" with "self-contained" in *The Reformed Pastor and Modern Thought* (Nutley, NJ: Presbyterian and Reformed, 1971), 74: "This reference point [for human thought] must be taken as *self-contained*, or ultimate, that is, self-sufficient and self-interpretative; in the nature of the case it cannot be impersonal." His point is that an impersonal principle cannot *speak* to bear witness to itself or interpret itself.

22. There are traces of the doctrine of aseity in Judaism and Islam, and in heresies such as the views of the Jehovah's Witnesses. On this fact, two remarks: (1) To the extent that they ascribe aseity to God, they do it because at that point they are influenced by the Bible. (2) Their divergence from Bible teachings leads them to compromise the aseity of God: Islam makes God unknowable and remote, fearing that his direct involvement in the world will relativize him. If the Islamic God were truly *a se*, he would not lose his transcendent glory by entering history. Islam also turns predestination into fatalism, thus veering toward an impersonal concept of God. Judaism today (whatever recent scholarship may conclude about first-century Judaism) is a religion of works, rather than of an *a se* God who gives what we cannot repay. And Judaism, like the Jehovah's Witnesses and other cults, rejects the Trinity, which, as we've seen, is closely related to God's aseity.

tinctives. So the phrase "self-contained ontological Trinity" summarizes the content that the apologist is called to defend.

Aseity and Biblical Epistemology

The second service that the doctrine of divine aseity renders to apologetics is that it determines what sort of knowledge we may have of God, or, indeed, of anything else. I noted earlier that Van Til uses terms like *self-interpreting* and *self-referential* in apposition to *self-contained*, and that he regards God as self-contained, not only in his being, but also in his "knowledge and will."[23] For Van Til, then, God's aseity has definite epistemological implications.

First, God knows himself and the world, both by knowing himself. He knows himself intuitively and perfectly. He knows the world also by knowing himself: he knows what is possible in the world by knowing his own powers; and he knows what is actual in the world (at all times) by knowing his own eternal plan, as well as by his perfect awareness of the temporal accomplishment of that plan. In other words, he does not depend on the creation for his knowledge even of the creation. His knowledge is exhaustive and perfect, because it is *a se*. Van Til says:

> God is absolute rationality. He was and is the only self-contained whole, the system of absolute truth. God's knowledge is, therefore, exclusively *analytic*, that is, self-dependent. There never were any facts existing independent of God which he had to investigate. God is the one and only ultimate Fact. In him, i.e., with respect to his own Being, apart from the world, fact and interpretation of fact are coterminous.[24]

This view of God has implications for human knowledge. Van Til says that only on the presupposition of the self-contained God "can

23. Van Til, *Christian Apologetics*, 7.

24. Van Til, *An Introduction to Systematic Theology*, 10. Note also Cornelius Van Til, *The Protestant Doctrine of Scripture* (Ripon, California: the den Dulk Christian Foundation, 1967), 19: "The Christian religion says that God is self-contained; that he can say 'I' without needing to relate himself to anything over against himself while doing so." And in *Christian Apologetics*, 7, Van Til says, "God is self-sufficient or self-contained in his being. He therefore knows himself and all created existence by a single internal act of intuition."

man know himself or anything else."[25] First, "from the Christian point of view, it is impossible to think of the non-existence of God."[26] If God alone provides the rational structure of all reality, then we cannot understand anything without presupposing him, even though we may verbally deny his existence. So all people know God, as Paul says in Romans 1:21, though apart from grace they repress this knowledge.

Yet God is also *incomprehensible*. This term "does not mean that God is incomprehensible to himself. On the contrary, man's inability to comprehend God is founded on the very fact that God is *completely self-determinative*."[27] A self-contained God is necessarily beyond our complete understanding: "If God does actually exist as a self-contained and eternally self-conscious being, it is natural that we, his creatures, should not be able to comprehend, that is, understand him exhaustively."[28]

So our knowledge of God is, in Van Til's terms, "analogical" rather than "univocal." He defines this distinction as follows:

> Christians must also believe in two levels of knowledge, the level of God's knowledge which is absolutely comprehensive and self-contained, and the level of man's knowledge which is not comprehensive but is derivative and re-interpretative. Hence we say as Christians we believe that man's knowledge is analogical of God's knowledge.[29]

25. Van Til, *Christian Philosophy* (privately reproduced by Lewis J. Grotenhuis; accessed from *The Works of Cornelius Van Til*, CD-ROM, which does not provide page numbers).

26. Van Til, *An Introduction to Systematic Theology*, 9–10.

27. Ibid., 10.

28. Ibid. I shall not enter into the discussion of divine incomprehensibility of God in the controversy of the 1940s between Van Til and Gordon H. Clark, a controversy in which the Van Til party defined incomprehensibility rather differently, as the lack of any identity between any human thought and any divine thought. See my *Cornelius Van Til*, 97–113. As a definition of incomprehensibility, I prefer the simpler definition used in the present quotation.

29. Van Til, *An Introduction to Systematic Theology*, 12. In *Cornelius Van Til*, 89–95, I argue that this terminology is misleading. Thomas Aquinas used these terms to distinguish between literal ("univocal") and figurative ("analogical") uses of language to refer to God. Van Til's distinction concerns a different, though related issue. He does not deny, as Aquinas does, the possibility of literal language about God. Nor does Van Til use these terms to suggest any form of agnosticism, though that has sometimes been inferred from Aquinas's distinction. Van Til does say, as did Calvin, that God's revelation is "anthropomorphic," that is, "an adaptation by God to the limitations of the human creature" (Cornelius Van Til, *A Christian Theory of Knowledge* [Nutley, NJ: Presbyterian and Reformed, 1969], 41), and therefore that the confessions of the church are "approximated statements" (ibid.). But, although he regards revelation

So our knowledge of God depends on God's original knowledge of himself. How do we gain access to that original divine self-knowledge? We can never know God as he knows himself. But we do have access to his thoughts in the revelation he has chosen to give us, his thoughts given to us through created media. Van Til, as the Reformed tradition generally, distinguishes special revelation (God's words to us in human language), general revelation (God's self-manifestation in the created world), and a divine revelation in ourselves as the image of God. Thus we receive knowledge of God from God, from the world, and from ourselves; knowledge of the world from the world, God, and ourselves; and knowledge of ourselves from ourselves, God, and the world.[30]

Van Til focuses especially on God's written revelation, Holy Scripture. For him, the authority of Scripture and God's aseity are related as follows:

> It is this God, as self-contained, who has spoken clearly while on earth in Jesus the Christ and who speaks clearly to men now in the Scriptures. The idea of the Scriptures as the Word of God is both the source and the result of knowledge of the self-contained triune God. To appeal to the one without appealing to the other is impossible.[31]

> [The message of Christianity] comes, in the nature of the case, by authority. The God of the Bible, as self-contained, cannot speak in any other way than by authority.[32]

Not only is God self-contained, but the Word of God is also self-contained.[33] So the Scripture does not depend for its truth on anything other than itself. It is not true because it accords with some higher

---

as anthropomorphic and approximated, he does not deny that we can confess it as true: true anthropomorphisms and true approximations.

30. Van Til, *An Introduction to Systematic Theology*, 62–109.

31. Cornelius Van Til, *The Great Debate Today* (Nutley, NJ: Presbyterian and Reformed, 1971), 33.

32. Cornelius Van Til, *The Case for Calvinism* (Philadelphia: Presbyterian and Reformed, 1964), 104–5.

33. Van Til, *Christian Theory of Knowledge*, 41. Van Til has much to say about the self-contained God and the consequent self-contained character of Scripture in his "introduction" to B. B. Warfield, *The Inspiration and Authority of the Bible* (Philadelphia: Presbyterian and Reformed, 1948), 3–68. On 23, for example, he says, "The self-contained circle of the ontological trinity is not broken up by the fact that there is an economical relation of this triune God with respect

standard. It is true because it is God's Word, and God's Word is true because he says it. And God "alone can identify himself."[34] Therefore, Scripture's testimony, even about itself, must be accepted on its own authority.

That we must accept the Bible on the Bible's own testimony raises the most standard objection to Van Til's apologetic, namely that it is circular. In reply, Van Til insists that (1) all systems of thought are circular when it comes to establishing their most basic principles: for example, rationalists must assume reason in order to prove reason; (2) unless one presupposes biblical theism, all human thinking, including non-Christian thought, becomes incoherent.[35]

To summarize: Scripture is God's Word, and therefore it is self-attesting. There is no higher authority than Scripture by which we can verify it, for there is no authority higher than God. God's Word is self-attesting because he is self-contained. He has within himself all the resources he needs to justify his Word to us.

So apologetics seeks to bring to unbelievers that self-attesting message. Apologetics also seeks to present reasons for believing that message. But the reasons may not contradict the message itself. So our ultimate appeal may not be to human reason, sense expression, feeling, or any merely human authority. Ultimately the apologist must appeal to Scripture in order to defend Scripture. To say that doesn't mean that we must simply say, "Believe Scripture because Scripture says so." As Van Til emphasizes elsewhere, we may use all sorts of rational arguments and evidences.[36] But we must allow Scripture to determine what evidences and arguments are appropriate. In this sense, the apologist must "presuppose" Scripture, not only in his own worldview, but also when defending that worldview before unbelievers.

---

to man. No more is the self-contained character of Scripture broken up by the fact that there is an economy of transmission and acceptance of the word of God it contains."

34. Van Til, *Christian Theory of Knowledge*, 41.

35. For more discussion, see my *The Doctrine of the Knowledge of God* (Phillipsburg, NJ: Presbyterian and Reformed, 1987), 130–33; *Apologetics to the Glory of God* (Phillipsburg, NJ: P&R, 1994), 9–14; *Cornelius Van Til*, 299–309; and "Presuppositional Apologetics," in *Five Views of Apologetics*, ed. Steven B. Cowan (Grand Rapids, MI: Zondervan, 2000), 208–10.

36. Van Til, *Christian Theory of Knowledge*, 293. For discussion, see Thom Notaro, *Van Til and the Use of Evidence* (Phillipsburg, NJ: Presbyterian and Reformed, 1980), and my *Cornelius Van Til*, 177–84.

Aseity and Apologetic Strategy

The third emphasis of Van Til's doctrine of divine aseity is that it shows us the most radical defect in non-Christian thought. Of course, non-Christian thought often errs in its statements of fact, and it often presents invalid arguments. These are fair game for apologists, though the apologist must be willing to admit it when unbelievers discover such flaws in his own thought and witness. But the main issue between Christians and non-Christians is not incidental facts and occasional logical mistakes. Rather, the issue is the self-contained ontological Trinity. And it is always important for the apologist to be properly focused on that big picture.

Let us see how that big picture is relevant to two areas of philosophical debate.

Non-Christian Metaphysics

Many non-Christian thinkers have sensed the need to find something in the world that is *a se*. That *a se* being may be the universe as a whole (Parmenides, Spinoza, Hegel) or something within the universe (Plotinus, Hinduism) that somehow encompasses the whole. It is the *a se* being that accounts for everything else. Others have been skeptical as to the existence of such a being. But Van Til points out that those who affirm an *a se* being are not terribly different from the skeptics. For what is *a se* in non-Christian thought either is the universe itself or is relative to the other aspects of the universe. The *a se* being is "correlative" to the rest of the world.

When Thales said that "all is water," for instance, he took water to be *a se*, the cause and explanation of all else. But on this view, the water that explains is no different from the water that needs explanation. The water that causes is the water that is caused. The mind that seeks to understand water is itself water, and therefore no more fit to analyze water than water itself is.

Plato considered his *forms*[37] to be *a se* and therefore to be a sufficient explanation for the changing world. But the forms could not cause

37. I.e., perfect, unchangeable archetypes of the things and qualities in our changing world.

the world, or be intelligibly defined, without the aid of the changing world. The forms cannot account for all reality, because some of that reality is by nature unformed matter and therefore irrational. So the forms are *correlative* to the world. As such, they are correlative to the irrational aspects of the world, the aspects that are not forms. So they cannot serve as the standard of rationality.

Aristotle's divine Prime Mover is supposed to be the cause of motion in the world. But it, like Plato's forms, is impersonal and can be defined only by contrast with the finite world. It too is limited by the irrationality of Prime Matter, which is just as eternal and immortal as the Prime Mover.

Hinduism regards Brahma as the explanation for the world. But Brahma is an impersonal principle, not a person. It cannot be known, except as the opposite of the changing world, or as the content of human mystical experience that transcends reason.

In Plotinus, Spinoza, and Hegel also, the *a se* absolute is similarly relative to the temporal, irrational world. So, in Van Til's terms, the rational principle is correlative to an irrational principle.

Skepticism and its opponents ultimately come to agreement. The proposed *a se* rational principles are not really *a se*, because they are correlative to the realities they try to explain. Therefore, they themselves need explanation. Indeed, there is no way to account rationally for the world apart from the self-contained God of Scripture.

Nor is skepticism, however, a legitimate option. For skepticism is itself a rational metaphysical statement, that the world is such that no sure knowledge is possible. Being a negative position, skepticism is even harder to prove than a positive principle would be. If one affirms it nevertheless, he affirms irrationalism by way of an arrogant rationalism. To be a skeptic, one must make, as Van Til says, a "universal negative statement."

The most radical attack on divine aseity in our day comes from the so-called open theists, Clark Pinnock, John Sanders, Gregory Boyd, William Hasker, and others. For these, God was once *a se* but he somehow renounced his aseity so that now he cannot accomplish his goals without the free[38] choices of creatures. So in the present world,

---

38. In open theism, *free* is always to be taken in the libertarian sense, defined below.

nothing is *a se*. In one sense, open theism wants to attribute aseity to human free will. On the open theists' libertarian concept of freedom, human free decisions have no cause: not God, not the natural order, not even their own desires. But if my decision is not caused by my desire, then it is something I don't want to do. So even I do not cause my free decisions. They are random, arbitrary, irrational events, like the realm of Prime Matter among the Greeks. Not only does this view fail to give a rational account of free choice, but it makes any such account impossible. The rationalism of the open theists (seeking a definitive explanation of divine sovereignty and human responsibility) has to posit a principle of sheer irrationality.[39]

Non-Christian Epistemology

So far we have looked mainly at metaphysical issues: philosophers trying to give an account of the nature of reality. But the same issues exist in epistemology. We saw earlier that aseity is both a metaphysical and an epistemological category. God, who is metaphysically self-contained, is epistemologically self-attesting. In non-Christian thought, it is man himself who becomes epistemologically *a se*. It is, of course, implausible to regard man as *metaphysically a se*, though mystics have frequently tried to identify themselves with the ultimate. But many others have claimed *epistemological* autonomy, which is epistemological aseity. When a thinker claims that human reason, experience, or feeling is the ultimate criterion of truth, he is claiming epistemological aseity. So Van Til says:

> The natural man virtually attributes to himself that which a true Christian theology attributes to the self-contained God. The battle is therefore between the absolutely self-contained God of Christianity and the would-be wholly self-contained mind of the natural man. Between them there can be no compromise.[40]

39. For more discussion of open theism, see Bruce A. Ware, *God's Lesser Glory: The Diminished God of Open Theism* (Wheaton, IL: Crossway, 2000); John Piper, Justin Taylor, and Paul Kjoss Helseth, *Beyond the Bounds: Open Theism and the Undermining of Biblical Christianity* (Wheaton, IL: Crossway, 2003); Douglas Wilson, *Bound Only Once: The Failure of Open Theism* (Moscow, ID: Canon, 2001); and John M. Frame, *No Other God* (Phillipsburg: P&R, 2001).
   40. Van Til, *Christian Apologetics*, 97.

The doctrine of epistemological autonomy can be made to seem plausible: Mustn't we think for ourselves, even in deciding what authority to submit to? Even if we embrace the God of the Bible, must we not do so on the basis of our own judgment? So Van Til refers to A. E. Taylor, who "cannot believe that any man could receive any revelation from such a [self-contained—J.F.] God without to some extent, in the very act of reception, confusing it with his own experiences that operate independently of this God."[41] On this basis, even the act of submitting to revelation is an act of our autonomous rationality, for revelation can never be clearly distinguished from our rationality.

But Van Til points out that Taylor's argument assumes the nonexistence of the self-contained God of Scripture. If that God does exist, he can reveal himself clearly in history. He is the Lord of history and the Lord of our experience. He can control, not only the initial revelatory events, but also our reception of that revelation, so that we can receive it with confidence. He has not chosen to make our subjective reception of that revelation infallible. But he has given us sufficient justification to affirm the infallibility of the revelation itself.

Of course we cannot appropriate God's revelation without making use of our own thought, our "epistemic apparatus," which is part of our subjectivity. The question is whether, as Taylor thinks, that subjectivity necessarily distorts the revelation or renders it uncertain. The Bible itself teaches that that is not the case.

A General Strategy

The aseity of God, therefore, suggests this general strategy for apologetic argument: We should make clear to the non-Christian that his substitutes for divine aseity (in the biblical term, "idols") cannot do their job. A principle within the world can never account for the world. For such principles are "correlative," as dependent on the rest of the world as the rest of the world is dependent on them.

Epistemologically, we must challenge the necessity of assuming intellectual autonomy. And we should show that such autonomy offers no adequate criterion of truth and falsity. At most it can come up with a standard of rationality that turns out, on inspection, to be correla-

41. Ibid., 93.

tive to irrationality. On the contrary, only on the assumption that the self-contained God exists and has revealed himself can we have any basis for claiming knowledge.

This kind of apologetic argument is not only cogent and persuasive (if the Spirit opens the heart of our opponent). It also focuses the apologetic encounter upon what is most important. Apologetic discussions are easily encumbered with complex syllogisms and factual detail. But the ultimate issue is the self-contained ontological Trinity. This is the doctrine that is most clearly distinctive of the Christian faith.

Let us remember, too, that apologetics is evangelistic, a communication of the gospel of Jesus Christ. Of course, apologetics is valuable in dealing with the doubts of believers. But in dealing with believers, as with unbelievers, apologetics should help them to look to Jesus as the answer to their questions. Van Til's argument from aseity has the virtue of leading people to Jesus, for these reasons: (1) It exposes the pretensions of unbelief as delusions, lies, and idols. (2) It convicts people of the sin of claiming intellectual autonomy, and thus provokes intellectual repentance. (3) It presents Jesus as Lord, for, as a member of the ontological Trinity, Jesus is himself *a se*, and therefore in control of all things in heaven and earth. (4) It presents a God who does not need our good works in order to bless us, who therefore offers grace most freely. (5) It presents God's Word as self-attesting, warranting assurance that the gospel is true. (6) It shows that salvation is by grace, not only in the atoning work of Christ, but even in the illumination of mind necessary to believe in that atoning work. (7) It presents Christ as Savior of the mind as well as all other aspects of human life.

With many kinds of apologetics it is exceedingly difficult to make a transition between the apologetic argument and the gospel. In Van Til's argument, the argument is already the gospel, *suaviter in modo*,[42] and it naturally leads to a more explicit presentation of the gospel. Of course, even Van Til's presuppositional argument can go off track, as when the apologist takes pride in presenting his transcendental refutations of Plato, Kant, and so forth. Satan tempts apologists of

---

42. Van Til often expressed appreciation for the Latin slogan, *suaviter in modo, fortiter in re*, which in a discussion of apologetics can be rendered "gentle (or subtle) in the mode of presentation, but strong in content."

all schools to display their own intellectual achievements rather than saying what is evangelistically helpful. Scripture urges us here as in all other situations to speak the truth in love. But Van Til's model is useful even here, for it rebukes our pride and magnifies the power, wisdom, and grace of God.

7

Consistently Reformed

The Inheritance and Legacy of Van Til's Apologetic

MICHAEL S. HORTON

he Hebrew word for "truth, faithfulness," *'emet* (אמת), thrives among its siblings *hesed* (חסד), "unfailing love," and *tsedaqah* (צדקה), "righteousness, justice." While they may share significant areas of superficial agreement with classical virtues, the biblical environment for these vital terms is the covenant—and not just any covenant, but the covenant that God made with humanity in Adam and the covenant that he made with the second Adam, executed in time with post-fall Adam, Abraham, David, and Jesus. As two cities emerge in redemptive history, one from the line of Cain and the other from Seth, two different sets of eschatologies, soteriologies, and, one might even say, ecclesiologies, emerge. It was Augustine's *City of God* that first gave considered attention to this historical development, but the tale of two cities is anchored in the history of redemption.

Truth, therefore, is not an abstract *notion* but a deeply contextualized *praxis*. I say *praxis* because it incorporates convictions about reality and the appropriate responses to that reality in its definition.

131

In biblical thought, truth is not simply the correspondence of words to things—a mirror of the eternal forms. It is a stance taken in relation to reality as God's creation and to oneself as God's creature—which creature in the covenant of grace is rightly related (justified) and rightly ordered (by the new birth and sanctification) to God's purposes for human flourishing.

The purpose of this brief essay is to provide an account of truth within that covenantal framework that specifically upholds the Creator-creature distinction. To do so, we will first consider the challenges that make this matter so crucial for apologetics today; second, I will provide a sketch of how Reformed theology has developed the epistemological corollaries to the Creator-creature distinction; and finally I will offer some very limited comments concerning whether this trajectory can do greater justice to the postmodern critique of "foundationalism" than the leading postmodern accounts themselves. In this essay our goal will be to consider what it means to think God's thoughts *after him* without presuming to think *God's thoughts*.

The State of the Controversy

While medieval theologies, generally speaking, affirmed divine transcendence and, consequently, denied noetic access to God's essence on the part of humans, this was often compromised in actual practice inasmuch as Plato and Aristotle provided the categories for theological discussion on these matters. Ancient and medieval theology and apologetics had inherited a basically Platonic and Neoplatonic conceptual scheme, which they often transformed to a remarkable extent through biblical revelation. For instance, Greek ontology was guided by *emanation*, the view that all of reality consists of a scale of being in which the highest (that which is eternal, invisible, spiritual) occupies greater being and the lowest (that which is temporal, visible, and material) occupies less being. This system is at once monistic (all reality participates in a scale of being) and dualistic (regarding spiritual reality as greater than material reality).

The early Christians, by contrast, though philosophically predisposed to this classical worldview (and never wholly divorced from it), accepted God's revelation that reality consists of two distinct types:

divine and creaturely. Instead of emanation, they embraced *creation* as the way of speaking about the nature of reality. Reality does not flow downward, Scripture teaches, from its pure origin to impure matter; rather, a good God created a good creation that is distinct from him and yet related to him—not essentially, but covenantally. This gave genuine space and freedom for the world (and specifically, humanity) to be itself—good as God created it, not ontologically "fallen" already by its very material existence.

Despite the impact of biblical theology, however, Christian theology has always struggled to break free from the pantheistic, rationalistic, and dualistic tendencies of its Western philosophical environment. In the Middle Ages, the synthesis "faith and reason" often meant "Christian faith and Platonism/Neoplatonism." Although Thomas Aquinas has often been the brunt of much unfair criticism by Reformed thinkers, he emphasized that if God is truly distinct from the world, there are epistemological as well as ontological implications. Thus, he insisted that just as God's existence and our existence are analogical rather than univocal (i.e., identical, as in a scale of being), God's knowledge and our knowledge must be analogically rather than univocally related as well.

These terms will be defined below; suffice it to say here that Thomas's answer was not universally embraced. Scotus, among others, insisted upon at least some "univocal core" if our attribution of being to God and ourselves is to have any legitimate purchase (anticipating in some ways the famous Van Til–Clark debate). Further, his own thought shows that he was still gripped by the Platonic vision of being. Like Augustine, he shifted the location of the eternal ideas from the realm of forms to the mind of God, but did not radically challenge this view of knowledge as a mirror of the divine ideas.

Roman Catholic thought generally coalesces around the notion that God's being and human being, God's knowledge and human knowledge, are related hierarchically on the same page. God's knowledge, to be sure, is greater, fuller, more comprehensive; but because the human mind participates in the eternal logos or universal forms, there are certain innate ideas that human beings hold independently of and antecedent to God's special revelation. While sin has inhibited the intellect to some extent, these eternal ideas remain fixed in the human mind. It is not such a large step to Descartes, trained in medieval philosophy and theology, to conclude that the goal of human knowledge is to obtain certainty of "clear and distinct ideas."

Modern foundationalism, as it has come to be called, emerged out of the efforts of Descartes and Locke, among others, to start from scratch by eliminating (so they thought) all prejudices and building from the ground up, this time with the right method and on a secure basis. Obviously, this meant that the self was now master, either through rational deduction (Descartes) or empirical induction (Locke), but for both, "truth" was what one got when one's propositions accurately (clearly and precisely) mirrored reality itself.

With the so-called "hermeneutical turn," this modern project has itself been seen to have no foundations except those agreed upon by a large circle of peers working in Western academies. We all interpret within a particular horizon of possible meanings, with no privileged access to a "God's-eye" view of reality, which Thomas Nagel characterized as "the view from nowhere." Far from Descartes' disembodied "thinking thing," every person is situated within a specific context that is not simply expressed in language but constituted by language and convention. This is not the place to offer a proper definition, much less analysis, of modern and postmodern approaches to the question of truth, but simply to suggest that a covenantal approach relativizes all autonomous approaches, whether they are explicitly (as in modernity) or implicitly (as in postmodernity) so.

It is within this situation, however, that evangelical apologetics has struggled to define itself. Cartesian epistemologies have produced "rational apologetics," while Lockean versions have generated "evidential apologetics." Cornelius Van Til's presuppositionalism was consequently regarded in its time as a *novum* in the history of apologetics, a conclusion that Van Til himself perhaps insufficiently challenged. But was it really new?

Archetypal/Ectypal Theology, or, The Creator-Creature Distinction

The Reformed scholastics, whose period began with Calvin and ended just before Descartes' appearance, rejected the Creator-creature confusion that still plagued the medieval synthesis, and thus they made methodologically central the distinction between archetypal and ectypal theology. Wolfgang Musculus (1497–1563) wrote that even the advanced believer does not attain a "plain and perfect" knowledge of "those things which concern the Majesty of God, which is so clothed and covered with inaccessible brightness, that the finest part of our mind or understanding can by no means comprehend it. . . . So we stand in a profound predicament—with the most mighty and unsearchable Majesty of God on the one side, and the necessity of our salvation on the other."[1]

Following Calvin (as well as Luther), the Reformed scholastics regarded the aim of theology as chiefly practical: "the necessity of salvation," and not abstract grasp of essences, was the hallmark of their exegesis and theologizing. Amandus Polanus (1561–1610) explained that God's theology is archetypal, but our theology (*theologia nostra*) is not only ectypal, but the ectypal theology of the pilgrim (*theologia viatorum*) rather than the theology of the blessed (*theologia beatorum*). No "beatific vision" was promised, or allowed, to even the most contemplative searcher. It is up to the hidden God to reveal as much of himself as he sees fit—that which will lead to our salvation and restoration, not that which would satisfy human curiosity.[2]

While officially maintained, this distinction became somewhat blunted even in certain Reformed and Presbyterian circles in which the standards of rationality and experience, along with their criteria, were established by the Enlightenment. Drawing on the Amsterdam school, but going beyond it, Van Til is actually closer to the Reformed scholastics than are his apologetic rivals within the Reformed family.

Examples of this are plentiful. For instance, although he never (as far as I can tell) uses the terms *archetypal* and *ectypal*, Van Til's emphasis on the Creator-creature distinction covers the same ground. He writes:

> Our knowledge of God is not and cannot be comprehensive. We are God's creatures. We cannot know God comprehensively now nor can we hope to know God comprehensively hereafter. We may know much

1. Cited in Richard A. Muller, *Post-Reformation Reformed Dogmatics: Prolegomena to Theology* (Grand Rapids, MI: Baker, 1987), 179.
2. Ibid., 127.

more in the future than we know now. Especially when we come to heaven will we know more than we know now, but we will not know comprehensively. . . . It is true that there must be comprehensive knowledge somewhere if there is to be any true knowledge anywhere but this comprehensive knowledge need not and cannot be in us; it must be in God.[3]

In his debate with Gordon Clark, Van Til defended the classical Reformed insistence on this distinction. Rationalism tends to relate divine and human minds, so that the difference between God's knowledge and ours is a matter merely of degree or, as Van Til says, "comprehensiveness."[4] Thus, it is as if the hierarchy of being rose like a ladder from the earth: from fifty stories high on the ladder the human beings could see more than the animal world at their mere ground level. But God sees things from an infinite height. Rationalism lends itself to these kinds of analogies, where the Creator-creature distinction is blurred and the epistemological difference (as all too often linked to ontology, as well) is one merely of degree. The intellect is where the divine and human first meet, rather than in the written and incarnate Word.

So what kind of knowledge can we have? Van Til insists that we can have true knowledge of God that is not comprehensive. In the words of the Reformed scholastics, he is saying that our knowledge is ectypal knowledge that is appropriate to pilgrims on the way (*theologia viator*), not archetypal knowledge, the sort of analytic and immediate knowledge that God alone possesses of everything. For this reason, Van Til insists that all knowledge *of* God is mediated *by* God through analogical predication. As far back as the Fourth Lateran Council, even the medieval church recognized that in every analogy between God and humans, there is always more dissimilarity than similarity.[5]

3. Cornelius Van Til, *The Defense of the Faith*, 3rd ed. (Philadelphia: Presbyterian and Reformed, 1967), 40–41.

4. Cornelius Van Til, *An Introduction to Systematic Theology* (Nutley, NJ: Presbyterian and Reformed, 1974), 34.

5. Analogy is distinguished, on the one hand, from equivocity (in which the relation of two terms is unknown) and univocity (in which they are identical at least at some point). The former tends toward irrationalism, the latter toward rationalism.

While much of medieval theology was inconsistent on this point, that rule was followed by the Reformers and, in fact, played a significant hand in their recognition that apart from Scripture there is absolutely no saving knowledge of God, since even the knowledge of the law that is implanted in all people is immediately distorted when its origin and ends are discovered. The natural revelation that surrounds them ("shining lamps," as Calvin called it) merely affords unbelievers with an opportunity to suppress the truth in unrighteousness. For instance, God's power is seen in the storms, but is attributed to "the forces of nature" in either a fatalistic or chance-oriented scheme. Regeneration does not suddenly give believers access to the divine mind either. In fact, not even the glorified saints in heaven overcome the Creator-creature distinction in their epistemology any more than in their ontology.

All knowledge of God, therefore, is analogical rather than univocal. In other words, any knowledge that we have of God is the result of divine accommodation.

This classic Reformed distinction is at least implied throughout Van Til's work. Without using these terms, he implies that equivocity leads to mysticism, while univocity tends toward rationalism. Hence, the "rationalist-irrationalist" dialectic of all pagan thought. "All of this may again be expressed from another point of view by saying that human knowledge is analogical of divine knowledge."[6]

> Roman Catholic theology seeks to serve two masters here. It too speaks of created being and human knowledge as being analogical of divine being and divine knowledge but it does not really take this seriously. In its philosophy and apologetics Romanism reasons as though man can, by himself, determine the nature and possibility of knowledge without reference to God. On the other hand it refers to mysteries as being above the understanding of man. But as Protestants we should definitely choose to make God the original in the knowledge situation.[7]

Thus, God's knowledge is original (archetypal), while human knowledge is analogical (ectypal). Univocity guarantees a clear view

6. Van Til, *The Defense of the Faith*, 39.
7. Ibid.

of the referent—not only *truth* but *Truth*. It sees reality not as it is interpreted by God for us (hearing in faith) but as it is in itself (possessing by sight). But this cannot be said of human knowledge of God or anything else, for that matter: "Our knowledge is analogical and therefore must be paradoxical. We say that if there is to be any true knowledge at all there must be in God an absolute system of knowledge. We therefore insist that everything must be related to that absolute system of God. Yet we ourselves cannot fully understand that system."[8] But apparent contradictions are just that: *apparent*.

If we insist on worshiping a god whom *we* have discovered, imagined, or experienced directly, we will surely have little interest in Scripture as revelation, that is, as a move that God has made toward us. Scripture may contain many of the great universal ideas or principles that are already present archetypally in the human mind (rationalism and idealism). The production of the Bible may be regarded as an instance of spiritually sensitive writers who were "inspired" by God as were the great poets and artists of all time (romanticism). But it will not be regarded as divine accommodation in speech and action, because unbelievers do not believe that this *can* happen, much less that it *has*. For God to accommodate in this way, he would have to actually communicate with human beings within a causal nexus that modern thought from Newton to Bultmann has regarded as a unified mechanism.[9] This *cannot* happen, we are told; therefore, it *does not* happen. Knowledge of God is either direct and immanent (ideas, universals, experience), or it is utterly nonexistent. This is the unbeliever's way of maintaining his claim to autonomy and asserting his control over that knowledge. (Despite their own unwillingness to carry their critique to its logical conclusion, many postmodern thinkers from Heidegger to Derrida have made similar points.)

The failure to make this sharp distinction between Creator and creature (a fuller exposition of the Reformed system's distinction between archetypal and ectypal theology) leads, Van Til correctly

8. Ibid., 44.
9. This Newtonian worldview has crumbled in the scientific community, just a half-century after Bultmann rallied his troops to a theological accommodation to it as an indubitable result of modern progress.

implies, to the swinging pendulum between the extreme poles of rationalism and irrationalism. No better example of this observation can be found perhaps than in his exposition of Augustine's earlier writings. After noting how in these writings the bishop of Hippo follows an essentially Platonic defense of theism, Van Til writes, "At least he does not recognize the fact that there is a difference, and that a basic difference, between the Christian and non-Christian defense of the doctrine of God." In the very act of apologetics, Augustine is subverting his own task: "A bare theism is a theism which thinks it needs not Christianity; the God of bare theism is such a God as does not need the work of Christ in order that men might be saved." Van Til points to the *Soliloquies*, where Augustine "personifies Reason and discourses with it. Reason asks Augustine what he would know. 'A. God and the soul, that is what I desire to know. R. Nothing more? A. Nothing whatever.'"[10] Although Van Til did not refer to it, Calvin's Genevan catechism seems to meet this idea when the following questions and answers are given:

> MASTER: What is the first head in this division of yours?
> STUDENT: To place our whole confidence in God.
> M.: How shall we do so?
> S.: When we know him to be Almighty and perfectly good.
> M.: Is this enough?

And right where the early Augustine says, "Yes," Calvin says,

> S.: Far from it.
> M.: Wherefore?
> S.: Because we are unworthy that he should exert his power in helping us, and show how good he is by saving us.
> M.: What more then is needful?
> S.: That each of us should set it down in his mind that God loves *him*, and is willing to be a Father, and the author of salvation *to him*.
> M.: But whence will this appear?
> S.: From his word, in which he explains his mercy to us in Christ, and testifies of his love towards us.

10. Cornelius Van Til, *A Christian Theory of Knowledge* (Nutley, NJ: Presbyterian and Reformed, 1969), 120.

M.: Then the foundation and beginning of confidence in God is
to know him in Christ?
S.: Entirely so.[11]

This echoes Luther's emphasis that the sort of knowledge that
theology teaches is who God is *for us* (God-in-relation), not who
God is *in himself*—for that would be deadly to sinners. Van Til points
out how Augustine's Platonism separates mind from body, the intellectual and phenomenal realms, linking eternal truth (viz., ideas)
to the former and uncertain opinion to the latter. When defending
mere theism, he is a rationalist; when defending Christianity on that
foundation, he is an irrationalist, Van Til argues from Augustine's *The
Profit of Believing*:

He speaks of words and signs by which men seek to communicate
with one another, and he asks what can be communicated by these
means from one man to another. The answer is nothing less than
startling. It is to the effect that nothing can be thus communicated.
"For when a sign is given me, if it finds me not knowing of what
thing it is a sign, it can teach me nothing, but if it finds me knowing
the thing of which it is the sign, what do I learn from the sign?" The
use of words and signs is therefore to remind us of what is already
known to us rather than to give us knowledge additional to what is
in our possession.[12]

Augustine himself offers that conclusion:

For it is the truest reasoning and most correctly said that when words
are uttered we either know already what they signify or we do not
know; if we know, then we remember rather than learn, but if we
do not know, then we do not even remember, though perhaps we
are prompted to ask. . . . To give them as much credit as possible,
words possess only sufficient efficacy to remind us in order that we
may seek things, but not to exhibit the things so that we may know
them.[13]

11. John Calvin, *John Calvin Selections from His Writings*, ed. John. Dillenberger (Missoula,
MT: Scholars Press for the American Academy of Religion, 1975), 249–50.
12. Van Til, *A Christian Theory of Knowledge*, 123.
13. Cited in ibid., 126.

This is Plato's (and before him, Socrates') doctrine of reminiscence (*mimesis*).[14] That which is rational is already in the mind. It is the eternal forms, which cannot perish, that yield truth. So where does that leave "knowledge" gained from the realm of appearances? Exactly the question, says Van Til.

> What this view does to history and the reporting of history may be gathered from Augustine's own treatment of the Scriptural story of the three young men who were thrown into the fiery furnace. "But we do accept the story of the boys, that they triumphed over the king and over the fires by faith and religion, that they sang praises to God, and that they won honor even from their very enemies. Has this been transmitted to us otherwise than by means of words? I answer that everything signified by these words was already in our knowledge. For I already grasp what three boys are, what a furnace is, and fire, and a king, what unhurt by fire is, and everything else signified by those words. But Ananias and Azarias and Misael are as unknown to me as *saraballae*; these names do not help me at all to know these men, nor can they help me." There can, therefore, be no communication of truth about individual historical happenings.[15]

As long as one is in the realm of bare theism, rationalism may appear at first glance to be getting us somewhere with unbelief. But the moment we begin to explain and defend Christianity on rationalist principles, the more irrational is that defense. No one learns anything from historical details, from narrated proclamation, from any communication that perishes, since "Truth" is an eternal universal (a form). While, happily, Augustine did not follow his own logic here, it could naturally lead to the belief that historic Christianity is simply meaningless, which is, by the way, exactly where Lessing ended up in his infamous "ditch" between the historical witness to Jesus and truth as purely rational. "Jesus of Nazareth," Van Til continues in relation to the implications of Augustine's view, "would be reduced to the Word which is eternal. All men, all souls, would be eternal in him as God, and

14. In Plato's *Meno* there is the famous example of the slave who is able to define the Pythagorean proposition of the three angles of a triangle without having had any education.
15. Van Til, *Christian Theory of Knowledge*, 126, quoting Augustine, *Confessions*.

thus we would be back with all the heresies of Origen."[16] Of course, Augustine did not follow the logic to that conclusion, because of his Christian commitment, but modernity could and in fact has.

So in this Platonic morass, there are two options: either Christianity is rational, in which case it is eternal and universal; or Christianity is irrational, since it is subject to that which is temporal and particular (historical). Early Augustine opts for the former, of course, but this renders Christianity an abstraction without any intelligible content. "An abstraction cannot perish. It has no content which can perish."[17] This is too high a price to pay for defending Christianity on the presuppositions of unbelief in general or Plato in particular. Furthermore, it need not be paid. Not only does this method do injustice to the form of scriptural knowledge (i.e., historical narrative); it cannot even live up to its own expectations.

Much more could be said on this point, but we will leave it here. As even Paul Tillich recognized (and exhibited), mysticism and rationalism often come from the same source, although we tend to see them as opposites.[18] This passing observation Van Til elaborates with considerable skill.

Needless to say, not all evangelicals (or even all Reformed) apologists have followed Van Til's legacy on these points, and many seem to have even been unaware that Van Til himself was only expanding in his day on the inheritance of Reformed thought. Gordon Clark, for example, apparently saw the endorsement of an analogical view of truth as Thomistic at best—"an elaborate and somewhat misleading way of saying that we have no knowledge of God"—and, in Van Til's expression, "neo-orthodox" at worst.[19] Despite his philosophical

16. Van Til, *Christian Theory of Knowledge*, 128.

17. Ibid., 129.

18. Paul Tillich, *A History of Christian Thought*, ed. Carl E. Braaten (New York: Simon and Schuster, 1968), 362.

19. Gordon H. Clark, "Apologetics," in *Contemporary Evangelical Thought*, ed. Carl F. H. Henry (Great Neck, NY: Channel, 1957), 160–61. Professor Clark not only fails to properly define analogy; he conflates analogy with "metaphorical or symbolic" language as employed by "the adherents of the dialectical theology" (ibid.). Analogy is distinguished from metaphorical or symbolic approaches in that it affirms the literal truth of its language while not reducing the relation of the two terms to one of *identity*. The view that all religious language is metaphorical or symbolic is simply a hyper-allegorical view that has nothing in common with an analogical view. That Clark apparently was not aware of the history of analogical predication as the dominant if not exclusive approach of the Reformed tradition is evidenced in the following comment: "The

expertise, Professor Clark assumed a seriously defective understanding of analogy, reducing it to equivocity. Not unlike Scotus's criticism of Aquinas, Clark insisted that if there is no univocal intersection between divine and human knowledge, the latter is left without foundation. But that is only true if God has not himself provided the analogies.

Clark was at best skeptical about the status of paradox, suggesting that paradox is nothing more than what a less learned student calls something he or she does not understand. In principle, then, there really is no paradox, but there are only difficult matters we have not yet resolved through careful reflection and logic.[20] "Let us then have done with paradoxes; let us restrict analogy to a literary embellishment; let us eschew fallacy, pursue valid reasoning, and acknowledge God as the source of all truth."[21] E. J. Carnell similarly dismissed an analogical in favor of a univocal view of knowledge:

> I am not unfamiliar with the claimant protests of those who say that if God and man have anything in common, the Creator-creature relation is effaced and God no longer rules man with a sovereignty that is metaphysically discontinuous with creation. But do these zealots realize what they are asserting? Unless God and man have something in common, it is impossible to make meaningful judgments about God. Hence, if one elects to guard God's sovereignty by denying that God and man share some points of identity, he should prepare for the fact that nothing significant can be known or said about God—not

Protestant Reformation swept away the superstitious idolatry of Romanism and the scholastic philosophy as well. But whereas it replaced the false worship with the pure Gospel, it failed to replace scholasticism with anything. Protestantism has never had an official philosophy—a fact of which we may be glad; but it is not so fortunate that we have not had a semi-official philosophy or at least a wide area of agreement." Professor Clark was apparently unaware that there even was such a thing as Protestant scholasticism, because it differed somewhat from medieval scholasticism on some of these crucial points.

20. In ibid., 61, Clark writes, "Theorem fifteen may be a paradox to the high school student, but not to the teacher. As an example of seeming contradiction, in fact, as 'one of the outstanding paradoxes of the Christian interpretation of things,' Van Til gives these two propositions: 'Prayer changes things and . . . everything happens in accordance with God's plan and God's plan is immutable.' Undeniably, this is a paradox, for the two statements seem contradictory to Van Til. Undeniably also this is not a paradox because they do not seem contradictory to some other people. A paradox is not a quality inherent in pairs of propositions, as the relationship of contradiction is. Since a paradox is only a seeming contradiction, it exists only insofar as these statements seem to some individual. But such irregular, personal reactions cannot be lifted to the level of principal importance."

21. Ibid.

even that there is a God, let alone that God is a person. God and man cannot be meaningfully compared unless they have something in common.[22]

So too Carl F. H. Henry equates the analogical view with Protestant liberalism, the evacuation of truth claims.[23]

Today there are a number of worthy claimants to this distinguished mantle of apologetics. There are others, impressed with the various postmodern critiques of modern foundationalism, who risk adopting (unwittingly) an equivocal view of truth that simply remains trapped in the rationalist-irrationalist dialectic and therefore are inhibited from making strong claims for Christian particularity despite the so-called "turn to the particular." Presuppositional apologetics in this time can affirm much of the critique of foundationalism but argue that it has not yet gone far enough; it is not yet radical enough. It does not yet expose the atheism of modern thought that is still present in postmodern discourse and can only yield nihilistic conclusions. It is therefore no time to retreat into the rubble of modernity or capitulate to an irrational immanentism, but to be addressed again from the God who has stooped to our meager and sinful prejudices to liberate us from every epoch of "this passing evil age."

Van Til's question is as relevant today as it has ever been since the days of Augustine and even before: Will our theology govern our view of reality (ontology) and access to it (epistemology)? Do we really believe in the Creator-creature distinction? Do we really believe that we are finite and that we can therefore only see reality as creatures? Do we really believe, furthermore, that we are fallen creatures and that reasoning is always a matter of interpreting things according to whether we are enemies of God or are reconciled to him by the death of his Son. If so, then we will be persuaded that we can know the truth as God has revealed it, but never as he knows it—either qualitatively or quantitatively.

22. E. J. Carnell, *Christian Commitment: An Apologetic* (New York: Macmillan, 1957), 138. Everywhere in this otherwise learned and useful volume where "analogy" is mentioned, it is vague and Carnell even moves back and forth between rejecting it and building arguments upon the divine-human *analogy*.

23. Carl F. H. Henry, *God, Revelation, and Authority*, vol. 1 (Waco, TX: Word, 1976), esp. 237–38.

Covenantal Epistemology

Adam blamed Eve, Eve blamed the Serpent, and the Serpent blamed God. At the end of the day, everybody blamed God, and ever since the fall, so do we. In ancient paganism (viz., Manichaeism), as in modern dualism, the problem of evil is identified with created nature in an effort to externalize sin by attributing it to evil structures, natural forces, and so forth. Shifting the issue from sin to ontology, metaphysics, and so forth, is one of the sources of dualism, ancient and modern. As with the Creator-creature (archetypal-ectypal) and rationalist-irrationalist categories, Van Til fleshes out the biblical and Reformed doctrine of covenant in relation to apologetics.[24] He lays this out especially in *The Defense of the Faith*:

> To the doctrine of creation must be added the conception of the covenant. Man was created as a historical being. God placed upon him from the outset of history the responsibility and task of reinterpreting the counsel of God as expressed in creation to himself individually and collectively. Man's creature-consciousness may therefore be more particularly signalized as covenant-consciousness. But the revelation of the covenant to man in paradise was supernaturally mediated. . . . Man is not in Plato's cave. . . . Man had originally not merely a capacity for receiving the truth; he was in actual possession of the truth. The world of truth was not found in some realm far distant from him; it was right before him. That which spoke to his senses no less than that which spoke to his intellect was the voice of God. . . . Man's first sense of self-awareness implied the awareness of the presence of God as the one for whom he had a great task to accomplish.[25]

Thus the deep problems of apologetics are not finally intellectual, but ethical. One cannot argue from autonomous presuppositions to the God of Scripture. Also like the Reformers and their successors, Van Til approaches the knowledge of God with a sensitivity to soteriological considerations. Unlike much of medieval scholasticism, which abstracted epistemology from the personal and existential situation of human beings

24. On its specific relation to mind-body dualism, for instance, see Van Til, *An Introduction to Systematic Theology*, 35.
25. Van Til, *The Defense of the Faith*, 90–91.

as enemies of God, Van Til asserts the authority of Scripture because this Word "comes to save from themselves those who do not want to be saved, because they think that they do not need to be saved." "It is this situation," he says, "as has been indicated by Reformed theologians, that accounts for the need of inscripturation of the authoritative and redemptive Word of God."[26] Across the yawning chasm separating the fearful divine majesty and our salvation, the bridge of Scripture is built. This is why evangelism and apologetics cannot be separated.

Thus, biblical authority is necessary not merely as an end in itself, but in order to teach us the truth about our sinful, autonomous orientation and to lead us to Christ for salvation from sin's judgment and terrible tyranny over our whole existence, including its intellectual aspects. Experience will not teach us that we are sinners, Van Til says.

> Only he who accepts the Scripture as the authoritative revelation of God and of the self-identifying Son of God, will accept what it says about himself as a sinner. So we are of necessity moving about in circles. Those who accept the fully biblical conception of sin will accept the Bible as authoritative. And those who accept the fully biblical view of sin do so because they accept the Bible as the authoritative Word of God.[27]

Evidences are essential in apologetics, as Van Til himself says, suggesting that we present "the message and evidence for the Christian position as clearly as possible, knowing that because man is what the Christian says he is, the non-Christian will be able to understand in an intellectual sense the issues involved."[28] He does not doubt that Christianity is built on evidences. But to suggest that the unbeliever is thus engaged in a process of neutral verification is to miss the point that he who "verifies" himself belongs to a circle, only in this case a vicious one, in which his refusal to face himself as a sinner is inextricable from the process of verification.

It is Van Til's emphasis on unbelievers as covenant-breakers that links soteriology and epistemology, and this is an inheritance from

26. Van Til, *Christian Theory of Knowledge*, 27.
27. Ibid.
28. Cornelius Van Til, "My Credo," in *Jerusalem and Athens: Critical Discussions on the Philosophy and Apologetics of Cornelius Van Til*, ed. E. R. Geehan (Nutley, NJ: Presbyterian and Reformed, 1971), 21.

classic Reformed thought, with Romans 1–3 as the *locus classicus*. "Fallen man cannot by his own adopted criteria make a true analysis of his own condition."[29] This is why the Reformed scholastics were suspicious of any granting to reason or experience the position of *principium cognoscendi*, as modern theology largely has done. As Turretin argued, human reasoning may point out the inherent weaknesses in our formulations, the contradictions in our faulty constructions, but it can never serve as a middle term of a syllogism.[30] In other words, it can critique our use of language and the logic of our argumentation, but it cannot supply the content of what is to be believed. As Richard Muller has pointed out, the Reformed scholastics did not understand prolegomena as pre-dogmatic, as Rome had.[31] This is to say that while Roman Catholic dogmatics (today as then) builds its church/theology on a foundation of universal ideas of moral reason, ontology, epistemology, and metaphysics, Reformed dogmatics builds its church/theology on the foundation of Scripture—which is to say, its foundation is actually made up of bits and pieces of the edifice itself. The narratives, doctrines, commands, and promises revealed in Scripture, then, are not merely the content of theology—after we have settled that content on a foundation firmer than God's Word. Rather, these doctrines revealed in Scripture are already active in determining the criteria of rightly ordered knowing in the first place.

Some Concluding Remarks on Ectypal Apologetics

Evangelical apologists (as well as biblical scholars, theologians, and pastors) are increasingly divided as to how to respond to the crisis of modernity. On one hand are those who apparently cling to the modern project, identifying the crumbling of autonomous foundationalism with the demise of truth itself. Many of these writers carry on the apologetic strategies of Gordon Clark, the medieval synthesis, or evidentialism—usually a combination of these.

29. Van Til, *Christian Theory of Knowledge*, 43.
30. Francis Turretin, *Institutes of Elenctic Theology*, 3 vols., ed. James T. Dennison Jr., trans. George Musgrave Giger (Phillipsburg, NJ: P&R, 1992–97), 1:24.
31. Muller, *Prolegomena to Theology*, 54.

But Christianity has never depended on the success or failure of the empires that wax and wane. The "crisis of Western civilization" is not the same as "the crisis of Christianity." Reformed theology, as we have seen, has long been a critic of the idolatries of the former and can continue to guide our response to the current situation.

The apologetic efforts of the past, even of the medieval synthesis and the various syntheses of contemporary evangelicalism, have not gone unrewarded. Many of us, I included, have had our faith strengthened through a reasonable argument and a well-presented summary of the evidences. Furthermore, while D. L. Moody's alleged rebuff of critics, "I like my way of doing it better than your way of not doing it," may be inadequate, it has often been the case that advocates of "rational apologetics" and "evidentialist apologetics" have actually engaged non-Christians in person and in print with greater frequency and passion than many of us.

On the other hand, in an era especially when the foundationalism of rationalism and empiricism seems to have crumbled, the Reformed impulses of presuppositional apologetics are more adequate not only to Scripture but to the times. The "myth of neutrality" is not just a Van Tilian shibboleth; it is now the by-word of postmodernity. Attacks on autonomy and the Promethean claims of reason are on every hand. But presuppositionalism is uniquely poised to indicate to the disillusioned children of modern hubris that their "horizon," "situation," "language game," "location," "paradigm," and "web" has a *name*: "this present evil age," "life under the sun," "vanity," "serving the creature rather than the Creator who is ever praised." Those who come with triumphant apologetics of absolute knowledge will rightly be rebuffed, but those who come as "pilgrims on the way," those who hear the Word that is preached instead of gazing on an autonomous vision of the True, the Good and the Beautiful, will be in a good position to lead others to "the God who commanded light to shine out of darkness, who has shone in our hearts to give the light of the knowledge of the glory of God in the face of Jesus Christ" (2 Cor. 4:6 NKJV).

8

A Confessional Apologetic

THOM E. NOTARO

pologetics concerns differences and things held in common. When the apostle Paul asks rhetorically, "What does
a believer have in common with an unbeliever?" (2 Cor. 6:15 NIV),[1] he
speaks of radical differences. The two have as little in common as do
light and darkness, righteousness and lawlessness, Christ and Belial (vv.
14–15).

Paul's application of this antithesis—"Do not be unequally yoked
with unbelievers" (v. 14), but "go out from their midst and be separate" (v. 17)—might seem to eliminate all connection with lost people,
and all compassion. But his words about separateness, purity, and the
newness of life in Christ (5:17) come not at the *expense* of but in the
interest of making real contact with people not yet in Christ. Putting
"no obstacle in anyone's way" (6:3), we have a "ministry of reconciliation" as Christ's ambassadors through whom God makes his appeal
to a world at odds with him (5:18, 20).

The task of making a reasoned appeal to opponents of the faith
raises questions about how to connect with them and where to

---

1. With the exception of this verse, Scripture quotations in this chapter are from The Holy
Bible, English Standard Version, copyright © 2001 by Crossway Bibles, a division of Good News
Publishers. Used by permission. All right reserved.

find common ground. While apologists differ over these questions, Reformed apologists do share common theological ground with each other. Differ as we may over what a Reformed apologetic looks like, or whether such a life form exists, the system of doctrine we profess supplies firm footing on which to begin a defense.

In this chapter we will revisit two Reformed confessional standards—the Westminster Confession of Faith and the Larger Catechism—to ask what, most basically, they say relevant to the challenges of doing apologetics.[2] The point of a confessional apologetic is to be biblical, to follow the counsel of Scripture regarding thought, life, and speech. Inasmuch as the confession, as a subordinate standard, is faithful to biblical revelation, it warrants application to all realms of life, including what we believe and say in apologetics.

It may seem odd to speak of a confessional apologetic when the truths and the God we confess are the issues in question. Confessions of faith are primarily for believers, and apologetics addresses people in need of saving faith. Moreover, the Westminster divines did not formulate an apologetic method. But they did lay a theological foundation that can help us understand and do apologetics. The confession and catechism articulate the truths of God's existence and character, the clarity of his revelation, the nature of unbelief, and how minds are transformed. They identify the primary means God uses to bring people from unbelief to a saving knowledge, and are highly suggestive as to the manner in which those means should be employed. So we may ask, How in apologetic contexts can we be faithful to the truths we profess when we subscribe to these Reformed standards? Let's look at a few of those truths.

The Covenantal Context

> The distance between God and the creature is so great, that although reasonable creatures do owe obedience unto Him as their Creator, yet they could never have any fruition of Him as their blessedness and reward, but by some voluntary condescension on God's part, which He hath been pleased to express by way of covenant. (WCF 7.1)

2. I will be quoting the Free Presbyterian Publications 1994 edition of the confession (hereafter WCF 1.1, etc.) and 1983 edition of the Larger Catechism (hereafter LC 1, etc.).

God in Plain View

The confession depicts all people—Adam's posterity (7.2)—as being in covenant with God. The need for this covenant predated the onset of sin. The first potential obstacle between God and humanity was not depravity but the sheer "distance" between Creator and creature, a distinction (in being, knowledge, power, etc.) so great that the only way to span the chasm was "by some voluntary condescension on God's part." God therefore formed a relationship with humanity "by way of covenant."

Vital to this covenant was God's revelation of himself through the things he made, including human beings. "The very light of nature in man, and the works of God, declare plainly that there is a God" (LC 2). But the standards say more than that a nondescript god exists:

> The light of nature showeth that there is a God, who hath lordship and sovereignty over all, is good, and doth good unto all, and is therefore to be feared, loved, praised, called upon, trusted in, and served, with all the heart, and with all the soul, and with all the might. (WCF 21.1)

General revelation reveals more than a god in general. The one revealed is Lord and sovereign over all. He is good and does good to all. The confession, quoting Paul, says that people have "the law of God written in their hearts" (4.2). This indicates an awareness of what God's goodness entails and what it requires of us (Rom. 2:14). Nature shows clearly that God is fearsome, lovely, worthy of praise, needed, trustworthy, and deserving of our wholehearted service (WCF 21.1). "It is the law of nature" that "a due proportion of time be set apart for the worship of God" (21.7). In short, "the light of nature and the works of creation and providence do so far manifest the goodness, wisdom, and power of God, as to leave men unexcusable" (1.1). "Reasonable creatures" owe obedience to this good, wise, trustworthy, and sovereign Lord.

Disbelief Is Covenant Rebellion

When someone denies that God exists or that he created all that we see and enjoy, when someone chafes at the idea that God is in charge, or denies that God can be both good and all-powerful, or refuses to trust and serve God, he or she does so in the face of condescending love whereby God did "so far manifest" himself. The clarity of God's revelation in nature, including human nature, eliminates excuses for disbelief. It invalidates "reasons" and "evidences" against God. No one may plead ignorance or indecision. There is no genuinely reasonable case for the nonexistence of this God or the existence of a substitute deity. The God of revelation is not one sensible, plausible option—not even the *most* credible object of belief—among several. There is no excuse, no valid defense, for denying the one "living, and true God" (WCF 2.1).

Failure to fear, love, praise, call upon, trust in, and serve this good, sovereign Lord (21.1) owes itself not to a dearth of evidence that he exists and is worthy of those responses. There is a problem within the doubter, one that begs, if only metaphorically, for a solution at the level of heart and mind. The unbeliever is at odds with Someone vastly greater, wiser, more powerful, and more wonderful than he or she has been willing to acknowledge.

It is said that problems identified become opportunities. We have the opportunity by faith to "destroy arguments and every lofty opinion raised against the knowledge of God" (2 Cor. 10:5). We do that only when "the weapons of our warfare are not of the flesh but have divine power" (v. 4). If we underestimate the covenantal rebellion behind arguments and lofty opinions raised against God, we will miss the opportunity to engage people powerfully at the focal point of their need.

God Is in the Details

To appreciate the scope of covenantal rebellion we need to consider the extent of God's self-disclosure in nature. Is God revealed in every thing, every event, every relationship, every fact? We saw that "the goodness, wisdom, and power of God" are vividly displayed in "the works of creation and providence . . . as to leave men unexcusable" (WCF 1.1). What, then, do creation and providence encompass?

In *creation*, "for the manifestation of the glory of His eternal power, wisdom, and goodness," God made "all things . . . visible or invisible" (4.1). His *providence* includes his governing "all creatures, actions, and things, from the greatest even to the least . . . to the praise of the glory of His wisdom, power, justice, goodness, and mercy" (5.1). Here natural revelation, in creation and providence, displays "eternal" attributes that echo the Shorter Catechism's answer to the question "What is God?"[3] Natural revelation is both content-rich and pervasive. It reveals the glory of God's character and does so in "all creatures, actions, and things." The Westminster divines did not exempt lesser things or incidental events from this purpose. Seemingly insignificant things and events, "from the greatest even to the least," have God's glory as their central purpose. When we look around us at all things great and small, we have every good reason to marvel at the Creator and Sustainer. Everything in God's good creation finds its meaning in relation to him. His creative activity, providence, and character are the preconditions for making sense of what we see.[4]

It is a small step from saying that all things reveal God's existence, character, and glory to saying that all states of things—all facts—reveal him. To the extent that we have knowledge of things, events, and relationships, we have an awareness (welcomed or suppressed) that points beyond them. The light of nature reflects the omnipresence of God, and thus his lordship, even in the seemingly trivial data we discover. The point here is not that all facts have equal evidential impact. Some offer, in effect, a larger lens or canvas for viewing the glory of God. The feeding of the five thousand testifies more boldly to God's goodness and power than does the fact that I had a tuna sandwich for lunch. Signs and wonders are more striking than common providence. But, as John Frame notes, even common providence, such as God's provision of food for humans and animals, is described in Scripture as wonderful.[5]

Providence is never simply mundane. We are not meant to view things in terms of a this-world, this-age perspective. Nor are we designed to see things as merely isolated data or disconnected aspects. Where there is bare perception, there is no knowledge. Facts find their meanings in contexts and connections. The light of nature, accompa-

---

3. "God is a Spirit, infinite, eternal, and unchangeable, in his being, wisdom, power, holiness, justice, goodness, and truth" (SC 4; cf. LC 7).

4. Only as we acknowledge those preconditions can we give an account that does not radically undermine, pollute, and distort what we know.

5. See Frame's comments on Pss. 107:8–9; 136:3–4, 25; 145:15–16 in reference to miracle and providence in John M. Frame, *The Doctrine of God* (Phillipsburg, NJ: P&R, 2002), 261.

nied by the Word of God, provides the fullest—covenantal—context. In that light all of God's gifts, including any bit of knowledge, carry with them responsibilities.[6] All facts call people to some kind of faithful, worshipful response to God: stewardship, thanksgiving (compare Rom. 1:21), delight, godly sorrow, just indignation, trust, patience, or combinations of these and other virtues. The facts are not just about people, places, and things. They are about Someone marvelous. They are not just about the creation. They are about the Creator, who is forever to be praised (Rom. 1:25).

Is it a stretch to say that we ought to (and, in a crucial sense, *do*) see the face of God in all the facts? Is that much different from saying that every thought should be captive to Christ? If, as the standards say, even "the least" features of providence speak of God, it would seem fair to say that all the facts mirror that same ultimate reality. The testimony of the facts is unanimous. They all call us to believe, love, and worship the covenant Lord.

Things and events are marinated in implications about their origins, design, legitimacy, coherence, sustenance, purpose, and future. Someone may ask how a remote fact, isolated from its larger context, reveals or proves God. The answer is that you can give up that covenantal context in theory or principle, but you cannot void it in practice. Everyone remains in relation to God as either a covenant-keeper or a covenant-breaker. As such, everyone needs him and depends on him, whether thankfully or thanklessly. In view of what is manifest by the light of nature, only an act of defiance against God can ignore what creation and providence display about him. You have to suppress the meaning of the facts—in effect, redefining each one and creating your own world—to miss their connections with the Lord.

Christ's lordship over the facts, over every thought as well as every thing, is the basis of our commitment to a Christian worldview and his lordship over every discipline and vocation. It is also why a Reformed apologetic has the luxury of beginning with any fact in order to investigate and challenge unbelieving systems. Starting with

---

6. Some would charge "naturalistic fallacy," which forbids our deriving obligation ("ought" language) from facts ("is" statements). But in God's creation, the character of reality is such that obligation (and privilege, to mention another covenantal feature) is built into the state of affairs. All things are for God's glory (and our enjoyment of him). Imperatives flow from indicatives.

any fact, the more you discuss it with your unbelieving friend, the more differences will surface, reflecting opposing systems of belief. If time allows and you are true to your biblical convictions, you will find yourself talking more and more about creation, fall, redemption, and consummation in contrast to your friend's unbiblical worldview. Playing out the starkness of that contrast is crucial to a caring and effective apologetic.

Creator above Creation

The confession's reference to the "distance" between the Creator and the creature (7.1) reminds us that God's thoughts and ways are above ours. Unlike us, he is not subject to principles higher than himself.

> The supreme judge by which all controversies of religion are to be determined, and all decrees of councils, opinions of ancient writers, doctrines of men, and private spirits, are to be examined . . . can be no other but the Holy Spirit speaking in the Scripture. (1.10)

"Religion" should not be taken narrowly here. God is supreme judge over all of life and thought. All measures of truth and goodness should be subservient to his Word. If anything is either above or independent of the triune God, something (or someone) else is supreme judge.

Some apologists, while not purporting to elevate reason above God, deem it necessary to reason *to* him in a way that is not dependent *on* him. While we who are called to renewed minds and reasonable service (Rom. 12:1–2) should of all people be committed to reason, the question is, How can we be sure we reach reasonable conclusions? Without the oversight of Scripture, our best efforts at reasoning soundly can yield false conclusions, such as denying the two natures of Christ, the Trinity, or other biblical mysteries. The problem is not that those doctrines are illogical. They are, in fact, "deduced from Scripture" "by good and necessary consequence" (WCF 1.6).[7] The problem is that logic, like any other gift from God, can be misused, and will be if it is

---

7. C. J. Williams, "Good and Necessary Consequence in the Westminster Confession," in *The Faith Once Delivered*, ed. Anthony T. Selvaggio, The Westminster Assembly and the Reformed Faith (Phillipsburg, NJ: P&R, 2007), 184, 188. Williams observes that the Westminster divines

not in submission to him. Logic is not independent of God. Even when used in unbelief, it is used in debt to the One whose self-consistent, divine nature is its source. Failure to acknowledge that debt does not free reason to sit in judgment of God.

Reason we must. How could we argue with that? The problem is not reason, but autonomous reason. Unless *sola scriptura* governs our discussions of what is reasonable and good, we will treat the supreme judge and covenant Lord like a subordinate, contingent being. The confession will not allow that: "There is but one only, living, and true God," among whose perfections is that he is "most wise, most holy, most free, most absolute" (2.1).

When an unbeliever comes to faith, she does so because she has been convinced of compelling reasons to believe. Yet she is not an autonomous judge granting that biblical claims measure up to her terms. Whether or not she uses words like *precondition* or *presupposition*, she now acknowledges dependence on God, whereas previously his existence and truth were the unacknowledged preconditions for thought and life itself, even her ability to argue against him. She comes to the conviction that Scripture speaks with authority from on high, that it scrutinizes her, and that the question is not whether she will accept God, but whether—and how—a holy judge would ever accept her.

We sometimes say that meaning and truth "presuppose" God and that we, for that reason, should consciously presuppose him too. But that term can be confusing because of its temporal and fideistic connotations, as if belief comes before and without reasons or evidence. Those connotations can distract us from the role of biblical truths, categories, and definitions *in* dialogue and persuasion. Nonetheless, building our lives, our thoughts, and our arguments on God's authority *is* the sensible thing to do. He *is* "the supreme judge." He *has* revealed himself in nature and Scripture to be "most wise." We represent him most faithfully—and most cogently—when we present him as the one who holds "all the treasures of wisdom and knowledge" (Col. 2:3).

---

considered "skill in logick and philosophy" a requirement for ordination, according to the Form of Church Government (p. 180).

The Persons Involved in Apologetics

The covenantal context of apologetics clarifies the persons involved in any apologetic encounter and, implicitly, their roles. There is the clearly revealed covenant Lord, opposed by the covenant-breaker. The apologist, in himself a covenant-breaker, is now by grace Christ's ambassador, with a ministry of reconciliation.

Though apologetics is ostensibly an encounter between believer and unbeliever, it is more importantly an encounter between covenant Lord and covenant-breaker. The object of apologetics is to reintroduce people to the God they refuse to see, in places they refuse to see him. We live and move and have our being not in a random, impersonal environment. There is a basis for human personhood and dignity, for purpose and value, for beauty and creativity, for love and community, for unity amid diversity—the tripersonal God (LC 9–11) who is there, and here, and in whose image we are made (17).

Apologetics is about inviting people to look into the face of this absolute, personal God. It dares them to see him for who he is and what he means for the world. It calls them to meet the Creator and covenant Lord on his holy and gracious terms.

The Noetic Effects

The light of revelation is never dim. We are. In clear view of God's stunning self-disclosure in nature and Scripture, sinners suppress the truth. The confession, often quoting Scripture, uses strong language to describe human depravity, including its effects on our thinking. Each of us possesses a "corrupted nature" (WCF 6.3). This "original corruption" leaves us "utterly indisposed, disabled, and made opposite to all good, and wholly inclined to all evil" (6.4; cf. LC 25). "Man, by his fall into a state of sin, hath wholly lost all ability of will to any spiritual good" (WCF 9.3). "By nature we and all men are not only utterly unable and unwilling to know and do the will of God, but prone to rebel against his word, to repine and murmur against his providence, and wholly inclined to do the will of the flesh, and of the devil" (LC 192). The inward effects of our sinfulness include "blindness of mind, a reprobate sense, strong delusions, hardness of heart, horror of conscience, and vile affections" (LC 28).

Considering all that unbelievers know, some apologists describe the effects of sin on the mind as indirect. "Something is wrong with the heart—not the mind."[8] "The mind itself is not reprobate."[9] It becomes darkened indirectly, through the influence of a totally depraved heart.[10]

The heart is indeed desperately wicked and, as the center of our being, wreaks moral havoc throughout us. But it would be wrong to cast the mind as a reluctant victim of the heart. Total depravity is total-person depravity. It cuts through all aspects of our being, not between them. "Mind," "sense," "heart," "conscience," and "affections" are all implicated in question 28. The person as a unit misuses all his abilities. They conspire against the truth. While sin compounds sin, resulting in further "punishments," such as deeper folly and greater hardening of hearts, there is never a time when our minds are unpolluted by original corruption. Nor is there a marginally affected compartment of our makeup. The list of effects under question 28 allows for no noetic immunity.

The confession is emphatic: "By this sin they ["our first parents" (6.1)] fell from their original righteousness and communion with God, and so became dead in sin, and wholly defiled in all the faculties and parts of soul and body" (6.2).[11] This whole defilement includes the minds of socially good, kind, reasonable people. Even model citizens fall far short of the glory of God on the heart level; and even the minds of brilliant, overtly sensible people suffer serious corruption. While total depravity does not imply that we are as evil as we could be, it does mean that we are corrupt through and through. It measures the extent of defilement, not the degree.

If depravity were total in degree, it would mean the *destruction* of all our faculties. But the theological (and apologetic) options are not a destroyed mind versus a properly functioning mind. The mind, along with soul and body, is "wholly defiled" without being nonfunctional. It functions often with great, God-given, powers. Tragically, those

8. R. C. Sproul, John H. Gerstner, and Arthur Lindsley, *Classical Apologetics* (Grand Rapids, MI: Zondervan, 1984), 242.

9. Ibid., 244.

10. Ibid., 243.

11. The confession's proof texts include references to the mind, "every imagination of the thoughts of [the] heart," and understanding.

cognitive powers are dedicated to denying, distorting, and displacing God and his truth. The knowledge of God that unbelievers retain (and must continually suppress) and the outward good that they do can be credited both to the clarity of revelation and to God's merciful restraint of the degree of human depravity. But all the unbeliever's good, all his motives, all his knowledge is compromised—mixed with idolatry—because all his faculties are employed toward ends other than the chief end of glorifying and enjoying God (LC 1).

It is difficult to describe how the unregenerate know (Rom. 1:19, 21, 32), see (v. 20), and understand (v. 20) the things of God at the same time they do *not* know (1 Cor. 1:21), see (Acts 28:26–27), or understand (Acts 28:26; Rom. 3:11; 1 Cor. 2:14) them. The solution is not to be found in regarding the carnal mind or intellect as a less tainted, truth-seeking cognitive faculty. Fallen humanity is not only "utterly indisposed . . . to all good" (WCF 6.4) and "unwilling to know," but "utterly unable . . . to know" God's will (LC 192). People suffer from an "utter inability and indisposition . . . to honour God aright" (LC 190).

If the whole person as a heart-mind-soul-and-strength complex is involved in suppressing the truth, then it is unwise to isolate one aspect as a relatively faithful terminal for accessing that suppressed truth. While minds are not destroyed by the fall, neither are hearts and consciences eradicated so that there is no point in talking with people. Because the whole person is in tension with realities he or she constantly struggles to suppress, the whole person is vulnerable to biblically shaped rational, aesthetic, and moral appeals and challenges. We may (and must) employ reasons of the heart as well as mind to connect with what is known but repressed.

Faith Comes by Hearing

Reformed apologists agree that only the internal work of the Holy Spirit can turn the heart and renew the mind, making a person "willing and able to believe" (WCF 7.3). Concurring with the confession, they would "acknowledge the inward illumination of the Spirit of God to be necessary for the saving understanding of such things as are revealed in the Word" (1.6). The doubter, "being quickened and renewed by the Holy Spirit . . . is thereby enabled to answer [God's] call" (10.2).

Given far less play in discussions of apologetics is that the Spirit works with and through Scripture.

The Spirit with the Word

The Westminster fathers never tired of describing the Spirit's use of the Word to change people profoundly. No fewer than eighteen times the confession and catechism credit Word and Spirit together with transforming unbelievers into people of faith. "The grace of faith, whereby the elect are enabled to believe to the saving of their souls, is the work of the Spirit of Christ in their hearts; and is ordinarily wrought by the ministry of the Word" (WCF 14.1).[12] God effectually calls his chosen people "by His Word and Spirit . . . enlightening their minds spiritually and savingly to understand the things of God" (10.1; see also LC 67). When justifying faith is "wrought in the heart of a sinner by the Spirit and word of God," the sinner is "convinced of his sin and misery, and . . . not only assenteth to the truth of the promise of the gospel, but receiveth and resteth upon Christ" (LC 72). Repentance is "wrought in the heart of a sinner by the Spirit and word," giving him "sight and sense, not only of the danger, but also of the filthiness and odiousness of his sins . . ." (LC 76).

These and other passages in the standards tell of the Spirit's use of the Word to convict, enlighten minds, give sight and sense, produce understanding, and persuade (WCF 1.5, 8.8; LC 4). The Word (read or proclaimed) is the Spirit's surgical instrument of choice, his "effectual means of enlightening, convincing, and humbling sinners" (LC 155).

Word content is indispensable for answering disbelief. "The light of nature and the works of creation and providence" are "not sufficient to give that knowledge of God and of His will, which is necessary unto salvation" (WCF 1.1). God's "word and Spirit only do sufficiently and effectually reveal him unto men for their salvation" (LC 2). The Word

---

12. The word "ordinarily" marks this as a rule, to which 10.3 is the exception: "Elect infants, dying in infancy, are regenerated, and saved by Christ through the Spirit, who worketh when, and where, and how He pleaseth: so also, are all other elect persons who are uncapable of being outwardly called by the ministry of the Word." "Uncapable" in this exceptional setting reminds us that an important cognitive function normally remains despite the noetic effects.

is the full and final revelation, "the supreme judge" over all our decisions and beliefs (WCF 1.10). "The whole counsel of God concerning all things necessary for His own glory, man's salvation, faith, and life, is either expressly set down in Scripture, or by good and necessary consequence may be deduced from Scripture" (1.6). There is no area of thought or life—including our perceptions, our understanding of what is reasonable, and our moral judgments—that does not need and is not answerable to the Word. It is "the only rule of faith and obedience" (LC 3). Even matters "ordered by the light of nature" are to be governed by "the general rules of the Word, which are always to be observed" (WCF 1.6).

Consider the Source

But don't people need reasons to believe the Bible before they can accept its rule? Shouldn't they first be persuaded that the Bible is credible?

People do (ordinarily) need reasons (such as in WCF 1.5 and LC 4), but the confession describes the ultimate reason first:

> The authority of the Holy Scripture, for which it ought to be believed and obeyed, dependeth not upon the testimony of any man, or Church; but wholly upon God (who is truth itself) the author thereof: and therefore it is to be received because it is the Word of God. (1.4)

Here is the consummate challenge to autonomous thinking. We should believe and receive the Word because it is the Word *of God*. The authority of Scripture depends on its Author. Though this confessional point may seem hopelessly circular, it is far from hopeless, though it is unavoidably circular. Just as there is no one greater by whom God can swear (so that "he swore by himself," Heb. 6:13), there is no higher authority to which we or God can appeal. Nor is there greater reason. The Author himself, "who is truth itself," is reason enough for people to receive and believe what he says.

This will strike some as naive or unfair—the unpardonable sin among logical fallacies, *petitio principii*. We would never allow self-authentication in other connections. What is different about this one?

God.

The confession's rationale for receiving Scripture is a ringing proclamation of the uniqueness of the Creator. Though in one sense we and God do the same thing when we both appeal to the highest authority to settle matters, the similarity stops at the distinction between him and everything else. *We* must appeal to principles and criteria independent of ourselves. But when God cites a principle, he is the ground for that principle. And when he appeals to the highest authority, he *is* that highest authority. He *must* appeal to himself. To object to his self-attestation is to disqualify God *for being God*. It is to rule out the notion of deity itself. And to object to circular arguments in defense of God is to say in effect, "I will accept (or defend) only a god who functions as less than the ultimate authority, and a system of belief that is less than coherent and unique." That is exactly what the nonbeliever does, thereby exchanging the one true foundation of reason and truth for a god of his own invention.

What distinguishes the Bible's circular argument from those we would readily dismiss as fallacious? What makes this claim to divine authorship unique? You meet the God of the Word in this Word. There you find someone who teaches with authority, not as mere men (Matt. 7:29). It is "the authority of God Himself speaking therein" (WCF 14.2). "The scriptures manifest themselves to be the word of God, by," among other things, "their light and power to convince and convert sinners" (LC 4).

Apologetics is intensely *about* God and *of* God. He is making a case through his Word and by his Spirit. The Word is not only the body of truth eventually received and believed. It is the "light and power" the Spirit uses to revolutionize perceptions of what is good and true. Conviction, persuasion, enlightened minds, new sight and sense, understanding—all these come via the Word.

Revelation Instead of Reason?

This may seem to reduce apologetics to making assertions. But the Westminster Confession by no means disparages reason, common sense (29.6), and evidence for believing the Word.

We may be moved and induced by the testimony of the Church to a high and reverent esteem of the Holy Scripture. And the heavenliness of the matter, the efficacy of the doctrine, the majesty of the style, the consent of all the parts, the scope of the whole (which is, to give all glory to God), the full discovery it makes of the only way of man's salvation, the many other incomparable excellencies, and the entire perfection thereof, are arguments whereby it doth abundantly evidence itself to be the Word of God. . . . (1.5)

To this endorsement of arguments we could add a wide range of evidences involving nature, history, moral conscience, teleology, human creativity, and so on. The evidence truly is abundant. But the confession continues:

. . . yet notwithstanding, our full persuasion and assurance of the infallible truth and divine authority thereof, is from the inward work of the Holy Spirit bearing witness by and with the Word in our hearts. (1.5; see also LC 4)

The confession seems at first to contrast the grounds for partial and full persuasion: evidence and arguments versus Word and Spirit. But reason and revelation should not be sharply separated here. Even the evidence assumes scriptural definitions. "The heavenliness of the matter, the efficacy of the doctrine, the majesty of the style, the consent of all the parts, the scope of the whole (which is, to give all glory to God)" all find their meaning in the theology of the Word itself. Whether the evidence appears in the Word or in the world, it calls for the Christ-centered interpretive framework of special revelation and thereby directs us to the One whom sinners try to erase from their worldview. The point is not only that spiritual persuasion lies beyond our powers of argument, being fundamentally a matter of the heart and requiring an inward supernatural transformation. Most significantly for apologetics, the Spirit does this inward work by means of the very Word in question.

Widening the Circle

Scripture is its own defender, but that does not mean that we should merely quote verses about biblical authority. We need not choose between developing full, rich, varied arguments for the faith and expressing what the Bible says, or between arguing from general revelation and arguing from special revelation. A wise apologist finds effective avenues to convey—humbly, mercifully, confidently, charitably—what the Bible says in various connections within a Christian worldview.

Because that worldview is comprehensive under the lordship of Christ, any topic, any thing, any event, offers a starting point. The more we reflect on and *live* life before the unbeliever, handle evidence, draw inferences from premises, respond to objections, and measure our agreement—that is, the more we engage in argument—the more we should find ourselves running into and reflecting upon the biblical truths of creation, fall, redemption, and consummation—the gospel. What is efficacious about this circular argument is not its formal structure but its personal content. Anybody can talk in circles. But this Word—because it is God's Word—has power to raise the dead, change hearts, open ears and eyes, and renew minds.

Revelation guides and informs reason. It fills out the logic of self-attestation with multidimensional portrayals of God in his relationship to all things. It gives definition to the terms we discuss when we set forth theistic proofs or say with the confession (1.5) that the Word ought to be believed and received because it is the Word of God. It turns a tight circle of reason into a wide orbit of truth viewing the many facets of God's character and his marvelous acts throughout space and time, culminating in his Son. Tight circles are in effect tight-lipped circles. They don't say enough unless their terms are understood. Arguments for the faith afford opportunities to play out implications of belief in contrast to the implications of unbelief, to paint two radically contrasting pictures of the world—one in reconciliation with the covenant Lord, and the other mired in the unlivable consequences of covenant rebellion.

Thy Word Have I Hid?

We have every reason to reason, but not apart from the definitions and priorities of Scripture. The catechism implicitly warns us not to withhold biblical truth when we have the opportunity to express it. "The duties required in the first commandment" include "the knowing and acknowledging of God to be the only true God, and . . . being zealous for him"(LC 104). Among "the sins forbidden in the first commandment" are "not . . . avouching him for God, and . . . the omission or neglect of any thing due to him," including "slighting . . . God" (105). The ninth commandment requires "clearly, and fully, speaking the truth, and only the truth" (144), and forbids "concealing the truth, undue silence in a just cause . . . doubtful or equivocal expressions" (145). If we argue at length for an undefined theism, do we not run the risk of slighting God, concealing his truth, or seeking to build a case on doubtful, equivocal expressions?

Granted, our case may need to unfold slowly. We do well to ask questions, as Jesus did, and wait patiently, attentively for replies. Eagerness to listen and slowness to speak are themselves evidences of the Lord's presence. They also tell us a great deal about what others believe. Bringing the Word to bear on thought and life from the outset does not mean that we should frontload conversations with our complete systematic theology. We cannot say everything at once, nor should we try. We do have to decide on an order in which to discuss things, and definitions of terms, especially *God*, will take time to fill out, perhaps over many conversations.

But that is not the same thing as hiding or deliberately withholding biblical truths when we have opportunity to express them. The sheer impulse to worship God should compel us to speak of him not merely as an abstract principle, but as the personal, triune God he is (LC 9). In speaking the Word, we give audience to the ultimate apologist, the Spirit of Christ, who as the consummate Prophet, fully reveals his truth; as the great King, overcomes unbelief; and as the great High Priest, reconciles sinners to God.[13]

For Argument's Sake

The world starves for truth without hungering for it. Such is the internal conflict wherein unbelievers depend on a wealth of knowledge just to live in God's world, yet bind the revelatory significance

---

13. WCF 8.1; LC 43–45.

of what they know. The doubter's central convictions severely clash with less-central beliefs uprooted and borrowed from God's truth. Something has to give.

By tracing out, for argument's sake, the logic of unbelief, we can help people to see that their presuppositions cannot account for the truth, reason, and morality they need. And if they will follow the logic of belief, for argument's sake, they may well discover that it leads them home to what they know deep down to be true. In the first case we connect with God's truth that is borrowed in order to show its debt to God's truth that is suppressed. In the second case we build on what is suppressed to show what borrowed and twisted truths look like when returned to their proper foundation. Both appeals work from biblical definitions and call for a biblical worldview to make sense of things.

Godless commitments form a holding cell in which the truth is incarcerated. When we find a semblance of agreement with the unbeliever's borrowed truths, how do we know that we are building on the truth and not on truth-repressing convictions? We make contact with suppressed truth when we say what Scripture says. Suppressed truths resonate to the voice of God in Scripture, thus intensifying the epistemic tension within the doubter. It is the Word and Spirit that shake the prison walls in which the doubter seeks to hold every thought captive, until, like the Philippian jailer, he asks, "What must I do to be saved?" (Acts 16:30). Ironically, our message must conflict with the core commitments of the unbeliever to make a connection with the knowledge he possesses. What brings true peace to a conflicted heart is the very thing the doubter lacks: a biblical view of reality—most of all, of God.

While our reasoning is obviously fallible, it is not a mark of humility to suggest that the Christian faith may actually be false. When, for argument's sake, Paul explores the implications of a hypothetical nonresurrection (1 Cor. 15), he never hints that Jesus may in fact still be in the ground or that our faith may be useless. Paul reasons from disbelief to futility, not in order to build on false premises, but in order to replace them. In so doing, he declares emphatically what the resurrection means and why it is necessary. His argument and his apostolic proclamation are inseparable.

Humbly Using Means of Grace

Nevertheless, true humility recognizes our own weakness and depends prayerfully on the Word and Spirit for results. We find pointed reminders of that in the catechism's instructions on preaching (see LC 159), Scripture reading (see 157), and prayer. Though I can only summarize them here, they deserve exploration in reference to our method and manner in apologetics.

We may confidently express the truths of Scripture "plainly, not in the enticing words of man's wisdom, but in demonstration of the Spirit, and of power; faithfully, making known the whole counsel of God," according to "the necessities and capacities of the hearers" (159), "with a firm persuasion that they are the very word of God, and that he only can enable us to understand them" (157). When we pray for God's name to be hallowed, we acknowledge "the utter inability and indisposition that is in ourselves and all men to honour God aright," and our own need for his grace in order "to know, to acknowledge, and highly to esteem him . . ." (190). And when we ask for his will to be done (192),

> we pray, that God would by his Spirit take away from ourselves and others all blindness, weakness, indisposedness, and perverseness of heart; and by his grace make us able and willing to know, do, and submit to his will in all things, with the like humility, cheerfulness, faithfulness, diligence, zeal, sincerity, and constancy, as the angels do in heaven.

9

Theologia Naturalis

A Reformed Tradition

JEFFREY K. JUE

*I*n his volume introducing systematic theology, Cornelius Van
Til wrote: "If the scholastics, with all their fine distinctions,
had been careful . . . they would not have fallen into the error of
giving as much credit to natural and to rational theology as they did.
Natural and rational theology were never meant to function, even in
paradise, apart from theology proper."[1] This precise statement reveals
an important theological assessment that marks one of Van Til's unique
contributions to contemporary debates regarding apologetic method.
Yet it also introduces Van Til's historical assessment of medieval and
post-Reformation Protestant scholasticism. For Van Til, scholasticism
was too positive in its use of rational or natural theology.

Classical or traditional Reformed apologists, such as R. C. Sproul,
Arthur Lindsley, and the late John Gerstner, would object to this historical criticism, claiming that the scholastic tradition's use of natural
theology as a starting point to engage the unbeliever is legitimate; and

---

1. Cornelius Van Til, *An Introduction to Systematic Theology* (Nutley, NJ: Presbyterian and
Reformed, 1974), 74.

likewise natural theology can provide a foundation from which one can move to supernatural theology. Subsequently, those who follow this traditional Reformed view of apologetics agree with the scholastics and claim that Van Til erred in his understanding of natural theology and its usefulness in the apologetic task. Sproul, Gerstner, and Lindsley argue that natural theology is precisely the point of contact between believers and unbelievers. The unregenerate, for the Reformed traditionalist, still possesses properly functioning rational capacities that are capable of engaging with evidence that demonstrates the verity of Christianity. "We contend that the '"facts" . . . most close at hand' are merely a starting point just because they are the only place at which anyone *can* start. If we do start at that point, we learn from the evidence that surrounds us that there is a God who alone can explain the ultimate meaning of everything."[2]

The traditional Reformed apologist's natural theology engages the unregenerate's reason by appealing to certain "common ground" assumptions. These assumptions include: the validity of the law of contradiction, the validity of the law of causality, and the basic reliability of sense perception.[3] While there have been philosophical challenges to these assumptions, Sproul, Gerstner, and Lindsley maintain that "all denials of these assumptions are forced and temporary."[4] Thus, these assumptions form the basis of a natural theology, which they argue is the proper starting point for Christian apologetics.

Van Til, however, opposes any position that begins with natural or rational theology as a starting point for engaging the unbeliever.[5] Instead, he insists that the function of natural theology must be conditioned always by the wider context of theology proper. This context would identify the function of and relation between natural theology and supernatural theology in the pre- and post-fall environment.[6] Natural and supernatural theologies form "one system of truth," revealed by God, and therefore they imply one another. In Van Til's terms, they are

2. R. C. Sproul, John H. Gerstner, and Arthur Lindsley, *Classical Apologetics* (Grand Rapids, MI: Zondervan, 1984), 215.

3. Ibid., 72.

4. Ibid.

5. Cornelius Van Til, *The Defense of the Faith*, 3rd ed. (Philadelphia: Presbyterian and Reformed, 1967), 114–22.

6. Van Til, *An Introduction to Systematic Theology*, 74.

"limiting concepts of one another."[7] As such, in the pre-fall state, natural theology and supernatural theology confronted Adam immediately and at every point with the knowledge of God as Creator and covenantal Lord. Subsequently Adam's reason functioned in paradise with this presupposition, and he was able to interpret his world correctly.[8] With the introduction of sin, this presupposition was abandoned and the functions of natural and supernatural theologies were radically altered. In the post-fall state, for Van Til, man lost the ability to rightly interpret not only supernatural theology, but natural theology as well.[9]

Van Til is not saying, as some have misinterpreted him, that the unbeliever knows nothing; with Calvin, he sees the distinction concerning the natural man's knowledge as "not primarily one of territory; his [Calvin's] distinction is primarily that of a blurred and wholly unsatisfactory knowledge on the part of the non-regenerate man and the true knowledge of the regenerate man."[10] In the post-fall state, natural theology still teaches the truth about God, who is both Creator and covenantal Lord, but now that knowledge is misinterpreted by rebellious creatures, who deny and suppress that truth.[11] Consequently, for Van Til, fallen man cannot possess a true natural theology, and thus it cannot provide a satisfactory starting point to engage the unbeliever.[12]

Natural Theology: A Historical Misunderstanding?

The purpose of this chapter is not to debate the specific merits of either Van Til's or the Reformed traditional apologists' methods

7. Ibid.

8. Van Til writes, "In paradise, man made his self-consciousness the immediate but wholly derivative starting point while he made the self-consciousness of God the remote but wholly ultimate starting point of all his knowledge. Hence he saw that his knowledge was, though finite, yet true. Hence he did not set before himself the false ideal of absolute comprehension. Hence, too, he did not despair and conclude to irrationalism simply because he himself could not fully comprehend the whole of reality." Ibid., 70.

9. Ibid., 75.

10. Ibid., 82.

11. Van Til's reading of Rom. 1 is crucial in arguing this point: "Paul assures us in Romans that all men know God. . . . All men at bottom know that theism is the only true interpretation of life. But it is precisely this knowledge which they do their best to repress in the actual self-conscious efforts that they make at interpreting human experience. And it is of these systems of their own interpretation that we speak when we say that men are as wrong in their interpretation of trees as in their interpretation of God." Ibid., 84.

12. Van Til, *The Defense of the Faith*, 94–95.

or conclusions. Instead we will assess historically the specific topic of natural theology in relation to the Protestant Reformed tradition. The traditional Reformed apologists claim that their view has historical precedence dating back to medieval and Protestant scholasticism, and continued by the Old School Presbyterian tradition of Princeton Seminary. Moreover it seems that Van Til agrees with the Reformed traditionalists' reading of historical theology, since he is critical of both scholasticism and Old Princeton.[13] Both traditional Reformed apologists and Van Til assume that scholasticism taught a positive use of natural theology, whereby a positive knowledge of God was available through human reason.

Of course, Sproul and others commend this use of natural theology, while Van Til condemns it. In their historical evaluations neither the traditional Reformed apologists nor Van Til distinguish between medieval and post-Reformation Protestant scholastics.[14] This is a costly historical error on the part of both camps, with significant implications. It is worth pointing out that this reading of scholasticism by Van Til and the traditional Reformed apologists was shared by the most unlikely theological bedfellows.

Surprisingly, Barthian historians likewise have followed this interpretation of Protestant scholasticism. In his debate with Emil Brunner in 1934, Karl Barth argued that Thomistic and scholastic influences led to the development of a rationalistic natural theology.[15] Subsequently Barth claimed it was the Protestant scholastics who revised Calvin's theology into a pre-enlightenment rational theology.[16] Following Barth, Ernst Bizer and Paul Althaus contended that this seventeenth-century scholastic theology separated natural knowledge from saving knowledge of God, and that it is possible to know God apart from Scripture and soteriology.[17] In fact, the Barthian historians

13. Ibid., 79–89, 261–66.
14. "That knowledge which Augustine, Anselm, and the early and late Scholastics (the Protestant scholastics included) confidently affirmed, Van Til as confidently rejects." Sproul, Gerstner, and Lindsley, *Classical Apologetics*, 259.
15. Emil Brunner and Karl Barth, *Natural Theology: Comprising "Nature and Grace,"* trans. Peter Fraenkel (London: G. Bles The Centenary Press, 1946), 101–10.
16. Ibid., 105.
17. Ernst Bizer, *Früorthodoxie und Rationalismus* (Zürich: EVZ-Verlag, 1963); Paul Althaus, *Die Prinzipien der Deutschen Reformierten Dogmatik im Zeitalter der Asritotelischen Scholastik* (Leipzig: Deichert, 1914).

claimed that the scholastics taught that natural knowledge functions independently and serves as the foundation for special revelation. Thus, "the gradual development of natural theology and the positive use of reason in post-Reformation Reformed theology represented a turn towards Enlightenment rationalism."[18] It seems that Van Til and the traditional Reformed apologists are not alone in their reading of Protestant scholasticism.

In his dictionary of theological terms drawn from Protestant scholastic theology, Richard Muller writes:

> *Theologia naturalis* can know of God as the highest good . . . and it can know of the end of man in God on the basis of perfect obedience to the natural law. . . . It is therefore insufficient to save man but sufficient to leave him without excuse in his sins. The Protestant orthodox include virtually no natural theology in their systems and never view natural theology, human reason, or the light of nature as a foundation upon which revealed theology can build.[19]

This succinct definition of natural theology according to the Protestant scholastics bears little resemblance to the caricature of scholasticism presented by either Van Til or traditional Reformed apologists like Sproul, Gerstner, and Lindsley. Muller claims that the Protestant scholastics did not grant a priority to natural theology or human reason; in fact, he contends that they had "virtually no natural theology." If Muller is correct, then Van Til and the Reformed traditionalists have misread and consequently misrepresented aspects of the history of scholasticism, particularly the significant period of Reformed orthodoxy in the seventeenth century. In order to provide some clarity to this historical confusion, it will be necessary to reexamine the intellectual context of the post-Reformation period and carefully reconstruct the Protestant scholastic understanding of natural theology by reviewing the writings of seventeenth-century theologians.

18. Willem J. van Asselt, "The Fundamental Meaning of Theology: Archetypal and Ectypal Theology in Seventeenth-Century Reformed Thought," *Westminster Theological Journal* 64 (2002): 320.
19. Richard A. Muller, *Dictionary of Latin and Greek Theological Terms: Drawn Principally from Protestant Scholastic Theology* (Grand Rapids, MI: Baker, 1985), 302.

The Scholastic Context: A Rational Culprit?

Before looking at the individual theologians, it is important to address a fundamental question. What is scholasticism? The answer to this important question will provide the necessary background for examining the topic of natural theology. Previous Reformation and post-Reformation historians operated with the premise that scholasticism was intrinsically rationalistic.[20] According to these historians the influence of Greek philosophy, particularly Aristotle, on Christian theology in the medieval and post-Reformation period was thought to have produced a theological school that prioritized the use of human reason. Writing about the seventeenth century, Brian Armstrong says:

> But the question remains, What specific effects did this scholasticism have upon Reformed theology? While it produced profound alterations in some of Calvin's doctrinal teachings, perhaps the most significant result was a change in methodology. . . . No longer was the primary approach the analytic and inductive, but rather the synthetic and deductive. . . . This approach was, then, primarily interested in the logical explanation of the source of theology.[21]

Armstrong is committed to a particular historiography that insists upon a dramatic discontinuity in the development of Reformed theology from the early Reformers of the sixteenth century, like John Calvin, to the Protestant scholastics of the late sixteenth and seventeenth centuries.[22] And the reason for the discontinuity between the early Reformation and the post-Reformation was precisely the influx of scholasticism and its uncritical appropriation of Aristotle's logic. For Armstrong, and other historians, the use of scholasticism

20. Richard A. Muller, *After Calvin: Studies in the Development of a Theological Tradition* (Oxford: Oxford University Press, 2003), 81–82.

21. Brian G. Armstrong, *Calvinism and the Amyraut Heresy: Protestant Scholasticism and Humanism in Seventeenth-Century France* (Madison: University of Wisconsin Press, 1969), 136.

22. For additional studies following this historiography, see Basil Hall, "Calvin against the Calvinist," in *John Calvin: A Collection of Distinguished Essays*, ed. Gervase Duffield (Grand Rapids, MI: Eerdmans, 1966), 23–27; R. T. Kendall, *Calvin and English Calvinism to 1649* (New York: Oxford University Press, 1979).

shaped the form and content of Protestant theology, and the results of his assessment produced the "Calvin versus the Calvinists" historical model. This historiographical definition of scholasticism is consistent with both Van Til's and the traditional Reformed apologists' comments about the state of Protestant theology in the seventeenth century. This suggests that Van Til, Sproul, Gerstner, and Lindsley were influenced equally by this historiographical reading of scholasticism.

Since the publications of Armstrong and others, studies in the history of Protestant scholasticism have undergone a massive revision. Newer studies attempt to examine seventeenth-century scholasticism within its intellectual-cultural context.[23] What has emerged is an assessment of Protestant scholasticism that exemplifies both continuity and discontinuity with its medieval and Reformation past. Carl Trueman and R. S. Clark write:

> The theologies of the Reformation and post-Reformation era are neither wholly continuous nor wholly discontinuous with the past—they are, rather changes in direction within the wider Augustinian, anti-Pelagian tradition of Western theology. As such, the era of orthodoxy must not be set over against its past but must be studied in the context of its medieval and Reformation roots.[24]

What are the lines of continuity and discontinuity between the post-Reformation and its medieval and Reformation roots? While post-Reformation theologians can be described accurately as scholastics, this use of scholasticism did not produce a rationalistic Protestant theology that broke with the content of the early Reformers. A close examination of scholasticism, both in its medieval and post-Reformation forms, reveals a method for structuring and ordering theological categories and not an Aristotelian system for propagating a particular rationalistic content.

23. See Richard A. Muller, *Post-Reformation Reformed Dogmatics: The Rise and Development of Reformed Orthodoxy, Ca. 1520 to Ca. 1725*, 4 vols. (Grand Rapids, MI: Baker, 2003); Carl R. Trueman and R. S. Clark, eds., *Protestant Scholasticism: Essays in Reassessment* (Carlisle, Cumbria: Paternoster, 1999); Willem van Asselt and Eef Dekker, eds., *Reformation and Scholasticism* (Grand Rapids, MI: Baker, 2001).

24. Trueman and Clark, *Protestant Scholasticism*, xiv.

In his seminal work on post-Reformation theology, Richard Muller writes:

> The term "scholasticism" can be applied to a theology that is not a duplication of medieval scholastic teaching and method, that is distinctly Protestant, and that is not nearly as concerned to draw philosophy into dialogue with theology as the great synthetic works of the thirteenth century. Scholasticism, then, indicates the technical and logical approach to theology as a discipline characteristic of theological system from the late twelfth through seventeenth century. Since scholasticism is primarily a method or approach to academic disciplines, it is not necessarily allied to any particular philosophical perspective, nor does it represent a systematic attachment to or concentration upon any particular doctrine or concept as a key to theological system. This latter point has always been clear with respect to medieval scholasticism, but it needs to be made just as decisively with regard to Protestant scholasticism.[25]

What Muller is describing is the movement of Protestant theology in the seventeenth century from the period of the initial Reformation to the era of institutional Protestantism. The seventeenth century witnessed the rise of the first Protestant universities and the accompanying need to construct a full academic Protestant curriculum to be taught to succeeding generations. This need was met by the reintroduction of a scholastic method used by Protestant professors to construct a "school theology." This was an attempt, not to alter radically the content of Reformed theology, but to provide "a theology designed to develop system on a highly technical level and in an extremely precise manner by means of the careful identification of topics, divisions of these topics into their basic parts, definition of parts, and doctrinal or logical argumentation concerning the divisions and definitions."[26] As a method, scholasticism can be and was applied to other academic disciplines. Consequently, the use of a scholastic method did not shape the content of the theology being taught, but only its pedagogical form. Of course the Protestant scholastic theology itself demonstrated differences with

25. Muller, *Post-Reformation Reformed Dogmatics: Prolegomena to Theology* (Grand Rapids, MI: Baker, 1987), 37.
26. Ibid., 34.

the medieval scholastics. Nonetheless seventeenth-century Protestant scholastics were attempting to maintain the theological heritage of the early Reformation. Muller elaborates:

> Where the Reformers painted with a broad brush, their . . . scholastic successors strove to fill in the details of the picture. Whereas the Reformers were intent upon distancing themselves and their theology from problematic elements in medieval thought and, at the same time, remaining catholic in the broadest sense of that term, the Protestant [scholastics] were intent upon establishing systematically the normative, catholic character of institutionalized Protestantism, at times through explicit use of those elements in patristic and medieval theology not at odds with the teachings of the Reformation.[27]

This new historiography, begun by Richard Muller and others, concludes that the seventeenth century built upon the theology of the Reformation by codifying and systematizing that theology. Scholasticism was not defined by a single dogma or a foundation of rationalism.

If it is the case that scholasticism should be defined as a method used to organize theological doctrines, and not as the content of the doctrines, then all of the specific loci of Protestant scholastic theology must be studied accordingly with this definition in mind. Likewise determining the use of natural theology within the context of Protestant scholasticism should not be preconditioned by rationalistic assumptions. It is the intent of this chapter to test the revised historiographical approach to scholasticism by examining the definition and function of natural theology in the works of Protestant scholastics.

Natural Theology and Theological Prolegomena

The place to begin our examination of natural theology is with the Protestant scholastic discussions of theological prolegomena. While the writings of the early Reformers for the most part addressed key theological issues, the seventeenth-century Reformed theologians began producing complete Protestant systematic theologies, covering the traditional loci. Understanding issues of prolegomena was extremely

---

27. Ibid., 37.

important for this project. Reformed theologians began by defining the fundamental principles of theology, which included the task of theology and its parts and divisions. Willem van Asselt writes:

> In their prolegomena the Reformed thinkers explicitly set out the premises, presuppositions, or principles of their system of thought and provided an interpretative paradigm. One of the fundamental issues in the prolegomena of the Reformed orthodox systems was the meaning and usage of the term "theology," its parts and divisions, genus, subject and object.[28]

Although it was being taught as a subject in the universities, theology, unlike other disciplines, was not pursued for intellectual gain alone. The study of theology was pursued for wisdom (*sapientia*), which included "things to be believed and things to be done."[29] Likewise it was carefully defined in terms of its various parts and divisions.

Understanding the parts and divisions of theology constructed by Protestant scholastic theologians will help us clarify their understanding of the place and use of natural theology. Van Asselt points out that Francis Junius (1545–1602) was one of the first Protestant scholastics to introduce a twofold division in his theological prolegomena.[30] Junius was a professor of theology at the University of Leiden. His comments on prolegomena are found in his work *De Theologia Vera* (1594).[31] Junius's divisions became a standard method for structuring the subcategories of theology used by Protestant scholastics in the seventeenth century.[32]

First, Junius distinguished between true theology and false theology. False theology was pagan or gentile theology that was nothing more than opinion, which was found in the mind and replaced the truth for dreams and mockeries.[33] This false theology contained no religious

28. Van Asselt, "The Fundamental Meaning of Theology," 321.

29. Ibid., 327.

30. Ibid., 321.

31. Franciscus Junius, *De Theologia Vera: Ortu, Natura, Formis, Partibus, et Modo* (Lugduni Batavorum: Ex officina Plantiniana, apud Franciscum Raphelengium, 1594).

32. This division can be found in the work of Johann Heinrich Alsted, Francis Turretin, Johannes Cocceius, and others. See van Asselt, "The Fundamental Meaning of Theology," 323.

33. Junius, *De Theologia Vera*, i. Muller writes, "Theologia falsa is a depraved judgment of the soul, falsehood posing as truth, vain and erratic opinion concerning divine powers . . . , ignorance

truth and produced nothing but rational errors. Those who engaged
in false theology included pagan philosophers, non-Christian religions,
and Christian heretics. While there did exist a natural theology under
the category of false theology, it had no positive benefit because it contained no religious truth. Consequently false natural theology provided
no common ground or foundation for establishing true theology.

Conversely, for Junius, true theology was both the knowledge and
wisdom of divine things. This theology was revealed by God for the
purposes of salvation.[34] Under the topic of true theology, Junius distinguished between what he called archetypal and ectypal theology.[35]
Archetypal theology was the wisdom of God himself. This was not to
be investigated but to be worshiped.[36] Muller writes, "The *theologia
archetypa*, then, is God himself, the identity of self and self-knowledge
in the absolutely and essentially wise God."[37] Ectypal theology was
the wisdom concerning divine things that had been revealed from
the archetype. For Junius archetypal theology was the source of true
theology, and the origin and cause of ectypal theology; but archetypal
theology was never fully grasped by the created recipients of the
ectype.[38] In other words the finite cannot contain the infinite.

Subordinate to ectypal theology were three additional divisions
in Junius's prolegomena. He discussed a theology of union, vision,
and revelation. The theology of union was the theology of the incarnate Christ. The theology of vision was the theology of the saints in
heaven. And finally the theology of revelation was theology given to
the pilgrim who continues on earth. The first two forms of ectypal
theology are not as significant for our purposes, but the third form is
important for understanding the place of natural theology.

Junius again divided ectypal revealed theology, this time into supernatural theology and also natural theology.[39] Supernatural theology

---

of God, fables about divine things. Such is all gentile or pagan theology." Muller, *Prolegomena to
Theology*, 159.

34. Junius, *De Theologia Vera*, i.

35. According to van Asselt this distinction has its origins in Johns Duns Scotus's concepts
of *theologia in se* and *theologia nostra*. See van Asselt, "The Fundamental Meaning of Theology,"
322.

36. Junius, *De Theologia Vera*, iv.

37. Muller, *Prolegomena to Theology*, 231.

38. Junius, *De Theologia Vera*, v.

39. Ibid., viii.

was the salvific knowledge of God given in his Word, while natural theology again was the knowledge of God gained from natural revelation through the use of reason. This seems to suggest a positive use of natural theology. However, it must be emphasized that Junius placed natural theology under ectypal revealed theology. He was describing a true natural theology revealed to and only comprehended by the regenerate person. The unregenerate's natural theology fell under the division of false theology. Muller explains, "As indicated by the Reformed orthodox paradigm of true and false, archetypal and ectypal theology, the true, ectypal *theologia naturalis* is founded not on the interaction of reason in general with the natural order . . . but on the examination of natural revelation by faithful reason."[40] Junius demonstrated a thorough Protestant Reformed approach by defining true natural theology as only available to the one who was able to exercise "faithful reason."

What are the implications for this understanding of natural theology in the context of Protestant scholastic theological prolegomena? Immediately we can see that the Protestant scholastics distinguished two forms of natural theology. The first is an ectypal revealed natural theology that is available to the regenerate and always must be discussed in subordination to supernatural theology. The second is the natural theology of the unbeliever. This is relegated to the category of false theology and has no positive religious value. Van Asselt summarizes:

> Natural theology is seen by Junius and his Reformed colleagues as belonging to the category of revealed theology and it is not used as a separate and independent source of knowledge. What is more, in the Reformed archetype-ectype paradigm, a clear distinction has been made between two totally different forms of natural theology which are so often confused in the literature: a pagan form of natural theology and a Christian form of natural theology. . . . Therefore, the modern attacks upon the Reformed distinction between natural and supernatural theology as being an inroad to the rationalism of the (early) Enlightenment rest upon a fundamental misinterpretation of the distinction insofar as natural theology is not viewed by the mod-

40. Muller, *Prolegomena to Theology*, 282; also see Junius, *De Theologia Vera*, xiv.

ern critics as a form of revealed theology or as distinct from the false natural theology of pagans. In other words, the bifurcation in Reformed theology made by the older scholarship between an independent positive locus of natural theology isolated from the revelation of the triune God and soteriology does not stand.[41]

Van Asselt has in mind the misinterpretation of Barthian scholars, but his comments are equally appropriate for others who assumed the same interpretation of Protestant scholastic natural theology.

Francis Turretin and the Role of Natural Theology

Returning to Muller's definition of natural theology, why does he state that the Protestant scholastics had "virtually no natural theology"?[42] We have observed the location of natural theology within the scholastics divisions, but did the scholastics cease to move beyond the basic prolegomena divisions? Within the discussion of prolegomena it seems that natural theology, as considered under false theology, had no positive benefit and it was pointless to investigate any further. False natural theology served only one purpose: it simply left the unregenerate without excuse in their sins.[43] Nevertheless the scholastics were willing to discuss the place of ectypal revealed natural theology, and to carefully distinguish its place within their theology proper.

It will be helpful to examine the work of Francis Turretin (1623–87) on this topic. Turretin was professor of theology in Geneva and renowned for his *Institutes of Elenctic Theology*.[44] In this work Turretin followed the same divisions of theology first set forth by Junius. He placed natural theology under the topic of ectypal revealed theology, but he further distinguished this form of natural theology.[45] Turretin described a natural theology that was "exquisite in Adam before his

41. Van Asselt, "The Fundamental Meaning of Theology," 333.

42. Cf. n. 19.

43. Muller, *Prolegomena to Theology*, 278.

44. François Turrettini, *Institutio Theologiae Elencticae in Qua Status Controversiae Perspicue Exponitur, Praecipua Orthodoxorum Argumenta Proponuntur & Vindicantur, & Fontes Solutionum Aperiuntur* (Genevae: Apud Samuelem de Tournes, 1688).

45. Francis Turretin, *Institutes of Elenctic Theology*, 3 vols., ed. James T. Dennison Jr., trans. George Musgrave Giger (Phillipsburg, NJ: P&R, 1992–97), 1:5.

fall, but is highly disordered in corrupted man."[46] The natural theology that was highly disordered in corrupt man was not the unregenerate's natural theology, since Turretin had clarified already that this division was under the topic of true theology as opposed to false theology. Yet he recognized that the regenerate's natural theology, due to the continual presence of sin, was not identical to the pre-fall natural theology of Adam.

Turretin's discussion of true-ectypal-revealed natural theology must be placed within the context of seventeenth-century theological polemics. In this context Turretin was very concerned about the teachings of the Socinians and Arminians.[47] The Socinians believed that God could not demand of humans that (obedience to his law) which he did not provide (knowledge of the law). Moreover the Arminians contended that natural theology could provide a basis on which supernatural theology could be built.[48] Turretin responded in his typical precise manner to both of these positions. Against the Socinians, Turretin clarified that that "which is sufficient to render inexcusable does not therefore suffice for salvation if used properly; for more things are requisite for the obtainment of salvation than for incurring damnation justly and without excuse."[49] Turretin explained that one act of sin is enough for condemnation, but it requires not just one act of righteousness, but perfect righteousness in order to obtain salvation; and to obtain perfect righteousness requires more than a singular or multiple actions—a change in the very nature of the individual.[50]

Furthermore, Turretin insisted against the Arminians that natural theology served no purpose but to leave individuals inexcusable in their sins. Here we observe a similarity between true and false natural theologies: neither can lead to salvation, yet both teach that God exists and must be worshiped.[51] However, Turretin's Reformed anthropology differentiated between the unregenerate's and regenerate's epistemology and moral ability. This natural knowledge of God left the unregenerate

46. Ibid.
47. For more on this context see John Platt, *Reformed Thought and Scholasticism: The Arguments for the Existence of God in Dutch Theology, 1575–1650* (Leiden: E. J. Brill, 1982).
48. Turretin, *Institutes*, 1:9; Muller, *Prolegomena to Theology*, 279–80.
49. Turretin, *Institutes*, 1:12.
50. Ibid.
51. Ibid., 1:6.

without excuse, but confirmed the truth of revelation for the regenerate.[52] Therefore, for Turretin, the doctrine of natural theology was not
a step toward rationalism, and any positive soteriological benefit that
could be derived is applicable only to the regenerate.

Joseph Mede and the Rational Shift

From the examples of Junius and Turretin, we can assert that
the Protestant scholastic view of natural theology was not inherently
rationalistic, nor did it serve a positive soteriological function for the
unbeliever. Scholasticism was not the rational culprit in the history
of Protestant theology, but historically there was a detectable shift
toward the end of the seventeenth century. The theological history
of Cambridge University illustrates this shift well.

In the late sixteenth and early seventeenth centuries, Cambridge
was considered the citadel of Puritan training. The names of William Perkins, William Ames, and Thomas Goodwin are legendary
for their theological contributions. But lost among this catalog of
notable Cambridge divines is the name Joseph Mede (1586–1638).
Mede was a fellow at Christ's College and was considered one of
the preeminent biblical scholars of his day. His biographer wrote,
"When Foreiners travelling into England came to visit the University
of Cambridge, they would carefully seek him out, and endeavoured
to gain his acquaintance, as much as any others then more eminent
in place."[53] He was most famous for his apocalyptic writings and
greatly influenced the rebirth of millenarianism in the seventeenth
century.[54]

---

52. Muller, *Prolegomena to Theology*, 286.
53. Joseph Mede, *The Works of the Pious and Profoundly-Learned Joseph Mede, B.D. Sometime Fellow of Christ's Colledge in Cambridge*, ed. John Worthington (London: Printed by Roger
Norton, for Richard Royston, bookseller to His Most Sacred Majesty, 1677), 7.
54. See Joseph Mede, *Clauis Apocalyptica ex Innatis et Insitis Visionum Characteribus
Eruta et Demonstrata. Ad Eorum Usum Quibus Deus Amorem Studiúmq[Ue] Indiderit Prophetiam
Illam Admirandam Cognoscendi Scrutandíque.* (Cantabrigiæ: [Printed by T. and J. Buck] impensis
authoris, in gratiam amicorum, 1627). This was translated into English in 1643 and published as
*The Key of the Revelation, Searched and Demonstrated Out of the Naturall and Proper Characters of
the Visions with a Comment Thereupon, According to the Rule of the Same Key*, trans. William Twisse
(London: Printed by R. B. for Phil Stephens, 1643). For an assessment of Mede's apocalyptic
thought, see Jeffrey K. Jue, *"Heaven Upon Earth": Joseph Mede (1586–1638) and the Legacy of
Millenarianism* (Dordtrecht: Springer, 2006).

In addition to his apocalyptic writings, Mede wrote a number of short theological treatises, including one containing a discussion of natural theology. In this discourse on Jeremiah 10:11, Mede articulated his definition of natural theology: "That the true God may be known by the Principles of Nature, and the Creation of the Heaven and Earth. . . . This is that which some call Naturall Theologie."[55] He continued by outlining three points for further explanation.

First, all men understand God as some person with a "living and Reasonable essence." Second, all men grant that God is the "most excellent of all Persons or Living Essences." Third, the perfections of God are threefold: in the understanding, in the will, and in the faculties of working. By "understanding," Mede referred to the wisdom of God; by "the will," God's goodness; and by "the faculties," God's power.[56] These three attributes compose the threefold sovereignty of God because "He alone is Almighty, He alone is All-good, He alone is All-wise."[57] It is no coincidence that Muller points to Peter Martyr Vermigli, Mede's theological predecessor by over twenty years, as establishing the same three points. Muller cites Vermigli's section on natural theology in his *Loci communes*: "In other words, 'the workmanship of this world' manifests both the almighty power of God and also the fact that this power is both wise and good in its creative exercise and providential care."[58] The consistency between Mede and one of the early Reformers suggests that Mede was following the received Reformed tradition on this point.

Subsequently another aspect of Mede's view must be more carefully examined to demonstrate his consistency with a broader Reformed understanding of natural theology. Mede followed the Reformed scholastic definition by recognizing that natural theology provides only the knowledge of God that renders man without an excuse. Mede stated that "God, in that he hath given them a Law, hath as it were stamped in

55. Mede, *Works*, 191.
56. Ibid.
57. Ibid.
58. Muller, *Prolegomena to Theology*, 170–71; also see Peter Martyr Vermigli, *The Common Places of the Most Famous and Renowned Divine Doctor Peter Martyr, Divided into Foure Principall Parts: with a Large Addition of Manie Theologicall and Necessarie Discourses, Some Never Extant Before*, ed. Anthony Marten and Josias Simmler (London: Henri Denham, Thomas Chard, William Broome, and Andrew Maunsell, 1583), 1.2.1.

them the character of his Will, which is the Law and Rule they observe in working."[59] As a result, one function of the law is to "admonish us of our duties."[60] Natural theology teaches that there is a God and it is man's duty to worship him; yet because of man's rebellion through sin, this knowledge of God now stands only to condemn him. At this point supernatural theology is needed to provide the knowledge of God unto salvation whereby man may be regenerated and thus given the ability to respond correctly to both the law of God and the gospel. Mede even posed the question in a manner that displayed the woeful condition of man:

> And tell me, from the circumference above unto the centre below, what one creature, what worst creature of God's making, what silly worm doth so transgress the Law of his creation as Man doth? And yet Man hath Reason given him, whereby he knoweth the Law and Rule he is to follow; Man hath also a liberty of Will: But what doeth he with them? His Reason he abuseth to make unreasonable actions; his Will, to most licencious and abominable liberty. It is a wonder the Earth can endure to bear him so vile a burthen, or the Sun to shine upon him the most unworthy creature in the world.[61]

Thus, Joseph Mede maintained the Reformed scholastic position in his articulation of a natural theology.

Mede died in 1638 just before the outbreak of the British Civil Wars. During the Interregnum and Restoration periods, Mede's generation of Cambridge dons was succeeded by the Cambridge Platonists, a group of scholars noted for their sympathies for Neoplatonism.[62] For the Cambridge Platonists the categories of "reason" and "nature" were the most distinguishing and controversial. The Platonists' view

59. Mede, *Works*, 192.
60. Ibid.
61. Ibid, 193.
62. Ernest Trafford Campagnac, et al., *The Cambridge Platonists* (Oxford: Clarendon, 1901); Isabel Rivers, *Whichcote to Wesley*, vol. 1 of *Reason, Grace, and Sentiment: A Study of the Language of Religion and Ethics in England, 1660–1780*, Cambridge Studies in Eighteenth-Century English Literature and Thought (Cambridge: Cambridge University Press, 1991); Sarah Hutton, "The Cambridge Platonists," in *A Companion to Early Modern Philosophy*, ed. Steven M. Nadler, Blackwell Companions to Philosophy (Malden, MA: Blackwell, 2002), 308–19.

of the "light of nature" became their hallmark doctrine. Isabel Rivers comments that they "were more interested in showing the essential congruity between natural and revealed religion and in interpreting the latter in the light of the former."[63] The most famous slogan for the Platonists was the "Candle of the Lord," coined by Benjamin Whichcote (1609–83), provost of King's College, which demarcated the relation between natural and supernatural theologies. Whichcote remarked, "God hath set up Two Lights; to enlighten us in our Way; the Light of Reason, which is the Light of his Creation; and the Light of Scripture, which is After-Revelation from him. Let us make use of these two Lights; and suffer neither to be put out."[64] Likewise, for Whichcote, revealed truth was superimposed upon natural truth and simply added more of the same thing.[65] Thus, within the theology of the Cambridge Platonists, reason and nature were given greater prominence than ever before.

Awareness of this began in a series of correspondences between Whichcote and his former tutor Anthony Tuckney, who served as a member of the Westminster Assembly.[66] On September 7, 1651, Whichcote delivered a Sunday sermon in Cambridge, shocking many of his listeners by expressing non-Puritan views.[67] This sermon sparked an immediate response from Tuckney, who admitted that it "hath very much grieved me."[68] Tuckney was concerned that Whichcote had placed within man's reason too much of an ability to gain salvation. "[Yet] to say, that the ground of God's reconciliation is from any thing in Us; and not from His free grace, freely justifying the ungodly; is to deny one of the fundamental truths of the Gospel, that derives from Heaven, which, I bless God, lyeth neer to my

63. Rivers, *Reason, Grace, and Sentiment*, 67.
64. Benjamin Whichcote, *Moral and Religious Aphorisms Collected from the Manuscript Papers of the Reverend and Learned Doctor Whichcote; and Published in MDCCIII, by Dr. Jeffery. Now Re-Published, with Very Large Additions . . . by Samuel Salter. . . . To Which Are Added, Eight Letters: . . .* (London: Printed for J. Payne, 1753), 109.
65. James Deotis Roberts, *From Puritanism to Platonism in Seventeenth Century England* (The Hague: Martinus Nijhoff, 1968), 116.
66. Benjamin Whichcote, "Eight Letters of Dr. Anthony Tuckney and Benjamin Whichcote," in *Moral and Religious Aphorisms*.
67. Ibid., 1–2.
68. Ibid., 2.

heart; it is dearer to me than my life," wrote Tuckney.[69] The fear, for Tuckney, was that Whichcote was laying too much stress on natural theology (specifically, the strength of man's reason), and exalting it over supernatural theology.[70] This was an unacceptable inversion of the theology set forth in the Canons of Dordt and the Westminster Confession.[71] Consequently, Tuckney's deductions led him to insinuate that Whichcote was capitulating toward two infamous heresies. Tuckney wrote, "Sir, those, whose footsteepes I observed, were the Socinians and Arminians; the latter wherof, I conceeve, you have bin everie where reading in their workes; and those very things, which You hint, They dilate."[72]

While Whichcote flatly denied any such accusations, his understanding of natural theology did deviate from the traditional Reformed scholastic formulation.[73] James Roberts comments that in "Whichcote we are closer to the *credo ut intelligam* of Augustine than the neat division of *theologia naturalis* and *theologia revelata* characteristic of Scholasticism."[74] Whichcote replaced the "neat division," including the true theology–false theology and archetype-ectype distinction, with a common foundation on which to build both natural and revealed theologies; that common foundation was Jesus Christ. Responding to Tuckney, he wrote:

> I am verie free to acknowledge Christ, the onlie foundation; since the apostasie and sinne of man: Hee alone gave the stoppe to God's just displeasure; His interposing prevayled with God, not to take the

69. Ibid., 4.

70. Roberts, *From Puritanism to Platonism*, 54; Roberts also added, "Just as natural truths are the first emanation from God, even so truths of after-revelation, saving truths are the second emanation from God and the proper supplement to the former." Ibid., 118.

71. Tuckney alluded to Whichcote's violation of the confession: "In the Assemblie, I gave my vote with others; that the Confession of Faith, putt-out by Authoritie, shoulde not bee required to bee eyther sworne or subscribed too; wee having bin burnt in the hand in that kind before: but so as not to be publickly preached or written against." Whichcote, "Eight Letters," 76.

72. Ibid., 27.

73. Whichcote wrote, "Trulie I have more read Calvine, and Perkins, and Beza; than all the bookes authors, or names you mention." Ibid., 54. Apparently Tuckney was convinced with Whichcote's defense and rescinded his previous accusation: "For that of Socinians and Arminians; seeing I ingenouslie cleared you, from those imputations; both in my own thoughts, and against other misprisions." Ibid., 78.

74. Roberts, *From Puritanism to Platonism*, 116.

forfeiture; or, if taken, Hee procured the restauration and recoverie. Upon this accounte I acknowledge Christ, in parts of nature, reason and understanding; as well as in gifts of grace: for that Christ is not by mee anie where leftout, nor faith neglected; no, nor not advanced to a superiorite and supereminencie everiewhere: for I beleeve, that I hold and enjoy my reason and understanding, by and under Christ.[75]

This emphasis on reason was to motivate men to exercise that Christ-given ability. However, Whichcote was careful to attribute any lack of exercise, not to some deficiency in Christ, but solely to a deficiency within the individual.[76] For Whichcote, natural and supernatural theologies served the same purpose and thus could be regarded as complementary. Likewise the positive benefits of natural theology far exceeded any previous formulations from Reformed theologians. Whichcote insisted on the value of reason and its worthy place even within preaching:

> I find that some men take offence, to hear reason spoke of out of a pulpit, or to hear those great words of natural light, of principles of reason, and conscience. They are doubtless in a mighty mistake, for these two things are very consistent, as I shall shew you by and by, and there is no inconsistency between the grace of God, and the calling upon me carefully to use, improve and employ the principles of God's creation. . . . And indeed this is a very profitable work to call upon me to answer the principles of their creation, to fulfil natural light, to answer natural conscience, to be throughout rational in what they do; for these things have a divine foundation. The spirit in man is the candle of the Lord lighted by God, and lighting men to God.[77]

The "candle of the Lord" signified the definite shift within the thought of Whichcote and the other Cambridge Platonists toward a more positive view of the use of human reason in natural theology.

75. Whichcote, "Eight Letters," 126.
76. Ibid.
77. Benjamin Whichcote, *The Works*, British Philosophers and Theologians of the 17th and 18th Centuries (New York: Garland, 1977), 2:370–71.

Conclusion

A reexamination of seventeenth-century Protestant scholastic sources results in the correction of the interpretation of scholastic natural theology by Van Til, the traditional Reformed apologists, and the Barthian historians. The scholastics were not capitulating toward a pre-Enlightenment rationalism; instead they carefully delineated the definition and function of natural theology within a wider theological context. The shift toward rationalism was a later development with movements such as the Cambridge Platonists and others. John Platt is correct in describing the Reformed scholastics' conclusion that "natural man's inexcusable culpability before God is thus the more forcibly underlined as the status of his rationality and consequent moral potentiality is exalted." According to the Protestant scholastics, natural theology has no positive function for the unregenerate and only a confirmatory role for the regenerate. Natural theology was never considered to be a rational exercise that would lead the unbeliever to the truth of the gospel.

As somewhat of an appendix to this historical study, it is worth noting a connection between the Protestant scholastics and Cornelius Van Til. While Van Til was mistaken in his assessment of the Protestant scholastics' teachings, his views are in fact quite similar. Van Til's understanding of the exclusively negative function of natural theology for the unbeliever resembles that of the seventeenth century. Moreover, Van Til's insistence on denying the use of natural theology as a starting point is a consistent implication of the Protestant scholastic position.

D. G. Hart has criticized Van Til for modifying the theology of Old Princeton because Van Til questioned Charles Hodge's and B. B. Warfield's epistemology. Hart claims that Old Princeton was holding fast to an "unoriginal Calvinism," and Van Til, along with others at Westminster Seminary, were innovators who deviated from traditional Calvinism. However, Van Til's understanding of natural theology had a greater affinity with the seventeenth-century Reformers, whereas Old Princeton arguably modified the Protestant scholastic understanding of natural theology.

Mark Noll writes, "I find the Princeton Theology weak on the relationship of natural and revealed theology, confused on the proper place of affective knowledge, and overly sanguine about the powers of rational apologetics." The influence of Common Sense Philosophy on the theology of Old Princeton probably accounts for Noll's comment. Nonetheless, the similarity between Van Til and the Protestant scholastics perhaps indicates that Van Til should not be accused of an alleged "originality." Much more needs to be explored as to how Van Til reached these similar conclusions without accurate historical knowledge; nevertheless, we can observe the unity and consistency of the Reformed tradition in the legacy of Cornelius Van Til.

10

The Eschatological Implications of Genesis 2:15 for Apologetics

WILLIAM D. DENNISON

*W*hat does eschatology have to do with apologetics? In terms of the traditional arrangement of the theological rubrics, it would seem that eschatology has nothing to do with apologetics. Eschatology is the last discipline of the theological encyclopedia, and it discusses subjects that relate to Christ's second coming. Apologetics is usually discussed in relationship to the first theological rubric, the doctrine of God, under the concept of theism.

In the twentieth century, however, many Reformed exegetes came to grips with the fact that the theological rubrics are intertwined with the eschatological revelation of God. For example, they came to understand that the glorious doctrines of soteriology are draped in the eschatological person and work of Christ, especially the efficacious power of his death and resurrection. In other words, Christ's death and resurrection form the core eschatological event in redemptive history, and as such are the ground, source, and power of every believer's eter-

190

nal union with Christ through the Holy Spirit (Rom. 6:1–14; 2 Cor. 4:11–5:8; Gal. 2:20; Col. 3:1–4). There would be no election, effectual calling, regeneration, faith and repentance, justification, adoption, sanctification, and glorification without that event.

We have come to realize, therefore, that Christ's eschatological kingdom has begun (Matt. 4:17; Mark 1:15; Luke 4:43). We are in the *eschaton* looking forward to its consummation (2 Cor. 6:2; Heb. 1:1–4; 1 John 2:18). Moreover, we are seated already by faith in the heavenly places with Christ even as we remain pilgrims on earth (Eph. 1:3; 2:6; Col. 3:1–2; 1 Peter 1:1). From this heavenly perspective every theological rubric must be shaped, including the doctrine of God and apologetics. With respect to apologetics, we *defend* the holy presence of Christ and our present union with him in the heavenly places against every evil advance in opposition to him and his kingdom.

A biblical text on the preredemptive state (pre-fall) of historical revelation has stimulated my thinking in regard to the eschatological dimension of apologetics. That text is Genesis 2:15: "Then the LORD God took the man and put him in the garden of Eden to serve and to guard it."[1] In my judgment, as eschatology is intertwined into the inner fabric of the history of revelation, this text will introduce and highlight some profound implications for apologetics.

From Christ to the Garden

The recent work of Gregory K. Beale and Meredith G. Kline has provided an insightful and stimulating interpretation concerning the garden of Eden.[2] Their basic thesis is that the garden is a creational representation of the heavenly temple or sanctuary of the Lord, which later will come to expression in the construction of the tabernacle and

1. Except where indicated, Scripture quotations in this chapter are my translations.
2. Although his interest is not apologetics, my essay is stimulated by the thoughts of Gregory K. Beale from his lectures, "Already and Not Yet Eschatology and the Temple," Overland Park, KS: Lectures presented at Park Woods Presbyterian Church on March 8–10, 2002. More recently, three publications by Gregory K. Beale have appeared that relate to the themes in those lectures: (1) "Garden Temple" (2003); (2) *The Temple and the Church's Mission* (Downers Grove, IL: InterVarsity Press, 2005); (3) "Eden, the Temple, and the Church's Mission in the New Creation," *Journal of the Evangelical Theological Society* 48, no. 1 (2005): 5–32. See also Meredith G. Kline, *Kingdom Prologue: Genesis Foundations for a Covenantal Worldview* (Overland Park: Two Age Press, 2000), 85–87.

the temple in Israel's history as these objects point us to the person and work of Jesus Christ, the true tabernacle/temple of the Lord (John 1:14; 2:19–22). Moreover, the eschatological vision concerning the new heaven and earth recorded in the book of Revelation presupposes this revelatory pattern (Rev. 21–22). In fact, in terms of God's knowledge of his eternal decrees, he knows the beginning from the end, and he knows the end from the beginning. God's knowledge is so comprehensive that he can foreknow a certain event in time and space, and know everything from that event retrospectively (past) and prospectively (future). Since God knows the beginning from the end, let me begin with God's revelatory vision to John about the new heaven and earth (Rev. 21–22), and then return to the garden in Genesis.

God's eschatological revelation of the new heaven and earth comes to John in the form of a city—the New Jerusalem (Rev. 21:2; cf. 21:10, 14, 16, 19, 21, 23; 22:2).[3] Interestingly, the city of John's vision does not contain any description of a typical geographical landscape, for example, the various sections of an urban environment or the aesthetic surroundings, such as mountains, plains, forests, and even a sea (21:1 notes that there is no more sea). Rather, the appearance, construction, and dimensions of the New Jerusalem are visualized as a temple-city (cf. Rev. 21:16 and 1 Kings 6:20; also Rev. 21:18–21 and Ezek. 40–48). Specifically, this temple imagery is grounded in God's final revelatory presence in his creation—the true tabernacle/temple, Jesus Christ (Rev. 21:3–8, 22–27; 22:5). This connection is verified as God provides an infallible interpretation of John's vision.

God immediately directs our attention to "the tabernacle of God," which dwells with his people (21:3). This tabernacle is a clear reference to Jesus Christ (John 1:14; Rev. 21:3, 6–7, 22–23). Herein, God is connecting the dots in the text; he composes an integrative picture that connects the new heaven and earth, the New Jerusalem, and the tabernacle to his presence in his Son, Jesus Christ. God's integrative picture is grounded, however, in his historic, progressive revelation. For example, just as the tabernacle/temple in the Old Testament points to

---

3. If one wishes to examine Rev. 21–22 more extensively, I would recommend Gregory K. Beale, *The Book of Revelation: A Commentary on the Greek Text* (Grand Rapids, MI: Eerdmans, 1999), 1039–157.

Christ, likewise Christ points us to the imagery of the New Jerusalem in the form of a temple-city. In John's vision, the order is *reversed*: in the Old Testament we move from tabernacle/temple to Christ, while in John's vision we move from Christ to temple-city.

God reverses the order in John's vision because the new temple-city begins with Christ's finished work (Rev. 21:6); all things are now viewed from the perspective that he is the beginning and the end (21:6; 22:13). Specifically, we are in the midst of a new heaven and earth in which Christ's finished work is the beginning of the new creation. If we use creational language, Christ is the origin as well as the source of all existence and life for the temple-city. The Lamb, who has been slain, and the Redeemer, who has been exalted, is the Creator of all things new and good! In terms of redemption accomplished, Christ's activity for the new creation is seen to be for sinners who have been brought into the eternal and final glory of their Savior (21:23–24). Those redeemed sinners are said to reside in the temple-city as the Lamb's bride—the church (21:9, 12–13). Herein, keep in mind, we are not presented with a city in one place and a separate temple in another place; rather, the city is a temple (21:22). The temple-city is the place of the glorious presence of God in his Son, and it is the place in whom he shines his glorious presence into the faces of his people—the church (cf. 2 Cor. 4:6).

Furthermore, not only is the new heaven and earth pictured as Christ's temple-city, but it is also pictured as Christ's garden-city (Rev. 22:2). As the eschatological Christ is the source for the new temple-city, likewise he is the source of the new garden-city (22:1). This pattern of God's revelation to John is written clearly upon the pages of the history of revelation. In the garden of Eden, God's presence dwells with his servant, Adam. After the fall, God's presence dwells in the midst of his people in the tabernacle, then in the temple. As we examine closely God's revelation to John (Rev. 21–22), the images transmitted to him are of places that reveal God's presence in the midst of his people: Christ, city-temple (tabernacle/temple), and city-garden (garden of Eden). John's vision is not about a generic garden or a generic city; rather, God is communicating life in the garden-city, and the temple-city, or more specifically, life in the garden-city and the temple-city as life is in Christ.

Again, one needs to note that the order in John's eschatological vision is *reversed*; in the sequence of history the movement is from garden to tabernacle/temple to Christ; in John's vision the picture pans from Christ to tabernacle/temple to garden. In God's progressive revelation in history, Christ is the consummation of the presence of God; moreover, Christ is the all-comprehensive presence of God in the eschatological life of his bride.

We realize now that an integral understanding of the fabric of God's revelation can be comprehended from its end rather than always starting at the beginning of the story. Specifically, we have moved from the end (new heaven and earth) to the beginning (garden), noting that the integrative revelatory relationship of the presence of God in Christ, the tabernacle/temple, and the garden is consummated in Christ's coming in history and his exaltation in glory. As God's revelation to John has moved from Christ to the garden, let us now direct our attention to the temple imagery in the garden with its eschatological end in mind.

The Temple-Garden and Genesis 2:15

As God performs his creative activity, the garden becomes the place of his localized presence in the midst of the creation, where he enters into covenant communion with man, who alone is made in his image (Gen. 1:26–27; 2:7–8; cf. Ezek. 28:13; 31:8f.; Isa. 51:3). Adam is placed immediately in the visible and created replica (the garden) of God's heavenly sanctuary as that sanctuary manifests the glorious presence of God (cf. Ezek. 47 and Rev. 21–22). The sanctuary idea is impressed upon us when we note the use of the hithpael form of the Hebrew word *halak* (הלך, "walk back and forth") in Genesis 3:8. There *halak* is used to describe God's presence as he walks in the garden; likewise, in the same manner, *halak* is used to describe God's walking back and forth in the future tabernacle/temple sanctuary (cf. Lev. 26:12; 2 Sam. 7:6). In the tabernacle/temple as well as the garden, God's walk is a special revelation of his glorious presence in covenant union with his people. Biblical revelation makes a clear connection between the heavenly sanctuary, the tabernacle/temple, and the garden. In terms of the revelatory imagery, Adam should be viewed as the first priest in the Lord's garden-temple (sanctuary). This observation will be solidified by turning our attention to Genesis 2:15: "Then the LORD God took the man and put him in the garden of Eden to serve and to guard it."

Typically Genesis 2:15 has been viewed as an extension of the cultural mandate found in Genesis 1:26–28. Specifically, Genesis 2:15 is thought to teach that Adam is fulfilling the cultural mandate as a gardener; he is dressing, tilling, tending, cultivating, and keeping the garden. Recently, closer attention has been given to the words '*abad* (עבד) and *shamar* (שׁמר) in Genesis 2:15, especially as those terms appear together elsewhere in the Old Testament. Beale has observed correctly that when the two words appear in the same context, they never refer to the gardening task (unless Genesis 2:15 is the only instance in the entire Old Testament for such a reference).[4] Rather, when '*abad* ("serve") and *shamar* ("keep, guard") appear together, Israel is told to serve the Lord and to keep his Word (Deut. 10:12–13; 1 Chron. 28:8–9). This same idea is taught when the people are instructed to keep God's Word and *not* to serve other gods (Deut. 30:16–17; Josh. 23:6–7; cf. also 1 Kings 9:6). For our purposes, however, there is a second manner in which '*abad* and *shamar* appear together; the terms appear together in reference to the duties of the priest to serve the Lord and guard the tabernacle/temple (Num. 3:6–8; cf. also the duties of the Gershonites, Kohathites, and the Merarites in Num. 3:17–4:49).

If we remain consistent with God's revelatory pattern, then the connection should be evident. In John's vision, the temple-city and the garden-city are correlative revelations. Likewise the use of '*abad* and *shamar* with respect to the tabernacle/temple and the garden-temple of Eden show that they are correlative revelations. In this revelatory pattern, '*abad* and *shamar* are priestly terms when they appear in the same context; they are not gardening terms. Hence, as the priest serves as a guard of God's presence and his Word in the tabernacle/temple, likewise Adam, as the first priest serves as a guard of God's presence and his Word in the garden. In fact, one of the important priestly duties of Adam and the Levites is to guard the garden and tabernacle/temple

4. "Already and Not Yet Eschatology and the Temple," session 2.

from any intruder—the unclean who would attempt to penetrate the sanctuary (Num. 18:7; cf. also Num. 3:38).[5]

Adam failed in his task as priest in the garden-temple; he permitted an unclean intruder to invade the premises. Adam, as priest, failed to serve (*'abad*) the Word of God and to guard (*shamar*) the holy and glorious presence of his Creator from that evil trespasser, Satan. To put it another way, Adam failed in his defense (*apologia*) of the Lord's sanctuary from the Serpent's evil advance. Hence, as federal head of humanity, Adam not only failed as the first priest, but also failed as the first apologist.

In my judgment, there is a clear connection between *shamar* (to "guard") and its synonym, to "defend" (*apologeomai*/ἀπολογεομαι) in the garden-temple. Simply put, to *guard* the presence of God in the garden-temple from any intruder is also to *defend* the presence of God in the garden-temple from any intruder. The instrument for such a defense is faithfulness to the Word of the Lord. However, as Adam failed his apologetic task, he, along with the woman, accepted the rebellious presuppositions of the invader who questioned the truth, integrity, and authority of God's Word. Satan convinced them that they were their own reference point for knowing good and evil, being like God himself (Gen. 3:1–5). In their act of rebellious sin, they exchanged the truth of God for a lie as they worshiped and served the creature rather than the Creator (Rom. 1:25). Hence, they surrendered their status of fellowship and communion in the intimate presence of their Lord for the sake of fellowship and communion with the embodiment of evil. As a consequence, God cast them out of his garden-sanctuary; they were no longer fit for his presence.

Genesis 2:15 and Apologetics

Genesis 2:15 has profound implications for apologetics. First, God created and placed Adam in the sanctuary of his created universe. In

5. I am fully aware that Genesis 2:15 can be used to demonstrate the constitution of man as prophet, priest, and king in accordance with the teaching of the Heidelberg Catechism, Q&A 32. For the purpose of this essay, however, I am concerned with only the priestly function, although it will be apparent that the prophetic office and its service to God's Word will constantly be placed before us. However, an outline or discussion of Adam's office as king is not the design of this essay.

the garden-temple Adam is immediately placed in God's presence. A crucial observation must be grasped here: Adam is not placed in the garden in order to begin reading natural revelation as he makes his way to special revelation. Nor is Adam placed in the creation in order to proceed by means of deductive and inductive logic from theism to the triune God of the Bible. As God places Adam in the garden, God does not design Adam so he would move intellectually from comprehending God naturally to comprehending God more fully. Rather, Adam is immediately in the presence of the personal God who made him; here God reveals himself clearly in this preredemptive state. If a movement is to be observed here, it is not with Adam moving rationally and empirically to God, but with the sovereign Lord condescending to Adam.

The true, personal, triune God has condescended in covenant bond to his servant. Immediately, Adam is encountered with God's supernatural and self-authenticating existence as the Lord's presence envelops Adam's existence in the garden-temple. Herein the eschatological nature of the garden-temple comes into view. If we comprehend the retrospective process of revelation that we have outlined from the city-temple (Revelation) back to the garden-temple (Genesis), we must note that Adam's apologetic state in the garden-temple is eschatological. The eschatological reality of being in the presence of the Lord forever (New Jerusalem) is forecasted in history as a present reality to Adam as the Lord's presence envelops the garden-temple. For this reason, it should be noted that to unfold the biblical doctrine of eschatology is to unfold the biblical doctrine of apologetics.

Second, Adam's task is to guard or defend the sacred presence of God from any intruder or invader into his created sanctuary, the garden-temple. Here is the core of Adam's priestly and apologetic task; he is to guard and defend the sanctuary of the Lord from unclean things. As the Lord places Adam in an apologetic setting, he defines his apologetic task; it is to keep every intruder and invader out of his presence. Herein the eschatological dimension of Adam's task becomes evident. In order to grasp this dimension of his task, however, one must think in terms of the eternal realm of God's eschatological glory. In the new heaven and earth, do unclean intruders and invaders reside in the eternal glory of the Lord's presence? Absolutely not; in God's eternal residence nothing unclean will be in the presence of the Lord—only those cleansed by the blood of the Lamb of God are permitted there. Hence, the eternal eschatological realm is injected upon Adam's apologetic commission in the preredemptive state in history. Adam is to maintain and secure the purity of the garden-temple from any contamination (cf. Ps. 84:10).

As God defines Adam's apologetic task in the garden-temple, there is absolutely nothing that suggests, or even hints, that Adam is to begin his defense with natural revelation, natural theology, or generic theism. Rather, according to Genesis 2:15, Adam is to perform his apologetic task by defending and serving the Lord and his Word; he is to live by every Word that proceeds from the mouth of the Lord. The eschatological dimension of God's revelation determines the *method* of the apologetic task: he must start with God, and he must end with God; or it can be said that he must start with God's Word, and he must end with God's Word.

Third, if we connect Adam's fall into sin (Gen. 3:1–7) with his stated task in Genesis 2:15, we note the pitfalls of his apologetic performance. Adam's breakdown is defined simply as a failure to guard and defend the sacred presence of God (garden-temple) from an unclean intruder (Satan). In other words, if Adam and Eve had adhered faithfully to God's Word, the invader would have been repelled from God's presence. Instead, the Word of the Lord was compromised, surrendered, and forfeited. Once this was done, Adam and the woman were doomed for failure. After all, Satan understood the situation well; if Adam and the woman would buckle under his seductive words, he could succeed in contaminating God's sanctuary and presence.

Indeed, Adam and Eve buckled; they exchanged eschatological glory for eschatological judgment. Instead of remaining faithful to the absolute authority of the Lord's Word, Adam and the woman allowed Satan to define the discussion; they surrendered to the "neutral" claims of Satan's reason. He seduced them to think of a world in which the Lord God is not the Lord God, and thus he convinced them that they needed to experience the empirical world outside the presence of the Lord. Or, to put it another way, Adam dropped his armaments against the intruder for the empirical experience of life outside the presence of God. Instead of savoring the presence of the Lord, Adam wished to experience the lying world of Satan (cf. John 8:44).

For Adam and Eve, God and the truth of his Word no longer defined what was rational and irrational; rather, they felt comfortable to turn such definitions over to the invader. Specifically, Satan presented Adam with a world in which his reason was autonomous in blatant rebellion against the truth of God's Word. Once Adam capitulated to Satan's summons, his security against the enemy was gone. That is, Adam relinquished the Word of God as the starting point and finishing point of his apologetic. He failed his apologetic task across the eschatological spectrum.

Genesis 2:15 and Christ, the Apologist

In contrast to the first Adam, the last Adam upheld the eschatological dimension of the apologetic task. Keep in mind that as we move prospectively, the garden-temple points us to the tabernacle/temple in Israel's history, which in turn points us to the true tabernacle-temple of God, the Lord Jesus Christ (John 1:14; 2:19–22; Rev. 21:3–7). Where the first Adam failed in his priestly and apologetic task to serve the Lord and his Word while guarding and defending the Lord's presence, the second Adam succeeds. Moreover, the second Adam is fully equipped as priest and apologist to deal with the stipulations of Genesis 2:15.

As Immanuel, he is the actual presence of God, whose own ontological identity as the Word of God provides him with the guard and defense against any intruder or invader of his being (Isa. 7:14; Matt. 1:23; John 1:1, 14). His effectual defense is seen at the beginning of his ministry when he confronts the intruder (Satan) in the wilderness (Matt. 4:1–11; Mark 1:12–13; Luke 4:1–13). Although the wilderness confrontation with Satan is primarily about Christ's faithful reenactment of Israel's failure in the wilderness, the event also points us back to the garden. Just as God's enemy intruded and invaded the residence of God's presence in the garden-temple, now Satan attempts to intrude and invade the ontological presence of God in the eschatological Son of God. Just as Satan seduced the first Adam, he attempts to seduce the second Adam to act with respect to an autonomous rational and empirical world outside of God's presence. Moreover, Satan challenges the second Adam to compromise, surrender, and forfeit the Word of God. But the second Adam *is* the Word of God!

As the Word of God, Christ is equipped ontologically to be *the* apologist who can recite the Word of God as part of his own essence against the onslaught of Satan. He will not be seduced to pursue a rational and empirical world outside his own ontological presence. The self-attesting Christ as the Word of God is sufficient to guard and defend his own ontological divine presence from Satan's evil intent. Specifically, Christ's own epistemological self-consciousness goes into effect; he uses the Word of God to repel each advance by his enemy. By beginning and ending with the Word of God (his ontological identity as well as his performance in Word and in deed), Christ's initial defense against his archenemy undermines Satan's malicious plot to divert him from the cross. Hence, in his initial confrontation with Satan, the eschatological Adam fulfills the apologetic task. He protects his own divine presence by faithfully adhering to the eschatological method of defense—beginning and ending with the Word of God. In Christ, therefore, we have entered into the realm of eschatological apologetics for the sake of guarding, protecting, and entering into the divine presence of the triune God forever!

Furthermore, Christ's initial apologetic act against Satan is consummated at the cross. As Christ makes his way to the cross, he protects the presence of the Lord within himself. He accepts freely the path his Father has ordained for him as revealed in the Word of God (Matt. 16:21; 26:42; John 20:9; Heb. 5:8). When we follow Christ's path to the cross, we must not overlook that his apologetic faithfulness directs him to suffering and death. In fact, like Christ, those who faithfully adhere to his apologetic mission may expect suffering, and the possibility of death in this world (e.g., Stephen, Peter, and Paul). Death came to Christ, and, perhaps, we may come to the same end.

Interestingly, the failure of the first Adam in his apologetic task brought the state of death, whereas the success of the second Adam in his apologetic delivers him to the cross. However, the act of the first Adam was grounded in pride and sin; the act of the last Adam, in servitude and righteousness. The path of death secured by the first Adam was destruction; the path of death secured by the eschatological Adam was life. Hence, Christ's faithfulness to the apologetic task destroys the works of the devil in order to secure a place for his elect in his presence.

For this reason, the believer's apologetic must comprise the central message of the cross and the resurrection to be effectual. It is the actual event that destroyed the works of the devil (Acts 17:1–4, 18, 31–32). As the church operates faithfully within the confines of this apologetic task, the Lord may provide the fruits of her faithfulness. Just as Christ's faithfulness was rewarded as his Father raised the Lamb of God from the dead for the sake of his elect, likewise, the Lord may reward the church for her faithfulness by raising those who are spiritually dead to life (his elect). Indeed, just as Christ is vindicated by the Spirit to life in his resurrection (1 Tim. 3:16), likewise, the unbeliever is vindicated by the Holy Spirit as he is transformed from death to life (Rom. 6:1–14; 8:9–11). Herein, the eschatological work of the Holy Spirit ushers the unbeliever into the presence of the eschatological sanctuary, Jesus Christ!

Genesis 2:15, the Church, and the Holy Spirit

As we consider the work of the Holy Spirit to convict, convince, and persuade sinners about the gospel, we return to the book of Revelation and the imagery of the Bridegroom and the bride (21:2, 9–13; 22:17). Christ and his bride are present in God's vision to John concerning the new heaven and earth. They play an essential role in the revelatory pattern of God in Christ, the tabernacle/temple, and the garden. Just as we have seen with the previously mentioned revelatory pattern, we may project the eschatological Bridegroom and bride into the garden-temple in Genesis. The marriage of the man and woman in the garden is the initial eschatological picture of the eternal marriage of Christ and his church; the eschatological future is thereby projected into the preredemptive state.

In the garden, the woman was created immediately to dwell in the presence of her husband just as Christ's bride dwells eternally in his presence. Moreover, from the beginning it was God's intent to have the man and the woman dwell in his presence as the man and the woman depict his bride. Hence, as we consider the original priestly and apologetic task of Adam, his task has been enriched and expanded.

Thus far we have established that apologetics is to guard and defend the presence of God by the Word of God; but in God's eschatological revelation to John, God's presence also includes his bride—his church! Adam's task to guard and defend the presence of God by his Word also included himself and his wife (the church in the garden). For this reason, since eternity is pictured as the wedding feast of Christ (Bridegroom) and his church (bride), and this eschatological dimension is revealed in the garden, apologetics is also the defense of the bride and Bridegroom against their intruders and invaders.

In order to combat the enemies of the church and the gospel, the eschatological work of the Holy Spirit is paramount. One function of the Spirit's eschatological work is that the church and the believer are now the dwelling place of God's presence. The body of the believer is the temple of the Holy Spirit; the believer's body is the place where the presence of Christ dwells by his Spirit (1 Cor. 3:16–17; 6:19). As the Spirit dwells in the body of believers in Christ's church, the apologetic task is defined by the fact that the apologist is placed immediately in the sanctuary of the Lord. He is engulfed by the revelation of Christ's exalted glory in the heavenly places as the Holy Spirit dwells in him. Encompassed by the revelation of Christ in the heavenly sanctuary, the apologist is not instructed to begin with an abstract concept, for example, reason, experience, feeling, or inner faith. Rather, consistent with the teaching of Genesis 2:15, *the apologist begins in the eschatological realm of the "fullness of time." In this realm, the apologist is to serve, guard, and defend the purity of Christ's holy presence in the heavenly places and his union with his church from any contamination by faithfully adhering to the Word of God.*

As God revealed to John, Christ's eschatological work cannot be separated from his church; the Bridegroom and the bride are part of her epistemological self-consciousness. In this eschatological situation, the apologist has no recourse; he must guard and defend the church and the believer against the continual seductions of Satan's advances to defile God's holy presence. Although already conquered and defeated by Christ, Satan will fight until his final destruction. But the church is equipped for his advances; as she continues to live as a pilgrim bride, she is the presence of Christ in this world. As such, she is not permitted to allow anything to defile the Spirit's holy presence of Christ; this includes the things her members see, the things they hear, and the thoughts they entertain.

Specifically, Christ's bride is to defend and guard herself in the marketplace by living the Word of God. Once again, we see that apologetics begins and ends with the Word of God, thus maintaining a true eschatological method. Blending our notion of apologetics with Cornelius Van Til's definition, we could say that *apologetics is the vindication of the presence of Christ and his church against the various forms of the non-Christian philosophy of life that constantly attempt to invade and intrude that presence.* And as the church is engaged in the marketplace, she has a confidence never enjoyed before in redemptive history. The second Adam has fulfilled the apologetic task of Genesis 2:15; the self-attesting Christ has already won the apologetic battle. In this context, Christ provides the presence, witness, and testimony of the Spirit to his bride to sustain his victory in this world.

Epilogue

Over the years, my interest in apologetics has been the issue of prolegomena; I have been concerned about the starting point of a Christian apologetic method. This essay continues to elaborate upon that concern, especially in association to the apologetic method of Cornelius Van Til. Those familiar with Van Til's method will recognize that this essay reflects upon two of his most salient points: the self-attesting Christ of Scripture as his starting point and the Word of God as the tool of apologetic engagement.

Taking Van Til's own acknowledgment that Geerhardus Vos was his most influential teacher, I have attempted to push Van Til's biblical apologetic deeper into the fabric of God's revelation. In other words, I want to understand how God and the historical revelation of himself shape the foundation (prolegomena) and method of Christian apologetics. For example, Vos and other Reformed exegetes have exposed the rich eschatological nature of God's revelation. It seems to me this understanding of revelation can only enhance and enrich what Van Til has placed before us. In terms of the self-attesting Christ of Scripture, the eschatological nature of revelation has actually placed the apologist and his method in the presence of God's sanctuary. He is actually placed in the presence of his glorious and holy Savior, who testifies about himself in Holy Scripture. Being in covenant union with the exalted Christ, the Christian apologist begins his defense and ends his defense with God's Word. After all, he is in the presence of, and he is in union with, the Word of God who has become flesh. He does not begin with reason and then appeal to God's Word, nor does he begin with God's Word and then finish with personal experience. Rather, God's Word is the starting point and the ending point; Christ, as the Word of God, is "the Alpha and the Omega, the Beginning and the End, the First and the Last" (Rev. 22:13 NKJV)!

As this essay attempts to solidify Van Til's apologetic in the historical revelation of God, pastors and laity in the church may be very curious about the next step, especially since I have closed by discussing the church and the work of the Holy Spirit. Such a concern is legitimate. Pastors and laity want to see what an eschatological apologetic looks like, that is, how the defense of Christ's presence by the Word of God comes to expression in the marketplace.

Everyone in Christ's true church realizes that Satan and his forces continue each day to attack Christ's sacred presence. Indeed, I realize that we must move beyond prolegomena issues. Next, we need to investigate how the Word of God provides the substance for the transcendental critique against all vain imaginations raised up against the knowledge of God. For pastors and laity, it becomes necessary to show how the transcendental critique exposes the folly of unbelief (eschatological judgment) for the sake of preserving the sanctity of the presence of Christ and his bride. Let us press forward in this discussion.

PART 3

REFORMED APOLOGETICS

Methodological Implications

II

The Old-New Reformed Epistemology

K. Scott Oliphint

*W*hat are the epistemological implications of a Reformed apologetic? The question is more easily asked than answered. Any Reformed approach to apologetics must itself be grounded in Reformed theology. It would be helpful, therefore, to see, first, the epistemological implications of a Reformed theology in order to link those implications to a Reformed apologetic.

In his influential work, "Reason and Belief in God,"[1] Alvin Plantinga began in earnest to argue for the proper basicality of theistic belief.[2] His concern, generally, was that the evidential objectors (to belief in God) had unduly placed requirements on the rationality of that belief that they themselves did not, and do not, maintain. His more

This chapter can be seen as a philosophical and epistemological development of the implications of Paul's discussion in Rom. 1:18ff. It may prove more helpful, therefore, to remember chap. 3, "The Irrationality of Unbelief," when reading this chapter, since much of the material here will depend on the conclusions in that chapter.

1. In Alvin Plantinga and Nicholas Wolterstorff, eds., *Faith and Rationality* (Notre Dame, IN: University of Notre Dame Press, 1983), 16–93.

2. This may not be completely accurate. Some would say that Plantinga began his argument in *God and Other Minds*. In any case, "Reason and Belief in God" was the beginning of a concerted effort toward the development of a new epistemological approach.

specific concern, up to the present day, is that the rationality of belief in God has been illegitimately rendered suspect. Those who demand evidential proof for such a belief relax those same demands when it comes to other, more popular, beliefs that they all hold. In the initial stages of this epistemological development, Plantinga referred to his approach as "The New Reformed Epistemology."[3]

He has since replaced this specific label with a more generic one; he now refers to his own approach as a "proper function epistemology," which has as its key concern, not the notion of the justification of knowledge (which was his initial concern), but rather of warrant.[4] In arguing more specifically for warranted *Christian* belief based on properly functioning cognitive faculties, Plantinga attempts to build what he calls the "Aquinas/Calvin model." That model, as I see it, has within it the (we could say) theological bases upon which Plantinga attempts to place the rationality of Christian belief.

Without elaborating the details of Plantinga's model, I would like to set forth a modification of his model in order to show how Reformed theology might begin to inform our epistemology, and then to note the apologetic implications of such an epistemology.[5] One caveat: this discussion should be seen as a beginning, an approximation that is open-ended. It is not meant to be the final (or the first) word on the subject. Much more development is needed.

Theological Foundations

The first thing that should be noted in any theological discussion worth its epistemological salt is that our understanding of the world is essentially related to our being created as the image of God. That is, the age-old epistemological conundrum of the subject-object relationship finds its resolution in the age-old*er* doctrine of creation; the triune God's creative and covenanting activity. When God determined

3. Note, just to cite two examples, Plantinga's articles, "The Reformed Objection to Natural Theology," *Proceedings of the American Catholic Philosophical Association* 54 (1980), and "On Reformed Epistemology," *The Reformed Journal* 32 (January 1981): 13–17.

4. There are numerous reasons for this change that do not directly affect our discussion here, and so they will be left for another time.

5. For the details of Plantinga's model see Alvin Plantinga, *Warranted Christian Belief* (Oxford: Oxford University Press, 2000).

to create man (male and female), he determined that they would have dominion over the creation: "Then God said, 'Let us make man in our image, after our likeness. And let them have dominion over the fish of the sea and over the birds of the heavens and over the livestock *and over all the earth* and over every creeping thing that creeps on the earth'" (Gen. 1:26).[6] This dominion includes (though is not exhausted by) the fact that there is a lordship relationship between man as male and female and the rest of creation. In order to understand just what this lordship relationship is, we look, in the first place, to God who is the Lord.

Two aspects of lordship should be highlighted here. (1) As Lord, God has committed himself to his creation for eternity. He has promised not to annihilate what he has made, but rather to keep it for himself forever. We call this commitment a covenant; it is a commitment of God the Lord to tie himself so inextricably to what he has made that creation, in being bound by God to God, will go on into and for eternity.[7] (2) As Lord, the relationship that obtains is not one of equality. Because God has committed himself to us does not entail that he has become an equal partner in this relationship. He is and remains God, and we are and will remain his creatures. He neither depends on us nor owes us anything (Rom 11:33–36.). We owe him allegiance and worship, and we owe it to him for eternity. He rules over us—lovingly, sovereignly, wisely—and we submit to that rule (either now or in the future—cf. Phil. 2:9–11).

When God created us in his own image, he intended for us to be lords over everything else that he made. This lordship over creation carries the same two implications, noted above, of God's lordship over us.

(1) God has committed us to creation in such a way that we are inextricably linked to it. It is instructive to notice that, in creating the animal world, God used the same "dust" that he used in creating Adam. In creating Adam, notice, "the LORD God formed the man of

---

6. Scripture quotations in this chapter are from The Holy Bible, English Standard Version, copyright © 2001 by Crossway Bibles, a division of Good News Publishers. Used by permission. All right reserved. Italics indicate emphasis added.

7. Whether or not the new creation at Christ's second coming is wholly new or is in some ways continuous with this creation, creation *per se* will continue.

dust from the ground" (compare Gen. 2:7 with Eccl. 3:20). This is intended to show us, at least, that we, like the beasts, are children of dust (Gen. 3:19). Adam (and, indirectly, Eve also since Eve came from Adam) came from the same "stuff" as the beasts (Gen. 2:19).[8] Thus we are linked with creation, in one sense, because we are taken from it; we are quite literally a part of it.

But there is a significant difference in the creation of Adam, a difference, we could say, that marks us off from everything else created: "Then the LORD God formed the man of dust from the ground and *breathed into his nostrils the breath of life*, and the man became a living creature" (Gen. 2:7). Of course, the beasts of the earth were living as well when God created them. But our living—that act of God that constituted man as a "living soul"[9]—was a result of God's own inbreathing. It was *that* inbreathing, the imparting of the very breath of God in us, that made us images of God.[10]

The point to be made here is that, in creating us as image, God bound us together not only with himself, but also with creation. There is a bond of humanity with (the rest of) creation such that, since creation, one will not, and cannot, exist without the other.

It is for this reason that Paul, in speaking of what we call "the problem of evil," can say confidently that, as a result of our sin, the whole creation groans and itself was subjected to futility (Rom. 8:19–20). It does not groan because of its own inherent deficiencies, but because, in our sinning, we subjected it to futility (cf. Gen. 3:16–19). Creation, in covenant with man, fell *because* we fell.

Thus, there is a covenant bond between man and creation; a bond that cannot be broken. In our lordship over creation, we subjected it to futility when we ourselves chose futility over obedience. This has sweeping implications for epistemology.

(2) As in God's lordship over us, our lordship over creation is not one of equals. We were meant to rule over—lovingly and wisely—all that God made. Because of the entrance of sin, matters have become

---

8. Note that, in Gen. 2:7 and 19, both Adam and the beasts are formed from הָאֲדָמָה.

9. That is, לְנֶפֶשׁ חַיָּה.

10. This should not be read dichotomistically, as if the image of God in us resides only in the spiritual, or "soulish" aspect of man. The point to be made in the text is that God constituted us, both body and soul, *as image* by virtue of his breathing into what was otherwise nonimage.

complicated (to say the least), and our ruling sometimes causes harm rather than good. The point to be made here, however, is that there is an inextricable link between ourselves and the world, a link that is both established by God and is intended to reflect his character. Because of that, we are people who are created to know and to interact with our world, all to the glory of the triune God, our Creator. It is this crucial but almost universally neglected truth—that our connection with the world is initiated, constituted, orchestrated, and sustained by the triune God—that is the theological key to a Christian epistemology.

One other theological point must be underscored. Because God is who he is, *all* of his dealings with us and with creation presuppose his voluntary condescension. In John Calvin's words:

> For who even of slight intelligence does not understand that, as nurses commonly do with infants, God is wont in a measure to "lisp" in speaking to us? Thus such forms of speaking do not so much express clearly what God is like as accommodate the knowledge of him to our slight capacity. To do this he must descend far beneath his loftiness.[11]

In relating himself to us, the triune God creates the means by which he condescends to us. He takes on human language, meaning, experience, and even flesh in order to faithfully maintain his covenant with us; and he does all of this while yet remaining fully and completely God.[12]

It may seem, therefore, that a "proper function epistemology" would most closely align itself with these truths. If man was created in covenant with God (primarily) and with creation (secondarily), and if our covenant with creation assumes an intrinsic connection between us and it, then an argument for the rationality of (at least some of) our beliefs based on the proper functioning of our cognitive faculties might seem to be the best way to formulate our epistemology.

Unfortunately, the story of creation is not the whole story. Something went wrong, terribly wrong. God's fellowship with Adam and Eve, which was a natural part of the created order, was radically and

11. John Calvin, *Institutes of the Christian Religion*, ed. John T. McNeill, trans. Ford Lewis Battles, Library of Christian Classics (Philadelphia: Westminster, 1960), 1.13.1.

12. This was, in large part, God's message to Moses in Ex. 3, and was climactically revealed to us in the person of the God-man, Jesus Christ.

decisively disrupted. The image of God as male and female, fully and completely revealed in the garden prior to sin, became a source of shame after the fall (Gen. 3:7). Though God graciously clothed Adam and Eve, the need for clothing, though necessary because of sin, was nevertheless fundamentally *un*natural, not a part of the created design or order. What was true physically was just as true spiritually; the image of God that Adam and Eve fully exhibited prior to sin, was now a source of shame and was covered up because of sin.[13]

This, then, is the serious problem, even the terminal condition, that confronts us. After the fall, the image of God becomes a source of shame; our visceral reaction to who we are as image (including the presence of God ever before us) is to hide and suppress whatever we can of that image (Gen. 3:8–10).[14]

It would seem, then, that any notion of "proper" function with respect to our cognitive faculties would need to take account, in the first place, of the radical, pervasive, and universal effects of sin on those faculties. Apart from sin, the presence of God would be a joy to us; we would be happily working in his world, walking with him in the cool of the day. We would acknowledge him and his gracious presence with every breath we took, and with everything we thought.

But our faculties no longer function that way. They have been damaged, fractured, broken, impeded, hindered, hampered, thwarted from doing what they were designed to do, since the effects of sin have enslaved and influenced them. Whereas we were designed to do all things to the glory of God—whether eating, drinking, thinking, or knowing—sin has constrained us so that, as enslaved to sin, we do all things to our own glory, or to the glory of something or someone other than God.

But his presence still remains. It is not only, as the hymn writer states, that "he shines in all that's fair," but he shines in all that's foul as well. In all that's fair we see his goodness and his mercy; in all that's foul we see his wrath and his justice. The point, however, is that God's presence was not removed from creation when sin entered it. Rather,

---

13. The theological implications of this "clothing" after the fall cannot be explored here. We should note, however, that according to Paul the graciousness of God's clothing Adam (which should be seen as both physical and spiritual) reaches its eschatological fulfillment at the *eschaton* (cf. 2 Cor. 5:1–5).

14. This is just another way of explaining what Paul details in Rom. 1:18ff.

he continues to show himself to all of his creatures made in his image. And he does that through all that exists in the creation itself.

Epistemological Applications

Beneath Plantinga's proper function epistemology is an epistemological structure he calls Reidian foundationalism. Without spelling out the details of this structure, we may note that it, like all "foundationalisms," has at its root the distinction between beliefs that are basic, and properly so, and those inferred from basic beliefs. Because of this category of properly basic beliefs, a foundationalist structure of knowledge is easily merged with the common sense realism of Thomas Reid and his followers.

As George Marsden has pointed out, however, it is just this "common sense" approach to knowledge that set the stage for the decline of Christianity's relationship to academia in the nineteenth century.[15] In arguing that nineteenth-century apologists and Christian academics were unable radically to challenge the Darwinism that sprang to life in their day, Marsden shows that, as a matter of fact, the common sense realism dominant during this time among evangelicals was ill-equipped for serious intellectual challenge. The reason it was ill-equipped, according to Marsden, was that "common sense could not settle a dispute over what was a matter of common sense."[16] This is just to say that common sense beliefs, while perhaps useful for a generic analysis of human beliefs, are not able to carry the weight of a final rationale for belief itself. The best one can hope for with such a scenario is a kind of majority vote. Granted, if the vote is a vast majority, the weight such beliefs can carry is significantly increased. But given that their status depends on human

15. See George Marsden, "The Collapse of American Evangelical Academia," in *Faith and Rationality*, ed. Alvin Plantinga and Nicholas Wolterstorff (Notre Dame, IN: University of Notre Dame Press, 1983), 219–64.

16. Marsden, "The Collapse of American Evangelical Academia," 244. At least one of the reasons for this seems obvious. If common sense beliefs function as presuppositions, then they take on the (religious) characteristic of authority, ultimacy, and so forth. But it is also "common" knowledge that common sense beliefs were only *generally* common and not absolutely so. Therefore, there was no criterion by which to determine which views are and which are not common sense. Or, to say it another way, there was no way to give a *rationale* for such common sense beliefs without, at the same time, appealing to that rationale, rather than those beliefs, as a presupposition.

behavior, it will never be possible to move toward anything more than probability with respect to the status of belief itself.[17]

What is needed, therefore, in order for the "commonness" of common sense realism to "have roots" is an epistemological structure that can support the "why and wherefore" of the knowledge situation. Because of God's creative activity, because he has made us as his image, because all of this presupposes God's revelatory activity to us, only revelation can provide such roots.[18] But just what is a revelational epistemology? According to Van Til:

> Primary and fundamental for revelational epistemology is the contention that man can have true knowledge of reality. No form of agnosticism is consistent with any form of Christianity. Oh yes, there have not been wanting those that have asserted the contrary, but they are not typical. Agnosticism is suicidal. Arguments from the possibility of error have amply demonstrated that we must choose between real knowledge or suicide. . . . All that the argument of the possibility of true knowledge can and does mean is a negation of agnosticism. Then comes the following question, not to be identified with the former, whether the possibility of true knowledge, which in this case must also be an actuality, is attained and can be attained by theistic argument or is in itself historically a product of revelation. . . . Suffice it here to state that all forms of revelational epistemology take their stand on the trustworthiness of the human consciousness in the most general sense of the term.[19]

Two elements of a revelational epistemology mentioned here by Van Til need some elaboration.

First, there is the affirmation that we can have knowledge of reality. This, of course, is what is maintained in common sense realism as

17. This is not to say that epistemic probability is essentially deficient. Some of our beliefs must necessarily remain probable. It is only to say that, if the very foundation on which our beliefs are built cannot rise above the status of epistemic probability, then *all* of our beliefs must themselves be probable beliefs. In that case, the best that we could say, just to use one example, is that God (most?) probably exists.

18. Here we must include general as well as special revelation. Just how these two relate cannot be detailed here. See Cornelius Van Til, "Nature and Scripture," in *The Infallible Word: A Symposium by the Members of the Faculty of Westminster Theological Seminary*, ed. N. B. Stonehouse and Paul Woolley (Nutley, NJ: Presbyterian and Reformed, 1978).

19. Cornelius Van Til, *The Works of Cornelius Van Til*, CD-ROM (New York: Labels Army Co., 1997).

well. Any belief thought to be basic, and properly so, is an affirmation that there is an intrinsic and intuitive connection between the subject and the object, at least in some cases. But that connection could only be asserted; it had to provide its own rationale, which, as Marsden maintains, rendered it relatively useless. The reason that a revelational epistemology can provide an affirmation of knowledge is that our knowledge of the world is inextricably tied to our knowledge of God. And our knowledge of God is a necessary element of who we are as image of God.[20] Since, as image, God has covenantally bound himself to us, we must, and do, necessarily know him. We know him because he makes himself known to us *through all that he has made*. Just as certainly as we know God, therefore, we know the world.[21] Therefore, "the trustworthiness of the human consciousness" has its foundation in God's revealing activity.[22]

Second, we should note that any idea of properly basic belief must find its ground in God's revelation (his revealing activity).

This brings us back to the beginning of our discussion. Under the general rubric of a "proper function" epistemology, Plantinga's Aquinas/Calvin model, designed to include the rationality of theistic belief, includes a capacity for the knowledge of God, which Plantinga (using Calvin's language) labels the *sensus divinitatis*. For a number of reasons, however, a modification is needed.[23]

We should first notice that any general theistic belief, unless it necessarily entails Plantinga's tripartite elements—Scripture, the work

20. There are differences, we should note here, between the knowledge of God that we have and the knowledge of the world that comes with it. The knowledge of God that comes by way of general revelation is incorrigible and infallible. Since God reveals himself such that his revelation always and everywhere gets through to us, we unavoidably and necessarily always have it. Because of sin, however, our knowledge of the world is neither incorrigible nor infallible.

21. In his explication of Van Til's epistemology, Hendrik Stoker argues for what he calls a phanerotic (revelational) investigation of reality. This, it seems to me, is fundamental to a revelational epistemology. See Hendrik G. Stoker, "Reconnoitering the Theory of Knowledge of Professor Dr. Cornelius Van Til," in *Jerusalem and Athens: Critical Discussions on the Philosophy and Apologetics of Cornelius Van Til*, ed. E. R. Geehan (Nutley, NJ: Presbyterian and Reformed, 1971), esp. 26–34.

22. This means, of course, that while we may trust our consciousness, generally speaking, just *why* we may trust it remains a mystery to those outside of Christ. They will do all within their power to attribute such trust to anything but the true God and his activity.

23. Further reasons for modification cannot be detailed here; see K. Scott Oliphint, "Epistemology and Christian Belief," *Westminster Theological Journal* 63 (2001): 151–82.

of the Holy Spirit, and faith[24]—is, *ipso facto*, irrational.[25] Any epistemology that sees such belief as rational can only do so in the context
of a deontological and internalist notion of justification. Given such
a notion, however, *any* belief is rational provided one has done one's
epistemic duties with respect to that belief. By the same token, Christian-theistic belief that entails the three elements mentioned above
will necessarily be rational.

But what of beliefs that correspond to something in reality, yet do
not include or entail rational theistic belief? What are we to think of a
person's belief, say, that she sees a tree (when, in fact, she does), while
she excludes belief in God entirely from the noetic structure?

Two things should be noted here with respect to a revelational
epistemology. First of all, it is the entrance of sin that has made the
knowledge situation so complex. Because of this complexity, we will
not be able to define precisely just where and when expressions of
sin, combined with the image of God (in its noetic expression), will
surface. Second, we can say that in general any person's belief that
(1) corresponds to some aspect of reality and (2) excludes belief in
God from the noetic structure is involved in a kind of rational/irrational
dialectic.[26] The belief, we could say, has a rational aspect to it since
it does in fact correspond to something in creation. But that rational
aspect is swallowed up in irrationality since the belief excludes the
most essential component of the fact believed: that it is created and
sustained by the triune God. The dialectic, therefore, is in reality an
antinomy that cannot be resolved apart from a person's conversion
to Christ.[27]

In other words, given the entrance and effects of sin, it seems
we cannot endorse, without significant modification, a notion of

24. See Plantinga, *Warranted Christian Belief*, chap. 8, for a discussion of these
elements.

25. Irrationality itself needs definition. For the sake of brevity, we can define it here as
holding a belief to which nothing in reality corresponds.

26. Van Til talks of the rational-irrational dialectic with respect to unbelieving thought. He
defines that dialectic, however, in the context of unbelieving thought *itself*, which is, of course,
correct. In the way I am using this dialectic here, it has reference, not first of all to the unbeliever's
own attempted coherence, but to the tension that obtains by virtue of our (prior to conversion)
enslavement to sin (and thus suppression of the truth), on the one hand, and remaining the
image of God (thus maintaining a correspondence with the world), on the other.

27. In which, as Paul reminds us, we are renewed *unto knowledge* (Col. 3:10).

proper function with respect to our cognitive faculties. Adam and Eve's faculties were functioning properly prior to the fall, but after the fall such was not the case. Given the complexity of the knowledge situation after the fall, perhaps it would be more accurate to speak of *adequate*[28] function (generally speaking), rather than proper function.

Proper function seems to be exactly what was lost at the fall.[29] If every fact is such that it reveals God, we may take that fact and believe it to be what it is, but since the fall we believe such without acknowledging the God who is revealed in that fact. In every aspect of knowledge or belief, therefore, in which the effects of sin's enslavement are operating, our cognitive faculties fail to function as they were designed to function. There is, we could say, in every functioning of our cognitive faculties in which sin dominates, an element, perhaps a strong element, of self-deception. While we know God, the covenant triune God, we hold down that knowledge in unrighteousness, and thus pretend that we can know the fact that is present to us, right before our very eyes, whether or not we know God.

Along with the implications of a revelational epistemology, we may, it seems, affirm that there are many beliefs that are, to use the language of foundationalism, properly basic. Our covenantal connection with the world (because, first of all, with God) ensures that we will always be a part of the created environment, and will be (in many cases intuitively) responding to it.[30] Much of that response will, of course, not be that of inference or argument, but will be "natural." The *ground*, however, of this "natural" reaction is precisely where apologetics has its focus.

28. One of the classic definitions of truth is this: *veritas est adaequatio rei et intellectus*. While not affirming a simple correspondence theory of truth, this definition does allow for a connection between belief and reality, without explaining the subjective situation with regard to the *adaequatio*.

29. Included in Plantinga's explanation of properly functioning cognitive faculties are a congenial environment and a teleological truth function. It would seem that all of these elements would need modification since both the environment and the end result of our cognitive processes are radically affected by sin.

30. This will be the case, it should be noted, even in the new heavens and the new earth, and in hell.

Apologetic implications

Because, as Marsden reminds us, common sense realism was unable to account for its own commonality (and thus was rendered virtually useless apologetically), we should set firmly in our minds the truth that, whatever "commonality" there is in our beliefs, such commonality can only obtain because God is who he says he is and he has done what he says he has done. The apologetic import of commonality, therefore, is that it cannot be accounted for except on the truth of the Christian position.

The apologetic challenge to epistemology, therefore, is in part to ask for a justification of that which is thought to be common. It is to challenge those outside of Christ to bring the subject-object relationship together while maintaining the random character of the universe, as well as the brute factuality of that to which our beliefs refer. This will be an impossible task. It will be a task that will arbitrarily import elements of Christian truth (borrowed capital) in order to attempt to make some sense of it all. But foreign organs cannot be transplanted into bodies that are bent on rejecting them. No matter how hard one may wish for such organs, a body built for rejection will never tolerate such foreign bodies.[31]

So, while we might affirm an adequate functioning of cognitive faculties, we will, at the same time, affirm that such adequacy itself depends on that which those same faculties will not have—an acknowledgment of the God who reveals himself, and who came to save his own in his Son.[32]

31. It should be noted here that Robert C. Koons argues for a definition of proper function that allows for a certain dysfunction. With respect to proper function, he notes: "Any organism will suffer from a certain degree of dysfunctionality. The standard is one of substantial harmony among functions, not ideal or optimal harmony." The problem with the noetic effects of sin, however, is not simply that *part* of our faculties function properly, while *part* of them malfunction; it is rather that the *essential* character of our cognitive faculties is radically damaged such that we exchange the truth given by God for a lie. This renders our faculties utterly *dis*harmonious at root. See Mieke Bal, Jonathan V. Crewe, and Leo Spitzer, *Acts of Memory: Cultural Recall in the Present* (Hanover, NH: Dartmouth College: University Press of New England, 1999), esp. 146.

32. It is encouraging that, at least formally, philosophers are arguing for the necessity of the ethical in any adequate analysis of human knowledge. While Christianity requires a necessary *Christian*-theistic component, it is nevertheless true that knowledge (as intellectual) is fundamentally ethically determined. See Linda T. Zagzebski, *Virtues of the Mind: An Inquiry*

In a revelational epistemology, therefore, the "structure" of knowledge is twofold, depending on one's covenant status. Those who remain covenant-breakers in Adam nevertheless maintain a knowledge of God that comes to them through the things that are made, by way of revelation. This knowledge of God expresses itself (generally speaking) in a connection to reality, to the world. Yet covenant-breakers suppress the truth that comes by way of the creation.[33] Knowledge, therefore, in this covenant context is still, fundamentally and at every step, dependent on revelation.

For those who, by grace, are in Christ, the true knowledge that comes through God's creation is joined together again with the true knowledge of God given in Scripture.[34] The knowledge of God that is given in general revelation becomes a subjective acknowledgment of his rule and reign over us, and we are given, by virtue of the Holy Spirit's work, true faith, in which, for the first time, we *acknowledge* God for who he is, and Jesus Christ his Son (cf. John 17:3).

When we are converted, therefore, the apologetic task begins. All of our properly basic beliefs are placed back in their proper context. We begin to understand Scripture so that we think God's thoughts after him. Through argument and persuasion (Acts 19:8–9), therefore, we plead with others to come to Christ, not simply to complete their epistemological journey, but in order to glorify God and enjoy him forever.

---

into the Nature of Virtue and the Ethical Foundations of Knowledge (Cambridge: Cambridge University Press, 1996).

33. And as Bavinck reminds us, we have, therefore, a certainty of faith: "In most earthly matters we can tolerate lesser or greater degrees of probability. But in religion, which in its deepest ground always concerns man's eternal salvation, total certainty is an indispensable requirement. The basis of our hope for eternity cannot be a human word, a result of scientific inquiry, an ideal shaped by our imagination, or a proposition built on human reasoning, for all these are shaky and fallible. They cannot support the building of our hope, for soon it would collapse into ruin. Faith—religious faith—can by its very nature rest only on a word, a promise from God, on something that proceeds from His mouth and is revealed to man either naturally or supernaturally." See Herman Bavinck, *The Certainty of Faith* (St. Catharines, Ontario: Paideia, 1980), 51.

34. Thus, Scripture is the interpretive grid through which this general revelation is understood. Scripture is, as Calvin reminds us, the spectacles through which we see everything else. Says Calvin, "Just as old or bleary-eyed men and those with weak vision, if you thrust before them a most beautiful volume, even if they recognize it to be some sort of writing, yet can scarcely construe two words, but with the aid of spectacles will begin to read distinctly; so Scripture, gathering up the otherwise confused knowledge of God in our minds, having dispersed our dullness, clearly shows us the true God." *Institutes*, 1.6.1.

12

The Fate of Apologetics
in an Age
of Normal Nihilism

MICHAEL W. PAYNE

*A*pologetics[1] has had a bumpy ride in recent years.[2] Paul Griffiths writes, "In almost all mainstream institutions in which theology is taught in the USA and Europe, apologetics as an intellectual discipline does not figure prominently in the curriculum."[3]

1. Richard Rorty playfully lowercased the word *philosophy* to indicate the lowered expectations of the game of philosophy construed along pragmatist lines as compared to Philosophy as traditionally construed since Plato (largely following "realist" or "representationalist" lines). I see a similar recent reconstruction of the discipline of apologetics by postliberals as indicative of lowered expectations in light of the impact of post-philosophical ideas. For Rorty's ideas on the subject see his *Consequences of Pragmatism* (Minneapolis: University of Minnesota Press, 1982), which gives a more complete illustration of his distinction between philosophy and Philosophy.

2. Particularly apologetics construed as a defense of the Truthfulness (Truth with a capital *T*) of one position as opposed to another (operating with some version of bivalence).

3. Paul J. Griffiths, *An Apology for Apologetics* (Maryknoll, NY: Orbis, 1991), 2. After doing an admittedly limited and random survey of my own (focusing exclusively on MDiv programs in evangelical and Reformed seminaries), I found that of the seven seminary catalogues consulted (Reformed Theological Seminary, Calvin Seminary, Covenant Seminary, Columbia Seminary, SC, Mid-America Seminary, Westminster Seminary California, and Westminster Seminary in

Any number of reasons can explain this decline: (1) the influence of postmodernism[4] and the attending skepticism it engenders toward all attempts to adjudicate between competing truth claims by employing putatively universal rational criteria[5] (a quest that has proven illusory according to post-secular philosophy);[6] (2) the rising awareness of "multiculturalism" and the unwillingness of many to engage in an enterprise that might imply any form of culturally based superiority. (Since all absolute claims are generally rooted in some

---

Philadelphia), only two (both Westminster seminaries) require more than one apologetics course. Two of the seven require no apologetics courses. Both the Westminster institutions likewise make apologetics central to the overall *raison d'être* of their respective institutions—as reflected in their purpose statements. This is of course not to suggest that the sheer number of courses adds up to much, but it does indicate that some thought has been given to the importance of courses in apologetics as central to the theological formation of students preparing for the gospel ministry.

4. John Milbank has offered a tantalizing twist on "postmodern[ism]" as really the second phase of modern critical thought. According to Milbank, "The Sublime in Kierkegaard," *Heythrop Journal* 37 (1996): 288: "In the first phase, inaugurated by Kant, the sublime or the indeterminable was safely off-limits for the proper exercise of theoretical reason, which is confined to notions that can be 'schematized' within finite space and time. In the second phase, by contrast, sublimity is perceived to contaminate even what is deceptively taken for finitude, so that it is precisely our 'here' and 'now' which cannot be finally characterized, but are only seized in their passing evanescence." There were according to Milbank pre-modern "postmodern" anticipations! Milbank elaborates further on this theme in "Problematizing the Secular: The Post-Postmodern Agenda," in *The Shadow of Spirit*, ed. Philippa Berry and Andrew Wernick (London: Routledge, 1992). Toulmin seems to suggest something similar in his *Cosmopolis* (see n. 7 below), as does Louis Dupre in his *The Way of Theology in Karl Barth: Essays and Comments*, in Princeton Theological Monograph Series (Allison Park, PA: Pickwick, 1986). Recent assessment of the "postmodern" include the incisive analysis provided by Pierre Manent, *The City of Man*, trans. Marc le Pain (Princeton: Princeton University Press, 1998); Nicholas Boyle, *Who Are We Now? Christian Humanism and the Global Market from Hegel to Heaney* (Notre Dame, IN: Notre Dame University Press, 1998); David Toole, *Waiting for Godot in Sarajevo: Theological Reflections on Nihilism, Tragedy, and Apocalypse* (Boulder, CO: Westview, 1998); Terry Eagleton, *The Illusions of Postmodernism* (Oxford: Basil Blackwell, 1996); Catherine Pickstock, *After Writing: On the Liturgical Consummation of Philosophy* (Oxford: Basil Blackwell, 1998); Philip Blond, ed., *Post-Secular Philosophy: Between Philosophy and Theology* (London: Routledge, 1998).

5. Jean-François Lyotard defines postmodern as "incredulity toward metanarratives" in *The Postmodern Condition: A Report on Knowledge*, in Theory and History of Literature (Minneapolis: University of Minnesota Press, 1984), xxii–xxv.

6. In this regard one should consult the article by William Edgar, "No News Is Good News: Modernity, the Postmodern, and Apologetics," *Westminster Theological Journal* 57 (1995): 277–97; likewise other recent articles bemoan the state of apologetics in a postmodern situation, e.g., J. P. Moreland, "Philosophical Apologetics, the Church, and Contemporary Culture," *Journal of the Evangelical Theological Society* 39, no. 1 (1996): 123ff.; David K. Clark, "Narrative Theology and Apologetics," *Journal of the Evangelical Theological Society* 36, no. 4 (1993): 493ff.; Karl Barth and Fernand Ryser, *Philosophie et théologie* (Genéve: Labor et Fides, 1960), 108ff.

Michael W. Payne

religious tradition, which is itself a sociological-cultural phenomenon, the conclusion should be obvious!) As Griffiths points out, in such an environment "to be an apologist for the truth of one religious claim or set of claims over against another is, in certain circles, seen as not far short of being a racist."[7]

Such antipathy toward apologetics reflects what Griffiths identifies as an "underlying scholarly orthodoxy" that sees "understanding" as the only goal of interreligious dialogue and "judgment and criticism of religious beliefs or practices other than those of one's own community as always inappropriate," thus avoiding any defense of the truthfulness of those beliefs or practices.[8] The consequent diffidence toward the practice of apologetics has been further exacerbated by the influence of George Lindbeck's work *The Nature of Doctrine*,[9] which seems to suggest, according to some at least, that since all religious experience is "cultural-linguistic" in nature, any attempt to engage in apologetic discussion should be at best *ad hoc*, and then only for the purposes of suing for peace and putting an end to hostilities; in other words, agreeing to disagree.

7. Griffiths, *An Apology for Apologetics*, 2. Robert Knudsen reflects with similar dismay on the increasing indifference toward the teaching of apologetics and discusses the historical context of this development in his inaugural address as professor of apologetics at Westminster Theological Seminary, titled "The Transcendental Perspective of Westminster's Apologetic," *Westminster Theological Journal* 48 (1986): 233–39. The attitude of "scholarly orthodoxy" described by Griffiths is ironic when one considers historically the motivation behind Descartes' own project of establishing a rational basis for adjudicating religious conflicts; one that is non-territorial or tradition-bound, hence obligatory to any "reasonable" person. See Stephen Toulmin's excellent discussion of this perspective in his *Cosmopolis* (Chicago: University of Chicago Press, 1990). Michael J. Buckley develops the negative implications of Descartes' project in his magisterial work, *At the Origins of Modern Atheism* (New Haven, CT: Yale University Press, 1987). Similar concerns on the role of apologetics in postmodern missions can be seen in the debate between Konrad Raiser and Lesslie Newbigin. The discussion arose from Newbigin's review of Raiser's book titled *Ecumenism in Transition: A Paradigm Shift in the Ecumenical Movement?* (Geneva: World Council of Churches, 1991). Newbigin's review was titled "Ecumenical Amnesia," *International Bulletin of Missionary Research* 18, no. 1 (1994): 2–5. Raiser subsequently wrote a response, "Is Ecumenical Apologetics Sufficient? A Response to Lesslie Newbigin's Ecumenical Amnesia," *International Bulletin of Missionary Research* 18, no. 2 (1994): 50–51.

8. Griffiths, *An Apology for Apologetics*, xi. Richard Rorty's "ironic stance" reflects this sentiment, whereby an attitude of "irony" should replace the "rule of judgment." In *Contingency, Irony, and Solidarity* (Cambridge: Cambridge University Press, 1989), he notes that the enlightened postmodern individual is one who recognizes "the contingency of his or her own most central beliefs and desires . . . which don't refer back to something beyond the reach of time and chance" (p. xv).

9. George Lindbeck, *The Nature of Doctrine* (Philadelphia: Westminster Press, 1984).

This appears to be the fate of religion and philosophy generally in an era that James C. Edwards (echoing the words of Nietzsche!) calls the "age of normal nihilism."[10] After all, truth only has currency in the philosophical economy of "representations," *ding an sich*, and forms. This, according to normal nihilism, is an economy that no longer exists with any philosophical credibility. There is nothing for representations to represent except more representations (e.g., Berkeley), until ultimately we are left only with interpretations, or *impositions of points of view* (Foucault's *regimes of truth?*). The *Ubermensch* of normal nihilism recognizes its role as self-creating and the author of all values. As Nietzsche writes, "Not 'know' but to schematize—to impose upon chaos as much regularity and form as our practical needs require." In the formation of reason, logic, and the categories, it was need that was authoritative: the need, not to "know," but to subsume, to schematize, for the purpose of intelligibility and calculation.[11]

We are left with "interpretation," which is the introduction of meaning—not explanation. "There are no facts, everything is in flux, incomprehensible, elusive; what is relatively most enduring is—our opinions."[12] There is no criteriological role played by some *Other*, some object (be it "reality" or otherwise) to which our thoughts must conform. "A 'thing-in-itself' is just as perverse as a 'sense-in-itself,' a 'meaning-in-itself.' There are no 'facts-in-themselves,' for a sense must always be projected unto them before there can be 'facts.'" The question, what is that? is an imposition of meaning from some other viewpoint. "Essence," the "essential nature," is something perspective and already presupposes a multiplicity. At the bottom of it always lies the question, what is that for me? (for us? for all that lives? etc.).[13]

What fate befalls "truth" in the Nietzschean world? For Nietzsche, truth is a vestige of our Platonic-Cartesian-Kantian past. Truth is "the kind of error without which a certain species of life could not live. The value for life is ultimately decisive."[14] Truth is no longer conceived

10. James C. Edwards, *The Plain Sense of Things: The Fate of Religion in an Age of Normal Nihilism* (University Park, PA: The Pennsylvania State University Press, 1997).

11. Friedrich Nietzsche, *The Will to Power*, ed. Walter Kaufmann, trans. Walter Kaufmann and R. J. Hollingdale (New York: Random House, 1967), sec. 515.

12. Ibid., sec. 604.

13. Ibid., sec. 556.

14. Ibid., sec. 493.

as the correspondence of thought-being, idea and immaculate fact, but rather as a value that *we* deem as ultimately decisive for life. What we value, we canonize as truth and all values are for Nietzsche functions/exercises of will, the *will to power* and for the purpose of self-preservation.[15] Values are "the basic filters through which raw experience is passed, thereby being modulated into a coherent and livable world."[16] All values, including truth, lose their universality or objectivity (not that they ever possessed such status in the first place!) and become nothing more or less than the strategic applications of force concretized in social practices.[17] Nothing is immune to this devaluation of all values. "What does nihilism mean? That the highest values devaluate themselves. The aim is lacking: 'why?' finds no answer."[18]

Nihilism is thus, according to Edwards, the "secret logic of Western culture: the worm in the bud all along."[19] We crave a full meal and have ingested all variety of cuisine from Plato to Descartes to the Bible. When we have finished, "when we have eaten all we can hold; three hours later you're hungry again."[20] Our highest values have become self-devalued and we must rest in our nihilism, not as some kind of brutish pathological beast, weary and pessimistic, but as those who

15. Nietzsche writes: "And do you know what 'the world' is to me? Shall I show it to you in my mirror? This world: a monster of energy . . . a play of forces and waves of forces, at the same time one and many, increasing here and at the same time decreasing there; a sea of forces flowing and rushing together, eternally changing, eternally flooding back, with tremendous years of recurrence, with an ebb and a flood of its forms, striving toward the most complex, out the stillest, most rigid, coldest forms toward the hottest, most turbulent, most self-contradictory, and then again returning home to the simple out of this abundance, out of the play of contradictions back to the joy of concord . . . a becoming that knows no satiety, no disgust, no weariness: this is my *Dionysian* world of the eternally self-destroying. . . . Do you want a name for this world? . . . *This world is the will to power—and nothing besides!* And you yourselves are also this will to power—and nothing besides!" Ibid., sec. 1067.

16. Edwards, *The Plain Sense of Things*, 37.

17. This Nietzschean perspective pervades Michel Foucault's notion of "regimes of truth." *In Power/Knowledge: Selected Interviews and Other Writings 1972–1977* (New York: Pantheon, 1980), he writes: "Truth is a thing of this world: it is produced only by virtue of multiple forms of constraint. And it induces regular effects of power. Each society has its regime of truth, its 'general politics' of truth: that is, the types of discourse which it accepts and makes function as true; the mechanism and instances which enable one to distinguish true and false statements, the means by which each is sanctioned; the techniques and procedures accorded value in the acquisition of truth; the status of those who are charged with saying what counts as true" (131).

18. Nietzsche, *The Will to Power*, sec. 2.

19. Edwards, *The Plain Sense of Things*, 43.

20. Ibid.

recognize "that our lives are constituted by self-devaluating values." Normal nihilism is

> just the Western intellectual's rueful recognition and tolerance of her own historical and conceptual contingency. To be a normal nihilist is just to acknowledge that, however fervent and essential one's commitment to a particular set of values, that's all one ever has: a commitment to some particular set of values.[21]

The fruits of this new economy can be seen in a variety of disputes from anthropological to scientific. A classic case is the one arising from the discussion between Peter Winch and Kai Nielsen over the question of what constitutes science and rationality when comparing different cultures.[22] Winch was critical of Evans-Pritchard's study of witchcraft among the Azande, which Evans-Pritchard concluded were unscientific and irrational. This, according to Winch, was an erroneous imposition of alien "outsiders'" criteria of what is rational (in this instance a Western view of science) upon a worldview and practice that could only be understood from "inside." They were simply engaged in a different language game: "Zande notions of witchcraft do not constitute a theoretical system in terms of which Azande try to gain a quasi-scientific understanding of the world."[23] The response by Winch was seen by Kai Nielsen as a logical extension of Wittgenstein's notion of "language games," which, according to Nielsen, results in a kind of social fideism, or what he regarded as "Wittgensteinian fideism":

> Religion is a unique and very ancient form of life with its own distinctive criteria. It can only be understood or criticized, and then only in a piecemeal way, from within this mode by someone who has a

21. Ibid., 46–47.

22. Peter Winch, *The Idea of a Social Science, and Its Relation to Philosophy* (London: Routledge & Kegan Paul, 1958); also see Peter Winch, "Understanding a Primitive Society," *American Philosophical Quarterly* 1 (1964); for a less-than-sympathetic analysis of Winch, see Robin Horton, *Patterns of Thought in Africa and the West* (Cambridge: Cambridge University Press, 1993), 138–60. For an African perspective on the same issue, see Kwame Anthony Appiah, *In My Father's House* (Cambridge: Cambridge University Press, 1992), 120–27; also see D. A. Masolo, *African Philosophy in Search of Identity* (Bloomington, IN: Indiana University Press, 1994), 124–26.

23. Winch, "Understanding a Primitive Society," 307–24.

participant's understanding. . . . Philosophy cannot relevantly criticize religion; it can only display for us the workings, the style of functioning, of religious discourse.[24]

Similar conflicts arose as a result of Thomas Kuhn's work on the philosophy of science[25] and the apparent threat such thinking posed to our purported objectivity in the matter of scientific methodology and discovery. Once notions of objectivity, neutrality, and invariability were cast by the wayside, all that seemed to be left was personal preference and the celebration of whatever seems to work or is seen to produce rewards of sufficient quantity that life is considered sufficiently better as a result.

What's an apologist to do under such circumstances? In the following I will consider one recent attempt by David Kamitsuka to re-introduce apologetics to the public realm of discourse, an attempt that comes from a hybrid of "liberation, postliberal and revisionary" perspectives.[26] In doing so I will attempt to explore in greater detail the use Kamitsuka makes of John Rawls's notion of "reflective equilibrium." Rawls is viewed by Kamitsuka as providing a useful tool by which competing religious and philosophical traditions can be assessed and an adequate defense of *the relative superiority/usefulness* of one over another presented. Although one might follow any number of paths in analyzing Kamitsuka's position, the focus that follows will be on his attempt to establish a common area of agreement based upon a fallibilist approach to apologetics that will provide the basis for serious critical dialogue between the Christian and the non-Christian. Further, some cautionary reflection will be provided concerning the way out of the impasse created by the position stimulated by Lindbeck and others, which seems to resolve into an "incorrigibility thesis" regarding the ineffectiveness of arguments for superiority of one position over another, as they are construed by Kamitsuka.

24. Kai Nielsen, "Wittgensteinian Fideism," *Philosophy* 62 (1967): 191–93.
25. Thomas S. Kuhn, *The Structure of Scientific Revolutions* (Chicago: University of Chicago Press, 1970).
26. The fact that Kamitsuka is arguing from within such a hybridized intellectual environment is made clear by Kamitsuka himself in his *Theology and Contemporary Culture: Liberation, Postliberal and Revisionary Perspectives* (Cambridge: Cambridge University Press, 1999), 1–11.

The Search for Common Ground in *ad hoc* Apologetics

The modern apologist finds himself in what appears to be a conundrum. Once he signs the death certificate for apologetics as it has been construed (on grounds more often than not that are philosophically justifiable!) in one or more of the traditional senses—for example, as a rational engagement with unbelief, built on a foundationalist epistemology, or as a "translational" methodology seeking in the fundament of human experience a suitable bed for apologetic exchange (Tillich)—what options are left? It is precisely this situation that David Kamitsuka describes and attempts to redress in his work on apologetics.[27]

Kamitsuka is interested in arguing for the theoretical justifiability of apologetics in light of nonfoundationalism and in this way offering an apology for the viability of argument between diverse "grammars" in a Lindbeckian framework. Kamitsuka in particular finds Rawls's theory of "reflective equilibrium" a means whereby meaningful conversation can transpire between people of different religious and philosophical traditions. In order to understand exactly how Kamitsuka develops his argument, we need some background on both Lindbeck and Rawls. We will keep our descriptions brief.[28]

Lindbeck's "Cultural-Linguistic Alternative" or a Performative Theory of Truth

According to George Lindbeck, previous approaches offered to explain doctrinal and religious diversity have failed to provide adequate concepts for explaining constancy and change, both intramurally (among the various Christian traditions) and extramurally between the world's religions. This is due, according to Lindbeck, to the continued employment of concepts and language that were born out

27. David Kamitsuka, "The Justification of Religious Belief in the Pluralistic Public Realm: Another Look at Postliberal Apologetics," *Journal of Religion* 76, no. 4 (October 1996): 588–606, as well as his *Theology and Contemporary Culture*, cited above. A more strictly "postliberal" approach without the "revisionary" (e.g., David Tracy) influences can be found in the work of William Werpehowski, "Ad Hoc Apologetics," *Journal of Religion* 66 (1986): 282–301.

28. I am not interested in criticizing Lindbeck's categorizations and especially the dissatisfaction individuals like David Tracy and others feel in his treatment of their ideas. Rather, granting Lindbeck's scheme as a working hypothesis, what are its implications for apologetics?

of a context that no longer exists. What worked at Nicea or Geneva simply won't work today.

He classifies these theories as fitting one of three models. For our purposes we will limit discussion to two of the models:[29] (1) cognitive-propositionalist and (2) experiential-expressivist. The former attempts to ground all doctrinal formulations as meeting truth conditions that follow neatly from correspondence or realist theories of meaning and reality. The latter reduces religious language and theology to fundamentally aesthetic expressions based on *Anschauung und Gefuhl*. For the former, any doctrinal change necessarily entails a change in meaning, since terms are understood to refer/correspond to the unchanging reality they identify and designate. For the latter, meanings may and in fact do change while the language itself may remain the same. For the experiential-expressivist, insofar as "doctrines function as nondiscursive symbols, they are polyvalent in import and therefore subject to changes of meaning or even to a total loss of meaningfulness."[30]

Lindbeck thus offers another alternative for justifying both constancy and change in theological formulations. This alternative he calls the "cultural-linguistic" approach to theology. Here the correspondence is found neither between words and the immutable reality to which they putatively refer, nor between feelings and their objectification in symbols, but rather between religion and language along with the practices they codify (culture). Here the emphasis is on "those respects in which religions resemble languages together with their correlative forms of life and are thus similar to cultures (insofar as these are understood semiotically as reality and value systems—that is, as idioms for the construction of reality and the living of life)."[31]

Religion is thus construed as a "system of discursive and nondiscursive symbols linking motivation and action and providing an ultimate legitimation for basic patterns of thought, feeling and behavior uniquely characteristic of a given community or society and its

29. Lindbeck actually describes a third model that is an attempted synthesis between the first two. However, he subsumes this third approach, which he refers to as the "two-dimensional" approach, under his discussions of the first two. He explains that he finds this third approach "awkward and complex." Lindbeck, *The Nature of Doctrine*, 17.

30. Ibid.

31. Ibid., 18.

members."[32] Doctrines thus become "communally authoritative rules of discourse, attitude and action," and serve as "regulative" or "rule" theories.[33] This constitutes a medium that then molds and directs the lives of the practitioners.

Lindbeck places the greatest emphasis upon the "outer" or *verbum externum* rather than the "inner" *verbum internum*. Rather than begin with the experience, both pre-conceptually and pre-symbolically, Lindbeck proposes that without the preexisting "scheme" or grammar functioning as the *a priori* of experience, there could not be the inner experience. He writes, "We cannot identify, describe, or recognize experience *qua* experience without the use of signs and symbols."[34] These signs and symbols take the form of myths or narratives that "structure all dimensions of existence," and are the "medium in which one moves . . . a set of skills that one employs," offering the practitioner a vocabulary and syntax for determining appropriate response and behavior.[35]

Rawls and Justice without Ontology

Like Lindbeck, John Rawls is concerned with mediation, accounting for change without surrendering to ultimate contingency. Whereas Lindbeck is principally concerned with theology and theological traditions, both inside and outside the church, Rawls wishes to "apply the principle of tolerance to philosophy itself."[36] Summarizing Rawls's ideas can be highly problematic, even for those who purport to be specialists in Rawlsian theory.[37] Having said this, we can tender a brief summary as follows:

32. Ibid., 62. Here Lindbeck is paraphrasing Clifford Geertz, *The Interpretation of Cultures* (New York: Basic Books, 1973), 90. This reflects Geertz's model of "thick" description as opposed to "thin" description. The former is semiotically enriched, whereas the latter tends toward more superficial description.

33. Lindbeck, *The Nature of Doctrine*, 18.

34. Ibid., 36.

35. Ibid., 32–35.

36. John Rawls, "Justice as Fairness: Political Not Metaphysical," *Philosophy and Public Affairs* 14 (1985): 225.

37. The question of whether one reads Rawls's *A Theory of Justice* in light of later formulations by Rawls or reads later formulations as consistent extrapolations from his earlier works has characterized much of the debate around Rawls's ideas and their interpretation. The most popular controversy surrounds Michael Sandel's analysis of Rawls, found in his *Liberalism and*

Rawls is attempting to find a "public conception of justice," which is suitable for a liberal democratic society like our own. This precludes the use of philosophical or moral conceptions of the self or society such as those memorialized by the Enlightenment or religion in general. He writes, "Philosophy as the search for truth about an independent metaphysical and moral order cannot . . . provide a workable and shared basis for a political conception of justice in a democratic society."[38] Why? Either one so generalizes religious or philosophical conceptions of the "self" so that everyone is "religious," or one falls prey to "essentialist" notions of the self (Kantian), which are philosophically specious.[39] Rather, Rawls starts from within an existing democratic tradition from which he then proceeds to extrapolate what appear to be common instances of justice. He states, "It tries to draw solely upon the basic intuitive ideas that are embedded in the political institutions of a democratic society and the public traditions of their interpretation."[40] These include religious toleration and rejection of slavery, to name but two. One then proceeds to arrange these into a coherent conception of justice.[41]

Since "fairness" is the good toward which Rawls aims in his formulations, he employs a methodology that is designed to ensure his outcomes. This precludes the need for any antecedent philosophical anthropology as a foundation for our conceptualizations of ends.[42]

---

the Limits of Justice (Cambridge: Cambridge University Press, 1982). For a different interpretation, see Richard Rorty, *Objectivity, Relativism, and Truth* (Cambridge: Cambridge University Press, 1991), esp. 175–96. An excellent collection of essays on Rawls can be found in Norman Daniels, ed., *Reading Rawls: Critical Studies on Rawls'* A Theory of Justice (New York: Basic Books, 1975).

38. Rawls, "Justice as Fairness," 230.

39. It is precisely here that Sandel sees Rawls's theory of the original position and the veil of ignorance breaking down. In *Liberalism and the Limits of Justice*, Sandel describes this as a "deontology with a Humean face" and writes that it "either fails as deontology or recreates in the original position the disembodied subject it resolves to avoid"(p. 14).

40. Rawls, "Justice as Fairness," 225–26.

41. Ibid., 230.

42. This is one of the disputed points in Rawls's theory that Michael Sandel argues in *Liberalism and the Limits of Justice*. It is Sandel's contention that Rawls in fact does argue for an antecedent theory of the "self," a Kantian self in fact, but without the implicit metaphysics of Kant. It is precisely here that Kamitsuka's attempt to have it both ways comes to a halt. The necessity for "revisionary" capabilities as *sine qua non* of the "conversation" between disputing parties is only possible if one de-Kantianizes Rawls. However, once one has accomplished this task, the conversation partners are now on purely "pragmatic" ground, where the background theory that is constitutive of Wide Reflective Equilibrium simply is not supposed to exist.

Rather, he proceeds by constructing what he calls the "original position," a position hidden behind a "veil of ignorance," where agents know less, rather than more, than "actual" human agents. Moving the "social contract" idea to the limit of higher abstraction, these agents do not know their social or economic position, which would include their assets, or their conceptions of the good.[43] They are in fact blind to the difference. The "original position" is "not an axiomatic (or deductive) basis from which principles are derived but a procedure for singling out principles most fitting to the conception of the person most likely to be held, at least implicitly, in a democratic society."[44] He writes:

> The upshot of these considerations is that justice as fairness is not at the mercy, so to speak, of existing wants and interests. It sets up an Archimedean point for assessing the social system without invoking a priori considerations. The long range aim of society is settled in its main lines irrespective of the particular desires and needs of its present members.[45]

Built on a historical-sociological description of the contemporary form our (American) democracy has taken, Rawls is simply asserting that such is "the most reasonable doctrine for us."[46]

David Kamitsuka and "Wide Reflective Equilibrium Apologetics"

Kamitsuka sharply rejects the criticism that postliberals are disinterested in apologetics and are in fact paralyzed by their commitment to the Lindbeckian program of religion as "cultural linguistic."[47] Consistent with the views of Werpehowski and others mentioned above, Kamitsuka also rejects any putatively neutral norms for rational discourse that would transcend historic situatedness (the Enlightenment

43. John Rawls, *A Theory of Justice* (Cambridge, MA: Belknap Press of Harvard University Press, 1999), 11–12.
44. John Rawls, "Kantian Constructivism in Moral Theory," *Moral Philosophy* 88 (1980): 572.
45. Rawls, *A Theory of Justice*, 261.
46. Ibid., 519.
47. This criticism is part of the stimulus for Kamitsuka's article and is reflected in an earlier article by Richard Lints, "The Postpositivist Choice: Tracy or Lindbeck?" *Journal of the American Academy of Religion* 61, no. 4 (1993): 658ff.

dream?), but doesn't want to leave us homeless with regard to the apologetic enterprise. Rather, the need is to develop more explicitly "the extent to which [postliberals] can and do . . . rely on a notion of a *shared rational space*."[48] Kamitsuka thus sets out to develop an apologetic method that he describes as a "kind of coherence approach to the justification of Christian beliefs, which utilizes a notion of contextually based shared rational space in public conversation."[49] Kamitsuka identifies this "coherence approach" as a "wide reflective equilibrium" methodology, borrowing from John Rawls's work on justice.[50]

According to Kamitsuka, such an approach is as "rational as one can get in any nonfoundationalist attempt to redeem the viability of one's claims."[51] Kamitsuka acquiesces to the postmodern delimitation of "truth" insofar as he limits his own procedural steps to questions of "validity" as opposed to an explicit analysis of truth conditions.[52] What are then needed in any discussion of competing rationalities are not "ultimate" criteria, which, after all (as we saw earlier), have been sundered by Nietzschean genealogical methods born of absolute historicism, but rather, greater "clarity." He is proposing a "wide reflective equilibrium" approach that suggests a third level beyond narrow reflective equilibrium. Some further elucidation is in order.

Kamitsuka is building his application of Rawls around the work of Norman Daniels and Kai Nielsen. Daniels in particular has applied Rawls's notion of reflective equilibrium to matters of ethical dispute. For example, narrow reflective equilibrium (NRE)[53]consists of (a) the articulated set of moral judgments held by a particular person and (b) a set of general moral principles that systematizes (a).[54] The ques-

48. Kamitsuka, "The Justification of Religious Belief," 589, emphasis mine.

49. Ibid., 589.

50. Rawls, *A Theory of Justice*. The follow-up book by Rawls on this subject, with some adjustments being made to his earlier formulations, is *Political Liberalism* (New York: Columbia University Press, 1993).

51. Kamitsuka, "The Justification of Religious Belief," 590.

52. This is consistent with Lindbeck's own cautious approach to questions of "truth" that reduce largely to "coherence" and "performatory" resolutions (cf. *The Nature of Doctrine,*, 63–69). We shall explore the implications of this later in the essay.

53. Narrow Reflective Equilibrium hereafter cited as NRE.

54. Here Kamitsuka is following Norman Daniels, "Wide Reflective Equilibrium and Theory Acceptance in Ethics," *The Journal of Philosophy* 76 (1979): 21–25 (reprinted in his *Justice and Justification: Reflective Equilibrium in Theory and Practice* [Cambridge: Cambridge University Press, 1996], 21–46).

tion that goes unaddressed and hence unanswered in NRE approaches is *why* one set of judgments and principles should be preferred over another.

Wide reflective equilibrium (WRE)[55] expands the circle of engagement and argument to encompass a third set of "relevant background theories," which would include the moral, social, political, and empirical.[56] Using Hans Frei's formulations,[57] Kamitsuka offers the following illustration of how we can configure NRE with (a) to (b) as follows:

(a) *Specific judgment (stable belief): the church's proclamation of Jesus' crucifixion and resurrection as told in the biblical narrative.*

(b) *General principle (regulative doctrinal principle): Westminster Confession of Faith, 8.4.*

This office the Lord Jesus did most willingly undertake, which, that he might discharge, he was made under the law, and did perfectly fulfill it; endured most grievous torments immediately in his soul, and most painful sufferings in his body; was crucified and died; was buried, and remained under the power of death, yet saw no corruption. On the third day he arose from the dead, with the same body in which he suffered; with which also he ascended into heaven, and there sitteth at the right hand of his Father, making intercession; and shall return to judge men and angels, at the end of the world.

What is lacking in NRE is any attempt "to show why one grammar (in this instance the WCF) is to be preferred over another."[58] Otherwise, we have simply the coherentist, that is, confessionalist picture of NRE, absent what could potentially make this "publicly intelligible." The answer is the inclusion of (c), which "helps to bring out the relative

55. Wide Reflective Equilibrium hereafter cited as WRE.
56. Cf., Kai Nielsen, *After the Demise of the Traditions: Rorty, Critical Theory and the Fate of Philosophy* (Boulder, CO: Westview, 1991), 199.
57. Hans W. Frei, "Theological Reflections on the Account of Jesus' Death and Resurrection," *Christian Scholar* 49 (1966): 263.
58. Kamitsuka, "The Justification of Religious Belief," 591; cf. Norman Daniels, "On Some Methods of Ethics and Linguistics."

strengths and weaknesses of . . . alternative sets of principles." For example, the addition of the following:

(c) *Background theory.* The Bible means what it says, that is, it fits into what Frei refers to as a "realistic narrative" framework (hence, a literarily justified theory of reading and interpretation). Such an approach also gives us the most complete picture of Jesus as he is portrayed in the narrative, which thus coheres with what a philosophically informed anthropology would expect from reading the text(s).

Such addition initiates a "give and take" or revisionary process whereby all three sets come in for adjustment and/or abandonment. According to Kamitsuka, "WRE marks an advance over the simple coherence of NRE by considering competing sets of principles and judgments and by using background theories (c) that are independent from (a) and (b)."[59] He goes on to suggest that even where (a) and (b) seem incapable of rapprochement, "workable debate can begin at the level of background theories." Such an approach is thus "coherentist, fallibilistic and contextual, thus satisfying any open minded conversation partner."[60]

Kamitsuka accuses most of Lindbeck's critics of misconstruing his "cultural linguistic" model in such a way that argument remains on the level of (a) and (b). Thus making the religious conversation purely intramural, without the potential for serious interreligious dialogue. For Kamitsuka, such a construal is unjustified since the postliberal model proposed by Lindbeck (and enhanced by Rawls) is representative of WRE and not NRE. This is reflected in what Kamitsuka describes as the two general apologetic approaches, which grow naturally out of the WRE model. He designates these as (1) *non-Christian specific* and (2) *Christian specific* approaches.

The *non-Christian specific* approach would be represented by Aquinas's "proofs," in which a general theistic context is created as a potentially useful background where "scriptural and creedal descriptions of who God is . . . can be given a specifiable referent."[61] Such an

59. Kamitsuka, "The Justification of Religious Belief," 592.
60. Ibid.
61. George Lindbeck, "Discovering Thomas: The Classic Statement of Christian Theism," *Una Sancta* 24, no. 1 (1967): 47, 50.

approach makes, according to Kamitsuka, specific Christian talk of God coherent and reasonable to the otherwise skeptical and secular mind.[62]

According to Kamitsuka, Werpehowski illustrates a *Christian-specific wide equilibrium* approach in his apologetic methodology. His construal of Werpehowski takes the form of a three-step procedure. First, we begin building a cumulative case by utilizing the test of coherence, whereby the non-Christian interlocutor is shown the inconsistencies of her specific judgments and understanding of the facts. This is followed by a more complete display of the web of Christian beliefs and practices as to their inner logic and coherence and connection with a distinct background theory. The final step is to show the superiority of Christianity in terms of its *assimilative power* (Lindbeck), its capacity to give a more plausible account of the way things are and the way things should be.[63] As Lindbeck describes the process, the demonstration of assimilative power is seen in "an accumulation of successes or failures in making practically and cognitively coherent sense of relevant data."[64]

Kamitsuka is quick to acknowledge, however, that the degree of success or failure in establishing or confirming this assimilative power will more than likely be mitigated by the degree of willingness on the part of the non-Christian to acknowledge it. After all, such an acknowledgment (surrender?) is driven by a host of paradigm-dependent notions. Consistent with Richard Bernstein's analysis, such admissions are matters not of understanding only, but of what is acknowledged as a "problem" and what "standard" is seen as admissible in measuring success or failure.[65]

62. In this context, Kamitsuka reintroduces a revised transcendental argument as potentially useful particularly in the postmodern environment. Following David Tracy, Kamitsuka limits the efficacy of such arguments in terms of their "relative adequacy," building on a notion of truth as "manifestation" that continually reminds us of the ongoing "disclosure-concealment-recognition process" whereby we are reminded that the conversation is never over (a kind of "infinite regress"?). David Tracy, *Plurality and Ambiguity* (New York: Harper & Row, 1987), 28–46.

63. Lindbeck discusses this in *The Nature of Doctrine*, 131. Bruce D. Marshall, "Absorbing the World," in *Theology and Dialogue*, ed. Bruce D. Marshall (Notre Dame, IN: University of Notre Dame Press, 1990), 69–104, develops this strategy further and with greater specificity.

64. Lindbeck, *The Nature of Doctrine*, 131.

65. Richard Bernstein, *Beyond Objectivism and Relativism* (Philadelphia: University of Pennsylvania Press, 1983), 85.

Conclusions: The Search for a Language of Perspicuous Contrast

Kamitsuka is to be commended for his attempt at reintroducing the subject of Christian apologetics as an important issue for post-liberal theology and theologians. Even Kamitsuka's appropriation of a "transcendental argument" is to be commended, even if it lacks the self-critical perspective that Van Til brings to its use. I would like to isolate two areas in particular that seem to beg for closer scrutiny by the Christian apologist: the search for common ground and the notion of revisability as essential to dialogue.

Kamitsuka has a major stake in securing common ground, or as he (following Rawls here) refers to it, "publicly shared rational space." After all, this has been one of the central criticisms leveled at Lindbeck from David Tracy and others; namely, that all the cultural-linguistic model produces is fideism, a celebration of the incommensurability that exists between diverse grammars (a kind of vulgar Wittgensteinianism). Without some notion of "translatability" that doesn't succumb to either the experiential-expressivist fallacy—that is, leaving nothing untranslated—or to a purely equivocal (incorrigibility-thesis) approach offering no hope of conversation, apologetics at best becomes pure monologue.

The difficulty emerges when the only rational way of securing "publicly shared rational space" is by allowing a purely "functional normativity" for core Christian beliefs, a limitation inherent in a post-modern, foundationless epistemological environment. As Kamitsuka describes it:

> Calling core Christian beliefs and principles functionally normative is all the epistemic primacy a nonfoundationalist stance permits. The benefit for apologetics is that this functional view of the normativity of core beliefs and principles allows postliberals to engage in genu-ine public debate, which entails not only defending one's theological claims but also openness to revising one's position in the process of mutually critical dialogue.[66]

The most that can be granted is a kind of "provisional" basicality that gives the "effect" of priority. Why? Because in theory (according

---

66. Kamitsuka, *Theology and Contemporary Culture*, 100.

to the implications derived from nonfoundationalism), "if a belief one initially held is found to be incompatible with some new considerations one finds compelling (e.g., background theories or aspects of a competing worldview), one may have to revise or even reject that initial belief."[67]

However satisfying to postliberal sensitivities this appears, one has to ask who in fact holds "core beliefs," especially paradigmatic biblical patterns that inform believers (*pari passu* Muslims and the Quranic patterns that inform followers of Islam!), with such open hands? There is a kind of liberal democratic "civility" informing this construct that questions how one could justify such a strategy while simultaneously positing a normative text supposed to be the lens whereby we translate/critique any and all "alternative" patterns (2 Cor. 10:5). The answer, according to Kamitsuka, is for believers to be reminded that the Scriptures provide only a "provisional fixed point" for engagement, with revision always a possibility. Utilizing Kai Nielsen's metaphor, Kamitsuka notes:

> Proponents of *WRE* are not suggesting that it is necessary or even possible to revise all one's beliefs and principles at the same time. We are, as Nielsen says, "sailors rebuilding the ship at sea, modifying and adjusting here and there until we get a coherent and consistent set of beliefs."[68]

But are "core beliefs" really only loosely held "frameworks" and possible scenarios? Or are they something more? Kamitsuka is surely correct in drawing the circle in terms of (c) wider reflective considerations (i.e., background theories), but there is something abstract and frankly unhelpful about the way he articulates the manner in which individuals hold on to certain beliefs.

A more suggestive approach can be seen in Charles Taylor's analysis of how we "understand" other agents or cultures. A basic premise he works with is: Why should we assume that the agent (or culture) we

67. Ibid.
68. Ibid., 603. The quote is from Kai Nielsen, *After the Demise of Tradition*, 203. Also see Ernest Sosa, "The Raft and the Pyramid: Coherence versus Foundations in the Theory of Knowledge," in *Midwest Studies in Philosophy, vol. 5, 1980 Studies in Epistemology*, ed. Peter French and Theodore Uehling (Minneapolis: University of Minnesota, 1980), 3–25.

are analyzing has a clear understanding of who he or she is (or they are)? Isn't Scripture forthcoming in this regard, that in fact people are dangerously in error, and their self-descriptions and world-descriptions are unreliable and self-serving (Rom. 1:21; Eph. 4:17–18; Col. 2:3–8)? This does not obviate the need or the appropriateness of calling for answers or self-descriptions from the unbeliever. After all, as Taylor writes:

> My identity is defined by the commitments and identifications which provide the frame or horizon within which I can try to determine from case to case what is good, or valuable, or what ought to be done, or what I endorse or oppose. In other words, it is the horizon within which I am capable of taking a stand.[69]

The point of analysis is then to pursue the development of the "essential link between identity and a kind of orientation." The orientation is one qualified as a "moral space," that is, "a space in which questions arise about what is good or bad, what is worth doing and what not, what has meaning and importance for you and what is trivial and secondary."[70] An individual's language of self-description makes up what are sometimes referred to as "desirability characterizations," conditions that in fact define an individual's world. In forcing someone to give an account of these characterizations, one may have to challenge not only what the "Other" sees, but also the way they describe what they see (Acts 17).[71] Are there lacunae, contradictions, and so forth, in the picture(s) they draw? There is no question that "judgments" are being made in the process—moral or value judgments!

What is not always as evident in Reformed apologetics is another side to this issue. It is a two-way conversation and not a monologue! In order to make this a two-way conversation (a path of self-criticism as well as criticism), however, one cannot simply translate without loss, directly from one language-game to another—that is, from one worldview to another—without a reflective moment. Why? Because

---

69. Charles Taylor, *Sources of the Self: The Making of the Modern Identity* (Cambridge, MA: Harvard University Press, 1989), 27.

70. Taylor, *Sources of the Self*, 28.

71. Paul at Lystra provides an even more dramatic illustration of how the unbeliever commonly draws the wrong conclusion (Acts 14)!

then one would be accused of simply restating in one's own language what advantages him or her over the "Other."[72] "Oh, so what you are really saying is . . ." Such reiterations simply won't do! Part of what the apologist is advancing is a hermeneutical enrichment of his or her fellow interlocutor's worldview (vocabulary, etc.), and this entails the possibility of an enrichment of the apologists' own language as well.[73] This is what is meant by being "called up short" by one's conversation partner. Areas of inconsistency (the link between background theory and regulative rule and even proclamation), as well as the need for a more robust understanding of a particular biblical theme or principle (social justice, racism, etc.), all come in for analysis and criticism through the process of identity clarification.

What is needed is a *language of perspicuous contrast*.[74] This would allow us to view our native moral language and theirs as

> alternative possibilities in relation to some human constants at work in both. It would be a language in which the possible human variations would be so formulated that both our form of life and theirs could be perspicuously described as alternative such variations. Such a language of contrast might show their language of understanding to be distorted or inadequate in some respects, or it might show ours to be so (in which case, we might find that understanding them leads to an alteration of our self-understanding, and hence our form of life—a far from unknown process in history); or it might show both to be so.[75]

However, this language of perspicuous contrast relies on something more ultimate, more basic—namely, a narrative that makes sense of the process altogether. What makes sense of what Taylor refers to as "human constants at work in both"? Scripture makes it clear that such constants are themselves evidence of the shared experience(s) of both believer and unbeliever as they live and participate in a world made by God (Rom. 1:19–21, 25).

---

72. Further to this issue, see Jeffrey Stout, *Ethics after Babel* (Boston: Beacon Press, 1988), 60–81.

73. Ibid., 64.

74. I am following closely the argument of Charles Taylor found in his "Understanding and Ethnocentricity," in *Philosophy and the Human Sciences*. Philosophical Papers (Cambridge: Cambridge University Press, 1985), 116–33.

75. Ibid., 125–26.

We are thus lead back to the question of normativity, whether of an ultimate or functional kind. Kamitsuka is clearly on the side of "functional normativity," whereas for the Reformed apologist the norm of Scripture is hardly functional—i.e., revisable or surrender-able—but rather absolute and demanding. It is a question of loyalty and not intellectual pride or superiority (Pss. 24:1; 103:19; 1 Cor. 10:31; Col. 1:16; 3:17; 1 Peter 4:11). After all, the core beliefs of the Christian faith are not grounded in reason (of whatever kind), but on the written testimony that speaks to events and people in history, what we call revelation. This "norm" is not to be located or justified in some domain of reason.

This normativity serves as the basis (foundation) of a scripturally guided reflection upon the whole of truth, not truth divided into parts and incrementally (piece by piece) assessed. The former accords with Van Til's remarkably prescient comments regarding the apologist's responsibility to "consider Christianity as a totality view of man and his environment, a view including every fact in the universe, involving them all in one grand drama of redemption or condemnation." The apologist's work then is "to take the totality picture of Christianity, and compare it with the totality picture of non-Christian thought."[76]

A language of perspicuous contrast begins then with what Van-hoozer calls a "philosophy of canonical sense."[77] Vanhoozer writes (echoing Van Til):

> It is the sum total of the biblical books, the various parts in their interrelatedness, that communicates the wisdom of the Christian way, which is the wisdom of Christ and the wisdom of the cross. Faith in the God of Israel and of Jesus Christ commits Christians to a supreme interpretive norm: the Scriptures.[78]

76. Cornelius Van Til, *The Reformed Pastor and Modern Thought* (Nutley, NJ: Presbyterian and Reformed, 1971), 36, 218.

77. Kevin Vanhoozer, "The Trials of Truth," in *To Stake a Claim: Mission and the Western Crisis of Knowledge*, ed. J. Andrew Kirk and Kevin J. Vanhoozer (Maryknoll, NY: Orbis, 1999), 130.

78. Ibid., 130. Van Til writes in *An Introduction to Systematic Theology* (Nutley, NJ: Pres-byterian and Reformed, 1974), 190–91: "We must begin with the actuality of the book. We must not pretend that we have established the possibility of the book and the necessity of it in terms of a philosophy that we did not get from the book. We have as Christians indeed learned with Calvin to interpret ourselves in terms of the book, and that on the authority of the book,

Unlike Nietzsche (the godfather of the age of interpretation)—who concludes that because there is only interpretation, there can be no truth or any claim to absolute normativity—a commitment to interpretation or understanding only reminds the apologist that, as fallen and finite readers of reality and of ourselves, we need constant revision, correction, and focus. Such an acknowledgment, however, does not sentence us to some version of functional normativity and relative conceptions of truth, but rather reminds us that the whole is in fact greater than the sum of its parts. The goal is more clearly and obediently to grasp or lay hold of the significance of the various parts as revealed in the biblical narrative itself (the truth as a whole).

---

and then we have looked to the book for the interpretation of the meaning of the facts. . . . We know nothing but such facts as are what the book, the authoritative revelation of God, says they are. *And we challenge unbelievers by saying that unless the facts are what the Bible says they are, they have no meaning at all"* (emphasis mine).

13

Turn! Turn! Turn! Reformed Apologetics and the Cultural Dimension

WILLIAM EDGAR

*I*s there life after postmodernism? In France, where the kind of thinking associated with the term got its strongest boost, current discussions display little or no interest in postmodernism. Instead, much to the surprise of the Anglo-Saxon world, the hot topic is humanism.

A Turn to Modest Humanism

This humanism is not the sort of overconfident brand proclaimed by *The Humanist Manifestos* (*I* in 1933, and *II* in 1973)[1] with their brash objections to theism and their naïve faith in science. Rather, it is a chastened, humble variety, which still believes in humankind, but not one that is good. Deeply sobered by the cataclysmic events of the last few decades, especially the Holocaust but including the savageries of Rwanda and the ethnic cleansing of the Balkans, this approach still

1. *The Humanist Manifestos I and II* (New York: Prometheus, 1973).

finds reasons for hope by beginning with human beings. The new humanism is an answer (an apology) to the question of meaning in the midst of the surrounding chaos. It is not a Christian answer, but the approach has much to teach us.

A perfect exhibit of the new humanism is Tzvetan Todorov's best seller, *Imperfect Garden: The Legacy of Humanism.*[2] The book is a wide-ranging essay building on the legacy of Montaigne, Montesquieu, Rousseau, and Constant, and faces the "dark prophets" like Louis de Bonald who condemned the history of Europe with all of its claims to surpass the state of nature by the use of reason. Todorov argues that the dark diagnosis of the anti-modernists is wrong, although he takes many of their points along the way. For example, he faults individualism for its excesses and potential lawlessness, but he believes in the individual. He faults "scientism" while believing in science. We may not be aggressively modernist, but we may, and must, embrace modernity, which is the brave desire to understand the universe without the crutch of religion. He denies Kant's ethics, which makes mankind into autonomous moral agents, but he accepts a modest idea of freedom, attained through careful, reasoned analysis of the options. Social relationships are the ultimate hope for any kind of meaningful life.

In the end, Todorov tells us, we can bet on the possibility of human progress. It is a wager, not a doctrine. The wager is Pascal-like, except God is not in the bargain! All we can do is live in the imperfect garden, not because God has given it to us, but because that is all we have.

The book is dedicated to his "philosopher friends, Luc and André." The reference is surely to Luc Ferry and André Comte-Sponville. It would be difficult for Americans to appreciate the role these two French philosophers have had in their context, because there is no equivalent in the States. Both Ferry and Comte-Sponville are accomplished professional philosophers. Yet they are best-selling authors. These pundits write regularly for the leading weekly magazines. Currently, Luc Ferry is Minister of Education. In effect, these men are *maîtres à penser*, mentors for a large portion of the French population. They move easily between highly technical analyses of philosophical issues and popular tracts.

---

2. *Imperfect Garden: The Legacy of Humanism*, trans. Carol Cosman (Princeton: Princeton University Press, 2002). The French original is *Le jardin imparfait: La pensée humaniste en France* (Paris: Bernard Grasset, 1998).

In 2002 Ferry wrote *Qu'est-ce qu'une vie réussie?* (*What Is a Successful Life?*).[3] The book remained high on the best seller lists for months. Such a title in America would probably signal a therapeutic guide within the enormous self-help industry. In fact, its 480 pages are filled with difficult, technical, though clearly and thoughtfully written arguments for humanism. Comte-Sponville is somewhat of a pessimist. While Ferry is agnostic, Comte-Sponville is an atheist. A modern Stoic, he has written a series, again best-selling, based on the myth of Icarus.[4] This mythical figure is the perfect foil for his view: Icarus is the son of Daedalus, who died trying to escape prison with wax wings, which melted when he flew too close to the sun.

Ferry and Comte-Sponville collaborated on a lengthy volume called *La sagesse des modernes* (*The Wisdom of the Moderns*).[5] It sets out broadly to answer the question, how should we live? Its ten chapters cover topics such as, how to be a materialist, neurobiology and philosophy and the question of natural grounds for ethics, religion after "religion," the quest for meaning, beauty, science, and so forth. Here, both their similarities and differences emerge. Ferry generally believes in human transcendence. As in his earlier writings, reversing the Anselmian epithet, he believes in the man-god. Comte-Sponville has no such exalted notions, although he does believe there is truth. But truth for him is "reality," which we can know only in small portions. We can have a moral absolute if we are honest, painfully honest at times, about the presence of reality, the naked truth that surrounds us. In a memorable phrase, he affirms, "God's mercy is *truly* infinite, because he does not exist."[6] To which he adds, only *truth* can be a moral guide, although its first effect, if we should encounter it honestly, might be to banish us from any moral absolutes.[7]

---

3. *Qu'est-ce qu'une vie réussie?* (Paris: Bernard Grasset, 2002).

4. André Comte-Sponville, *Le mythe d'Icare*, 3 vols. (Paris: Presses universitaired de France, 1984).

5. Luc Ferry and André Comte-Sponville, *La sagesse des modernes* (Paris: Robert Laffont, 1998).

6. Ibid., 282.

7. A bold attempt at answering this book from a Roman Catholic point of view was made by Isabelle Prêtre, *La folie des modernes* (Paris: François-Xavier de Guibert, 2000). She sees nothing in Ferry's and Compte-Sponville's views that cannot be resolved by trusting in God.

Sounding closer to a Christian point of view, but nevertheless still fundamentally a humanist, the prolific Jean-Claude Guillebaud has been arguing that the Enlightenment project still has much to offer us, as long as we conjoin it with the right kind of "Judeo-Christian" faith. In a series of books on *La refondation du monde*,[8] he argues that we have overreacted to the excesses of modernity and must "refound" it in order to benefit from its undeniable attainments. Like Todorov, Ferry, and Comte-Sponville, he is fully cognizant of the evils of recent times, many of them the fruit of a perverted modernity. And like them, he espouses a soft humanism. But more than they, he is sharply critical of the claims of postmodernists. The postmodern attack on the subject and its claimed final death-blow to metaphysics can only lead to destruction and resignation across the board. Only after dismissing the entire twentieth century and its follies, especially the "falling star" of postmodernism, can we recover freedom.

What is striking about this move toward modest humanism is that it feels very much like modernism, albeit a somewhat less-confident version than earlier ones. As such, it represents a massive rejection of the postmodern turn. The irony is that postmodernism had claimed that no attempt to salvage modernity was possible or even desirable. Jean-François Lyotard had famously claimed that modernity died its death of "tragic incompletion" after Auschwitz.[9] According to one way of seeing it, postmodernism was a massive attack on the human self. But here we are, back again, or almost. Are we simply moving around and around in an endless cycle?

Turn! Turn! Turn!

In a way, we are. It is significant that often the move to another plateau in philosophy—or, for that matter, in other disciplines—is called a *turn*. The postmodern turn, then, appears to be a cover for various inner turns, such as the "cultural turn," the "linguistic turn,"

8. *La refondation du monde, vols. 1–3* (Paris: Seuil, 1999).
9. Jean-François Lyotard, *The Postmodern Explained* (Minneapolis: University of Minnesota Press, 1992), 18.

the "technical turn," and even the "religious turn."[10] And today, we are seriously questioning the postmodern turn itself, not only in French humanism, but across the disciplines and across the geographical boundaries.[11] One might even say that the search for meaning was bracketed, dismissed for a while, in the postmodern turn. But such avoidance was not possible for very long. We are God's image-bearers after all. It is now permissible to look for meaning and order. But how deep is this new turn?

It is hard not to become cynical about the endless preoccupation with new dimensions, new perspectives, turns to the right and to the left. There is something reminiscent of the book of Ecclesiastes here. In 1965 the remarkable British folk-rock group the Byrds came out with their greatest hit, "Turn! Turn! Turn!" The words were adapted by Pete Seeger from the third chapter of Ecclesiastes. The refrain interweaves the words of Ecclesiastes 3:1 with the ritornello on "turn, turn, turn":

> To everything, turn, turn, turn
> There is a season, turn, turn, turn
> And a time to every purpose
> Under heaven

The four stanzas loosely run down the verses that follow. It was in a way the perfect 1960s song. Coming at the end of the year, it marked the midway point of a decade in which much was happening. Kennedy had been assassinated, the Vietnam War was escalating, and rock music itself was well into its second generation. From the blues-like sounds

10. Just for starters, consider these titles: Ihab Hassan, *The Postmodern Turn: Essays in Postmodern Theory and Culture* (Columbus, OH: University of Ohio Press, 1987); Steven Best and Douglas Kellner, *The Postmodern Turn* (New York: Guilford Press, 1997); Fredric Jameson and Perry Anderson, *Cultural Turn: Selected Writings on the Postmodern, 1983–1998* (London: Verso, 1998); David R. Hiley, Richard Shusterman, and James Bohman, eds., *The Interpretive Turn: Philosophy, Science, Culture* (Ithaca, NY: Cornell University Press, 1991); Cristina Lafont, *The Linguistic Turn in Hermeneutic Philosophy*, trans. Jose Medina (Cambridge, MA: MIT Press, 1999); Andrew Feenberg, *Alternative Modernity: The Technical Turn in Philosophy and Social Theory* (Berkeley: University of California Press, 1995); Hent de Vries, *Philosophy and the Turn to Religion* (Baltimore: Johns Hopkins University Press, 1999).

11. See, for example, Victoria E. Bonnell and Lynn Hunt, eds., *Beyond the Cultural Turn: New Directions in the Study of Society and Culture* (Berkeley: University of California Press, 1999).

of Chuck Berry and Elvis Presley, the scene had shifted to the Mersey sounds of the early Beatles. Bob Dylan was moving from pure folk to a more electronic and rock-based music. The Beatles themselves were becoming more philosophical, even brooding.

Was "Turn! Turn! Turn!" ultimately fatalistic? On the surface, it would seem so. Tellingly, the song was used in the sound track of the movie *Forrest Gump*, in which a simpleminded man visits different pockets of history, without making much progress. Yet the song has a deliberate ambiguity, one that leaves a window open for hope, despite its litany of times to do this and times to do that. In the last stanza, Seeger inserted desperate words of admonition, not found in Ecclesiastes:

> A time to gain and a time to lose
> A time to rain, a time to sow
> A time for love, a time for hate
> A time for peace
> I swear it's not too late

The song captures both the sense of resignation of the biblical book, and its window of hope. Is it not in that way a prophetic word to understand the turns in the human sciences? Resigned and yet hopeful.

The new humanism's rejection of postmodernism can be traced back to certain European debates not very common in America. In 1947 Martin Heidegger wrote his *Letter on Humanism* to one of his former students.[12] It can be argued that this text, more than any other, would forge the direction and nature of Continental philosophy, particularly in France, for the next forty years. The *Letter* is an open critique of the views of Jean-Paul Sartre, expressed the year before in his landmark essay, *Existentialism Is a Humanism*.[13]

To put it succinctly, Sartre claims that human beings are the only real channels of the values of this world. Nothing *causes* the choices they make, for there is only the self: "Existentialists believe

---

12. Martin Heidegger, *Über den Humanismus* (Frankfurt am Main: Vittorio Klostermann, 1947).

13. *L'Existentialisme est un humanisme* (Paris: Nagel, 1970).

that existence precedes essence, or, if you wish, that we must begin with subjectivity." He opposes the traditional view that holds God to be the Creator, in favor of the existentialist view that denies any causality to human functioning. He contrasts the nature of a paper cutter, which has a purpose assigned to it by its maker, to the human being, which has no such essence. One just *is*. "There is no other universe than a human universe, the universe of human subjectivity. . . ."[14] Because of this, we cannot make excuses for who we are. We are free because first we are nothing, but then we become what we decide to become.[15]

This is a tragic philosophy, but ultimately a hopeful one according to Sartre. For, in view of our nothingness, while we are tempted to flee and to exercise *bad faith*, if we become *engaged*, we may then undertake a courageous *praxis* and be rid of anxiety. And thus we are humanists.

Heidegger overwhelmingly rejects this view. In his *Letter on Humanism* he faults Sartre for being unable to grasp the true dignity of man. Cartesian subjectivism binds humans to metaphysics, making them oblivious to the higher calling of the "light of Being."[16] Sartrian humanism promises mastery over nature, but only delivers a reduced human being. Reason becomes the calculation of cause and effect, and human gifts are merely resources.

The problem is that in rejecting all authority other than subjectivity, we have lost both God and all human value in the bargain. Our relations become mere struggles for advantage. The root cause of this false and dangerous view is that it accepts Hegelianism as the norm for doing philosophy.[17] In this tradition, philosophy is the pursuit of knowledge in an attempt to reconcile human thought and experience with the way things are. The history of philosophy is but a succession of worldviews that come closer and closer to the reconciliation of the rational and the real. Hegel himself is a sort of culmination of this particular history of philosophy, because he seems to add up all the

---

14. Ibid., 17, my translation.

15. Ibid., 21.

16. Heidegger, *Über den Humanismus*, 17–18.

17. See Martin Heidegger, "The End of Philosophy and the Task of Thinking," in *On Time and Being*, trans. Joan Stambaugh (New York: Harper & Row, 1973).

insights that have survived, and then goes on to obliterate any difference between the rational and the real.

Heidegger responds to this by saying that such a victory actually masks a gigantic failure. The Hegelian approach is indeed the end of philosophy. It is the height of metaphysics.[18] But the whole project is not valid to begin with. Discussions of the rational and the real distract us from the central task of philosophy, which is to discover being. Heidegger's discourse is quite religious, suggesting that our vocation should center on being "shepherds of Being," who preserve the precious disclosure (*Lichtung*) of the ultimate meaning transmitted to us out of the hidden ground of the universe. By claiming that reality is rational, even including the horrors of evil and war, Hegelian thinking disregards the mystery of existence. Heidegger famously touts poetry and pre-Socratic writers as the conduits toward being, rather than the successors of Plato, who sold their birthright of the search for identity and meaning for a mess of rational thought potage.

Heidegger himself struggled with vestiges of metaphysical thinking, which the West cannot easily shake off. That was one of the reasons he could not write the third section of the first part of *On Time and Being*. Having written most of the text on the urgent need to dismantle metaphysics and ordinary language, through techniques of destruction (*Destruktion Abbau*), the next step should have been the deeper exploration into being itself, with full appreciation for the "ontological difference" with objects. But he could not, because the only language he had at his disposal was still corrupted by the Greek model of a simple presence of a being accessible to rational thought. When revelations of involvement with the Nazi Party came to light in the 1980s, Heidegger's defenders blamed a residual humanism that clung to him.[19]

Sartre's doctrine still depends on the Enlightenment. Heidegger's philosophy is a dark, counter-Enlightenment romanticism. He was drawn to the somber German poets Rilke, Trakl, and Mörike, who were so many "unsafe" companions on the dark path of alienation. He

18. Ibid., 55–73.
19. Philippe Lacoue-Labarthe confidently asserted that Nazism is a humanism, because of its ambition to dominate the entire world. See *La fiction du politique: Heidegger, l'art et la politique* (Paris: Bourgois, 1998).

showed no interest in the big schemes of Marx or Freud. He thought of technology as the end of Western thought and welcomed its demise as the sign of the utter failure of humanity to rule the earth. Crucially, Heidegger is really the father of postmodernism, whether in its more philosophical forms or in its cultural approach.

It would not be entirely fair to say that the new humanists, especially Ferry and Comte-Sponville, call for a return to Sartre in order to leave Heidegger behind in a cloud of dust. Indeed, they show some sympathy with Heidegger's critique of Hegelian systems, even though Heidegger's heirs are generally thinkers they recuse, such as Michel Foucault.[20] If they return to anything, it is to Immanuel Kant. In an important essay from 1994, the team Ferry and Renaut ask us point blank to reconsider not only Kant but Fichte.[21] They begin by describing two places where philosophy had an end point, Hegel and Heidegger. But they go on to suggest that there is a third, less known, "end of philosophy," which is *criticism*.[22] In essence, Kant's criticism, fully carried out in Fichte's *Doctrine of Science*, declares the end of philosophy as a system, but the open field of philosophy as the "thinking through of contemporary thought," thus restoring the possibility of true reflection.[23] This, in turn, ought to free us up to engage in two philosophical activities: first, an ethics of communication, and, second, looking for meaning within the facts that surround us.

Ferry and Renaut go on to propose a way to think that avoids both the irrational mysticism of Heidegger and the rationalistic systematization of Hegel. The discussion is intriguing. First, they point out that Heidegger's irrationalism makes coming to any conclusions impossible. Then they show how Hegel's systems leads to a shouting match between worldviews, with no hope of resolving the "war between the gods." They could be echoing Van Til. But then they opt for a third way, which they call "internal criticism": using reason, not

20. Luc Ferry came into prominence with his collaborator Alain Renaut by attacking the likes of Foucault, Derrida, and Bourdieu. See, for example, Luc Ferry and Alain Renaut, *La pensée 68: Essai sur l'anti-humanisme contemporain* (Paris: Gallimard, 1985). The book is dedicated to Todorov!

21. Luc Ferry and Alain Renaut, "Kant and Fichte," in *New French Thought: Political Philosophy*, ed. Mark Lilla (Princeton: Princeton University Press, 1994), 74–81.

22. Ibid., 75.

23. Ibid., 77.

magisterially, but purely methodologically. This should mean that we can discuss the events of history, not by looking for some sort of cause, but by "constructing its intelligibility."[24] Their quest is to make the facts discovered in the social sciences philosophically meaningful without falling into cold systems: "The human sciences have indeed suffered too long from the illusion that the accumulation of an enormous apparatus of archives, investigations, and statistical data would allow them to escape the problems with which philosophy has long struggled."[25]

In the Turns but Not of Them

How should the wanderings of recent scholarship be approached by Reformed apologists? How would Cornelius Van Til view these turns? We cannot always know directly, for Van Til was no longer active when some of the most significant landmarks were reached. He certainly made comments on Heidegger and on some of the more theologically oriented scholars of various turns. In a remarkable essay from 1964, Van Til juxtaposes Karl Barth, Rudolf Bultmann, and the later Martin Heidegger based on a chapter in the volume edited by James M. Robinson and John B. Cobb Jr.[26] After describing Heidegger's *Umkehr*, his "turn" away from nothingness toward the rediscovery of being, Van Til concludes that Barth's transcendent God is almost identical with Heidegger's idea of being, which is, in effect, wholly hidden and wholly revealed at the same time. Somewhat shockingly, at first blush, because Barth himself disavowed any such connection, Van Til defends this comparison with the help of Heinrich Ott's essay in the volume Van Til is reviewing.

Van Til notes the importance of Heidegger's essay on humanism. He is aware of the debate with Sartre. Not to be confused with Sartre's position, "Man is what he is because he is *thrown* into the truth of Being. As such he must be the watchman of Being. . . . And Being, what

24. Ibid., 78.
25. Ibid., 79.
26. Van Til's article is entitled "The Later Heidegger and Theology" and appears to be an extended review of Robinson and Cobb's *The Later Heidegger and Theology*, in the New Frontiers in Theology series (New York: Harper & Row, 1963). See Cornelius Van Til, "The Later Heidegger and Theology," *Westminster Theological Journal* 26 (1964): 121–61.

is it? Future thought must teach us."[27] Thus, "being," for Heidegger, is really utterly different from what we can conceive. It is something like Parmenides' unattainable ground. But, unlike Parmenides, Heidegger wants to avoid all attempts at conceptualization. In effect, we have a sort of postmodern turn here. There is no meaning, and no grace. Thus, "Barth adds nothing of importance to the philosophy of the later Heidegger."[28] Van Til notes that there is no grace in Heidegger's gospel, anymore than there is, he reckons, in Barth's.

So there is plenty here to suggest what Van Til would do with what eventually would be known as postmodernism. More importantly, we can develop and apply his material from the rich commentary he made on Kant and the idealists, and, for that matter, on the more classical philosophers and theologians. What we will discover, surely, is that the diagnosis of the central failures of these successive trends as simply *impossible* will hold, no matter what they are. In the tensions between the modern and the postmodern we have something like the tension between rationalist and irrationalist forces described by Van Til.

A culture slouching toward unbelief will be one that is groping to reconcile immanence and transcendence, the nearby god and the faraway god. Reformed apologetics points out that unbelief is a sort of counterfeit of these two truths about God. Thus, it comes in two phases, a rationalist and an irrationalist commitment. Cornelius Van Til viewed the two as codependent, so to speak. Sometimes rationalism seems to carry the day, as it did under Spinoza and Leibniz. Sometimes irrationalism is in the saddle, as it began to be under Kant, who "limited reason so as to make room for faith." But in the end, "irrationalism has a secret treaty with rationalism by which the former cedes to the latter so much of its territory as the latter can at any time find the forces to control."[29] Francis Schaeffer talks of the "lower storey" and the "upper storey" in the non-Christian worldview. Herman Dooyeweerd discusses the dialectical tension within the pretended autonomy of human thought in recent times between the motives of "nature" and "freedom."

27. Van Til, "The Later Heidegger and Theology," 150.
28. Ibid., 158.
29. Cornelius Van Til, *The Defense of the Faith*, 3rd ed. (Philadelphia: Presbyterian and Reformed, 1967), 125.

It makes sense to think of these giant cultural trends as examples of the dialectical tension. And thus, persuasive arguments for the gospel message must attempt to lay bare the inner tension here, and challenge the very heart of the dialectic. The God of the Bible is neither material nor mystical, but he is both truly immanent and truly transcendent at the same time. Neither modernity nor the postmodern can ever succeed because they cannot square with reality.

Understanding the Times for Israel's Sake

But is that all we can say? Can we not learn something from the ongoing cycles before us? Are there tools for apologetics made available to us in the succession of trends? Those are probably harder questions than those surrounding the diagnosis above. As we try to answer them we will face the temptation, ever present, to confuse a useful tool for its framework. One of the cautions ever strong in Van Til's writings is against uncritically embracing someone's baseline philosophy in an attempt to build a bridge for critical communication. He often warned of becoming an empiricist to the empiricist so that God could pass *summa cum laude* a test to which he should never have been subjected. Proper attention to the history of modern thought ought to give us some sense of the dangers, but also of the opportunities. We can be like the children of Issachar, who had understanding of the times, in order to know what Israel ought to do (1 Chron. 12:32).

The succession of turns is itself instructive in view of our understanding of our culture. There is a sense of exhaustion to the endless recital of facts, and a sense of futility to the infinite succession of "turns" in the human sciences. The new humanism is a refreshing oasis away from the cultural web. But how long can it last? When will it succumb to its own inner weaknesses? Our task as apologists is clearly to note the weaknesses and predict the next turn! At the same time, we need to learn from the insights of the human sciences, whether postmodern or humanist, whatever their weaknesses, so that we have a better understanding of our times, and so that we can plead for meaning and coherence. We are curiously in a very similar place to that of the apostle Paul when he faced the audience at Mars Hill (Acts 17). There people lusted after the new. They had the nearby gods of small idols, and deterministic philosophy, and the faraway gods of an agnostic altar. Paul knew the context well. His own diagnostic tools benefited from theirs. But he found the inner contradiction and was able to proclaim judgment persuasively (one truth, not a web of new trends).

Traditional Christian apologetics too often has become a series of air-tight logical arguments that never touch the deep issues of meaning, evil, purpose, and so on. That is because it never really connects to where people are. We would do well to appropriate the insights of cultural anthropologists who have helped us correct the functionalist and mechanistic approaches to human experience in favor of a more complex, *meaningful* view. Culture studies have been building momentum from the early days of the Frankfort School and the Birmingham group until now. We do well to listen and learn.[30] On the whole, apologetics has not interacted much with culture studies.

Perhaps no thinker has helped to advance the cause of challenging empiricist materialism more than Clifford Geertz. In this way, he is quite close to the humanism of Ferry and the other French thinkers. Geertz did not simply bring culture back in or teach us that "culture matters," but introduced a genuine cultural turn. His most influential text is no doubt, *The Interpretation of Cultures: Selected Essays.*[31] Simply put, Geertz rejects positivism and pleads for the centrality of meaning for human experience. He understands culture to be a series of webs that cannot be interpreted by experimental science alone. There must be "thick description," which does justice to the whole range of human possibilities, and is not ashamed to relate it to the "big questions" posed by philosophy.

In his studies of the Balinese, or the Navajos, Geertz notes the strong concern in those people groups with the problem of evil and the relation of suffering to a good God. He asks that we take religion seriously as a cultural system that attempts to make sense of suffering. He invites us to study the symbols, even the moods and motivations of various groups, as

---

30. Harvie Conn's study, *Eternal Word and Changing Worlds: Theology, Anthropology and Mission in Trialogue* (1984; repr., Phillipsburg, NJ: P&R, 1992), is a fine example of this awareness.

31. Clifford Geertz, *The Interpretation of Cultures: Selected Essays* (New York: Basic Books, 1973).

clues to the way they face reality.[32] Christian apologetics should need no particular prompting in order to recognize the central place of meaning and human suffering in human existence. But curiously, many who are writing as professional apologists are insensitive to it.

Ronald Grigor Suny has recently written about the influence on the cultural turn for doing history.[33] Following the work of Geertz and others, he points out that in history and social science at least seven influences can be detected.[34]

First, recognizing the turn leads to opposing all social naturalism. Rather than espousing timeless judgments or essentialism (humans are instrumentally rational, Armenians are good merchants, women are nurturing, etc.), people and events must be placed in a context. Identities are more fluid; culture is dynamic. Second, culture is understood to be more constitutive than language or technology or even history. Culture, though not simple, has its own coherence, and is not reducible to a text (contra Derrida). Third, culture is practice. Politics are involved. We can no longer compare "advanced" cultures to "primitive" ones, but must look for examples of contestation and contrast between worlds. Fourth, with Foucault, the historians of the cultural turn become suspicious of all kinds of agents. They do not necessarily create history (ideas make the world turn 'round), but they emerge from its pages. Fifth, again, with Foucault, and moving beyond Geertz, power is taken far more seriously than before. Science is not neutral, nor is social organization. They mask power plays of all kinds. Sixth, stories are taken much more seriously than before. The assumed metanarrative of the Enlightenment is a great story from the past that is not so solid as once thought. Seventh, the cultural turn recognizes that the observer is not a neutral outsider, but becomes a part of the cultural process.

We do not have time to look into each of these implications. In a way, they all belong to the general trend of recognizing diversity, interest, the great variety of contexts, the lack (if we will) of a metanarrative. They are all part of a hermeneutic direction. Are we doomed to an indeterminate world, with no central meaning, no internal coher-

32. Ibid., 87–125.
33. Ronald Grigor Suny, "Back and Beyond: Reversing the Cultural Turn?" *The American Historical Review* 107, no. 5 (2002): 1476–99.
34. Ibid., 1484–88.

ence? Is the postmodern turn another guise for relativism? Already, social scientists are moving beyond the cultural turn and asking the key question of meaning. Suny himself asks us not to abandon "thin coherence" within the diversity of the cultural web.[35] Sherry B. Ortner recently organized a colloquium called, *The Fate of "Culture": Geertz and Beyond*, which featured seven scholars, including William Sewall, who are wrestling with the need to stay anchored in some kind of coherence, even while benefiting from the cultural turn.[36]

Again, it seems to me that apologetics has not profited very much from this kind of scholarship. To be sure, there is considerable material on postmodernism, including specifically apologetic-oriented research.[37] But much of it is limited. Some simply embraces the various features of the postmodern turn without significant critique.[38] Much of it ignores the lynchpins of the anthropology of Geertz and the historicism of Foucault.[39] Further, much of it is incapable of separating what is descriptive and what is prescriptive in the vast material on culture studies in order to vindicate the Christian position. Perhaps the embarrassing truth is that we simply have not spent enough time studying the material itself, and doing our own case work, to be effective.

35. Ibid., 1498. The term is William Sewell's, who argues for a semantic coherence within a culture whose language and symbols otherwise display instability. See his "The Concept(s) of Culture," in Bonnell and Hunt, *Beyond the Cultural Turn*, 49–50.

36. Sherry B. Ortner, *The Fate of "Culture": Geertz and Beyond* (Berkeley: University of California, 1999).

37. For example, Timothy R. Philips and Dennis L. Okholm, eds., *Christian Apologetics in the Postmodern World* (Downers Grove, IL: InterVarsity Press, 1995); Stanley J. Grenz, *A Primer on Postmodernism* (Grand Rapids, MI: Eerdmans, 1996); and Gene Edward Veith Jr., *Postmodern Times: A Christian Guide to Contemporary Thought and Culture* (Wheaton, IL: Crossway, 1994).

38. Kathryn Tanner's *Theories of Culture: A New Agenda for Theology* (Minneapolis: Fortress, 1997) connects with apologetics but ends up almost purely with postmodern virtues like diversity, creativity, and "relational identity." Richard J. Middleton and Brian J. Walsh, *Truth Is Stranger than It Used to Be: Biblical Faith in a Postmodern Age* (Downers Grove, IL: InterVarsity Press, 1995), do a better job than most of recognizing the turn and using it for apologetics (though they would not use the term), although it ends with uncritical generalities on a narrative approach to truth.

39. David K. Naugle's fascinating work *Worldview: The History of a Concept* (Grand Rapids, MI: Eerdmans, 2002) notes the role of Heidegger, Davidson, Derrida, and Foucault (though no mention of Geertz) as critics of simplistic worldview thinking, but does not apply their strengths and weaknesses to apologetics, nor even to specific evaluations of cultural trends. Os Guinness is very much committed to apologetics. He interacts thoughtfully with cultural and political trends, almost from a history of ideas perspective. See his *Time for Truth: Living Free in a World of Lies, Hype, and Spin* (Grand Rapids, MI: Baker, 2000).

The opportunity is there, provided we recognize it. Geertz himself calls for a certain kind of apologetics in order not only to make sense of the world but also to prescribe virtuous ways to live in it. In a thoughtful review of Tyler Cowen's *Creative Destruction: How Globalization Is Changing the World's Cultures*, Geertz opens with a historical note about the role of Christian apologetics, "the demonstration that, despite appearances to the contrary on almost every hand, our universe is rationally put together, and is good."[40] He then launches a strong criticism of Cowen's book, which justifies the current culture of globalization as a good thing. The apologetics of *Creative Destruction* boils down to economics. Despite the craziness of what is going on in the arts, buying and selling makes everything available, thus making us aesthetically richer. Skeptical of this market model, Geertz ends with a plea:

> If we are to come to any conclusions about "how globalization is changing the world's cultures," other than the simple fact that it is indeed changing it and profoundly, we need a language of perception and sensibility capable of sorting it out and guiding us through it. It is not clear that economics can produce that.[41]

Geertz is asking for language that helps us make sense of the world in order to guide us through it. Pure economics only makes us complacent. What would take the higher ground? A Christian apologetics well steeped in the scholarship before and after the postmodern turn. Solid grounding in biblical theology. And to do justice, and to love kindness, and to walk humbly with your God (Mal. 6:8). These are qualities that characterize Reformed apologetics at its best. But so far, we have been far better at asserting the principles, and applying them to older battles, than at developing a sense of the cultural issues of today and vindicating the gospel in the face of them.

---

40. Clifford Geertz, "Off the Menu," *The New Republic* (February 2003): 27.
41. Ibid., 30.

14

Van Til and Transcendental Argument

DON COLLETT

Central to the apologetic of Cornelius Van Til is the claim that a Reformed apologetic and the transcendental method of argumentation go hand-in-hand. Back of this claim lies the conviction, oft stated by Van Til, that the theology of Scripture entails a distinctive apologetic method. For example, in the opening pages of *A Survey of Christian Epistemology* Van Til writes that "every system of thought necessarily has a certain method of its own."[1] Thus Christian theism, considered as a system of thought, requires an apologetic defense that is methodologically distinctive. For Van Til, this in turn requires the Christian apologist to employ a transcendental method of argument, since "the only argument for an absolute God that holds water is a transcendental argument."[2]

An earlier edition of this essay appeared in the Fall 2003 issue of *The Westminster Theological Journal*. For the purposes of this book I have condensed my earlier essay, especially its second section, and a number of clarifications have been added to the third and fifth sections.

    1. Cornelius Van Til, *A Survey of Christian Epistemology* (Nutley, NJ: Presbyterian and Reformed, 1969), 5.

    2. Ibid., 11.

Criticism of Van Til's transcendental methodology has not been lacking over the years, especially among Christian apologists who remain committed to inductive and deductive methods,[3] or who prefer to adopt a more integrative and methodologically diverse approach to the practice of apologetics.[4] In recent years the distinctive character of Van Til's transcendental approach has also generated critical debate within Van Tilian circles.[5] This debate is especially significant for apologists who share a basic commitment to Van Til's transcendental approach, inasmuch as it raises the question whether transcendental arguments can be distinguished from traditional arguments, and if so, on what grounds. Insofar as Van Til himself attempted to justify this distinction, he typically did so in terms of theological concerns rather than formal argument *per se*. While I am far from suggesting that Van Til's theologically oriented approach to this issue lacks merit, ongoing debate over these matters attests to the fact that a formal basis for distinguishing Van Til's approach from traditional approaches is needed.

The present essay seeks to address this lacuna in Van Tilian scholarship by drawing upon certain insights into the concept of presupposition that have arisen within the tradition of analytic philosophy.[6] To that end I will begin with a survey of some important theological concerns underlying Van Til's commitment to the distinctive character of transcendental argument, then attempt to provide a motivation for this commitment by drawing upon the work of Peter Strawson.[7]

3. By way of qualification, one should note that Van Til's commitment to a transcendental method did not lead him to reject the use of inductive and deductive methods of argument *per se*. However, in keeping with his belief that Reformed theology entails an apologetic method that is distinctive, namely the transcendental method, Van Til called for the methodological reconstruction of deductive and inductive argument along transcendental lines (see ibid., 8–11, 201). It lies beyond the purview of this paper to enter into the question why Van Til himself chose not to provide us with *explicit* examples of such a reconstruction in his writings.

4. Most, if not all, non–Van Tilian apologists fall into this category.

5. See John M. Frame, *Apologetics to the Glory of God* (Phillipsburg, NJ: P&R, 1994), 69–88; *Cornelius Van Til: An Analysis of His Thought* (Phillipsburg, NJ: P&R, 1995), 317–20; "Presuppositional Apologetics," in *Five Views of Apologetics*, ed. Steven B. Cowan (Grand Rapids, MI: Zondervan, 2000), 220–21n18; Greg L. Bahnsen, *Van Til's Apologetic: Readings and Analysis* (Phillipsburg, NJ: P&R, 1998), 499ff.

6. See especially P. F. Strawson, *Introduction to Logical Theory* (London: Methuen, 1952), 174–79; Bas van Fraassen, "Presupposition, Implication, and Self-Reference," *Journal of Philosophy* 65 (1968): 136–52.

7. Readers should note that my purpose in this paper is to defend the methodological distinctiveness of transcendental arguments on a *formal* level. Such a defense, if successful, does

Van Til and Transcendental Argument

To appreciate the reasons why Van Til believed in the distinctive character of transcendental argument,[8] we may begin by surveying a few of the more prominent apologetic concerns Van Til believed to be safeguarded by the transcendental method.[9] This should also help to clarify some of the reasons why Van Til believed that traditional methods of argument failed to do justice to his theological and apologetic concerns.

First, Van Til believed that the transcendental method of argument safeguards the doctrine of God's transcendence.[10] Closely related to this belief was his insistence that a Christian apologist "take seriously" the *absolute* character of God's being when formulating an argument for Christian theism. The problem with both "deductive" and "inductive" methods of argument, says Van Til, is that they typically begin with the assumption that certain axioms are more ultimate and certain than God's existence (e.g., the principle of causality) and then proceed to reason in "a straight line" fashion to the conclusion that God exists.[11] In so doing they unwittingly assign to the concept of God's existence a logically derivative rather than logically primitive status.[12]

---

not entail the conclusion that inductive and deductive arguments have no place whatsoever in a presuppositional apologetic. In general I agree with Bahnsen (and Frame) that "there is no transcendental argument that 'rules out all other kinds of arguments' . . . either in general philosophy and scholarship or particularly in apologetics" (Bahnsen, *Van Til's Apologetic*, 502n64). Frame apparently believes that Van Til himself would not have agreed with such a claim, and thus he calls for the "supplementation" of transcendental argument "by other arguments" (Frame, *Apologetics to the Glory of God*, 73; *Cornelius Van Til*, 316–17). While I would differ with Frame's interpretation of Van Til at this point, the question whether Van Til himself allowed the use of other argument forms should be distinguished from the question whether Van Til was justified in his belief that transcendental arguments are methodologically unique. Again, this paper primarily addresses the latter question.

8. It cannot be stressed enough that Van Til embedded the transcendental argument within a distinctly Christian worldview. Failure to reckon with the implications of this fact has lead to a great deal of misunderstanding on the part of Van Til's critics over the years.

9. For a brief overview of Van Til's methodological concerns, consult Van Til, *A Survey of Christian Epistemology*, 4–13.

10. "It should be particularly noted, therefore, that only a system of philosophy that takes the concept of an absolute God seriously can really be said to be employing a transcendental method. A truly transcendent God and a transcendental method go hand-in-hand." Ibid., 11.

11. Ibid., 8–11.

12. To my knowledge, Van Til never stated the matter in precisely these terms or categories ("logically derivative" vs. "logically primitive"). Their usage here is meant to clarify the language

By way of contrast, the transcendental argument preserves the logically primitive and absolute character of God's existence by *starting* with the premise that God's existence is a necessary precondition for argument itself.[13] In this way argument is made to depend upon God, rather than vice versa, since argument is possible if and only if God's existence is true from the outset of argument itself. Thus in contrast to both deductive and inductive forms of argument, a transcendental argument allows the concept of God to function as a logically primitive rather than logically derivative proposition, thereby bearing witness to the nonderivative character of God's existence on an argumentative level.

To state matters another way, in Van Til's Christian-theistic construction of the transcendental argument, the truth of God's existence is not a deductive consequence of the premises of the argument, but rather the metaphysical and logical ground for the very possibility of the premises themselves.[14] This is undoubtedly one of the reasons, if not the chief reason, why he believed that transcendental arguments were uniquely suited for the task of placing into sharp relief the *nondeductive* character of the truth of God's existence.

Second, for Van Til the transcendental argument alone does justice to the clarity of the objective evidence for God's existence, in that it highlights the *necessary* character of God's existence—that is to say, it does not grant the possibility that God's existence is falsifiable, and thus it does not "tone down the objective claims of God upon men."[15] Inasmuch as creation clearly testifies to the necessary character of God's existence, it follows that the Christian apologist cannot do

---

that Van Til often uses when he states this point in his writings ("straight line" reasoning vs. "indirect" reasoning).

13. "It is not as though we already know some facts and laws to begin with, irrespective of the existence of God, in order then to reason from such a beginning to further conclusions. It is certainly true that if God has any significance for any object of knowledge at all, the relation of God to that object of knowledge must be taken into consideration from the outset. It is this fact that the transcendental method seeks to recognize." Van Til, *A Survey of Christian Epistemology*, 201.

14. "The best, the only, the absolutely certain proof of the truth of Christianity is that unless its truth be presupposed there is no proof of anything. Christianity is proved as being the very foundation of the idea of proof itself." Cornelius Van Til, *The Defense of the Faith* (Philadelphia: Presbyterian and Reformed, 1955), 396; subsequent references to *The Defense of the Faith* are to this first edition unless otherwise noted.

15. Ibid., 197.

justice to the objective evidence for Christian theism unless he or she insists on the necessary character of the concept of God's existence in theistic argument.

Van Til often buttressed this claim by means of an argument from predication. A transcendental argument, theistically constructed, begins all argument upon the premise that predication requires for its possibility the necessary truth of God's existence. In this manner the concept of God's existence is brought into a necessary relation with predication from the outset of argument itself, thereby precluding any future possibility of using argument to falsify God's existence. Argument cannot proceed without predication,[16] and predication necessarily presupposes the existence of God.[17]

On the other hand, Van Til was convinced that traditional constructions of the "theistic proofs" fail to do justice to the necessary character of God's existence. Responding to criticisms made by S. J. Ridderbos in this connection, Van Til reminds him that for an argument to serve as a "witness" to God, it cannot bear witness to any other god but the "living and true God." Thus it must bear witness to God as he truly is, and that requires in turn that it bear witness to God as "the One who cannot but exist."[18] In short, theistic argument must bear witness to the *necessary* character of God's existence. Or, to state the matter in more philosophical terms, in theistic argument the concept of God's existence must not be allowed to function on the level of logical contingency. To do so is to grant the possibility that God's existence is falsifiable.

It is true, of course, that Van Til would sometimes argue the premise that God's existence is falsifiable in order to perform a *reductio ad absurdum* of the non-Christian position. It is important to note,

16. Van Til has in mind predication that affirms that something is the case (i.e., *it is* the case that John is tall) *and* predication that *denies* that something is the case (i.e., *it is not* the case that John is tall). In terms of assigning truth values to the propositions in an argument, this amounts to the claim that it is (logically) impossible to predicate truly *or* falsely about any proposition in an argument unless the proposition "God exists" is true.

17. Van Til's argument from predication is closely related to his criticism of the cosmological argument—to wit, that the cosmological argument, as traditionally constructed, assumes that the principle of causality is intelligible apart from God. For Van Til, the only way to avoid this consequence in apologetic argument is to insist upon the necessary relation of God's existence and predication from the outset of argument itself.

18. Van Til, *The Defense of the Faith*, 197.

however, that his use of the *reductio* was the second part of a two-phase apologetic strategy wherein he adopted *the unbeliever's argument* solely "for the sake of argument." In view of this, Van Til's "practical strategy"[19] of adopting the unbeliever's stance for the sake of refuting it should be distinguished from his transcendental argument *per se*.[20]

At this point advocates of the traditional method might argue that Van Til's endorsement of the transcendental method overlooks the fact that Anselm's version of the ontological argument reasons from the necessary character of God's being, and as such would be capable of addressing Van Til's concern. In a debate over apologetic method with Greg Bahnsen at Reformed Seminary in Jackson, Mississippi, R. C. Sproul went even further and expressed the opinion that Van Til's so-called transcendental argument was merely a sophisticated version of the ontological argument.[21]

Despite formal resemblances between the two, the transcendental argument and the ontological argument are not merely two sides of the same coin. In this connection two points should be noted. The first is that Van Til believed the ontological argument to be incapable of doing justice to *the revelational sense* in which God's existence is necessary, since it "proves" a god who exists "by the same necessity as does the universe," and thus a god who is no more than "an aspect of, or simply the whole of, the universe."[22] Van Til was aware that advocates of the ontological argument, Anselm in particular, make a distinction between two different senses of "necessity" in order to distinguish God's existence from that of the universe. For Van Til, however, this distinction is fatally undermined by the initial starting point of the argument itself. The ontological argument begins by defining God's being as that being "than which nothing greater can be thought,"

---

19. Frame, *Cornelius Van Til*, 320.

20. According to John Frame, Van Til's version of the transcendental argument is "essentially a reductio" (ibid., 319). While the two are closely related in Van Til's apologetic, especially on a practical level, putting the matter in this way tends to obscure the distinction between a transcendental argument and the method of *reductio ad absurdum*. See further the discussion in the fourth section of this essay.

21. The audio tape of this debate (titled "The Bahnsen/Sproul Debate over Apologetic Method") is available from Covenant Media Foundation, 3420 Piccadilly Circle, Nacogdoches, TX 75961.

22. Cornelius Van Til, *The Reformed Pastor and Modern Thought* (Nutley, NJ: Presbyterian and Reformed, 1971), 64–65.

thereby identifying God's being with humanity's highest thought. In other words, the ontological argument begins by identifying God's being with an order of thought and existence that is, on a Christian worldview, metaphysically contingent. Moreover, even if a logical transfer into the realm of necessary being were possible by means of the ontological argument, such a transfer would not leave us with "the biblical notion of God."[23]

This brings us to the second point of contrast between Van Til and the proponents of the ontological argument. In arguing for God's existence Van Til believed one could distinguish a transcendental argument from deductive arguments, in this case the ontological argument. Those who equate the ontological argument with the transcendental argument implicitly assume that transcendental argument is reducible to deductive argument; yet they typically fail to provide grounds for this assumption, thus begging the very point in dispute.

Although the preceding discussion calls attention to some important reasons why Van Til regarded transcendental arguments to be distinctive, there is yet another reason why he believed that transcendental arguments were uniquely suited for the task of Christian apologetics. Unfortunately this aspect of Van Til's transcendental argument has not been given its due weight, even though it is precisely this feature that allows us to distinguish it on a formal level from traditional methods of argument. At this point we must zero in, so to speak, on a particular theological and apologetic concern of Van Til's, namely, the question of the metaphysical foundations of the possibility of predication.

In his writings Van Til frequently stresses the need for apologetic argument to engage this question from a Christian-theistic point of view. Consider the following statement from *A Christian Theory of Knowledge*, which occurs in the context of Van Til's stated purpose "to indicate in a broad way the method of reasoning that is to be pursued" in the vindication of Christian theism:

23. "If we take the highest being of which we can think, in the sense of have a concept of, and attribute to it actual existence, we do not have the biblical notion of God. God is not the reality that corresponds to the highest concept that man, considered as an independent being, can think." Cornelius Van Til, *An Introduction to Systematic Theology* (Nutley, NJ: Presbyterian and Reformed, 1974), 206.

How then we ask is the Christian to challenge this non-Christian approach to the interpretation of human experience? He can do so only if he shows that man must presuppose God as the final reference point in predication. Otherwise, he would destroy experience itself. *He can do so only if he shows the non-Christian that even in his virtual negation of God, he is still really presupposing God.* He can do so only if he shows the non-Christian that he cannot deny God unless he first affirm him, and that his own approach throughout its history has been shown to be destructive of human experience itself.[24]

Here we are reminded that for Van Til, God himself constitutes "the final reference point in predication," which is but another way of saying that God's existence provides us with the metaphysical and epistemological basis for the possibility of predication. We are also reminded that Van Til directly identified presuppositional (or transcendental) argument with the task of justifying this possibility on Christian-theistic grounds. In other words, by means of a transcendental argument from predication, Van Til sought to make definite the claim that *all* human predication, whether that of affirmation or that of negation, presupposes the truth of God's existence:

It is the firm conviction of every epistemologically self-conscious Christian that no human being can utter a single syllable, *whether in negation or affirmation*, unless it were for God's existence. Thus the transcendental argument seeks to discover what sort of foundations the house of human knowledge must have, in order to be what it is.[25]

The last two quotes highlight the central position occupied by the transcendental argument from predication in Van Til's apologetic, and this prominence has been noted by John Frame as well.[26] Often overlooked, however, is Van Til's concern to emphasize that the argument from predication is not limited to cases of affirmation, but also

24. Cornelius Van Til, *A Christian Theory of Knowledge* (Nutley, NJ: Presbyterian and Reformed, 1969), 13, emphasis mine.

25. Van Til, *A Survey of Christian Epistemology*, 11, emphasis mine.

26. Frame summarizes Van Til's approach to theistic proof as the belief that "all legitimate theistic proof reduces to the 'proof from the possibility of predication.' God exists, in other words, because without him it would not be possible to reason, to think, or even to attach a predicate to a subject." Frame, *Apologetics to the Glory of God*, 70.

extends to cases of negation. Might not this emphasis merit closer scrutiny, especially in light of the distinction he drew between his own method and the methods of traditional argument?

Implicit in Van Til's argument from predication is the criticism, albeit undeveloped on a formal level, that traditional methods of argument are inadequate because they proceed upon the assumption that *at least some* types of predication are possible apart from the truth of God's existence. By way of contrast, Van Til believed that the method of argument used by a Christian apologist must make it clear that even the negation of God's existence is impossible, philosophically speaking, unless God's existence is true. To put it another way, the method of argument used by the Christian apologist must make it clear that God's existence is the basis for *all* predication, such that one cannot predicate truly *or falsely* about anything unless God exists.[27] Hence the argument a Christian apologist utilizes must not grant the non-Christian assumption that predication, either *in part* or *in toto*, can be justified independently of the truth of God's existence, and for Van Til this was a concern that only a transcendental method of argument could satisfy.

The question naturally arises as to whether Van Til was justified in thinking thus. Is it actually the case that the traditional methods of argument fail to do justice to the necessary relation that obtains between God's existence and the possibility of predication? On the other hand, what are we to make of Van Til's confidence in the ability of the transcendental method to succeed where traditional methods of argument have failed? Is his conviction in this regard something that can be justified or is it merely a case of misdirected zeal on his part? In light of the preceding discussion, it would seem that the answers to these questions are to be found in a more precise clarification of the presuppositional nature of Van Til's argument from predication. Before entering into this project, however, it is necessary to briefly

---

27. Cf. also the remarks of Greg Bahnsen in this regard: "Van Til's stunning application of this feature of transcendental argumentation to apologetics is that the truth of the Christian worldview is established not only by theistic premises and opinions, but also by antitheistic beliefs and opinions. As Van Til said, 'Antitheism presupposes theism' (*Survey of Christian Epistemology*, xii). Even if the unbeliever wants to start with the assertion that 'God does not exist,' a transcendental analysis of it would show that the possibility of its coherence and meaningfulness assumes the existence of the very God that it denies" (Bahnsen, *Van Til's Apologetic*, 502n63).

consider what I will call "the reductionist objection" to Van Til's belief in the distinctive character of transcendental argument.

The Reductionist Objection

Objections to the distinctive character of transcendental arguments are of some vintage in the history of philosophy, going back at least as far as Kant. The decade following the publication of Kant's *Critique of Pure Reason* in 1781 witnessed a number of critical responses to the distinctive claims of Kant's transcendental program. Indeed, a number of Kant's German contemporaries insisted that insofar as Kant's transcendental program constituted an answer to Hume, it was merely restating arguments that had already been voiced by the rationalist philosopher Leibniz.[28] Such criticism paved the way for later, more sophisticated attempts to deny the distinctive character of transcendental argument. To take but one example, in a series of articles published during the latter third of the twentieth century, Moltke S. Gram mounted a sustained attack on the notion that transcendental arguments are *formally* distinct from deductive arguments.[29] On Gram's view, statements of the form "*p* presupposes *q*" are *reducible* to statements of the form "*p* implies *q*."[30] Hence there is at least some justification for classifying arguments of this type under the title "the reductionist objection."[31]

28. See Henry E. Allison, *The Kant-Eberhard Controversy* (Baltimore: Johns Hopkins University Press, 1973). Eberhard was a contemporary critic of Kant who argued, according to Allison, "that whatever is true in Kant is already found in Leibniz, and that wherever Kant differs from Leibniz he is wrong" (p. 9). Kant's own response to Eberhard came in 1790 in the form of a short essay entitled "On a Discovery according to Which Any New Critique of Pure Reason Has Been Made Superfluous by an Earlier One." Although Eberhard never argued that a formal equivalence obtains between transcendental and deductive arguments, he nevertheless opened the door to such criticism by questioning whether Kant's transcendental philosophy differed in substance from the deductive rationalism of Leibniz.

29. See the helpful bibliography provided in Stephen Wentworth Arndt, "Transcendental Method and Transcendental Arguments," *International Philosophical Quarterly* 27 (1987): 43n1.

30. Moltke S. Gram, "Transcendental Arguments," *Nous* 5 (1971): 15–26.

31. The term "reductionist," like the term "rationalist," admits of a broad range of uses. Its application in this paper is somewhat restricted and refers primarily to someone who claims that a deductive relationship obtains between the form of a transcendental argument and the various forms of implicational argument (e.g., *modus ponens* and *modus tollens*).

It should be noted that while Van Til himself never provided a formal defense of the proposition that transcendental arguments are irreducible to either deductive or inductive arguments, it does not follow from this that he was unaware of the reductionist objection to his position. In *A Survey of Christian Epistemology*, a book that traces back to the earliest years of his teaching career, Van Til speaks of the distinction that exists between the transcendental method, on the one hand, and the inductive and deductive method, on the other:

> To us the only thing of great significance in this connection is that it is often found to be more difficult to distinguish our method from the deductive method than from the inductive method. But the favorite charge against us is that we are still bound to the past and are therefore employing the deductive method. Our opponents are thoughtlessly identifying our method with the Greek method of deduction. For this reason it is necessary for us to make the difference between these two methods as clear as we can.[32]

This passage serves as a reminder that the reductionist objection to the transcendental argument is not new, nor was Van Til unaware of it. Nevertheless, there is truth in Frame's claim that Van Til himself never provided us with an actual argument for its distinctiveness.[33] What follows is a tentative attempt to do so by making use of twentieth-century philosophical discussion of the concept of presupposition and the subsequent application of this discussion to transcendental argument. Admittedly this will involve making use of ideas that, strictly speaking, do not appear in Van Til's writings. Nevertheless, I believe that the clarity they lend to the exposition of Van Til's presuppositional argument, and especially his argument from predication, will eventually justify their introduction. Perhaps not all Van Tilians will find my argument convincing. At the very least, however, it should

---

32. Van Til, *A Survey of Christian Epistemology*, 9. This work represents the second edition of a syllabus originally written by Van Til in 1932 under the title *The Metaphysics of Apologetics*.

33. "The first thing to note is that in this discussion Van Til has not presented us with an actual argument. He has presented (1) a conclusion, (2) a logical model, and (3) a practical strategy. . . . I confess that I am not convinced that a transcendental argument for Christian theism must of necessity be indirect rather than direct. To my knowledge, Van Til never argues the point, but merely asserts it. But it is by no means obvious." Frame, *Cornelius Van Til*, 317.

serve to suggest a new avenue of approach to the question, which others may perhaps build upon.

Presupposition and Implication

The failure of traditional argument forms to capture what is meant by the concept of presupposition points up the need for a more precise way of construing the semantic relation between statements related by it. The most promising option to emerge is arguably that of Peter Strawson. According to Strawson, a statement A may be said to *presuppose* a statement B if B is a necessary precondition of the truth-or-falsity of A.[34] Strawson's interpretation of the concept of presupposition has been restated in succinct fashion by Bas van Fraassen as follows:[35] A presupposes B if and only if A is neither true nor false unless B is true.

This may also be stated as follows:[36]

(1) A presupposes B if and only if:
     (a) if A is true, then B is true.
     (b) if $\sim A$ is true, then B is true.

Van Fraassen's formulation is helpful for two reasons. First, it enables us to articulate more precisely Van Til's claim that "no human being can utter a single syllable, *whether in negation or affirmation*, unless it were for God's existence."[37] Second, it provides us with more formal language by which to articulate the differences between transcendental and traditional argument forms. To illustrate this, let us begin by applying the semantic relation embodied in (1a) to the

34. "A statement S presupposes a statement S' in the sense that the truth of S' is a precondition of the truth-or-falsity of S." Strawson, *Introduction to Logical Theory*, 175.

35. Van Fraassen, "Presupposition, Implication, and Self-Reference," 136–52. Cf. also the application of van Fraassen's work to Kant's transcendental argument in Gordon G. Brittan, *Kant's Theory of Science* (Princeton: Princeton University Press, 1978), 28–42. The argument that follows builds upon the work of both these scholars. I recognize, of course, that neither of these men would be likely to agree with the particular application I make here of their work.

36. Since A has no truth value (i.e., is neither true nor false) unless B is true, the truth of B must be presupposed whenever A has a truth value (i.e., whenever A is either true or false). Thus van Fraassen's definition may be restated in terms of the conjunction given in (1) above.

37. Van Til, *A Survey of Christian Epistemology*, 11, emphasis mine.

causal argument for God's existence. Letting C = causality, and G = God's existence, we translate as follows:

(2)   C presupposes G   (premise 1)
       C   (premise 2)
       Therefore G   (conclusion)

A comparison of this argument form with *modus ponens* makes it clear, as van Fraassen has noted, "that an analogue of *modus ponens* holds also for presupposition."[38] Formal differences become apparent, however, when we negate the minor premise in (2) as follows:

(3)   C presupposes G   (premise 1)
       ~C   (premise 2)
       Therefore G   (conclusion)

Note that in terms of the characterization provided by (1), the corollary principle (1b) shows that (3) is *valid*, whereas this argument would be *invalid* for implication.[39]

We are now in a position to identify a distinguishing feature of arguments based upon the concept of presupposition as we have formulated it here. That feature concerns what logicians refer to as "truth-functionality." In arguments of the form (3), the truth value of the conclusion is *not* a function of the truth value of the antecedent minor premise (i.e., premise 2), since the conclusion remains true whether C or ~C obtains. By way of contrast, in the case of standard implicational or direct argument forms such as *modus ponens* or *modus tollens*, the truth value of the conclusion is a direct function of the truth value of the antecedent minor premise. In *Van Til's Apologetic*, Bahnsen calls attention to this peculiar feature of transcendental arguments. He summarizes the matter as follows:

38. Van Fraassen, "Presupposition, Implication, and Self-Reference," 137.
39. Because the minor premise of (3) does not begin by affirming the antecedent, it is neither an instance of *modus ponens*, nor an analogue to it (see Irving M. Copi, *Introduction to Logic*, 7th [New York: Macmillan, 1986], 296). In other words, the argument form represented by (3) is *unique* to arguments based upon the semantic relation of presupposition.

To put it simply, in the case of "direct" arguments (whether rational or empirical), the negation of one of their premises changes the truth or reliability of their conclusion. But this is not true of transcendental arguments, and that sets them off from the other kinds of proof or analysis. A transcendental argument begins with any item of experience or belief whatsoever and proceeds, by critical analysis, to ask what conditions (or what other beliefs) would need to be true in order for that original experience or belief to make sense, be meaningful, or be intelligible to us. Now then, if we should go back and negate the statement of that original belief (or consider a contrary experience), the transcendental analysis (if originally cogent or sound) would nevertheless reach the very same conclusion.[40]

Generally speaking, then, presuppositional or transcendental arguments may be distinguished from implicational or "direct" arguments in terms of "the truth-functional relation of their conclusions to their premises."[41] In view of this distinction, the claim that traditional forms of the causal argument yield "a transcendental conclusion"[42] becomes questionable. To qualify as a transcendental conclusion, the truth of the conclusion in a direct argument would have to be in some sense independent of the truth value of its antecedent premise. However, both *modus ponens* and *modus tollens*, two classic forms of direct argument, fail to meet this criterion.[43]

The same must be said with respect to the claim that we can reach a "transcendental conclusion by many kinds of specific arguments, including many of the traditional ones."[44] In the nature of the case, the truth of a "transcendental conclusion" does not depend upon the truth value of its antecedent premise, regardless of whether this premise affirms causality or any other principle, since a transcendental conclusion constitutes the very ground for the proof of that premise.[45]

40. Bahnsen, *Van Til's Apologetic*, 501–2.
41. Ibid., 501.
42. Frame, "Presuppositional Apologetics," 220–21.
43. Noteworthy at this point is the fact that Frame construes the traditional causal argument in terms of *modus ponens* (Frame, *Apologetics to the Glory of God*, 76).
44. Frame, "Presuppositional Apologetics," 220.
45. The classic definition of a transcendental principle in argument was given by Kant in his *Critique of Pure Reason*: "But though it needs proof, it should be entitled a *principle*, not a *theorem*, because it has the peculiar character that it makes possible the very experience which is its own ground of proof, and that in this experience it must always itself be presupposed."

Formal differences between the concepts of presupposition and implication also emerge when we consider the analogue to *modus tollens* for presupposition:

(4)   C presupposes G
        ~G
        Therefore ~C

Again, whereas this argument would be valid for implication as an instance of *modus tollens*, it is *not* valid when C and G are joined by the semantic relation of presupposition, since in the latter case C has no truth value unless G is true.[46] Thus the possibility of assigning a truth value to C depends upon the logically anterior truth of G. To put the matter another way, if ~G obtains, we have what Strawson refers to as "a failure of presupposition," in which case the possibility of assigning a truth value to C does not even arise.[47]

John Frame has rightly noted that Van Til's apologetic method "seeks to show that *all* intelligibility depends on, or presupposes, Christian theism."[48] In light of the preceding arguments, however, there is reason to question whether direct argument forms such as *modus tollens* meet this criterion. In argumentative instances where causality (C) and God's existence (G) are related by implication, ~C follows from ~G. In other words, an argument formulated in terms of *modus tollens* contains the implication, albeit subtle, that *at least some* types of predication are possible in cases where God's existence fails to obtain. By way of contrast, Van Til desired to argue that even cases of predicational negation presuppose the truth of God's existence. In light of this, *modus tollens* would seem to be incapable of sustaining the apologetically radical goal he was aiming at with his argument from predication.

Immanuel Kant, *Critique of Pure Reason*, trans. Norman Kemp Smith (New York: St. Martin's Press, 1958), B765.

46. Recall that in terms of the way we have construed the presuppositional relation, the truth value of C (i.e., its truth or falsity) depends upon the truth of G. Thus if G fails to obtain, then the possibility of predicating a truth value for C also fails to obtain.

47. Cf. the traditional maxim *non entis nulla sunt attributa*, "of nothing, nothing can be attributed." Since a property cannot be truly or falsely predicated of what does not exist, predication requires an existential. For Van Til, predication requires God's self-existence, since God's existence is the only "existential" that can ultimately justify the possibility of predication.

48. Frame, *Cornelius Van Til*, 314–15, emphasis mine.

In summary, the problem with traditional argument forms is that they do not allow one to argue the proposition "~G, therefore neither C nor ~C," nor do they allow one to argue its corollary proposition "~C therefore G." The transcendental character of these propositions is evident from the fact that both of them depend upon the assumption that G constitutes a necessary precondition for the very intelligibility of C. Since Van Til clearly sought to establish these propositions via apologetic argument, and since traditional argument forms do not allow one to do so—indeed, in at least two cases actually invalidate these propositions—it follows that traditional argument forms simply cannot do justice to Van Til's apologetic goals. Moreover, it remains questionable whether there is any meaningful sense in which one may continue to say that traditional arguments yield "transcendental conclusions." At best such a statement is highly ambiguous and ultimately misleading.

Transcendental Argument and *Reductio ad Absurdum*

Strawson's concept of presupposition, as formulated by van Fraassen, also allows us to sharpen the distinction between the method of *reductio ad absurdum* and Van Til's transcendental argument from predication. In a *reductio*, a position is refuted by deducing a contradiction from its premises. In Van Til's transcendental argument from predication, the possibility of assigning a truth value—and thus by extension the very possibility of generating a contradiction—fails to obtain unless God's existence is true. In other words, Van Til's transcendental argument from predication makes a stronger claim than the claim generated by the *reductio*. The latter generates a contradiction from the non-Christian position, while Van Til's transcendental argument from predication makes the more radical claim that contradiction itself is impossible apart from the truth of God's existence. To state the contrast in slightly different terms, if God's existence is a necessary condition for the mere truth of causality, then denying God's existence while affirming causality results in contradiction. However, if God's existence is a necessary condition for both the truth or falsity of causality, then denying God's existence results in a failure to predicate anything at all.[49]

49. Strawson argues that the logical absurdity involved in self-contradiction should be distinguished from the logical absurdity involved in a failure of presupposition: "It is self-contradictory

This points up an important reason why the transcendental argument should not be confused or equated with the method of *reductio ad absurdum*. For Van Til it was not enough to deduce a contradiction from the non-Christian's position and leave matters at that. Indeed, had Van Til stopped there, it is doubtful whether he would have ruffled as many apologetic feathers as he did. Rather, Van Til insisted on going further and making the *transcendental* claim that the very intelligibility of the non-Christian's claims, whether true *or* false, *necessarily* presupposes the truth of Christian theism. If there is an apologetic equivalent to the "offense of the cross" in Van Til's method, this would be it. To be sure, the *reductio* helps make definite the nature of the presuppositional relation between God's existence and causality, and it does this by pointing out contradictions that arise in the non-Christian position when God's existence is denied. Strictly speaking, however, the *reductio* does not establish God's existence, since the truth of God's existence is a necessary precondition for the possibility of argument itself, and it is precisely the latter claim that Van Til's transcendental argument from predication seeks to prove.

As noted in an earlier section of this paper, the reductionist objection to the unique character of transcendental argument rests upon the assertion that "*p* implies *q*" and "*p* presupposes *q*" are deductively equivalent propositions. However, if the arguments developed above are valid, as I am inclined to believe, then it follows that semantic differences between the concepts of presupposition and implication do in fact translate into differences on the level of formal argument and method. As such, it is not possible to reduce "presuppositional" or transcendental arguments to standard instances of implicational argument, all of which is to say that the reductionist objection to the transcendental argument fails.

Van Til's transcendental argument from predication helps us to see that the most fundamental question in logic and argument turns

---

to conjoin S with the denial of S' if S' is a necessary condition of the truth, simply, of S. It is a different kind of logical absurdity to conjoin S with the denial of S' if S' is a necessary condition of the *truth or falsity* of S. The relation between S and S' in the first case is that S entails S'. We need a different name for the relation between S and S' in the second case; let us say . . . that S *presupposes* S'." Strawson, *Introduction to Logical Theory*, 175.

out to be a metaphysical one, namely that of God's existence.[50] For Van Til, God's existence is a metaphysical presupposition that grounds the very possibility of logic, and by extension argument itself. This is doubtless the reason why Van Til's apologetic method takes very seriously the essential character of the relation between God's existence and argument—so much so that on Van Til's view of things, the negation of God's existence renders argument impossible. How so? By rendering impossible the task of assigning truth values in argument (i.e., predication). In this way Van Til's transcendental argument from predication takes us beyond the analysis of particular arguments and raises the question of argument itself.

Further Objections

A few closing caveats in anticipation of possible objections:[51] First, one might object that while the preceding analysis serves to clarify the concept of presupposition in Van Til's apologetic, it fails to provide an actual example of transcendental argument. In response to this objection one should call attention to the contradiction involved in asserting that the following is an argument,

(5)   Causality implies God
      Not God
      Therefore not causality,

while at the same time asserting that the following is *not* an argument:

(6)   Causality presupposes God
      Not God
      Therefore neither causality nor not causality
      (i.e., neither C nor ~C).

50. The primacy of metaphysics in Van Til's apologetic traces back to his earliest writings, as evidenced by the title *The Metaphysics of Apologetics*, a work originally written by Van Til in 1932 (cf. n. 32 above). Viewed from this perspective, Van Til's apologetic method is thoroughly anti-Kantian.

51. I would like to thank John Frame for reading over an earlier version of this essay and offering many helpful criticisms and suggestions. His critical interaction provided the catalyst for many of the clarifications I make in this section.

Note that (6) is neither invalid nor unsound, *given* the definition of presupposition stated in (1), above. Hence the ground for privileging (5) as an example of argument while rejecting (6) ultimately rests upon the refusal to allow the introduction and integration of the concept of presupposition into one's definition of what counts as "argument." One must resist the Procrustean notion that the arguments worthy of the name are only those based upon the semantic relation of implication. Van Tilians in particular should be wary of adopting a form of rationalist dogmatism that refuses to admit the limitations inherent in a formal logic based exclusively upon implication.

One may, nevertheless, object that the argument begs the question, inasmuch as it assumes that a certain semantic relation between God and causality obtains from the outset. However, other commonly accepted forms of argument, for instance arguments based upon material implication, also begin with a semantic relation that is assumed. The relation of presupposition, like the relation of implication, is a semantic relation. Thus there is no reason why, *prima facie*, an argument that begins with the premise "C presupposes G" should be assigned a lesser status than an argument that begins with the premise "C implies G." Indeed, one may go further and raise the question whether finite creatures can begin any argument without making assumptions of some sort or other. The real question is not whether initial assumptions can be avoided, but whether subsequent argument can demonstrate their *necessary* character.

The latter observation provides a convenient opportunity to address a possible misunderstanding of the nature of the claim being made here. In defending the right of (6) to lay claim to the title of "argument," the additional claim is *not* being made that (6) proves the whole of Christian theism in one argument. While in my opinion (6) constitutes a legitimate instance of transcendental argument, it obviously does so in an abbreviated form. For this reason it is more accurate, and for apologetic purposes more useful, to regard (6) as an abbreviated transcendental argument. Other arguments can, and in fact should, be utilized in order to demonstrate the necessary character of the presuppositional relation between causality and God expressed in the major premise of (6). What (6) serves to illustrate is that an argument may be both valid and sound from a formal point of view, yet insufficient from a practical point of view. In the concrete world of apologetic engagement one is certainly bound to make use of a variety of arguments. Admitting this does not entail the conclusion, however, that transcendental and traditional arguments cannot be distinguished from one another on formal grounds, or that they are somehow deductively equivalent to one another.

Finally, some might object that the arguments advanced in this paper entail the conclusion that Christian apologists, and Van Tilians in particular, are somehow obliged to stop using implicational arguments altogether. After all, if certain forms of argument (e.g., *modus tollens*) are formally invalid when arguments like (6) are operative, what place remains for implicational arguments in a presuppositional apologetic? It should be kept in mind that in terms of the concept of presupposition set forth in this essay, both *modus ponens* and its presuppositional analogue represent valid forms of argument. This arises from the fact that semantic differences between the latter two argument forms, while clearly present, nevertheless do not register themselves on a formal level. Thus in the particular case of *modus ponens*, there is in fact *formal* overlap between an argument based upon the concept of implication and its presuppositional analogue. Commenting on the nature of this overlap, van Fraassen writes: "Thus presupposition and implication are not the same, but they have something in common. What they have in common is that, if A either presupposes or implies B, the argument from A to B is valid."[52]

To this observation one may add that the formal notion of "validity" itself is not an abstraction, but a contextual notion that is relative to, and therefore conditioned by, the particular semantic relation that is operative in a given argumentative context. Taken together, these considerations indicate that in those argumentative contexts where *modus ponens* is operative, or where the operative semantic relation is that of implication proper, methodological differences between presuppositional and traditional approaches do not register themselves on a *formal* level. In such contexts implicational arguments continue to have their proper function and place.

52. Van Fraassen, "Presupposition, Implication, and Self-Reference," 138.

It is important to add, however, that in the case of *modus ponens* this statement holds only when one views it in reference to its purely formal aspect. Even though one cannot distinguish *modus ponens* from its presuppositional analogue on formal grounds, it nevertheless does differ from its presuppositional analogue on a semantic level. Moreover, even if such a semantic distinction were absent, it would still be possible, as Bahnsen's argument suggests, to distinguish these two argument forms in terms of the truth-functional relation of their premises to their conclusions.

Conclusion

The philosophical journal *Nous* featured a symposium on transcendental arguments in 1971. Among the contributors to that symposium was Moltke S. Gram, who began his paper as follows: "The problem about transcendental arguments is whether there are any."[53] Obviously the passage of three decades has not rendered this question moot by any means. Secular philosophers certainly have not reached anything like a consensus on this question. From this it does not follow, however, that Christian apologists are somehow bound to share in Gram's skepticism with respect to transcendental arguments. One must also grant that neither van Fraassen nor Strawson has said the last word on presupposition, and there may in fact be better ways to construe the relation of presupposition. There may also be different, and even better, ways of stating the case for the distinctive character of "presuppositional" argument.

At the very least, however, the arguments advanced here call into question the assumption that the concept of presupposition lacks formal and methodological significance. A plausible case can be made for the distinctive character of Van Til's transcendental argument, provided one keeps an eye on the concept of presupposition and the distinctive way that it functions in argument. My hope is that this essay may at least contribute to the ongoing discussion in that regard.

---

53. Gram, "Transcendental Arguments," 15.

Cornelius Van Til and the Reformation of Christian Apologetics

K. Scott Oliphint

*T*hough it is difficult at times, as one reads Van Til's works, to tell whether he is first of all a philosopher who is developing an apologetic or an apologist developing a Christian philosophy, there was never any question in *Van Til's* mind as to which came first. He considered himself to be a defender of the faith, first and foremost.[1]

This appendix is an edited version of a larger chapter, K. Scott Oliphint, "Cornelius Van Til and the Reformation of Christian Apologetics," in *Die idee van reformasie: Gister en vandag*, ed. B. J. van der Walt (Potchefstroomse: Potchefstroomse Universiteit vir Christelike Hoër Onderwys, 1991). Space constraints here preclude some needed updating and elaboration since that earlier publication. This essay is reprinted in its present form in order to emphasize aspects of Van Til's thought that remain in need of highlighting.

1. See "Response by C. Van Til," in *Jerusalem and Athens: Critical Discussions on the Philosophy and Apologetics of Cornelius Van Til*, ed. E. R. Geehan (Nutley, NJ: Presbyterian and Reformed, 1971), 348.

He was a theologian of the highest order,[2] as well as a penetrating philosopher,[3] but it was the apologetic of Dr. Cornelius Van Til that set him apart as a twentieth-century Reformer. It is interesting to note that while Van Til was without peer in his pursuit of a truly Reformed apologetic, he was without competition as well. Any historical survey of Christian apologetics would show that, since Aquinas, the church has done little to develop the discipline of apologetics until Van Til.

It was early in his academic career[4] that Van Til began to see the problems inherent in the "traditional"[5] approach to a defense of Christian theism. He realized that there was an inherent theological and methodological weakness in any thought, system, or method that attempted initially to exclude God and his revelation in order to bring him in surreptitiously at a later point. Because all things are "from him, through him, and unto him,"[6] Van Til knew that God must be the ultimate explanation for any argument, any conversation, any "proof"—anything at all.

Van Til's influence will be seen by future generations as a "Copernican revolution" in apologetics. Though there are myriad approaches one could take when delineating the vast influence of Van Til's approach, I would like to approach his thought from three distinct, yet interconnected, perspectives: (1) A Worldview Apologetic, (2) A Trinitarian Apologetic, and (3) A Covenantal Apologetic.

2. See, for example, John M. Frame, *Van Til: The Theologian* (Phillipsburg, NJ: Pilgrim, 1976).

3. For a discussion of Van Til's "more philosophical" approach see, for example, Geehan, ed., *Jerusalem and Athens*, 23–127; Van Til, *A Survey of Christian Epistemology* (Nutley, NJ: Presbyterian and Reformed, 1969), 14–64.

4. Van Til was arguing presuppositionally even as far back as his doctoral dissertation in 1928. See K. Scott Oliphint, "The Consistency of Van Til's Methodology," *Westminster Theological Journal* 52 (1990): 27–49.

5. By "traditional" approach I mean any one of the historic apologetic methods that attempts to absolutize aspects of created reality, be it reason (rational apologetics), empirical facts (evidential apologetics), or some combination of the two (various forms of Thomistic apologetics).

6. In Cornelius Van Til, "At the Beginning, God: An Interview with Cornelius Van Til," *Christianity Today* 22 (December 30, 1977): 22, when asked how he would like to be remembered, Dr. Van Til replied, "as one who was faithful to him, 'from whom, through whom, and unto whom are all things.'"

A Worldview Apologetic

Van Til summarizes what a worldview apologetic entails:

It is not as though we are at the outset dealing with the question of knowledge of the world about us and that the only point in dispute is whether or not God can be and need be known. We . . . make the question whether God need be and can be known *so inclusive* that it coincides with the question whether anything can be known.[7]

It is Van Til's commitment to Reformed theology that causes him to make such an all-inclusive statement. Van Til's approach to a defense of Christianity turned apologetics on its head. While traditional apologetic approaches ask the unbeliever to understand his world *in order to* understand God, Van Til affirms (with Reformed theology) that because God controls "whatsoever comes to pass," because it is "in God that we live, move, and exist," the world can never be understood aright at any point without reference to God. Rational apologists seek to agree with the unbeliever on such all-encompassing concepts as being, essence, infinity, cause, effect, contradiction, and so forth. Evidentialists want the unbeliever simply to observe the "facts" and to agree on the "evidence." Van Til is convinced that no concept of being, essence, cause, fact, or evidence can be understood truly without first understanding the Creator of being, essence, fact, and so on. In other words, there is no neutrality in thought or in life for any of God's creatures. Because all people are creatures of God, every thought, every act, every word is either for or against God, *whether we want to recognize it or not*.

To quote Van Til again, "There is not a spot in heaven or on earth about which there is no dispute between the two opposing parties."[8] This is what separates Van Til's apologetic from all others. This is what makes Van Til's apologetic truly Reformed. Only Van Til's approach allows for the obedient application of a truly Reformed theology. There are two and only two classes of people in the world. Such has always been the case. Such will always be the case. There are those who know

7. Van Til, *A Survey of Christian Epistemology*, 116, emphasis mine.
8. Ibid.

God and love him because they have been called out of darkness into his marvelous light. There are also those who know God and hate him because they refuse to acknowledge the truth that is known, and they worship and serve the creature (Rom. 1:18ff.). There is no third party, no "honest seeker," no "confused questioner." There is none righteous, no not one. There is none who seeks for God, none who understands, none who does good. All have turned aside (Rom. 3:10ff.).

Those who have been delivered from death by the sovereign grace of an omnipotent Father seek subsequently to interpret all things in light of the God who has saved them from the wrath to come. They are the ones who are renewed unto knowledge (Col. 3:10). In a very real sense, they are the ones who for the first time know their God, their world, and themselves.

Van Til's apologetic method, because it *starts with* the existence of the God of Scripture, encompasses absolutely everything that exists in the world. Because all is created, all relates directly and absolutely to the Creator. It is biblically insufficient, therefore, to attempt to start with some supposedly neutral "fact" and from it to extrapolate the existence of "a god." As Van Til has said, those who seek such an approach, "ought first to justify the contention that 'facts' exist in total independence of God."[9] This view of "facts" is all-encompassing. It includes not only empirical facts but rational facts as well. It is not only that man cannot make sense of what he observes (if he attempts to do so and indeed is encouraged to do so by the traditional method) apart from the existence of God. It is also that the fact of existence itself cannot be intelligibly discussed without reference to God. In speaking of the unbeliever, Van Til says, "What our opponents mean by *existence* of any 'fact' is *existence apart from God*."[10] Existence itself, or we could say "being" itself (for Aquinas and Thomists, who follow the traditional approach), is thought to be the transcendental notion, fundamental to every other notion. But as Van Til has consistently and persistently shown, "being" or "existence" cannot be discussed apart from the more fundamental presupposition of *God's* existence.

9. Ibid., 122.
10. Ibid., 117.

"Being" has been one of the thorns in the flesh of philosophy only because philosophy historically has dogmatically presupposed its own epistemological autonomy. Parmenides was no closer to a proper understanding of being than was Heraclitus. Aquinas was no closer than Hegel. Once one assumes any fact to be apart from God, that fact will never be *truly* known. "Facts are unaccounted for if Scripture is left out of account."[11] It is for this reason that Van Til's approach is seen as a worldview apologetic. Only in a consistently Reformed apologetic can we see not just "being" or "reason" or "evidence" or "cause" as inexplicable apart from God, but all "things"[12] are inexplicable apart from the presupposition of the God of Scripture.

What has been said above about Van Til's worldview approach, though thoroughly penetrating, seems impossible for a Bible-believing or particularly Reformed Christian to disagree with. Reformed Christianity has always held that God is the source of all things, all facts, all existence. The problem has come, however, whenever Van Til has attempted to apply consistently his own approach. It is the application of this worldview approach that has caused great controversy among theologians and apologists. Particularly, the great controversy seems to center on Van Til's understanding of human reason. For Van Til, "reason and revelation should not be contrasted as two sources of knowledge."[13] "Reason as one 'fact' among others is itself a revelation."[14] Van Til sees reason as itself coming under this all-encompassing worldview approach. God is the author and revealer of *all* things.

The fundamental question is whether or not reason can reason aright apart from any reference to or renewal from God. If it can, then it would be biblically legitimate to point the unbeliever to any "fact," be it conceptual or empirical, and to ask him to reason from that fact to the fact of God's existence. Reason's role, given this scenario, would be not to contradict revelation but to lead us to the revelation of the God of Scripture. There would be, then, a legitimate reasoning process

11. Ibid., 125.
12. I take the word "things" here in a wide sense, meaning observable facts as well as consciousness of any and every fact, including self. I take my idea from Hendrik G. Stoker, "Reconnoitering the Theory of Knowledge of Professor Dr. Cornelius Van Til," in Geehan, ed., *Jerusalem and Athens*, 29n14.
13. Van Til, *A Survey of Christian Epistemology*, 123.
14. Ibid., 124.

that the believer could engage in with the unbeliever in order to prove God's existence. Reason would be the *Anknüpfungspunkt*,[15] the point of contact, between believer and unbeliever. Unfortunately, while this approach is sensitive to the plight of the unbeliever, it severely restricts rather than encourages the apologetic mandate (1 Peter 3:15). If one holds to this view of reason, one of two things is true, depending on one's theology.

First, from the standpoint of a less consistent theology that self-consciously holds to some form of independence from God, man's reason becomes the final arbiter as to whether or not God's revelation is authoritative, whether or not God's salvation is acceptable, whether or not God's character is comprehensible. These questions can be answered by an appeal to human reason. This, of course, follows consistently from any theology that limits the all-controlling plan of God. If God is not sovereign in salvation, as some would contend, neither is he sovereign over our total thought and life. Autonomy is the inevitable result. The inherent problem is that *neutrality* means *autonomy*. And autonomy is the opposite of *theo-nomy*;[16] it is sinful.

The second thing that occurs is perhaps prevalent more in Reformed circles. It is the problem of rationalism or, the absolutization of reason. This type of approach seeks arbitrarily to assign to our reasoning process the ability to distinguish itself from a depraved heart and to be the final authority as to whether or not God actually did reveal himself in the world.

The problems inherent in such a rationalistic view are many from a Reformed perspective. At stake fundamentally and primarily in these discussions of reason is the character of God himself and, more specifically, the Creator-creature distinction. When it is said, for example,

15. It is said of Van Til that upon entering his apologetics classroom one day at Westminster Theological Seminary, he had forgotten that he had scheduled an hour-long exam for his students. Having been reminded of his lapse and having no exam prepared, he wrote one word on the blackboard: *Anknüpfungspunkt*. His students proceeded to write for an hour. I tell this story only to cast light on the importance in Van Til's mind of the problem of "point of contact." For Van Til, *the* point of contact in apologetic reasoning is not "reason" or "facts," but the knowledge of God that *all* of us possess (Rom. 1:18–20).

16. I hyphenate *theo-nomy* in order to distance myself from the reconstructionist movement in the United States, a subdivision of which is called theonomy. This movement has claimed Van Til as one of its major influences, though Van Til never aligned himself with it, nor did he ever endorse its theological tenets.

that God cannot resolve a bona fide contradiction, the natural question is, why not? If the answer given is that logic carries with it such force, such compelling consent in and of itself that God is subject to it, we must disagree with such a claim. Logic, like all else save God himself, is *created*. All things created are absolutely, totally, and completely subsumed under their Creator and, by definition, never equal to him. Logic (like light, for example) may reflect the character of its Creator but cannot be said to be above him (in the sense of being in any way superior to him); nor does it, in and of itself, constrain him, which brings us to one of the fundamental problems in rationalistic thought.

Whenever the word *logic* is debated or used in a rationalistic context (and this is inevitably true of secular thought, but regretfully true of some Reformed thinking), it is used without reference to the fundamental difference between human logic and God's thought. Those who exalt logic as Lord of the mind fail to distinguish between the Lord and logic. When it is said that even God cannot square a bona fide contradiction, we must ask whether or not a bona fide contradiction is contradictory for man or for God or for both. If it is contradictory for man, what criterion will we use to prove that it is contradictory for God as well? Is *everything* that man proves contradictory *ipso facto* contradictory for God also? Because man is unable to resolve a contradiction does not mean that God has the same inability.[17]

Let's assume for the sake of argument that God has logic as one of his attributes.[18] Would this mean that God has the need to analyze and evaluate reality and himself in order to understand it? Would we say that God "needs" logic in order to distinguish himself from all else? If so, then his logic is of a temporal rather than eternal necessity, since there was a time when "all else" was nothing. How can an

17. In the original version of this essay, I used our understanding of the Trinity as an example of our limited use of logic. Because I would need to elaborate the point more significantly than I did originally, I have chosen rather to delete it here in the interest of space.

18. Though theologians and apologists are quick to speak of *God's* logic, I have yet to hear an adequate explanation of what his logic would be. Because God thinks what he is and is what he thinks, logic in God would have to include the Trinitarian resolution just delineated, thus making it of quite a different sort of thing than human logic, not to mention that it would be infinite, eternal, and exhaustive.

infinite, eternal God make use of a tool designed to facilitate the thinking *process*?

This is not to say that God is in any way irrational or inconsistent with himself. It is only to say that "rationality" in God and "logic" in God mean that he is consistent with who he is, not with some exterior principle that determines his consistency. If logic is a part of God's character, then because he is pleased to act only in accordance with his attributes, he will act rationally or logically. God always acts in accordance with who he is. We know that he is consistent with himself and thus in that sense is "logical." The important question that has yet to be addressed by the rationalist (though emphasized by Van Til) is, however, the distinct and necessary difference that must obtain between God's thinking and man's logic. Because God is consistent with himself, man must be consistent, not fundamentally with *man* or with *logic*, but with God. God is our final reference point, not logic. It is true that God cannot resolve a "bona fide contradiction" if by "bona fide contradiction" we mean any proposition or "fact" that is opposed to the nature and character of God.[19]

Similarly, in discussing a Reformed view of mathematics, one scholar says, "If we identify part of creation with God or part of God with creation, we are guilty of serious idolatry."[20] Of course, God does communicate to man in a way that requires the use of human logic in order to understand God and his world. Van Til goes so far as to say that "no one can say anything intelligible about God's revelation through Christ in Scripture without the use of the process of syllogistic reasoning."[21] Van Til goes on in the next sentence to affirm his worldview approach.

> But to say anything intelligible about God's revelation through Christ
> in Scripture and in particular to do so in the interest of challenging

---

19. This would include God's decisions to create the world in a particular way, thus making certain things (createdly) necessary that were not so prior to creation.

20. Vern S. Poythress, "A Biblical View of Mathematics," in *Foundations of Christian Scholarship*, ed. Gary North (Vallecito, CA: Ross House, 1979), 159–88. This entire discussion is relevant to our discussion on logic. Poythress grounds mathematics in the knowledge of God, revelation, and the righteousness of God. So must logic be grounded.

21. Cornelius Van Til, *The Sovereignty of Grace: An Appraisal of G. C. Berkouwer's View of Dordt* (Philadelphia: Presbyterian and Reformed, 1969), 27.

the natural man to repent and to seek forgiveness of his sin through Christ, such reasoning (syllogistic reasoning) must be subject to the presupposition of the absolute authority of Christ's Word.[22]

As a matter of fact, Van Til insists that the Christian alone can be logical. "The anti-theist has," says Van Til, "in effect, denied the very law of contradiction, inasmuch as the law of contradiction, to operate at all, must have its foundation in the nature of God."[23]

This brings us back to the original contention that Van Til's apologetic is a worldview apologetic. With Van Til's approach, one may *start anywhere* with the unbeliever and challenge him *at any point*. Van Til is conscious of the enmity against God that flows from unbelief:

> It is therefore pointless for Christians to tell non-Christians that Christianity is "in accord with the law of contradiction" unless they explain what they mean by this. For the non-Christian will take this statement to mean something entirely different from what the Christian ought to mean by it. The non-Christian does not believe in creation. Therefore, for him the law of contradiction is, like all other laws, something that does not find its ultimate source in the creative activity of God.[24]

Because of the Christian's foundation in God, because the Christian is redeemed by Christ through whom all things (including logic) came into being, then it is the Christian who can use (and justify) created logical principles in accordance with created reality. It is the Christian who can unashamedly use (and justify) logic to its fullest.[25] If the unbeliever claims to be fully logical, one may either challenge the consistency of using logic apart from its Creator or ask the unbeliever as to the basis of logic itself.

But Van Til's worldview approach not only allows for argumentation at the rationalist's level, it allows for apologetic debate at the evidentialist's level as well. The unbeliever may want to talk about the

---

22. Ibid.
23. Cornelius Van Til, *An Introduction to Systematic Theology* (Nutley, NJ: Presbyterian and Reformed, 1974), 37.
24. Ibid., 256.
25. For an elaboration of the use of reason and logic in a Christian context, see Oliphint, *Reasons for Faith: Philosophy in the Service of Theology* (Phillipsburg, NJ: P&R, 2006), part 1.

evidences or the facts of the Christian position, whether in archeol-
ogy or in history. Again, the Christian may talk with the unbeliever
about his objections:

> Every bit of historical investigation, whether it be in the directly
> Biblical field, archeology, or in general history, is bound to confirm
> the truth of the claims of the Christian position. But I would not talk
> endlessly about facts and more facts without ever challenging the
> non-believer's philosophy of fact. A really *fruitful historical apologetic*
> argues that every fact *is* and *must* be such as proves the truth of the
> Christian theistic position.[26]

If one understands the biblical emphasis that all things are created
and sustained by a personal God, then one can understand that at any
point in thought or in life the unbeliever can be challenged about
unbelief. This, indeed, is a worldview approach to apologetics. Christ
reigns and is Lord of all of life. All of life can therefore be used against
those, in apologetic argument, who insist on denying the God whom
they already know (Rom. 1:18f.) and in whom they live, move, and
exist. "The Bible claims to have the ultimate *truth* about *all facts*,"[27]
including logic, reason, and evidence.

A Trinitarian Apologetic

It deserves careful thought that Van Til immediately and without
embarrassment *begins* his apologetic with the self-contained *triune
God*. Those familiar particularly with Thomistic apologetics know
that Thomas and his followers can never begin with the tri-unity of
God in apologetics because such truth "exceeds all the ability of the
human reason."[28]

For Aquinas, there is a "twofold mode of truth in what we profess
about God."[29] There are truths that can be proved by natural reason,

---

26. Van Til, *The Defense of the Faith*, 199. Italics in the phrase *fruitful historical apologetic*
my emphasis; other italics his.

27. Van Til, *A Survey of Christian Epistemology*, 124, emphasis on "all facts," mine.

28. Thomas Aquinas, *Summa contra Gentiles*, trans. Anton C. Pegis (Notre Dame, IN:
Notre Dame University Press, 1957), 1:63.

29. Ibid.

unaided by revelation. "Such are that God exists, that He is one, and the like."[30] Truths that, according to Aquinas, exceed reason's ability are in need of supplementation by divine revelation. This supplementation cannot disagree with that which comes by way of unaided reason. There are not two *different* truths but, says Thomas, two ways of knowing. Because the tri-unity of God is one of those truths that exceeds the ability of human reason, Aquinas is never able to affirm such a truth in his defense of Christianity.[31]

Van Til, however, *starts with* the triune God of Scripture in his apologetic. He is not content simply to attempt proof of the oneness of a god, only to bring in the three-in-oneness of *the* God later. He is quick to question any method of reasoning that concludes with a kind of half-truth (which in reality is a falsehood) in order to convince "Reason" that *some* god *somewhere* exists. So, it is with the triune God that one must begin one's defense: "The demand of the doctrine of the Trinity is that reality be interpreted in exclusively eternal categories inasmuch as the source of diversity lies in the Trinity itself and could never be found in a sense world beyond God."[32]

What Van Til means here, at least in part, is this: The problem of unity and diversity is another of the fundamental thorns in the flesh of philosophy and consequently of apologetics. All attempts in philosophy to unify the diversity without diversifying the unity have ended in failure. Thomas Aquinas will serve well again as an example of this failure (given the fact that he self-consciously, as a Christian philosopher, refused to start his reasoning with the triune God).

Aquinas was keenly aware of the problem of the one and the many. For him, as for much of philosophy, the one, the unity, must have metaphysical and epistemological priority over the many, the diversity. In order for man to know the essence of a thing, according to Aquinas, he must organize and perfect the diversity that he sees by universalizing those diverse things through the intellect. Being, according to Aquinas, diversifies itself in all things in the universe. Being is limited only by the essence (or quiddity) of a thing. Being is a transcendental notion because it includes all classes and thus

30. Ibid.
31. Ibid.
32. Van Til, *A Survey of Christian Epistemology*, 96.

transcends them all. But in order for one to know what a thing is, he must unify the diversity around him through the intellect. The job of reason according to Aquinas is to organize the diversity into a unit and thus end up with knowledge of a thing.

For Aquinas, truth and knowledge are the *adequation* of the immanence in act of our thought with that which exists outside our thought.[33] What our reason does, therefore, in gaining knowledge is to abstract from sensible reality (i.e., diversity) that which does not exist in reality *as such* (i.e., as unity). To put it in Aristotelian terms, the form is abstracted from the matter and, though existing in the mind as immaterial and immobile, the form is analogous to, though not identical with, the matter. The form, according to Aquinas, is that in the real (in *re*) which makes knowledge of it possible.[34] Aquinas puts it this way:

> Nevertheless, it cannot be said that the character *universal* belongs to nature so understood, because commonality and unity belong to the character *universal*. . . . For if commonality were included in the notion of man, commonality would be found whenever humanity was found. But this is false, because in Socrates no commonality is found. On the contrary, whatever is in him is individuated.[35]

The problem of unity and diversity in knowledge becomes acute in Aquinas when one begins to realize that, according to his existential metaphysic, that which is in the mind, the universal, is *not* in individuating matter, and that which exists in individuating matter *cannot* be in the mind as individuated, but only as universalized. There is, then, no possible way to connect the mind (or reason) with reality. There is no way of knowing if that which is in the mind as immaterial and immutable is also in reality (which is material and mobile). There is no way, on Aquinas's own basis, to account for knowledge of anything.

But the problem does not stop with knowledge of reality. Aquinas encounters the same kind of problem when he attempts to account

33. Jacques Maritain, *Existence and the Existent* (New York: Pantheon, 1964), 11.

34. Etienne Gilson, *The Christian Philosophy of St. Thomas Aquinas: With a Catalog of St. Thomas's Works* (New York: Random House, 1956), 31.

35. Aquinas, *Summa contra Gentiles*, 1:48.

for knowledge of God. According to Aquinas, God is one in whom essence and existence are identical. Because God is pure act, knowledge of him, as knowledge of all else, must be knowledge by way of analogy.[36] Aquinas's doctrine of analogy asserts that being belongs to each and every thing *analogically*, that is, *in proportion to its nature*.[37] The ultimate basis of such a doctrine, therefore, lies in the proportion that exists between the essence (*quod est*) and existence (*esse*) of a thing.[38] Goodness, for example, does not mean the same thing (univocally) when predicated of men and food. The way in which a thing is good is proportionate to its being. This is called "analogy of proper proportionality." Such a view of analogy is calculated to overcome the problem of unity and diversity.

However, because the analogy of proper proportionality deals exclusively with the relation that obtains between essence and existence, it is not able to allow for the possibility of One in whom essence and existence are identical. Aquinas is forced to introduce a second type of analogy in order to allow for the existence of a god. This second type, based on the causal process, is called "analogy of intrinsic attribution." The analogy of intrinsic attribution relates to the existence of One in whom essence and existence are identical and is calculated to affirm some sort of relationship between God (pure act) and his creation (which *always*, according to Aquinas, combines the transcendental notion of being with essence).

We must ask at this point how one can know God, given this type of metaphysical structure. If it is the case that God is one in whom existence and essence are identical, then it would seem that God is of a piece with the metaphysical, transcendental, all-inclusive notion of "being" as that in which potential existence determines its act of existence. Being, in this case, is the same for God and for man such that God himself is of a piece with the transcendental notion of being. Though Thomists would remind us that the analogy of proper

36. Those familiar with Van Til's writings will recognize immediately that he also affirmed the analogical character of all knowledge. It must be made clear here, however, though it cannot be expanded, that Van Til's analogical knowledge and Aquinas's doctrine of analogy are two totally different ideas.

37. G. B. Phelan et al., *Saint Thomas and Analogy* (Milwaukee: Marquette University Press, 1941), 8.

38. Ibid., 25.

proportionality does not apply to God, they must still account for the so-called transcendental notion of being.

If they claim that such a notion is accounted for by way of the analogy of intrinsic attribution, which seeks to affirm that God is the unparticipated being, we could only respond by reminding them that, *on their own basis*, if God's being is unparticipated, then it has absolutely no relation to the transcendental notion of being and thus to existence itself. It seems that at this point Thomists are forced to conclude either with pure univocism, in which the being of God is identical to the being of man (though their respective essences may differ), or with pure equivocism, in which the being of God has absolutely no relation to the being of his creation. Either result shows that the God of the Bible (as neither identical in being to his creation nor separated from it) is not and cannot be known within the framework of Thomistic metaphysics.

It is important to understand that one of the primary reasons that Aquinas, with all of his genius, could not account for the existence of the God of the Bible is that he refused to start with the triune God of Scripture. For Van Til, "Human knowledge ultimately rests upon the internal coherence within the Godhead; *our knowledge rests upon the ontological Trinity as its presupposition.*"[39]

It is the Trinity, the "self-contained" Trinity (which is primarily what Van Til means by "ontological"), that is the basis for all human knowledge. Unless one starts the reasoning process by affirming the necessity of God's existence, the process itself becomes meaningless, as we have seen in Aquinas. If we begin our reasoning, our philosophy, our defense of Christianity with the truth of the self-contained triune God of Scripture, the "problem" of unity and diversity is properly understood. That is not to say that the relationship between unity and diversity is exhausted by man, but that the problem is answered only within a Christian framework.

---

39. Van Til, *An Introduction to Systematic Theology*, 23, emphasis mine. This problem of unity and diversity in philosophy extends itself automatically into apologetics if one chooses Thomism as his apologetic approach. See, for example, Ronald B. Mayers, *Both/and, a Balanced Apologetic* (Chicago: Moody, 1984) and my review of that book in the *Westminster Theological Journal* 67 (1985). See also Norman Leo Geisler, *Christian Apologetics* (Grand Rapids, MI: Baker, 1976), 151–262.

But what is it that makes the Trinity so crucial? Why is it that Van Til says that unless we presuppose the Trinity *first of all*, all "proofs" for the existence of God as well as all predication are meaningless?[40] The fundamental answer to these questions is that in the Trinity we understand that unity and diversity are equally ultimate. Because the three persons of the Trinity are mutually exhaustive of each other, that which is diverse within the Godhead is at one and the same time unified. There is no more of a priority to the essential unity of the Godhead than to the essential diversity. The Holy Spirit is no more or less God than is the Father. All that the Father is, the Spirit is also. The two are two and one at the same time and in the same way. Though they have distinct roles in history, "ontologically" (as Van Til would say), there is equal ultimacy. There is no pressure, therefore, to assign absolute priority to unity or to diversity. Our task is no longer to attempt to universalize the diversity or to diversify the unity. Our task is to attempt to understand the great richness of the world that is understood only within the context of the equal ultimacy of the diverse Godhead. In other words, if unity and diversity are equally ultimate in eternity, and if creation reveals the triune God of Scripture, we can expect that the world and all things in it are understood in the context of this equal ultimacy and are to be interpreted as such. While there may in any investigation be an emphasis on unity or diversity, there is no need, indeed there is no way, to ascribe ultimate priority to one or the other.

This does not mean that one's methodology is something completely new and otherwise unknown. Van Til affirms the use of methods of reasoning such as *a priori* or *a posteriori*. He says, however, that such methods cannot be absolutized so that one method is given ultimate status over all others. There are times when we may employ the empirical method of reasoning (which for Van Til is *a posteriori* reasoning) and other times when we may employ deductive (*a priori*) methods.[41] Each and every method has no more priority than the other.[42] Van Til

---

40. Cornelius Van Til, *Common Grace and the Gospel* (Philadelphia: Presbyterian and Reformed, 1972), 49.

41. Van Til, *A Survey of Christian Epistemology*, 10. Van Til explains that *a priori* and *a posteriori* are synonymous to deductive and inductive reasoning, respectively.

42. Those who have accused Van Til of being simply an a priorist have not understood the basic thrust of his apologetic. See for example discussions in Geehan, ed., *Jerusalem and Athens*, 380–403, 420–27.

has always insisted that we need not fear any approach or method that takes seriously the existence of the God of Scripture from the outset. The diversity of reality (including thoughts, things, methods, perspectives, etc.) coheres because all things come from the one God who is three persons.

In Van Til's syllabus *An Introduction to Systematic Theology*, he develops this equal ultimacy principle in connection with the biblical view of revelation.[43] In that syllabus, Van Til is concerned to show that disciplines such as physics, psychology, science in general, and theology are all understood within the context of the Creator's revealing himself to the creature and of creation's being itself revelational.

> It is customary on the part of some orthodox theologians to depreciate the objects of sensation as a source of knowledge. They would therefore substitute an a priori approach for that of the empiricist, thinking that thus they represent biblical thought. Two points may be mentioned with respect to this. In the first place, to flee to the arms of an a priorism from those of empiricism is in itself no help at all. *It is only if an a priori is self-consciously based upon the conception of the ontological Trinity* rather than upon the work of Plato or some other non-Christian philosopher that it can safeguard against skepticism. The a priori of any non-Christian thinker will eventually lead to empiricism. It can keep from doing so only if it keeps within the field of purely formal predication. In the second place, *if we do place the ontological Trinity at the foundation of all our predication* then there is no need to fear any skepticism through the avenue of sense. Sensation does "deceive us" but so does ratiocination. We have the means for their corruption in both cases. *The one without the other is meaningless. Both give us true knowledge on the right presupposition*; both lead to skepticism on the wrong presupposition.[44]

Notice that Van Til is quick to affirm the mutual interdependence both of ratiocination and empiricism within the context of presupposing the self-contained (ontological) triune God.

---

43. Perhaps this is what Dr. Stoker was suggesting in "Reconnoitering," 456n6. In that footnote, Stoker calls for a phanerotic investigation of human thought. Van Til seems to approach this in *An Introduction to Systematic Theology*, 64, 109.

44. Van Til, *An Introduction to Systematic Theology*, 66, emphasis mine.

It might be argued that the doctrine of the Trinity is one of the fundamental doctrines of the Christian faith and therefore not exclusive to Calvinism. That is true in one sense. What *is* exclusive to Reformed apologetics is the *application* of a doctrine as mysterious as the Trinity to the perennial and persistent problems of Christian philosophy and apologetics. Because Van Til is willing to admit that "mystery is the lifeblood of Dogmatics,"[45] he is not afraid to develop and apply that which is mysterious, nor is he content simply to deal with the less problematic fundamentals of the faith. In this sense, Van Til's apologetic as a Trinitarian apologetic is thoroughly Reformed. He has been able to glory in the mystery while at the same time seeing its application for the development of a truly Reformed apologetic.

A Covenantal Apologetic

There is a sense in which Van Til's covenantal emphasis in his apologetic could be seen as his most important contribution. Anyone who is familiar with Van Til's chalkboard graffiti will think first of all of his now famous illustration of the two circles, one larger and above the other, both connected by two vertical, parallel lines. This illustration has been used by Van Til and others to sum up, in picture form, the essence of his entire approach. It is a picture of the covenant. It is a picture of the necessity of revelation from God to man in order for man to know anything at all. The Westminster Confession of Faith says it this way:

> The distance between God and the creature is so great, that although reasonable creatures do owe obedience unto him as their Creator, yet they could never have any fruition of him as their blessedness and reward, but by some voluntary condescension on God's part, which he hath been pleased to express by way of covenant. (7.1)

45. Herman Bavinck, *Reformed Dogmatics: God and Creation*, ed. John Bolt, trans. John Vriend (Grand Rapids, MI: Baker, 2004), 29. The Dutch influence of Van Til could arguably be the most significant influence that has contributed to his Reformed apologetic. While American Christianity accepts the mysterious, there is a tendency to relegate it to secondary status with regard to application. Van Til, like Bavinck, *begins with* mystery. Van Til makes a distinction between mystery for a Christian and mystery from a non-Christian perspective in, among other works, *The Sovereignty of Grace*, 27.

Though Van Til's "circles" represent a broad range of his thinking, fundamentally that picture represents the covenant as explained in chapter 7 of the Westminster Confession, and Van Til's innovative and ingenious application of the truth of the covenant to apologetics and Christian philosophy. For Van Til, covenant theology and the Trinity are two mutually dependent truths within Reformed theology.[46] In elaborating on this mutual dependence, Van Til wants to emphasize not only the tri-unity of the Godhead, but the tri-personality as well. Since the omnipresent God is personal ("Absolute Personality," to use Van Til's words), both in his unity and in his diversity man always and everywhere lives his life *coram deo.*[47]

The implications of the personal God being everywhere and always in relation to men are far-reaching for apologetics (and for philosophy). The fundamental premise apologetically is this: "Covenant theology is the only form of theology which gives a completely personalistic interpretation to reality."[48] It is of the nature of non-Christian philosophy/apologetics, as well as inconsistent Christian philosophy/apologetics, to assume that man is placed in an impersonal universe. Though not expressed so boldly in non-Christian thought, this line of thinking seeks to give credence to, indeed to argue for, the necessity of what Van Til calls "brute fact." Brute facts are those facts discovered by science or used by the philosopher or appealed to by the inconsistent apologist which are assumed simply to be "there," uninterpreted, manipulated ultimately by man and his activity. Correlative to this view of brute fact is an appeal to neutrality, that is, an assumption that such facts are neither created by God nor interpreted by him in his Word. The only way that such an argument can be presented is by neglecting the covenantal emphasis of reality as expressed in a Reformed apologetic.

For Van Til, there are no brute facts, there is no neutrality, and the universe is not impersonal. Every fact, every interpretation, every spot in the universe reveals the covenant God; and every man, in living in God's universe, is responsible for his use of the facts, the laws, and

46. Van Til, *A Survey of Christian Epistemology,* 96.
47. Ibid., 97.
48. Ibid., 128–29.

the interpretation of such. To put the matter simply, men, *all men*, are either covenant-keepers or covenant-breakers:

> To speak of man's relation to God as being covenantal at every point is merely to say that man deals with the personal God everywhere. Every manipulation of any created fact is, as long as man is not a sinner, a covenant-affirming activity. Every manipulation of any fact, as soon as man is a sinner, is a covenant-breaking activity.[49]

One can begin to see how Van Til's worldview apologetic is intertwined with his covenantal emphasis. *Every* fact *everywhere* is revelational of the God of Scripture. Thus man is always and everywhere either denying God or submitting to him, depending on how he uses God's facts. The environment of man is by no means impersonal, but is exhaustively personal and, *as* personal, is revelational of the triune God.

  In traditional apologetics, not only is the reason of man considered to be a brute fact, but the very facts to which the traditional apologist appeals (the order of the cosmos, the design of the universe, the cause of the effect) are all thought to be initially uninterpreted until interpreted by us. The initial assumption in the traditional proofs for the existence of God is that the facts require an unbeliever's interpretation in order to lead to a god. If Van Til is right in his application of the covenant, however, every fact is, fundamentally, *God's* interpretation and is therefore only truly known if re-interpreted in light of God's initial interpretation (revelation) of and through that fact. Traditional apologetical approaches seek to exclude God from the analysis and understanding of certain facts, certain laws, in order to include him later as a kind of "concluding unscientific postscript" to the main body of argumentation. For Van Til, "when man faced any fact he would *ipso facto* be face-to-face with God."[50] Man always and everywhere either breaks or keeps covenant with God by the way he sees and lives life in God's world.

  In the paragraph quoted above, Van Til affirms that the covenant relation should go hand-in-hand with natural revelation. The two

49. Van Til, *Common Grace and the Gospel*, 69–70.
50. Van Til, *A Survey of Christian Epistemology*, 97.

should be thought of as mutually interdependent. Van Til has always wanted to maintain the correlativity of natural and special revelation. He has wanted to show that the two have always gone together and that the so-called "attributes of Scripture" apply also to natural revelation.[51] Both have always been necessary for man to live in God's world, even before the fall:

> Being from the outset covenantal in character, the natural revelation of God to man was meant to serve as the playground for the process of differentiation that was to take place in the course of time. The covenant made with Adam was conditional. There would be *additional* revelation of God in nature after the action of man with respect to the tree of the knowledge of good and evil.[52]

Van Til goes on to discuss the necessity both of natural and special revelation in the garden. Natural revelation provided the substance of Adam's covenant-keeping activity as he subdued the earth to the glory of God, as he ate from any tree in the garden, save one. Yet that one tree, to be covenantally qualified, needed interpretation by God through special revelation in order for Adam's task to be clearly delineated.

Covenant-keeping and covenant-breaking depended on God's gracious revelation of himself through his handiwork and through his verbal communication to Adam. Both were required. Both necessitated the covenant activity of Adam. Adam's world was as covenantally qualified, as personalistic, as our own. Natural revelation must be seen as just that, *revelation*, of the God of history. For a man to take the things of nature and to use them for his own glory is to break God's covenant based on the revelation given to that man in nature. While God is revealed through nature, man is suppressing that revelation by abusing it (Rom. 1:18f.). Man's task, man's calling, man's responsibility, is defined for him and delimited for him by the revelation of God.

---

51. See Cornelius Van Til, "Nature and Scripture," in *The Infallible Word: A Symposium by the Members of the Faculty of Westminster Theological Seminary*, ed. N. B. Stonehouse and Paul Woolley (Nutley, NJ: Presbyterian and Reformed, 1978).

52. Ibid., 267–68.

To use Van Til's terminology, rather than thinking of himself as *creatively constructive* of the facts of the world, man is to view himself as *receptively reconstructive* of the facts of God's world. This is covenantal epistemology. The covenant of God forms the backdrop for all *knowing*, all *analyzing*, all *perceiving*. The things of this world must first of all be seen as revelatory both of what the thing itself is and of its Creator. It has the character, therefore, both of transcendence (in revealing its Creator) and of immanence (in revealing itself). Because it is revelation (and that revelation is *given* to revealing man, not only *discovered* by him),[53] man is responsible and held accountable for its use, both to know it in its relation to the world and to know it as a fact of God's creation.

The application of the covenantal approach to Reformed apologetics is almost limitless. Unlike the traditional approach, the covenantal approach gives full reign to the facts of God's existence and of his activity in the world. Rather than seeking to discover the existence of a god by an appeal to uninterpreted facts, the Reformed apologist realizes and challenges unbelief on the basis of the real states of affairs in the world. The Reformed apologist does not come to the unbeliever with a pretended scenario of reality in order to "jump" to the real states of affairs in his conclusion. He comes to the unbeliever with the full realization that by definition the unbeliever is taking and will continue to take the facts of God's world and Word and twist them beyond recognition. He is, at bottom, always and everywhere a covenant-breaker.

The Reformed apologist takes seriously the covenant-breaking status of the unbeliever. He knows that, no matter how "moral," "acceptable," or "civil," the unbeliever is a much busier man than he appears to be, day and night suppressing the constant and persistent truth that bombards him from the God whom he knows. How "reasonable" is it to approach such a one and ask for an "honest" inquiry? How "rational" can it be to ask someone to make a moral judgment who, by virtue of his

---

53. The revelation of God that is given to man is intuitive knowledge. It could not be articulated knowledge because of the inherent depravity of man, but it must form the *basis* for all articulated knowledge. See Vincent Brummer, *Transcendental Criticism and Christian Philosophy: A Presentation and Evaluation of Herman Dooyeweerd's "Philosophy of the Cosmonomic Idea"* (Franaker: T. Wever, 1961), 172–73; and H. G. Stoker, "Calvinistiese Wysbegeerte," *Tydskrif Vir Wetenskap en Kuns* 15 (1950): 107.

very nature, has an ax to grind against God? How can God be honored in apologetic argumentation when the covenant-keeper approaches the covenant-breaker as a close relative rather than an enemy of Christ and his family? The unbeliever's mind is of the flesh, hostile toward God and unable to please God at any point (Rom. 8:7–8).

The Reformed apologist, because he is a covenant-keeper by the grace of God, approaches the unbeliever at the root of his unbelief. The unbeliever cannot make sense of his "facts," he cannot put a foreign organ into another body and expect it to survive. The challenge to the covenant-breaker is just that—to challenge his covenant-breaking. To ask him, as the traditional apologist wants to do, simply to reason together with the believer without making the fundamental covenantal distinction is to encourage him in his covenant-breaking efforts. To get him to agree, perhaps, that a god exists is to assure him that *the covenant God*, whom he knows to exist, does not in fact exist after all. It is to encourage rather than discourage the suppression that is the warp and woof of the entire thinking and doing of the unbeliever. This is what Van Til means by "argument by presupposition." Argument by presupposition, for Van Til, is argument by covenant, argument that takes for granted, at the outset, that each and every person with whom we come in contact is fundamentally and covenantally related to God. It is this covenantal relationship to God that makes man's unbelief culpable. The necessity of a proper understanding of Romans 1 for a Reformed apologetic must be emphasized here. Even Reformed theologians who want to emphasize a Thomistic approach to apologetics affirm the covenantal emphasis of this passage.[54] At the same time, however, in order to hold fast to their Thomism, they must reject the implications of the very truth they derive from Scripture.[55]

Van Til's emphasis on a covenantal apologetic has also to do with the controversial question of one's starting point in apologetics.

54. "We conclude that the apostle Paul teaches clearly and unambiguously that humans possess a natural knowledge of God which rests upon the foundation of general revelation." R. C. Sproul, John H. Gerstner, and Arthur Lindsley, *Classical Apologetics* (Grand Rapids, MI: Zondervan, 1984), 62.

55. "But people do not necessarily consider themselves in opposition to God, *whose existence they do not even know at the outset*. They simply operate according to human nature." Ibid., 233, emphasis mine.

Though Van Til sometimes uses the idea of starting point with differing emphases, his primary meaning is that one's starting point is his "launching pad" or the place where one self-consciously stands to begin his apologetic reasoning. Those who criticize Van Til for insisting that God, not the self, must always be the ultimate starting point in apologetic reasoning, attempt to do so by making Van Til sound as if people must get outside of themselves in order to start somewhere else besides themselves.[56] What he actually says, however, is this:

> The question at issue is not that of what is the immediate starting point. All agree that the immediate starting point must be that of our everyday experience and the facts that are close at hand. Neither Augustine nor Calvin would have objected to saying that knowledge of self was their immediate and temporary starting point.[57]

Van Til goes on to compare Calvin and Descartes. It was Calvin who began with the self as a *proximate* starting point and Descartes who began with the self as an *ultimate* starting point.[58] Notice, however, that both men began with the *self*. Van Til knows (and his critics should realize) that all men argue, think, and know as *selves*. His only contention, however, is that the self who begins his argumentation must self-consciously argue from the "launching pad" of the personal, face-to-face encounter with God when considering any fact or any experience. The rational apologist *self*-consciously stands on the bruteness of the fact of, for example, cause and effect, design, and being, while at the same time assuming the neutrality of unregenerate man's reason. The reason that Van Til accuses Descartes of seeing himself as the ultimate starting point is that Descartes contends that knowledge of his existence is *foundational* (a "launching pad"), the place on which he stands, only later to affirm the existence of a god. So the rationalistic apologist wants to affirm that unregenerate man can know the facts of the Word truly without recognizing that to know a fact truly is to know it as created by God. The ultimate starting point for the rationalistic apologist is himself and his world.

56. See for example, ibid., 212–40.
57. Van Til, *A Survey of Christian Epistemology*, 120.
58. Ibid., 132.

Because Van Til's apologetic takes seriously the implications of the covenant, he knows (with Calvin) that self-knowledge and God-knowledge are coterminous. One cannot simply seek the facts without answering the fundamental question of the possibility of those facts themselves. Covenantal apologetics assures us of the proper starting point for reasoning with the unbeliever because the Creator-creature distinction is taken seriously at the outset by a proper view of revelation within a covenant context. No fact can be truly known without reference to the One who created that fact and who consequently reveals himself through that fact. The ultimate starting point, God, therefore, is the decisive element in apologetic reasoning.

Conclusion

In our analysis of Cornelius Van Til, we have tried to avoid some of the most familiar terms and categories applied to him, particularly in the United States. Van Til has been called "the father of presuppositionalism," a "presuppositional apologist." The problem with this kind of category has been that Van Til has been included with other apologists, some non-Reformed, who use the word *presupposition* yet are more in line with rationalistic apologetics than with a truly Reformed apologetic.[59] The reason that we have looked at Van Til from the three different perspectives of worldview, Trinity, and covenant is in order to highlight the specifically and truly Reformed emphasis of Van Til's approach, an emphasis that escapes others in Reformed circles who have yet to implement his unique and innovative efforts.

If we agree with B. B. Warfield that Calvinism is "Christianity come to its own," then we would also agree that Van Til's Reformed

---

59. Among other apologists who are called "presuppositional" yet who stray significantly from Van Til's approach are E. J. Carnell and Francis Schaeffer. See, for example, E. J. Carnell, *An Introduction to Christian Apologetics* (Grand Rapids, MI: Eerdmans, 1948); and Francis A. Schaeffer, *The Complete Works of Francis A. Schaeffer: A Christian Worldview* (Westchester, IL: Crossway, 1982). Though Carnell was self-consciously opposed to Van Til's approach, Dr. Schaeffer used many of the tenets of Van Til's position to speak to the problems of the twentieth century. Van Til taught both men at Westminster Theological Seminary and expressed personal regret to me that neither man had followed him in his attempt to develop a truly Reformed apologetic.

defense of Christianity is "Christian apologetics come into its own." No other approach in the history of the church is so liberating to the believer at the same time that it is so challenging to unbelief. For this reason, Van Til's approach must be seen as one of the most significant advances in Reformed theology of the twentieth century.

Bibliography

Allison, Henry E. *Benedict de Spinoza: An Introduction*. Rev. ed. New Haven, CT: Yale University Press, 1987.

————. *The Kant-Eberhard Controversy*. Baltimore: Johns Hopkins University Press, 1973.

Althaus, Paul. *Die Prinzipien der Deutschen Reformierten Dogmatik im Zeitalter der Asritotelischen Scholastik*. Leipzig: Deichert, 1914.

Appiah, Kwame Anthony. *In My Father's House*. Cambridge: Cambridge University Press, 1992.

Aquinas, Thomas. *Summa contra Gentiles*. Translated by Anton C. Pegis. Notre Dame, IN: Notre Dame University Press, 1957.

Armstrong, Brian G. *Calvinism and the Amyraut Heresy: Protestant Scholasticism and Humanism in Seventeenth-Century France*. Madison, WI: University of Wisconsin Press, 1969.

Arndt, Stephen Wentworth. "Transcendental Method and Transcendental Arguments." *International Philosophical Quarterly* 27 (1987): 43–58.

Arnold, Clinton E. *The Colossian Syncretism: The Interface between Christianity and Folk Belief at Colossae*. Grand Rapids, MI: Baker, 1996.

Bahnsen, Greg L. "Machen, Van Til, and the Apologetic Tradition of the OPC." In *Pressing toward the Mark: Essays Commemorating Fifty Years of the Orthodox Presbyterian Church*, edited by C. G. Dennison and R. C. Gamble, 259–94. Philadelphia: The Committee for the Historian of the Orthodox Presbyterian Church, 1986.

———. *Van Til's Apologetic: Readings and Analysis*. Phillipsburg, NJ: P&R, 1998.

Bal, Mieke, Jonathan V. Crewe, and Leo Spitzer. *Acts of Memory: Cultural Recall in the Present*. Hanover, NH: University Press of New England, 1998.

Barth, Karl, and Martin Rumscheidt. *The Way of Theology in Karl Barth: Essays and Comments*. In Princeton Theological Monograph Series; 8. Allison Park, PA.: Pickwick, 1986.

Barth, Karl, and Fernand Ryser. *Philosophie et Théologie*. Genéve: Labor et Fides, 1960.

Bavinck, Herman. *The Certainty of Faith*. St. Catharines, ON: Paideia, 1980.

———. *Reformed Dogmatics: God and Creation*. Edited by John Bolt. Translated by John Vriend. Grand Rapids, MI: Baker, 2004.

Beale, Gregory K. *The Book of Revelation: A Commentary on the Greek Text*. Grand Rapids MI: Eerdmans, 1999.

———. "Eden, the Temple, and the Church's Mission in the New Creation." *Journal of the Evangelical Theological Society*, 48, no. 1 (2005): 5–32.

———. *The Temple and the Church's Mission*. Downers Grove, IL: InterVarsity Press, 2005.

Berkouwer, G. C. *Sin*. Studies in Dogmatics. Translated by Philip C. Holtrop. Grand Rapids, MI: Eerdmans, 1971.

———. *The Triumph of Grace in the Theology of Karl Barth*. Grand Rapids, MI: Eerdmans, 1956.

Bernstein, Richard. *Beyond Objectivism and Relativism*. Philadelphia: University of Pennsylvania Press, 1983.

Best, Steven, and Douglas Kellner. *The Postmodern Turn*. New York: Guilford, 1997.

Bizer, Ernst. *Früorthodoxie und Rationalismus*. Zürich: EVZ-Verlag, 1963.

Blocher, Henri. "The 'Analogy of Faith' in the Study of Scripture: In Search of Justification and Guidelines." *Scottish Bulletin of Evangelical Theology* 5 (1987): 17–38.

Blond, Philip, ed. *Post-Secular Philosophy: Between Philosophy and Theology*. London: Routledge, 1998.

Bonnell, Victoria E., and Lynn Hunt, eds. *Beyond the Cultural Turn: New Directions in the Study of Society and Culture*. Berkeley: University of California Press, 1999.

Boyle, Nicholas. *Who Are We Now? Christian Humanism and the Global Market from Hegel to Heaney*. Notre Dame, IN: Notre Dame University Press, 1998.

Breen, Quirinius. *John Calvin: A Study in French Humanism*. Grand Rapids, MI: Eerdmans, 1931.

Brittan, Gordon G. *Kant's Theory of Science*. Princeton, NJ: Princeton University Press, 1978.

Brummer, Vincent. *Transcendental Criticism and Christian Philosophy: A Presentation and Evaluation of Herman Dooyeweerd's "Philosophy of the Cosmonomic Idea."* Franaker: T. Wever, 1961.

Brunner, Emil, and Karl Barth. *Natural Theology: Comprising "Nature and Grace."* Translated by Peter Fraenkel. London: G. Bles, The Centenary Press, 1946.

Buckley, Michael J. *At the Origins of Modern Atheism.* New Haven, CT: Yale University Press, 1987.

Calvin, John. *Institutes of the Christian Religion.* Edited by John T. McNeill. Translated by Ford Lewis Battles. Library of Christian Classics. Philadelphia: Westminster, 1960.

———. *John Calvin Selections from His Writings.* Edited by John Dillenberger. Missoula, MT: Scholars Press for the American Academy of Religion, 1975.

Campagnac, Ernest Trafford, Benjamin Whichcote, John Smith, and Nathanael Culverwel. *The Cambridge Platonists.* Oxford: Clarendon, 1901.

Carnell, E. J. *Christian Commitment: An Apologetic.* New York: Macmillan, 1957.

———. *An Introduction to Christian Apologetics.* Grand Rapids, MI: Eerdmans, 1948.

Carson, D. A. "Athens Revisited." In *Telling the Truth: Evangelizing Postmoderns*, edited by D. A. Carson, 384–98. Grand Rapids, MI: Zondervan, 2000.

Clark, David K. "Narrative Theology and Apologetics." *Journal of the Evangelical Theological Society* 36, no. 4 (1993): 499–516.

Clark, Gordon H. "Apologetics." In *Contemporary Evangelical Thought*, edited by Carl F. H. Henry, 135–61. Great Neck, NY: Channel, 1957.

Comte-Sponville, André. *Le mythe d'Icare.* Paris: Presses universitaired de France, 1984.

Conn, Harvie M. *Eternal Word and Changing Worlds: Theology, Anthropology and Mission in Trialogue.* 1984; reprint, Phillipsburg, NJ: P&R, 1992.

Copi, Irving M. *Introduction to Logic.* 7th ed. New York: Macmillan, 1986.

Cowan, Stephen B., ed. *Five Views on Apologetics.* Grand Rapids, MI: Zondervan, 2000.

Craig, William Lane. *Time and Eternity: Exploring God's Relationship to Time.* Wheaton, IL: Crossway, 2001.

Daniels, Norman. *Justice and Justification: Reflective Equilibrium in Theory and Practice.* Cambridge: Cambridge University Press, 1996.

———. "Wide Reflective Equilibrium and Theory Acceptance in Ethics." *The Journal of Philosophy* 76 (1979): 21–25.

———, ed. *Reading Rawls: Critical Studies on Rawls' A Theory of Justice.* New York: Basic Books, 1975.

de Vries, Hent. *Philosophy and the Turn to Religion.* Baltimore: Johns Hopkins Press, 1999.

Dennison, William D. *Paul's Two-Age Construction and Apologetics*. Lanham, MD: University Press of America, 1985.

Du Plessis, P. J. *TELEIOS: The Idea of Perfection in the New Testament*. Kampen: Kok, 1959.

Dunn, James D. G. *The Epistle to the Colossians and Philemon*. The New International Greek Testament Commentary, Grand Rapids, MI: Eerdmans, 1996.

———. *The Theology of Paul the Apostle*. Grand Rapids, MI: Eerdmans, 1998.

Eagleton, Terry. *The Illusions of Postmodernism*. Oxford: Basil Blackwell, 1996.

Edgar, William. "No News Is Good News: Modernity, the Postmodern, and Apologetics." *Westminster Theological Journal* 57 (1995): 277–97.

Edwards, James C. *The Plain Sense of Things: The Fate of Religion in an Age of Normal Nihilism*. University Park, PA: Pennsylvania State University Press, 1997.

Ellis, E. E. *Paul's Use of the Old Testament*. Grand Rapids, MI: Baker, 1981.

Esmail, Aziz. *Reason, Interpretation and Islam: Essays in the Philosophy of Religion*. Richmond, Surrey: Curzon, 2004.

Fee, Gordon D. *The First Epistle to the Corinthians*. Grand Rapids, MI: Eerdmans, 1987.

———. *God's Empowering Presence: The Holy Spirit in the Letters of Paul*. Peabody, MA: Hendrickson, 1994.

Feenberg, Andrew. *Alternative Modernity: The Technical Turn in Philosophy and Social Theory*. Berkeley: University of California Press, 1995.

Ferry, Luc. *Qu'est-ce qu'une vie réussie?* Paris: Bernard Grasset, 2002.

Ferry, Luc, and André Comte-Sponville. *La sagesse des modernes*. Paris: Robert Laffont, 1998.

Ferry, Luc, and Alain Renaut. "Kant and Fichte." In *New French Thought: Political Philosophy*, edited by Mark Lilla, 74–81. Princeton: Princeton University Press, 1994.

———. *La pensée 68: Essai sur l'anti-humanisme contemporain*. Paris: Gallimard, 1985.

Frame, John M. *Apologetics to the Glory of God*. Phillipsburg, NJ: P&R, 1994.

———. *Cornelius Van Til: An Analysis of His Thought*. Phillipsburg, NJ: P&R, 1995.

———. *The Doctrine of God*. Phillipsburg, NJ: P&R, 2002.

———. *The Doctrine of the Knowledge of God*. Phillipsburg, NJ: Presbyterian and Reformed, 1987.

———. *No Other God: A Response to Open Theism*. Phillipsburg, NJ: P&R, 2001.

———. "Presuppositional Apologetics." In *Five Views of Apologetics*, edited by Steven B. Cowan, 207–31. Grand Rapids, MI: Zondervan, 2000.

———. *Van Til: The Theologian*. Phillipsburg, NJ: Pilgrim, 1976.

Frei, Hans W. "Theological Reflections on the Account of Jesus' Death and Resurrection." *Christian Scholar* 49 (1966): 263–306.

Gaffin, Richard B., Jr. *The Centrality of the Resurrection: A Study in Paul's Soteriology*. Grand Rapids, MI: Baker, 1978.

———. *Perspectives on Pentecost*. Phillipsburg, NJ: Presbyterian and Reformed, 1979.

———. "Some Epistemological Reflections on I Cor. 2:6–16." *Westminster Theological Journal* 57, no. 1 (1995): 103–24.

Gamble, Richard C. "*Brevitas et Facilitas*: Toward an Understanding of Calvin's Hermeneutic." *Westminster Theological Journal* 47 (1985): 1–17.

Geehan, E. R., ed. *Jerusalem and Athens: Critical Discussions on the Philosophy and Apologetics of Cornelius Van Til*. Nutley, NJ: Presbyterian and Reformed, 1977.

Geertz, Clifford. *The Interpretation of Cultures: Selected Essays*. New York: Basic Books, 1973.

———. "Off the Menu." *The New Republic* (February 2003): 27–30.

Geisler, Norman Leo. *Christian Apologetics*. Grand Rapids, MI: Baker, 1976.

Gilson, Etienne. *The Christian Philosophy of St. Thomas Aquinas. With a Catalog of St. Thomas's Works*. New York: Random House, 1956.

Gram, Moltke S. "Transcendental Arguments." *Nous* 5 (1971): 15–26.

Grenz, Stanley J. *A Primer on Postmodernism*. Grand Rapids, MI: Eerdmans, 1996.

Griffiths, Paul J. *An Apology for Apologetics*. Maryknoll, NY: Orbis, 1991.

Guillebaud, Jean-Claude. *La refondation du monde, vols 1–3*. Paris: Seuil, 1999.

Guinness, Os. *Time for Truth: Living Free in a World of Lies, Hype, and Spin*. Grand Rapids, MI: Baker, 2000.

Hall, Basil. "Calvin against the Calvinist." In *John Calvin: A Collection of Distinguished Essays*, edited by Gervase Duffield, 23–27. Grand Rapids, MI: Eerdmans, 1966.

Harris, Murray J. *Colossians and Philemon*. Grand Rapids, MI: Eerdmans, 1990.

Hart, D. G. "Systematic Theology at Old Princeton: Unoriginal Calvinism." In *The Pattern of Sound Doctrine: Systematic Theology at the Westminster Seminaries, Essays in Honor of Robert B. Strimple*, edited by David VanDrunen, 3–26. Phillipsburg, NJ: P&R, 2004.

Hassan, Ihab. *The Postmodern Turn: Essays in Postmodern Theory and Culture*. Columbus, OH: University of Ohio Press, 1987.

Heidegger, Martin. "The End of Philosophy and the Task of Thinking." In *On Time and Being*, trans. Joan Stambaugh. New York: Harper & Row, 1973.

———. *Über den Humanismus*. Frankfurt am Main: Vittorio Klostermann, 1947.

Helm, Paul. *Calvin and the Calvinists*. Carlisle, PA: Banner of Truth, 1982.

Henry, Carl F. H. *God, Revelation, and Authority*. Waco, TX: Word, 1976.

Hiley, David R., Richard Shusterman, and James Bohman, eds. *The Interpretive Turn: Philosophy, Science, Culture*. Ithaca, NY: Cornell University Press, 1991.

Hodge, Charles. *Commentary on the Epistle to the Romans*. Grand Rapids, MI: Eerdmans, 1994.

Horton, Robin. *Patterns of Thought in Africa and the West*. Cambridge: Cambridge University Press, 1993.

The Humanist Manifestos I and II. New York: Prometheus, 1973.

Hutton, Sarah. "The Cambridge Platonists." In *A Companion to Early Modern Philosophy*, edited by Steven M. Nadler, 308–19. Blackwell Companions to Philosophy. Malden, MA: Blackwell, 2002.

Jameson, Fredric, and Perry Anderson. *Cultural Turn: Selected Writings on the Postmodern, 1983–1998*. London: Verso, 1998.

Jue, Jeffrey K. *"Heaven upon Earth": Joseph Mede (1586–1638) and the Legacy of Millenarianism*. Dordtrecht: Springer, 2006.

Junius, Franciscus. *De theologia vera: Ortu, natura, formis, partibus, et modo*. Lugduni Batavorum: Ex officina Plantiniana, apud Franciscum Raphelengium, 1594.

Kaiser, Walter. "A Neglected Text in Bibliology Discussions: I Corinthians 2:6–16." *Westminster Theological Journal* 43 (1981): 301–19.

Kaiser, Walter C., Jr., and Moisés Silva. "The Case for Calvinistic Hermeneutics." In *An Introduction to Biblical Hermeneutics*, 251–69. Grand Rapids, MI: Zondervan, 1994.

Kamitsuka, David. "The Justification of Religious Belief in the Pluralistic Public Realm: Another Look at Postliberal Apologetics." *Journal of Religion* 76, no. 4 (1996): 588–606.

———. *Theology and Contemporary Culture: Liberation, Postliberal and Revisionary Perspectives*. Cambridge: Cambridge University Press, 1999.

Kant, Immanuel. *Critique of Pure Reason*. Translated by Norman Kemp Smith. New York: St. Martin's Press, 1958.

Kattenbusch, F. "Theologische Studien und Kritiken" (1930).

Kendall, R. T. *Calvin and English Calvinism to 1649*. New York: Oxford University Press, 1979.

Kline, Meredith G. *By Oath Consigned*. Eugene, Oregon: Wipf and Stock, 1998.

———. *Images of the Spirit*. Grand Rapids, MI: Baker, 1980.

———. *Kingdom Prologue: Genesis Foundations for a Covenantal Worldview*. Overland Park, KS: Two Age Press, 2000.

Knudsen, Robert D. "The Transcendental Perspective of Westminster's Apologetic." *Westminster Theological Journal* 48 (1986): 233–39.

Kuhn, Thomas S. *The Structure of Scientific Revolutions*. Chicago: University of Chicago Press, 1970.

Kümmel, W. G. *The New Testament: The History of the Investigation of Its Problems*. Nashville: Abingdon, 1972.

Lacoue-Labarthe, Philippe. *La fiction du politique: Heidegger, l'art et la politique*. Paris: Bourgois, 1998.

Lafont, Cristina. *The Linguistic Turn in Hermeneutic Philosophy*. Translated by Jose Medina. Cambridge, MA: MIT Press, 1999.

Lang, F. *Die Briefe an die Korinther*. Neue Testament Deutsch 7. Göttingen: Vandenhoeck & Ruprecht, 1986.

Lindbeck, George. "Discovering Thomas: The Classic Statement of Christian Theism." *Una Sancta* 24, no. 1 (1967): 588–606.

———. *The Nature of Doctrine*. Philadelphia, PA: Westminster Press, 1984.

Lints, Richard. "The Postpositivist Choice: Tracy or Lindbeck?" *Journal of the American Academy of Religion* 61, no. 4 (1993): 655–77.

Lyotard, Jean-François. *The Postmodern Explained*. Minneapolis: University of Minnesota Press, 1992.

Lyotard, Jean-François, Geoffrey Bennington, and Brian Massumi. *The Postmodern Condition: A Report on Knowledge*. Theory and History of Literature, vol. 10. Minneapolis: University of Minnesota Press, 1984.

Machen, J. Gresham. *The Virgin Birth of Christ*. New York: Harper & Row, 1932.

Manent, Pierre. *The City of Man*. Translated by Marc le Pain. Princeton: Princeton University Press, 1998.

Maritain, Jacques. *Existence and the Existent*. New York: Pantheon, 1964.

Marsden, George. "The Collapse of American Evangelical Academia." In *Faith and Rationality*, edited by Alvin Plantinga and Nicholas Wolterstorff, 219–64. Notre Dame and London: University of Notre Dame Press, 1983.

Marshall, Bruce D. "Absorbing the World." In *Theology and Dialogue*, edited by Bruce D. Marshall, 69–104. Notre Dame: University of Notre Dame Press, 1990.

Martin, Troy W. *By Philosophy and Empty Deceit: Colossians as Response to a Cynic Critique*. Sheffield: Sheffield Academic Press, 1996.

Masolo, D. A. *African Philosophy in Search of Identity*. Bloomington, IN: Indiana University Press, 1994.

Mayers, Ronald B. *Both/and, a Balanced Apologetic*. Chicago: Moody, 1984.

Mede, Joseph. *Clauis Apocalyptica ex Innatis et Insitis Visionum Characteribus Eruta et Demonstrata. Ad Eorum Usum Quibus Deus Amorem Studiúmq[Ue] Indiderit Prophetiam Illam Admirandam Cognoscendi Scrutandique*. Cantabrigiæ: (Printed by T. and J. Buck) impensis authoris, in gratiam amicorum, 1627.

———. *The Works of the Pious and Profoundly-Learned Joseph Mede, B.D. Sometime Fellow of Christ's College in Cambridge*. Edited by John Worthington. London: Printed by Roger Norton, for Richard Royston, bookseller to His Most Sacred Majesty, 1677.

Mede, Joseph, Philemon Stephens, Richard More, William Twisse, and Thordarson Collection. *The Key of the Revelation, Searched and Demonstrated Out of the Naturall and Proper Characters of the Visions with a Comment Thereupon, According to the Rule of the Same Key*. Translated by William Twisse. London: Printed by R. B. for Phil Stephens, 1643.

Middleton, Richard J., and Brian J. Walsh. *Truth Is Stranger than It Used to Be: Biblical Faith in a Postmodern Age*. Downers Grove, IL: InterVarsity Press, 1995.

Milbank, John. "Problematizing the Secular: The Post-Postmodern Agenda." In *The Shadow of Spirit*, edited by Philippa Berry and Andrew Wernick, 30–44. London: Routledge, 1992.

———. "The Sublime in Kierkegaard." *Heythrop Journal* 37 (1996): 298–321.

Moo, Douglas J. *The Epistle to the Romans*. The New International Commentary on the New Testament. Grand Rapids, MI: Eerdmans, 1996.

Moreland, J. P. "Philosophical Apologetics, the Church, and Contemporary Culture." *Journal of the Evangelical Theological Society* 39, no. 1 (1996): 123–40.

Muller, Richard A. *After Calvin: Studies in the Development of a Theological Tradition*. Oxford: Oxford University Press, 2003.

———. *Dictionary of Latin and Greek Theological Terms: Drawn Principally from Protestant Scholastic Theology*. Grand Rapids, MI: Baker, 1985.

———. *Post-Reformation Reformed Dogmatics: Prolegomena to Theology*. Grand Rapids, MI: Baker, 1987.

———. *Post-Reformation Reformed Dogmatics: The Rise and Development of Reformed Orthodoxy, Ca. 1520 to Ca. 1725*. 4 vols. Grand Rapids, MI: Baker, 2003.

Murray, John. *Collected Writings of John Murray: Vol. 2, Selected Lectures in Systematic Theology*. Edinburgh: Banner of Truth, 1977.

———. *The Epistle to the Romans: The English Text with Introduction, Exposition, and Notes*. The New International Commentary on the New Testament. Grand Rapids, MI: Eerdmans, 1995.

Naugle, David K. *Worldview: The History of a Concept*. Grand Rapids, MI: Eerdmans, 2002.

Newbigin, Lesslie. "Ecumenical Amnesia." *International Bulletin of Missionary Research* 18, no. 1 (1994): 2–5.

Nielsen, Kai. *After the Demise of the Traditions: Rorty, Critical Theory and the Fate of Philosophy*. Boulder, CO: Westview, 1991.

———. "Wittgensteinian Fideism." *Philosophy* 62 (1967): 191–209.

Nietzsche, Friedrich. *The Will to Power*. Edited by Walter Kaufmann. Trans. Walter Kaufmann and R. J. Hollingdale. New York: Random House, 1967.

Noll, Mark. "Introduction." In *The Princeton Theology 1812–1921: Scripture, Science, and Theological Method from Archibald Alexander to Benjamin Warfield,* edited by Mark Noll, 11–48. Grand Rapids, MI: Baker, 2001.

———. "The *Princeton Review.*" *Westminster Theological Journal* 50 (1988): 283–304.

Notaro, Thom. *Van Til and the Use of Evidence.* Phillipsburg, NJ: Presbyterian and Reformed, 1980.

Oliphint, K. Scott. "The Consistency of Van Til's Methodology." *Westminster Theological Journal* 52, no. 2 (1990): 27–49.

———. "Cornelius Van Til and the Reformation of Christian Apologetics." In *Die idee van reformasie: Gister en vandag.* Edited by B. J. van der Walt. Potchefstroomse: Potchefstroomse Universiteit vir Christelike Hoër Onderwys, 1991.

———. "Epistemology and Christian Belief." *Westminster Theological Journal* 63, no. 1 (2001): 151–82.

———. *Reasons for Faith: Philosophy in the Service of Theology.* Phillipsburg, NJ: P&R, 2006.

Ortner, Sherry B. *The Fate of "Culture": Geertz and Beyond.* Berkeley: University of California Press, 1999.

Phelan, G. B., et al. *Saint Thomas and Analogy.* Milwaukee: Marquette University Press, 1941.

Philips, Timothy R., and Dennis L. Okholm, eds. *Christian Apologetics in the Postmodern World.* Downers Grove, IL: InterVarsity Press, 1995.

Pickstock, Catherine. *After Writing: On the Liturgical Consummation of Philosophy.* Oxford: Basil Blackwell, 1998.

Piper, John, Justin Taylor, and Paul Kjoss Helseth. *Beyond the Bounds: Open Theism and the Undermining of Biblical Christianity.* Wheaton, IL: Crossway, 2003.

Plantinga, Alvin. "On Reformed Epistemology." *The Reformed Journal* 32 (January 1981): 13–17.

———. "The Reformed Objection to Natural Theology." *Proceedings of the American Catholic Philosophical Association* 54 (1980): 49–63.

———. *Warranted Christian Belief.* Oxford: Oxford University Press, 2000.

Plantinga, Alvin, and Nicholas Wolterstorff, eds. *Faith and Rationality.* Notre Dame, IN: University of Notre Dame Press, 1983.

Platt, John. *Reformed Thought and Scholasticism: The Arguments for the Existence of God in Dutch Theology, 1575–1650.* Leiden: E. J. Brill, 1982.

Poythress, Vern S. "A Biblical View of Mathematics." In *Foundations of Christian Scholarship,* edited by Gary North, 159–88. Vallecito, CA: Ross House, 1979.

———. "God's Lordship in Interpretation." *Westminster Theological Journal* 50 (1988): 27–64.

Prêtre, Isabelle. *La folie des modernes.* Paris: François-Xavier de Guibert, 2000.

Raiser, Konrad. *Ecumenism in Transition: A Paradigm Shift in the Ecumenical Movement?* Geneva: World Council of Churches, 1991.

———. "Is Ecumenical Apologetics Sufficient? A Response to Lesslie Newbigin's Ecumenical Amnesia." *International Bulletin of Missionary Research* 18, no. 2 (1994): 50–51.

Rawls, John. "Justice as Fairness: Political Not Metaphysical." *Philosophy and Public Affairs* 14 (1985): 223–51.

———. "Kantian Constructivism in Moral Theory." *Moral Philosophy* 88 (1980): 515–72.

———. *Political Liberalism.* New York: Columbia University Press, 1993.

———. *A Theory of Justice.* Cambridge, MA.: Belknap Press of Harvard University Press, 1999.

Ridderbos, Herman N. *Aan de Romeinen.* Commentaar op het Nieuwe Testament. Kampen: Kok, 1959.

———. *The Coming of the Kingdom.* Philadelphia: Presbyterian and Reformed, 1962.

———. *Paul: An Outline of His Theology.* Translated by John Richard DeWitt. Grand Rapids, MI: Eerdmans, 1975.

———. *When the Time Had Fully Come: Studies in New Testament Theology.* Grand Rapids, MI: Eerdmans, 1957.

Rivers, Isabel. *Whichcote to Wesley.* Vol. 1 of *Reason, Grace, and Sentiment: A Study of the Language of Religion and Ethics in England, 1660–1780.* Cambridge Studies in Eighteenth-Century English Literature and Thought. Cambridge: Cambridge University Press, 1991.

Roberts, James Deotis. *From Puritanism to Platonism in Seventeenth Century England.* The Hague: Martinus Nijhoff, 1968.

Rorty, Richard. *Consequences of Pragmatism.* Minneapolis: University of Minnesota Press, 1982.

———. *Contingency, Irony, and Solidarity.* Cambridge: Cambridge University Press, 1989.

———. *Objectivity, Relativism, and Truth.* Cambridge: Cambridge University Press, 1991.

Sandel, Michael. *Liberalism and the Limits of Justice.* Cambridge: Cambridge University Press, 1982.

Sartre, Jean-Paul. *L'existentialisme est un humanisme.* Paris: Nagel, 1970.

Schaeffer, Francis A. *The Complete Works of Francis A. Schaeffer: A Christian Worldview.* Westchester, IL: Crossway, 1982.

Schaff, Philip. *History of the Christian Church.* 5th ed. New York: Scribner, 1885–1920.

Schellenberg, J. L. *Divine Hiddenness and Human Reason.* Cornell Studies in the Philosophy of Religion. Ithaca, N.Y.: Cornell University Press, 1993.

Schoonhoven, Calvin R. "The 'Analogy of Faith' and the Intent of Hebrews." In *Scripture, Tradition and Interpretation: Essays Presented to Everett F. Harrison by His Students and Colleagues in Honor of His Seventy-Fifth Birthday*, edited by W. W. Gasque and W. S. LaSor, 92–110. Grand Rapids, MI: Eerdmans, 1978.

Schrage, W. *Der erste Brief an die Korinther*. Evangelisch-katholischer Kommentar zum Neuen Testament, 7, 1. Zürich: Benziger, 1991.

Schreiner, Thomas R. *Paul, Apostle of God's Glory in Christ: A Pauline Theology*. Downers Grove, IL: InterVarsity Press, 2001.

Seifrid, Mark A. "Unrighteous by Faith: Apostolic Proclamation in Romans 1:18–3:20." In *Justification and Variegated Nomism*, edited by D. A. Carson, Peter T. O'Brien, and Mark A. Seifrid, 105–45. Grand Rapids, MI: Baker, 2004.

Silva, Moisés. *Has the Church Misread the Bible? The History of Interpretation in the Light of Current Issues*. Grand Rapids, MI: Zondervan, 1987.

———. "Ned B. Stonehouse and Redaction Criticism." *Westminster Theological Journal* 40 (1977–78): 77–88, 281–303.

———. "The New Testament Use of the Old Testament: Text Form and Authority." In *Scripture and Truth*, edited by D. A. Carson and J. W. Woodbridge, 147–65. Grand Rapids, MI: Zondervan, 1983.

———. "Systematic Theology and the Apostle Paul." *Trinity Journal* 15 (1994): 3–26.

Sosa, Ernest. "The Raft and the Pyramid: Coherence versus Foundations in the Theory of Knowledge." In *Midwest Studies in Philosophy, vol. 5, 1980 Studies in Epistemology*, edited by Peter French and Theodore Uehling, 3–25. Minneapolis: University of Minnesota Press, 1980.

Sproul, R. C., John H. Gerstner, and Arthur Lindsley. *Classical Apologetics*. Grand Rapids, MI: Zondervan, 1984.

Stoker, Hendrik G. "Calvinistiese Wysbegeerte." *Tydskrif vir Wetenskap en Kuns* 15 (1950): 107.

———. "Reconnoitering the Theory of Knowledge of Professor Dr. Cornelius Van Til." In *Jerusalem and Athens: Critical Discussions on the Philosophy and Apologetics of Cornelius Van Til*, edited by E. R. Geehan, 25–71. Nutley, NJ: Presbyterian and Reformed, 1971.

Stout, Jeffrey. *Ethics after Babel*. Boston: Beacon Press, 1988.

Strawson, P. F. *Introduction to Logical Theory*. London: Methuen, 1952.

Stuhlmacher, P. "The Hermeneutical Significance of I Cor 2:6–16." In *Tradition and Interpretation in the New Testament*, edited by G. F. Hawthorne, 328–47. Grand Rapids, MI: Eerdmans, 1987.

Suny, Ronald Grigor. "Back and Beyond: Reversing the Cultural Turn?" *The American Historical Review* 107, no. 5 (2002): 1476–99.

Tanner, Kathryn. *Theories of Culture: A New Agenda for Theology*. Minneapolis: Fortress, 1997.

Taylor, Charles. *Sources of the Self: The Making of the Modern Identity*. Cambridge, MA: Harvard University Press, 1989.

———. "Understanding and Ethnocentricity." In *Philosophy and the Human Sciences. Philosophical Papers*. Cambridge: Cambridge University Press, 1985.

Tillich, Paul. *A History of Christian Thought*. Edited by Carl E. Braaten. New York: Simon and Schuster, 1968.

Todorov, Tzvetan. *Imperfect Garden: The Legacy of Humanism*. Translated by Carol Cosman. Princeton: Princeton University Press, 2002.

Toole, David. *Waiting for Godot in Sarajevo: Theological Reflections on Nihilism, Tragedy, and Apocalypse*. Boulder, CO: Westview, 1998.

Toulmin, Stephen. *Cosmopolis*. Chicago: University of Chicago Press, 1990.

Tracy, David. *Plurality and Ambiguity*. New York: Harper & Row, 1987.

Trueman, Carl R., and R. S. Clark, eds. *Protestant Scholasticism: Essays in Reassessment*. Carlisle, Cumbria: Paternoster, 1999.

Turretin, Francis. *Institutes of Elenctic Theology*, vol. 1. Edited by James T. Dennison Jr. Translated by George Musgrave Giger. Phillipsburg, NJ: P&R, 1994.

van Asselt, Willem J. "The Fundamental Meaning of Theology: Archetypal and Ectypal Theology in Seventeenth-Century Reformed Thought." *Westminster Theological Journal* 64, no. 2 (2002): 319–36.

van Asselt, Willem, and Eef Dekker, eds. *Reformation and Scholasticism*. Grand Rapids, MI: Baker, 2001.

van Fraassen, Bas C. "Presupposition, Implication, and Self-Reference." *Journal of Philosophy* 65 (1968): 136–52.

van Genderen, J., and W. H. Velema. *Beknopte gereformeerde dogmatiek*. Kampen: Kok, 1992.

Van Til, Cornelius. "At the Beginning, God: An Interview with Cornelius Van Til." *Christianity Today* 22 (December 30, 1977): 18–22.

———. *The Case for Calvinism*. Philadelphia: Presbyterian and Reformed, 1964.

———. *Christian Apologetics*. 2nd ed. Edited by William Edgar. Phillipsburg, NJ: P&R, 2003.

———. *A Christian Theory of Knowledge*. Nutley, NJ: Presbyterian and Reformed, 1969.

———. *Christianity and Idealism*. Philadelphia: Presbyterian and Reformed, 1955.

———. *Common Grace*. Philadelphia: Presbyterian and Reformed, 1947.

———. *Common Grace and the Gospel*. Philadelphia: Presbyterian and Reformed, 1972.

———. *The Defense of the Faith*. Philadelphia: Presbyterian and Reformed, 1955, 1967.

————. *The Great Debate Today*. Nutley, NJ: Presbyterian and Reformed, 1971.

————. *An Introduction to Systematic Theology*. Nutley, NJ: Presbyterian and Reformed, 1974.

————. "The Later Heidegger and Theology." *Westminster Theological Journal* 26 (1964): 121–61.

————. "My Credo." In *Jerusalem and Athens: Critical Discussions on the Philosophy and Apologetics of Cornelius Van Til*, edited by E. R. Geehan, 3–21. Nutley, NJ: Presbyterian and Reformed, 1971.

————. "Nature and Scripture." In *The Infallible Word: A Symposium by the Members of the Faculty of Westminster Theological Seminary*, edited by N. B. Stonehouse and Paul Woolley, 263–301. Nutley, NJ: Presbyterian and Reformed, 1978.

————. *The New Modernism: An Appraisal of the Theology of Barth and Brunner*. Philadelphia: Presbyterian and Reformed, 1946.

————. *Paul at Athens*. Nutley, NJ: Presbyterian and Reformed, 1978.

————. *The Protestant Doctrine of Scripture*. The den Dulk Christian Foundation, 1967.

————. *The Reformed Pastor and Modern Thought*. Nutley, NJ: Presbyterian and Reformed, 1971.

————. *The Sovereignty of Grace: An Appraisal of G. C. Berkouwer's View of Dordt*. Philadelphia: Presbyterian and Reformed, 1969.

————. *A Survey of Christian Epistemology*. Nutley, NJ: Presbyterian and Reformed, 1969.

————. *The Works of Cornelius Van Til*. CD-ROM. New York: Labels Army Co., 1997.

Vanhoozer, Kevin. "The Trials of Truth." In *To Stake a Claim: Mission and the Western Crisis of Knowledge*, edited by J. Andrew Kirk and Kevin J. Vanhoozer, 120–56. Maryknoll, NY: Orbis, 1999.

Veith, Gene Edward, Jr. *Postmodern Times: A Christian Guide to Contemporary Thought and Culture*. Wheaton, IL: Crossway, 1994.

Vermigli, Peter Martyr. *The Common Places of the Most Famous and Renowned Divine Doctor Peter Martyr, Divided into Foure Principall Parts: with a Large Addition of Manie Theologicall and Necessarie Discourses, Some Never Extant Before*. Edited by Anthony Marten and Josias Simmler. London: Henri Denham, Thomas Chard, William Broome, and Andrew Maunsell, 1583.

Vos, Geerhardus. *Biblical Theology: Old and New Testaments*. Grand Rapids, MI: Eerdmans, 1948.

————. "The Eschatological Aspect of the Pauline Conception of Spirit." In *Redemptive History and Biblical Interpretation: The Shorter Writings of Geerhardus Vos*, edited by R. B. Gaffin Jr., 91–125. Phillipsburg, NJ: Presbyterian and Reformed, 1980.

———. "The Eschatology of the New Testament." In *Redemptive History and Biblical Interpretation: The Shorter Writings of Geerhardus Vos*, edited by R. B. Gaffin Jr., 25–58. Phillipsburg, NJ: Presbyterian and Reformed, 1980.

———. *The Pauline Eschatology*. Grand Rapids, MI: Baker, 1979.

———. *The Kingdom of God and the Church*. 1903. Reprint, Nutley, NJ: Presbyterian and Reformed, 1972.

Vos, Geerhardus, and Johannes Geerhardus Vos. *The Teaching of the Epistle to the Hebrews*. 1956. Reprint, Phillipsburg, NJ: Presbyterian and Reformed, n.d.

Ware, Bruce A. *God's Lesser Glory: The Diminished God of Open Theism*. Wheaton, IL: Crossway, 2000.

Warfield, B. B. *The Inspiration and Authority of the Bible*. Philadelphia: Presbyterian and Reformed, 1948.

Werpehowski, William. "Ad Hoc Apologetics." *Journal of Religion* 66 (1986): 282–301.

Whichcote, Benjamin. "Eight Letters of Dr. Anthony Tuckney and Benjamin Whichcote." In *Moral and Religious Aphorisms Collected from the Manuscript Papers of the Reverend and Learned Doctor Whichcote; and Published in MDCCIII, by Dr. Jeffery. Now Re-Published, with Very Large Additions . . . by Samuel Salter. . . . To Which Are Added, Eight Letters:* . . . London: Printed for J. Payne, 1753.

———. *The Works*. British Philosophers and Theologians of the 17th and 18th Centuries. New York: Garland, 1977.

Wilson, Douglas. *Bound Only Once: The Failure of Open Theism*. Moscow, ID: Canon, 2001.

Winch, Peter. *The Idea of a Social Science, and Its Relation to Philosophy*. London: Routledge & Kegan Paul, 1958.

———. "Understanding a Primitive Society." *American Philosophical Quarterly* 1 (1964): 307–24.

Witherington, Ben. *The Acts of the Apostles: A Socio-Rhetorical Commentary*. Grand Rapids, MI: Eerdmans, 1998.

Wright, N. T. *The Climax of the Covenant: Christ and the Law in Pauline Theology*. Minneapolis: Fortress, 1992.

Zagzebski, Linda T. *Virtues of the Mind: An Inquiry into the Nature of Virtue and the Ethical Foundations of Knowledge*. Cambridge: Cambridge University Press, 1996.

Contributors

Don Collett is a PhD candidate at the University of St. Andrews.

William D. Dennison (PhD, Michigan State University) is professor of interdisciplinary studies at Covenant College.

William Edgar (DTh, University of Geneva) is professor of apologetics, and department coordinator, at Westminster Theological Seminary.

John M. Frame (MPhil, Yale University; DD, Belhaven College) is professor of systematic theology and philosophy at Reformed Theological Seminary, Orlando.

Richard B. Gaffin Jr. (ThD, Westminster Theological Seminary) is professor of biblical and systematic theology, and department coordinator, at Westminster Seminary.

Michael S. Horton (PhD, University of Coventry and Wycliffe Hall, Oxford) is J. Gresham Machen professor of systematic theology and apologetics at Westminster Seminary California.

319

Jeffrey K. Jue (PhD, University of Aberdeen) is associate professor of church history, and department coordinator, at Westminster Theological Seminary.

Thom E. Notaro (ThM, Westminster Theological Seminary) is senior editor at P&R Publishing Company.

K. Scott Oliphint (PhD, Westminster Theological Seminary) is professor of apologetics and systematic theology at Westminster Seminary.

Michael W. Payne (PhD, Westminster Theological Seminary) is visiting professor of international relations and military ethics at the Air War College, Maxwell Air Force Base.

Moisés Silva (PhD, University of Manchester) is a writer, editor, and biblical scholar. He formerly taught at Westminster Theological Seminary and at Gordon-Conwell Theological Seminary.

Lane G. Tipton (PhD, Westminster Theological Seminary) is associate professor of systematic theology at Westminster Seminary.

Index of Scripture

Index of Subjects
and Names